THE LINCOLN PERSUASION

PRINCETON STUDIES IN AMERICAN POLITICS:
HISTORICAL, INTERNATIONAL, AND COMPARATIVE
PERSPECTIVES

SERIES EDITORS

IRA KATZNELSON, MARTIN SHEFTER, THEDA SKOCPOL

THE LINCOLN PERSUASION

REMAKING AMERICAN LIBERALISM

J. David Greenstone

PRINCETON UNIVERSITY PRESS

PRINCETON, NEW JERSEY

LIBRARY OF CONGRESS CATALOGING-IN-PUBLICATION DATA

GREENSTONE, J. DAVID.

THE LINCOLN PERSUASION : REMAKING AMERICAN LIBERALISM /

J. DAVID GREENSTONE.

P.   CM. — (PRINCETON STUDIES IN AMERICAN POLITICS)

INCLUDES BIBLIOGRAPHICAL REFERENCES AND INDEX.

ISBN 0-691-08790-3

1. UNITED STATES—POLITICS AND GOVERNMENT—1783–1865.   2. LINCOLN,

ABRAHAM, 1809–1865—INFLUENCE.   3. POLITICAL CULTURE—UNITED STATES—

HISTORY.   4. UNITED STATES—POLITICS AND GOVERNMENT—PHILOSOPHY.

I. TITLE.   II. SERIES.

E302.1.G84   1993

973—DC20   92-40075

THIS BOOK HAS BEEN COMPOSED IN LINOTRON GALLIARD

PRINCETON UNIVERSITY PRESS BOOKS ARE PRINTED ON ACID-FREE PAPER
AND MEET THE GUIDELINES FOR PERMANENCE AND DURABILITY OF THE
COMMITTEE ON PRODUCTION GUIDELINES FOR BOOK LONGEVITY OF THE
COUNCIL ON LIBRARY RESOURCES

PRINTED IN THE UNITED STATES OF AMERICA

1   3   5   7   9   10   8   6   4   2

CONTENTS

CHARTS AND TABLES

ACKNOWLEDGMENTS

AUTHORS invariably thank others for inspiration, guidance, criticism, emotional support, and technical assistance. My husband and our father, David Greenstone, who died in February 1990, recognized that he was always learning from colleagues and students with whom he enthusiastically shared his ideas. We know that he greatly appreciated the interest many others took in helping him develop the ideas in this book.

It is now left to us to convey heartfelt gratitude to four University of Chicago political scientists—Dave Ericson, Louisa Bertch Green, Carla Hess, and John Mearsheimer—who were determined not to let David's book remain unpublished after he died. Their personal and intellectual devotion to David and to *The Lincoln Persuasion* has been extraordinary, with each of them making significant sacrifices, often putting David's book ahead of their own scholarly interests.

John Mearsheimer, a close friend of David's, and chair of the University of Chicago's political science department, directed the project. His leadership always showed enthusiastic organization, with sensitive management, unfailing good humor, and moral support toward the accomplishment of a very challenging task. He often said he would be happy only when he could hold the completed book in his hand.

Louisa Bertch Green was David's research assistant in the early stages of the book. She also had prior experience editing scholarly works, which allowed her to assume primary responsibility for editing David's manuscript after his death. She generously gave her time, energy, and wisdom to providing a very carefully edited manuscript.

Carla Hess was David's research assistant when he died. She worked caringly with him until the end, at which time she expressed her strong desire to help prepare the manuscript for publication. She has devoted herself to the difficult job of assembling the chapters and notes from David's files, looking up footnotes, and writing the book's introduction.

Dave Ericson, a former student of David's, who is now a faculty member at Wichita State University, kindly and ably did the preliminary editing of chapters nine and ten and wrote the introduction to part five of the book.

Special thanks are also owed to David's colleague and friend, Nathan Tarcov, who read the manuscript closely, contributed a number of helpful questions and suggestions, and provided several footnote citations. Bradley Thayer did the final checking of David's footnotes, and we greatly appreciate his help. We are also grateful to Lorraine Dwelle for her valuable administrative support and to Fay Booker for her computer expertise and assistance.

David would wish to thank all the students and research assistants who read and commented on various parts of the work over the last twelve years. Along with Dave, Carla, and Louisa, the list includes Chris Ansell, Peter Frett, Carol Horton, Darryl Hushaw, Jim Johnson, Jack Knight, Gayle McKeen, David Menefee-Libey, Anne Norton, Bart Schultz, Andrew Siegel, Kimberly Stanton, Vickie Sullivan, and David Vega. We know there are many other people whom David would have thanked, and we hope that they realize how much their contributions were appreciated by him and also by us.

Finally, we would like to thank Lauren Osborne of Princeton University Press for her consistent enthusiasm about David's book and for her sensitivity to the special circumstances of its posthumous publication. She has shown tremendous grace and skill in helping to turn David's manuscript into this book.

Joan, Michael, and Daniel Greenstone
Chicago, 1992

· · · · ·

Permission to publish the following material, which has appeared elsewhere, is gratefully acknowledged:

Much of chapter two was first published as the first half of "Political Culture and American Political Development: Liberty, Union, and the Liberal Bipolarity," in *Studies in American Political Development*, ed. Karen Orren and Stephen Skowronek (New Haven: Yale University Press, 1986), 1:1–49.

The section of chapter two entitled "The Bipolarity in American Liberalism" appeared in another version as "Against Simplicity: The Cultural Dimensions of the Constitution," in *The University of Chicago Law Review* 55 (1988): 428–49.

Some of the ideas in chapters three and four were explored in "Covenant, Process, and Slavery in the Thought of Adams and Jefferson," in *What Happened to Covenant in the Nineteenth Century?* ed. Daniel J. Elazar (Lanham, Md.: University Press of America for the Center for the Study of Federalism, forthcoming 1993).

A version of chapter four appeared as "Adams and Jefferson on Slavery: Two Liberalisms and the Roots of Civic Ambivalence," in *"The Constitution of the People": Reflections on Citizens and Civil Society*, ed. Robert E. Calvert (Lawrence: University Press of Kansas, 1991), 18–46.

Chapter nine was first published in a slightly different version as the second half of "Political Culture and American Political Development: Liberty, Union, and the Liberal Bipolarity," in *Studies in American Political Development*, ed. Karen Orren and Stephen Skowronek (New Haven: Yale University Press, 1986), 1:1–49.

A slightly different version of chapter ten was published with the same title, "Lincoln's Political Humanitarianism: Moral Reform and the Covenant Tradition in American Political Culture," in *American Models of Revolutionary Leadership: George Washington and Other Founders*, ed. Daniel J. Elazar and Ellis Katz (Lanham, Md.: University Press of America for the Center for the Study of Federalism, 1992), 195–225.

EDITOR'S NOTE

Louisa Bertch Green

THROUGHOUT the twelve or more years that David Greenstone worked on the manuscript for the present book, he coaxed and badgered a good many of his colleagues into listening to, reading, and challenging or confirming all or parts of his thesis about the American liberal bipolarity. It is not surprising, then, that after Greenstone's death, along with members of his family, quite a number of his colleagues and friends were concerned to see his manuscript published. To that end, some of them formed a committee of consulting members, which included Joan Greenstone, Michael Greenstone, Daniel Greenstone, and Erika Fromm from his family; and, from the Department of Political Science at the University of Chicago, Dave Ericson, Carla Hess, John Mearsheimer, John Padgett, Bernard Silberman, Cass Sunstein, Nathan Tarcov, and myself.

Greenstone left a clear book plan; he had written ten of the projected twelve chapters; and he had written introductions to four of the five parts of the book. In the shared judgment of the committee, the assembled manuscript presented a strong and coherent thesis, quite sufficiently complete for publication even without the unwritten chapters. Despite the committee's strong desire to honor Greenstone's plan to include a chapter on Daniel Webster and his special desire to include a chapter on Lydia Maria Child and Frederick Douglass—and despite Michael Greenstone's eloquent and heartfelt support for doing so—the committee accepted finally that there was not enough original material. There was as well a prevailing reluctance to confuse the authorship, especially in view of the strength of the existing work. Although the general thesis of the book was judged to stand without the unwritten chapters, the absence of the particular cases is to be regretted, since they would have been important contributions to the literature in their own right.

The task of preparing a manuscript for publication without the consultation of the author is a sobering one. The members of the committee agreed that as few changes as possible should be made. Despite the length of time over which the chapters were written, the substance and the underlying structure of the thesis had remained remarkably stable. Consequently, the editing was conformed to the time-honored principles of oriental laquerwork—the application of many thin coats with light sandings in between—in order to highlight and preserve the substance and shape of the original. The changes that have been made are commensurate with standard editing practices and were made with the single objective of providing clarity and consistency of expression to the work as a whole. Where an occasional phrase was needed, it was borrowed from nearby passages. Some minor corrections of fact were made, utilizing Greenstone's own sources; for example, the Jeffersonians supported the rechartering of the first Bank of the United States in 1811—not 1816, the year of the chartering of the second bank. The footnotes are Greenstone's, except for a few editor's notes, which are enclosed in square brackets. Greenstone's footnotes have been amended only as they would be in any check of footnotes. In some instances, a footnote reference was unclear or incorrect; with two exceptions, the correct citations were located, and the two that remain missing are so marked.

Only three editorial changes merit specific acknowledgment. First, in the introduction to part four, one of the last things he wrote, Greenstone introduced two new terms for the liberal bipolarity—*structural* and *volitional*—but he used them without explication. Although he changed the terms for the two poles a couple of times over the years, throughout the present manuscript he consistently used the terms *reform* and *humanist*— with that one exception. Over the years, the changes of terminology were a deliberate part of his ongoing exploration; they were a way of testing his thesis, of meeting colleagues' challenges, and of searching for more complex and complete descriptions of the basic split he saw in American liberalism. *Motivational* and *intentional*, for example, had a relatively brief but intense life in an essay on Lincoln that predates the essay that became chapter ten; and *interests* and *standards* liberalisms had a run in the early eighties. Nevertheless, in his schema there were never more than two liberalisms, and, despite the changes of name, the basic dichotomy and the substance of each pole remained consistent. In addition, in correspondence, Greenstone repeatedly referred to John Quincy Adams (the only figure treated in part four) as a reform liberal. Consequently, in the introduction to part four, *structural* and *volitional* have been changed to *reform* and *humanist*, respectively.

A further note on *reform* liberalism: Greenstone used both *reform* and *reformed* liberalism in the present manuscript (in Greenstone 1988, he cited Gamwell 1984 as the source of *reformed*). From the discussions in his writings overall, however, it is clear that he meant a liberalism devoted to reform and not a liberalism that was itself reformed. In addition, because *humanist* and *reform* liberalism are each a distinct, evolved "form" of the original republican liberalism, the use of *reformed* to refer to one pole compounded the grammatical ambiguity. *Reform* has therefore been substituted consistently wherever *reformed* modified liberalism.

Second, in chapter ten, the initial discussion of Lincoln's motives appeared to state for the first time material that was also stated in chapter one.

The argument in chapter ten therefore was summarized and edited from seven pages into four, and two brief transitions were added.

Third, the material that now makes up the epilogue to chapter ten was composed by drawing together in one place a number of scattered single examples and references. Together these constitute Greenstone's projection of his thesis into a second book, which would have traced the reform and humanist traditions from Lincoln forward: through the Progressives, Jane Addams and the settlement house movement, the programs of the New Deal, and the political and social reform movements of the late 1960s. Separately, the references to Addams—who exemplified the continuation of the reform tradition begun by Dorothea Dix (see Greenstone 1979), Horace Mann, and the abolitionists—and to the other, later social reformers did not do justice either to the importance of her and their place in the development of the thesis or to the full scope and context of the thesis as Greenstone envisioned it. It seemed appropriate, therefore, to collect these references in one place and allow them to constitute such a statement.

I share in the Greenstones' expressions of thanks, especially to John Mearsheimer, Dave Ericson, Nathan Tarcov, Brad Thayer, and Lauren Osborne. I would also like to thank Douglas Jaenicke of the University of Manchester for a sustained correspondence over the missing notes for chapter seven; Sterling Bland of Princeton University Press; J. Ronald Green of the Ohio State University for assistance in the transcription of critical passages of the final pages of chapter eight, which Greenstone left written out in longhand; David Apter of Yale University and Bat Sparrow of the University of Texas at Austin for their turnaround responses to last-minute queries; several anonymous readers for thoughtful suggestions; and David Nelson Blair for the copyediting.

．　．　．　．　．

I would like to add a personal note here. I first met David Greenstone when he was working on the first of the Lincoln chapters and beginning to formulate the bipolarity thesis. As one of his research assistants for more than six years, I regularly read, edited, and discussed with him successive versions of many of his papers, including those on Lincoln that became chapters one, two, nine, and ten of the book. David took great pleasure in gently prodding his readers into active engagement. In the process of working with him, I, like others, developed a profound respect for the elegance and complexities of his thinking, as well as a great affection for his boundless intellectual energy, and a working familiarity with his writing. Despite that experience, however, as one of the central dilemmas in Wittgenstein's work exemplifies, one cannot know another's mind with certainty. Decisions about David's book have necessarily been made without knowing what he would have done in this or that instance. That the edited manuscript was not precisely the one David himself would have sent to the publisher is simply the case and a consequence of the circumstances. He would certainly have understood the efforts of all those involved in the project to be a mark of their professional respect and personal affection.

A special roundtable in David's memory, "The Legacy of J. David Greenstone," was organized by Ronald Kahn of Oberlin College for the 1991 meetings of the American Political Science Association in Washington, D.C. Ronald Kahn, Paul Peterson, Karen Orren, Carol Nackenoff, Anne Norton, Dave Ericson, Carla Hess, and I shared reminiscences with about two hundred of David's family, friends, and colleagues. In the course of her talk, Anne Norton noted what she called David's "passionate curiosity that would not be still." Most of those present were familiar with the singular dedication and infectious enthusiasm with which David followed that curiosity through subjects as diverse as Lincoln's role in history, the status of undergraduate education at the University of Chicago, and the Chicago Bulls basketball team. All those whom he engaged or tried to engage in those particular enthusiasms over a quarter of his life must be saddened that David should miss both the publication of his book on Lincoln and the Bulls' two consecutive NBA championships—to say nothing of the Bulls' contributions to the 1992 Olympic "Dream Team." It is not possible even to guess whether the book or the Bulls would have given him the greater pleasure of the moment, nor does it matter. In the course of the editing, time and again a moment arose in which David was palpably present in the words and argument of the text and, simultaneously, irrevocably beyond the reach of the very engagement he loved to provoke. Yet he might simply have stepped out in the hall for a few minutes, leaving us, as he often had, to engage each other in the issues he left behind, on the table and in the air. In provoking us to such engagement, he wove himself into the forms of our lives and showed us, in the words of that "philosopher chosen at random," how to go on.

Columbus, Ohio 1992

INTRODUCTION TO THE BOOK

Carla M. Hess

HISTORY OF *THE LINCOLN PERSUASION*
Contra Hartz *and Wittgenstein*

THIS BOOK AROSE from both David Greenstone's questions about Louis Hartz's claim that liberalism in the United States constituted a single tradition of understanding and practice and from Greenstone's interest in using the later work of Ludwig Wittgenstein to analyze political practice. In Greenstone's early work in American urban and labor politics, he took issue with Hartz in the specific context of labor politics (see Greenstone 1977 [1969]). Then, while he chaired the Department of Political Science at the University of Chicago (1972–1975), David became interested in Wittgenstein's epistemological conclusions. He began to wonder whether Wittgenstein's observations could be useful in studying American politics. Specifically, could Wittgenstein provide insight in those areas where David found Hartz's arguments inadequate?

Greenstone collected the earliest notes for the book in a file made between September 1976 and December 1977, called "contra Hartz." In the first entry in that file, Greenstone argued that "a causal analysis works only if it is directed toward explaining political activity that goes on *within* a particular setting (what [Wittgenstein] would call a language game or, more satisfyingly, a form of life). It is this context . . . which gives the entire affair its legitimacy, its *meaningfulness* for the actors." That is, causal analyses require that the actors agree on the context, on the terms and the uses and meanings—on the "rules of the game." In addition, causal analyses do not necessarily regard the *use* of a rule as an *interpretation* of a rule. What Wittgenstein recognized, however, was that every use of rules was, in fact, an *interpretation* of those rules. This is unproblematic, Greenstone argued, when all the actors interpret the rules the same way, but when the actors' interpretations differ, causal analyses are inadequate. As Greenstone noted, "One can then say that it is when the assumptions of the given form of life (or mode of discourse) are challenged that the 'great' moments of modern political history occur." The Civil War was just such a "great" moment: "The bloodshed and suffering came because the game/form of life was itself in danger."

It was precisely here, Greenstone thought, that Hartz's analysis was insufficient. Hartz argued that liberalism was a single more or less coherent set of beliefs and practices; however, that argument could identify only continuity in the tenets of liberalism. It was unable to address the challenges to fundamental assumptions about American political practice that the Civil War exemplified. What troubled Greenstone was, first, that Hartz's theory required us to regard the Civil War as an aberration, one not explicable within the framework of American liberalism, and, second, that Hartz's implicit causal argument (what Greenstone calls his "metatheory," in chapter two) was mistaken.

Greenstone did not intend to enclose all of American politics in some new, grand theory; rather, he wanted to understand how politics was and is conducted in the American context and also to provide a methodological alternative to strictly causal analyses. He thought that if political actors were operating according to different versions of the rules, there would likely be times when some player or players must devise a means by which those different sets of rules could be reconciled or rewritten, else the polity could not continue. Greenstone thought that the Civil War was such a time and that Lincoln devised the means to change some of the rules of the game of American politics so that a single American polity could continue to exist.

Wittgenstein's work suggested to Greenstone that in such a case it would be necessary to turn to the meanings and interpretations of the rules—the grammar, as it were—that various participants used. Thus, Greenstone argued, in order to provide a thorough analysis of political culture or to illuminate a political crisis (such as the Civil War), the analyst had to explicate the language and practices, what Wittgenstein called the language games and forms of life, used by the political actors. As Greenstone put it, "We must draw upon our literature and not any contractual reading of Madison." Such analyses would not show us causes in the usual sense, but, rather, would show us the boundaries of meaning and practice (e.g., of *liberalism*).

Greenstone continued to explore these thoughts in his early notes, drawing upon such diverse sources as Weber, Kant, Calvin, the New Deal, and modern labor movements. It is also in these notes that the idea of more than one strain of liberalism in the United States began to emerge. Greenstone saw the distinctions within American liberalisms as one of the keys to an understanding of the complexities of American politics. One crucial question raised by those complexities concerned slavery; another concerned the methods by which we might analyze and understand American politics. That is, insofar as the founders left us with the institution of slavery and with a liberalism with important and sometimes contradictory strands to it, how could the problem of slavery, and the additional dilemmas it signaled, be solved? At the same time, how were we to interpret and understand American political thought?

The Jacksonians and Lincoln

In Winter 1980 Greenstone taught a course, "Polarities in American Politics: The Jacksonian Era," in which he explored the idea of more than one American liberalism. The course description read, in part:

> This course begins with the assumption that, for better or worse, American politics has been and continues to be pervasively liberal—i.e., individualist and pluralist—in its thought and practice. It asserts, however, that this liberalism exhibits a fundamental polarity that has shaped many of the most important conflicts in American political history but has not conformed very closely to patterns of partisan conflict. Rather, I believe this division must be understood as an ultimately philosophical disagreement over the character of the individual human personality. At the same time, I believe this disagreement first emerged in recognizable form in the Jacksonian era, that is the generation that led up to and culminated in the Civil War.

Greenstone thought that although Adams and Jefferson were clearly the spiritual forebears of the bipolarity he had identified, the second generation was forced to negotiate the political shoals left unmapped by the founders. What had been implicit in but unacknowledged and unresolved by the work of the founders only took shape as the Jacksonians conceptualized and institutionalized both the problems and their proposed solutions. Thus, Greenstone thought, an explication of the various Jacksonian solutions to the problem of slavery would (1) show the different ways in which some of the second generation carried out the programs of the founders, (2) illuminate the varying philosophical commitments of the founders, and (3) show the genius of Lincoln in solving these problems. The second generation had come up with numerous answers, no one of them satisfactory along all the important spectra. To understand the full meaning and complexities of American liberalism, Greenstone envisioned explicating three aspects of American political culture. First, he thought it would be necessary to trace the roots of American liberalism to the founders, specifically to Adams and Jefferson. Second, he meant to show the various solutions proposed by second-generation figures, detailing both their liberal commitments and how those commitments affected their approach to the issue of slavery. Finally, Greenstone meant to show how Lincoln addressed both the moral and political problem of slavery and the tensions between forms of American liberalism. Accomplishing these tasks would require a multilevel, cross-cutting analysis.

By 1982, Greenstone had concluded that Lincoln was the key to understanding both the Jacksonians and the liberal bipolarity. Lincoln, he thought, by resolving many of the conflicts left by the founders and only partly—and in different ways—resolved by their successors, was truly the key to understanding the late-nineteenth-century reworking of American politics and political culture. In a letter from September 1982, he wrote: "As it turns out, in a way I never really expected, my book about the Jacksonian period will turn out to be a book about Lincoln. What I have discovered is that I am trying to state the respects in which Lincoln, in his genius, synthesized the many different currents that made up Jacksonian politics and political culture."

Liberalism in the United States

Greenstone began to explicate his notion of a bipolarity in American liberalism; the substance of the terms Greenstone used and their relationships to each other are important. He thought that Americans did share a broad agreement on three specific tenets of liberalism: individual rights, private property, and government by popular consent. *Genus liberalism* (or *consensus* or *republican liberalism*) entails the belief in these three features of republicanism shared by all American liberals; collectively, these features constitute the substance of the liberal consensus about which Hartz wrote. In addition, however, there was a broad split among Americans on other tenets of political thought and practice. This split was, generally speaking, between those who focused on the satisfaction of preferences—*humanist* liberals, who assigned a central place to humankind rather than a deity—and *reform* liberals, who focused on the development of human faculties. In chapter ten, Greenstone traces connections between the two liberalisms and earlier kinds of ethical and political reasoning, first in the Puritan culture of the seventeenth century and then in the New England Calvinism of the eighteenth and nineteenth centuries. Instrumental, or means-end, reasoning belongs to the humanist liberal tradition; consummatory or perfectionist reasoning belongs to the reform liberal tradition.

The Actors

Lincoln, Webster, and Douglas, and then John Adams and Thomas Jefferson, were long included as parts of the book. Part of what has become chapter nine of this book was begun in the early 1980s, and the chapters on John Adams and Jefferson (chapters three and four) were written soon after, around 1984. As Greenstone began to explicate the tenets of humanist and reform liberalism—the heirs to Jefferson and Adams, respectively—he searched for second-generation figures who could exemplify the complexity of liberal thought and practice in American politics. He was interested in discussing people who, being assuredly both consensus liberals and either humanist or reform liberals, used those liberal beliefs to reach different institutional and philosophical solutions to the intertwined problems of liberty and union.

The humanist liberals on whom Greenstone settled were William Leggett, Stephen Douglas, and Martin Van Buren, each of whom suggested different solutions to the problems posed by the issue of slavery and the tenets of their beliefs. Each of these figures was indeed both a consensus liberal and a humanist liberal, but they reached different conclusions on both the issue of slavery and the institutions through which they thought that issue could be or ought to be discussed.

On the reform-liberal side, Greenstone originally planned to write about Wendell Phillips, Daniel Webster, and John Quincy Adams, and the class he taught in 1988 that drew on materials for this book still included writings of Phillips and Adams on the syllabus. Not long afterward, however, Greenstone decided to write about Lydia Maria Child and Frederick Douglass instead of Wendell Phillips and had begun research on both. Child and Douglass, he thought, better exemplified the radical abolitionist wing of reform liberalism, those who would rather see the union split apart than tolerate slavery anywhere in the union, and Child would enable him to discuss the conjunction of feminism and abolitionism.

Greenstone died before he could write the chapters on Child, Douglass, and Webster. (Material on Webster does appear in chapter nine and in Greenstone 1986.) He wrote chapter eight, on John Quincy Adams, before he started the chapters on Child, Douglass, and Webster, because he thought that John Quincy Adams was the key to understanding Lincoln. He dictated that chapter to me a few weeks before he died; his notes and outlines for the chapter indicate that it is not quite complete. We have not attempted to write the missing chapters on Child, Douglass, and Webster or to finish chapter eight; references to the (unwritten) chapters on Douglass, Child, and Webster appear sporadically in the book.

Arguments of *The Lincoln Persuasion*

As Greenstone worked out the arguments and how best to present them, the book evolved into five sections. Greenstone wrote introductions for all but the last, which was written by Dave Ericson. These introductions give clues to the evolution of Greenstone's thought. The first section sets out to explain Lincoln's political genius, from both a personal and a political point of view. The first chapter asks how we are to understand Lincoln the person. The second asks how we are to understand the (liberal) context in which he operated. Just as language is intertwined with a practice, so we cannot understand *only* a political actor, or politics in an abstract sense, but only politics as human activity, with particular meanings for the actors.

The second section traces the political context and meanings of the liberal bipolarity to the founding generation, specifically to Thomas Jefferson and John Adams. Chapter three examines the liberalism and republicanism they shared, as well as the epistemology on which they differed, in the context of the founding. Chapter four introduces the issue of slavery and connects Adams's and Jefferson's epistemologies to their beliefs about slavery, an issue that was nevertheless unresolved, both between Adams and Jefferson and for the union as a whole. This section was important for elaborating the *rules* of American politics, that is, the social, political, and philosophical context established by the founders, and, especially, for elaborating the tenets of humanist and reform liberalism.

Part three discusses the Jacksonian attempts to reconcile questions of slavery and politics by means of reconciling preferences, that is, by humanist liberal solutions; the section examines William Leggett, Stephen Douglas, and Martin Van Buren. All three agreed, with each other and with Jefferson, that decisions ought to be made by reconciling preferences among humans; they disagreed, however, on the exact mechanism for that reconciliation, and they disagreed somewhat on whether the preferences (or utility) of some set of people were more important than those of some other set. Thus, Leggett could oppose slavery, Douglas could consign the decision to individual communities, and Van Buren could consign the politics of slavery to political parties—three very different institutional answers—while all agreed on the fundamental epistemology.

Part four was to trace the responses of four heirs of John Adams: Frederick Douglass, Lydia Maria Child, Daniel Webster, and John Quincy Adams. All, like Adams, were motivated by some transcendent notion of duty or morality or union, though they disagreed on precisely how to carry out that duty. Child and Douglass focused on individual freedom, Webster believed that the *union* was the "transcendent good," and John Quincy Adams attempted to reconcile political necessity with the demands of duty and morality. Though this section is not complete, we can see three very different institutional responses despite epistemological agreement among the actors.

The last two chapters focus specifically on Lincoln's solution to the linked problems of liberty and union, problems that arise directly from the bipolarity in American liberalism in combination with the issue of slavery. This section shows how Lincoln reformulated the grammar of American politics; Lincoln recognized both the link between morals and politics and the link between individuals and the union. The section is also, implicitly, a discussion of forms of explanation in social science.

Thus, there are several arguments running through this book. One concerns the republican values shared by the actors as well as the epistemological positions that divided them. A second claim considers the question of what it is that people share, or do not share, when they engage in political, social, or economic communities; this claim argues that rules are only comprehensible in (or about) the context of the practices they describe or create. In addition, this claim examines particular American practices as proposed solutions to political problems—themselves a product of the American context—and evaluates them in the terms of discourse set out by the founders and elaborated by the second generation. A third claim, more implicit than the others, concerns the attempt to use Wittgenstein to provide a philosophical analysis of political practice. Finally, a fourth argument examines Lincoln's genius in the context of rewriting the rules of political institutions and discourse and examines what such a rewriting involves.

Shared Republicanism and the Liberal Bipolarity

There are two important aspects to the argument about shared republicanism and the liberal bipolarity. One focuses on the commitment to liberal republican institutions that is shared by all of the figures discussed in the book, while the second details the epistemological variations that separate those same people, that exemplify a bipolarity within consensus liberalism, and that help form the grounds for very different approaches to the question of slavery. Throughout the book, Greenstone shows how each of the people he discusses is committed to republican institutions and republican values, broadly described; each of the figures does share the genus liberalism described by Hartz, to some degree.

However, as discussed in chapter two, Hartz's focus on the aspects of liberalism that are shared so widely obscures the deep divides on beliefs about human nature, the bases and institutions for political activity, and the place of duty in political life. This epistemological line of cleavage divided humanist liberals from reform liberals. Humanist liberals focused on identifying and coordinating preferences among humans according to a utilitarian calculus and, in the case of some humanist liberals, according to a view of human nature that regarded African-Americans as inferior to European-Americans. By contrast, reform liberals focused on a moral imperative to develop one's own faculties and to assist others in doing so as well. Although in practice at least some reform liberals regarded African-Americans as *intellectually* inferior, they nevertheless agreed that African-Americans were *morally* on a par with others. (Similarly, some abolitionists advocated suffrage for women on the grounds that men and women were equally human, and civic rights ought not be assigned according to sex.)

Although for some reform liberals the union was the transcendent good or the means by which development of faculties could best be enabled, what reform liberals all shared was belief in the possibility of a duty that transcended political commitments and institutions. Humanist liberals shared a belief that moral issues ought to be decided or negotiated through political institutions, because they thought such issues could not be solved in any other way. In addition, humanist liberals in general applied what Greenstone calls "instrumental" reasoning, while reform liberals engage in deontic reasoning (and some had perfectionist leanings as well). This is not to say that humanist liberal reasoning is somehow *unprincipled* or merely utilitarian; nor does it mean that all reform liberals were unconcerned with the means to reach goals. (As we will see in chapter ten, some perfectionist reform liberals did not consider goals, per se, but duties, and they left the consequences of their actions to God.) Rather, as the syllogisms in chapter four show, instrumental reasoning does not concern itself with what people's preferences should be, only with how best to satisfy or reconcile them. Some humanist liberals focus on individual rights, while others stress collectivities of one kind or another. In contrast, reform liberal reasoning explicitly proceeds on the basis of how the proposed action fits in with one's moral tenets and the duties they imply, or even determines what actions are required by duty, according to those tenets. Of course, disagreements may arise over just what one's duties are, or over just what actions are prescribed by moral tenets.

The important distinction of this argument is the contrast between shared republicanism and the different epistemologies held by the various actors. What we begin to see is that, though shared commitment to republican institutions is important, epistemological commitments are important as well. One cannot merely declare a shared belief in, for example, private property or human rights. Depending on what may count as property (a person?) and depending on what rights are to be protected, and their source (a god?), these shared beliefs may result in quite different polities. This leads to the question of what it means to share meanings or to share a grammar of belief and action.

Shared Meanings

What all Americans—all liberals—shared was a commitment to certain kinds of rights and institutions, especially pluralism and individual liberty, much as Hartz had claimed. It is also true that it is insufficient to examine only what is shared; we must also examine what differs—humanist and reform liberalisms. The questions raised by consideration of these liberalisms in turn raise questions of what, exactly, it means to *share* an epistemology or a grammar of meaning and use. This book addresses these latter questions in light of Wittgenstein's writings.

In the American political context, the second generation, especially the Jacksonians, attempted to fashion a single game of American politics. The various institutional solutions proposed might have allowed political actors to subsume areas of disagreement under areas of agreements, much as Jefferson and John Adams did. As it was, slavery became an overriding issue, not least because it pointed out the failures of the institutions proposed to address or ignore it. It was not so much that slavery caused the Civil War. Rather, the issue of slavery made it clear that all the players of the game of American politics were not playing by the same rules, and the importance of slavery as a moral issue made it certain that the slavery question would retain its centrality, forcing the issue of institutional solutions and approaches.

This book argues that shared values should be thought of as *boundary conditions* rather than as causes. The shared values, as well as the ones on which the actors differed, formed the grammar of political discourse, language, and practice; this claim points to the complexities of language games, in contrast to Hartz but also in contrast to simple pluralist explanations or descriptions of American politics. As noted earlier, causal analyses are only possible when all of the actors share the same rules of the game and share interpretations of those rules. When actors disagree about the rules of the game or the terms of political discourse, disagreements will take on a different character: such are the "great moments" to which Greenstone alluded. In addition, such disagreements about the grammar of discourse are quite common, though they are not always expressed in as extreme a fashion as in the Civil War. Even if we know whether an actor adopted Adams's or Jefferson's epistemological view—even when people agree on the rules and their interpretations—we cannot predict how that actor would come down on the slavery issue. One can know what will be important in deciding that issue—the satisfaction of preferences or the development of human faculties, for example—but epistemology alone does not enable us to predict the *particular* solution an actor will adopt or recommend.

Rules are only comprehensible in the context of the game they describe; people must settle on what a community is for *and* the rules by which it will operate. These rules include not just the apparently purely procedural rules of political life (though, according to this view, there is no such thing as a purely procedural rule: the rules *are* the game), but the assumptions, for example, about human nature or about duty, that the participants bring with them. There may be—are likely to be—disagreements, though those disagreements will not always be immediately apparent and, as this book shows, may be quite subtle. For example, the profound disagreements between John Adams and Thomas Jefferson must be seen alongside their agreements, despite what we will see to be the depth and profundity of their disagreements. For another example, William Leggett and Lydia Maria Child both opposed slavery, but they opposed it on different grounds. Leggett believed that slavery impinged too much on the individual rights of slaves, and Child that it was a moral evil that prevented both slaves and their owners from fully developing their faculties. At the same time, although Leggett and Stephen Douglas shared the Jeffersonian/Jacksonian belief in satisfying preferences, those beliefs led them to different conclusions on the issue of slavery. This book shows us how a Wittgensteinian attention to these differences can illuminate the disagreements among actors.

Shared meanings (chapter two) include shared standards of correct performance, or what Wittgenstein described as standards of mastery. Thus, John Quincy Adams made reference to the "influence of Society on man," recognizing that not just preferences, but meaning and belief, as well, were a product of living in a community. One certainly had individual duties—to develop one's faculties—but John Adams and John Quincy Adams (and Lincoln) expected that such development would take place in the context of a community. Therefore, the morality of the community itself was important, though reform liberals did not all agree on how the morality of the community was important. In addition, of course, beliefs change: as Wittgenstein noted, languages develop much the way cities develop and grow, and each use is an interpretation. That is, standards of correct performance are not immutable, though they may be quite durable; in addition, though they are mutable, they are no less standards that communities use (or dispute). Finally, as we can see by noting the agreements among the actors Greenstone discussed, not all rules or standards are disputed at once: though the particular commitments of the actors varied, all had some commitment to liberal republican institutions, what Greenstone has called "genus" liberalism.

Understanding the epistemology of the actors is important for an analysis, but not because of the predictive power of these epistemologies. Greenstone's analyses help us understand the inadequacies of the institutional solutions of the second generation as well as see the complex beliefs that motivated actors to propose particular institutional solutions. For example, the Jacksonian efforts to keep morals out of politics were bound to conflict with the abolitionists' attempts to structure politics along the lines of (particular) moral beliefs. Thus, in the symmetry of parts three and four we see that, although Lydia Maria Child and William Leggett were both abolitionists, they arrived at that position by different paths. Similarly, Stephen Douglas and Daniel Webster both wanted to preserve the union and thus emphasized the importance of communities, though Douglas focused on communities' preferences while Webster focused on the union's mission in the world. Finally, both Van Buren and John Quincy Adams were troubled by the combination of morals and politics: Van Buren attempted to eliminate the divisions through the strategy of political parties, while Adams could only combine them in ways that threatened neither the union nor his own political position (and this latter was important insofar as his seat was an opportunity to inject morality into politics).

The conflicts between humanist and reform liberals existed not because the former were willing to allow slavery to exist and the latter were not; William Leggett does not fit into such a framing. It was also not because the former were devoted to the union in a way the latter were not: Daniel Webster was so committed to the union that he refused to condemn slavery publicly, but John Quincy Adams remained committed to the union even while he deplored the practice of slavery. In short, then, knowing the epistemology of the actors does not mean that one will know the institutions those actors will choose to settle the slavery (or any other) issue.

Understanding actors in the American political context requires realizing that there are several contexts, and these contexts cannot simply all be subsumed under one label (e.g., *liberalism*). One can best analyze major political events by examining the language and practice of the participants, or, as Greenstone put it, by attempting to "account for the solutions in terms of the situations the individuals found themselves in." That is, one must examine the rules by which people participated in politics and the particular interpretations those participants had of the rules they followed. Such an examination, as Greenstone has shown, provides a more complex picture of political life. It also enables the analyst to see that difficulties are never merely procedural (or only substantive, for that matter): The rules of the game *are* the game; when one changes the rules of basketball, one changes what happens when a game of basketball is played. Thus, we can see the importance of different kinds of reasoning as well as the political and institutional importance of the epistemological commitments of the actors.

Wittgensteinian Practice and the Lincoln Persuasion: Changing the Rules, I

One of the motivating questions for this book was whether one could use Wittgenstein to perform a philosophical analysis of political practice, and, if so, how one might do that. This book is Greenstone's attempt to provide a least one answer to that question. Though Wittgenstein himself never did social science or even gave instructions for doing so, his epistemology instructs us to look not for causes, in the usual social science model, or for psychologies, but for language games and forms of life, for grammars of meaning and use, especially ones that are being contested. Wittgenstein also did not elaborate on just how agents use the tools of their languages and practices to change those languages and practices. Finally, Wittgenstein often instructed his readers that one must show rather than say some things. Greenstone's thought that these dicta implied that the analyst must focus on the grammar of meaning and use employed by the participants in politics, on the motivating philosophical positions as well as the institutional practices and solutions the actors used.

David Bloor (1983), John Danford (1988 [1978]), and Hannah Pitkin (1972) all argued that, in principle, Wittgenstein could be used to conduct social science investigations. However, all of those authors made primarily *theoretical* arguments. It seemed to Greenstone that in order to answer the question of whether Wittgenstein could be used for philosophical analyses of political practice, one had to *attempt* such an investigation. Such an attempt would not focus on causes, at least not as generally understood. Instead, the focus would have to be on the grammar of politics. In such an investigation, the epistemological beliefs of the actors would be important, though not predictive; one would not know the particular solution an actor would suggest, only the language he or she would use to suggest and defend it. Similarly, though several actors might advocate the same position, they might do so because of very different philosophical commitments. The previously noted symmetry of parts three and four shows us just how complex the grammar of politics can be—and just how complex philosophical analyses must be.

A Wittgensteinian investigation would also emphasize the inseparability of language and practice. Several of the figures addressed in this book thought that morals and politics had to be separated, and that a commitment to some procedure or institution was not a moral commitment but was, instead, a way to avoid discussion of moral commitments. The inadequacy of such an approach becomes evident as various attempts to separate morals and politics fail; we see that this analysis challenges the possibility of neutral procedures, for either the actors or the analyst. All politics shape and are shaped not just by the grammar of meaning and use but also by grammars of what is important to, or contested by, the actors. In turn, Lincoln's achievement can be understood in this light: He was successful precisely because he managed to combine firm moral commitments—to the union as well as to abolishing slavery—with institutional solutions that addressed those issues. He agonized over and was haunted by the Civil War, but he was also not willing to let the slave states go: such a move would neither abolish slavery nor preserve the union.

Thus, as is shown most explicitly in the first and last parts of this book, one must examine not just the motives and actions of the actors, but also the political context(s) in which they operated. One must understand the logics of the discourses in use by the actors. Human activity, politics included, takes place in shared, as well as conflicting, communities of meaning and practice, and understanding and analysis of those activities—and, especially, of upheavals and disagreements in those activities—must address this. To analyze such disagreements, one must be able to analyze disputes over the rules, which is precisely what a causal analysis cannot do. A Wittgensteinian analysis, with its emphasis on the grammars of meaning and use, thus provides an alternative to, for example, a strictly causal analysis: causal analyses require that the actors not dispute the rules of the game, while a Wittgensteinian analysis may be most illuminating in just those situations where participants *disagree* on the rules. The book shows that not only is it possible to use Wittgenstein, it is *preferable* to do so for at least some analyses.

The Lincoln Persuasion and Wittgensteinian Practice: Changing the Rules, II

In this light, Lincoln's achievements become all the more remarkable. Lincoln fashioned a solution that retained the moral concerns of the abolitionists and the political whole of the union. He did all this in a language that retained a commitment to *both* individuals and their communities, and provided a solution that combined a reform liberal outlook with humanist liberal institutions. Lincoln's achievement was not merely a patching together of various elements; rather, his outlook was a distinct reinterpretation and reformulation—a refounding. To discuss Lincoln's solutions as superior to those offered by, for example, Martin Van Buren or John Quincy Adams, we must discuss the criteria by which Lincoln's solution can be regarded as superior, and here Greenstone again turned to Wittgenstein and notions of practice and language.

Lincoln used the tools of political discourse of his culture to accomplish this task, *and* he reformulated some of the rules of political discourse. For one thing, he believed morals and politics were not separate, or separable, spheres. More specifically, he coupled a commitment to political institutions—to party, but also, more importantly, to the union—with a commitment to moral principles: that slavery was wrong, and ought to be condemned and, eventually, abolished. It was insufficient to sever the union and thus distance at least part of the American polity from the institution of slavery; a union that did not condemn and attempt to end slavery was morally inadequate. That is, the union was *only* exemplary if it committed itself to condemning and eventually abolishing slavery. None of the people who preceded Lincoln—neither the founders nor the second generation— were able to fashion such an interpretation of American political practice. Lincoln's reform liberal commitments drew on Calvinist and Yankee belief (chapter ten); indeed, John Quincy Adams, for example, combined a commitment to the union with a loathing for slavery.

Greenstone wrote in notes for this book:

What the Puritans bequeathed to Lincoln was not a predisposition to a particular position or commitment on a policy question or moral issue. There were, after all, many pressures outside the New England Protestant tradition and Whig culture that encouraged a dislike of human slavery. What that tradition did give, instead, was a certain logic of discourse—a framework within which choices could be made. For one thing, that framework required explicit attention to the tension between one's responsibilities as a citizen and one's concern with moral duty. For another, it demanded that one weigh the competing claims of conscience and the goal of ethical perfectionism against the obligation to use one's rational faculties to shape the world in the most effective possible way.

In other words, if that logic did not determine the substance of Lincoln's position—or that of any other Republican—it nevertheless had an important impact on the form that that position could take. On one side, the tradition insisted that *if* an individual took a position on a major social issue, it was not enough to worry about the impact on the regime. One also had to consider the consequences for one's own personal activity. On the other side, the tradition insisted that no policy could be evaluated entirely in instrumental terms—that is, its likely impact on the nation's material or social well being. Ultimately, such policies and institutions must be appraised in terms of a finally perfectionist standard that would indeed be worthy of a saint.

But the point here is not simply the impact on Lincoln himself. In fact, the tradition put a great emphasis on both ethics and political responsibility, and on both rational calculation and moral duty. And it followed that any position, any political ethic, that could effectively invoke all these values was likely to appeal powerfully to those who were molded by this tradition.

Thus, Lincoln's solution can be regarded as superior because he solved two sets of problems (precisely what was required to solve either). He solved the institutional question of how to solve the moral question of slavery; he solved the moral question of how to rework institutions. This understanding is available to us only if we recognize the multiple aspects of Lincoln's position; we cannot talk about either Lincoln's solution or its superiority in the context of a causal analysis of American consensus liberalism or of the causes of the Civil War.

Greenstone's point was that we can only fully appreciate Lincoln (or any political actor) if we fully acknowledge the complexity of his views, his moral commitments, his political and institutional solutions, and, finally, the contexts in which he lived. Neither mythologized nor demystifying accounts of Lincoln capture his genius, because, in the end, neither is sufficiently complex; their lack of complexity, in turn, is related to their implicitly causal accounts of politics. What Greenstone has shown us is that, contrary to demystification accounts, Lincoln did refound the union, but not because he was the saint of the mythologizing accounts. Rather, Lincoln combined certain moral commitments, and a particular view of the place of morality and duty—as exemplified by John Adams and John Quincy Adams—with political and philosophical acumen.

REFERENCES FOR CARLA HESS'S INTRODUCTION

Bloor, David. 1983. *Wittgenstein: A Social Theory of Knowledge*. New York: Columbia University Press.

Danford, John. 1981 [1978]. *Wittgenstein and Political Philosophy: A Reexamination of the Foundations of Social Science*. Chicago: University of Chicago Press Midway Reprint.

Easton, Susan M. 1983. *Humanist Marxism and Wittgenstein's Social Philosophy*. Manchester: Manchester University Press.

Pitkin, Hanna Fenichel. 1972. *Wittgenstein and Justice*. Berkeley: University of California Press.

THE LINCOLN PERSUASION

PART ONE

INTRODUCTION TO PART ONE

MORE THAN thirty years ago, Marvin Meyers began his classic study, *The Jacksonian Persuasion*, by identifying a persuasion as "a matched set of attitudes, beliefs, projected actions. . . . At a given social moment some of these [shared values of a community] acquire a compelling importance. The political expression given to such values forms a persuasion."[1] A few years later, in the introduction to a new edition, Meyers added an implicit invitation to other scholars. At certain points, he noted, "the tired language of party politics" acquires a surprising new force, "a relevance and vitality." "Characteristically, a commanding presidential voice and figure—Jefferson, Jackson, Lincoln, Theodore Roosevelt, Wilson, FDR—immediately worked the change by giving moral direction, programmatic purpose to a conventional rhetoric."[2] Fifteen years ago, Lance Banning responded to Meyers's invitation by taking up the case of Jefferson. Although Banning's concept of *persuasion* was not identical to Meyers's, *The Jeffersonian Persuasion* offered an incisive account of "the more or less coherent body of assumptions, values, and ideas that bound [Jeffersonian] Republicans together as it shaped their common understanding of society and politics and lent a common meaning to events."[3]

Whereas Banning examined the era prior to the period of the Jacksonian persuasion, *The Lincoln Persuasion* examines the outlook that brought Jacksonianism's cultural hegemony to an end. *The Lincoln Persuasion* examines both the political and philosophical dimensions of the complex outlook—the persuasion—ultimately adopted by most northern Americans with regard to chattel slavery. As were Meyers and Banning, I am concerned with political culture, with a broad-gauged orientation toward politics and government—at mid-century in the present case—rather than with a creed so tightly organized that believers must accept or reject it whole. With all its intellectual elegance, Lincoln's outlook was indeed a persuasion, in part because it was genuinely eclectic. It can be understood, that is, only in terms of the many and diverse sources, philosophic as well as cultural, that Lincoln drew upon in constructing it. These sources included not only the Whig and Yankee reform perspective, from which Lincoln drew his major inspiration, but also the Jeffersonian and Jacksonian perspectives against which the Whigs contended. For the men of the second, the "silver generation," such as Webster, Clay, Calhoun, and Jackson, the central political challenge was to preserve the legacy of the founders and still make marks in politics of their

[1] Meyers 1960, 10.
[2] Ibid., vii.
[3] Banning 1978, 15.

own. In so doing, the second generation had to confront the remarkable dimensions of the founders' achievements, a task at which they only partially succeeded. The present account argues that Lincoln can best be understood as the great third-generation politician and political thinker, who reflected on both the achievements and the shortcomings of his predecessors; that the contribution, and genius, of the Lincoln persuasion was that it took up the same challenge that had faced the second generation and offered more satisfactory solutions.

Moreover, Lincoln developed his outlook, his persuasion, during the course of a national crisis so profound that it forced all who grappled with it to examine the basic commitments of their regime. Partly because the crisis forced such an examination and partly because Lincoln elaborated his position with great care and logical rigor, the Lincoln persuasion illuminates liberalism in American political culture. A study of the Lincoln persuasion must therefore turn from time to time to the philosophical and theological perspectives that it embraced. This study will argue that at its core American political culture is pervasively liberal—but not consensually so; that although American liberalism excludes nonliberal alternatives, it is nevertheless fundamentally divided, philosophically as well as politically. It is divided by an opposition between what I have called reform liberals, who were concerned primarily with the development of the faculties of individuals, and what I have called humanist liberals, who were concerned primarily with the satisfaction of the preferences of individuals. This opposition, this liberal polarity, began to emerge in the 1830s, most starkly in the conflict over slavery that eventually consumed almost all Lincoln's thoughts and energies.

The Lincoln persuasion can best be understood as one major episode in the development of that polarity. The polarity does not always correspond precisely to partisan political divisions, because it has philosophical as well as political dimensions. During the second generation of the republic, the polarity accounts for the attention paid by that generation to two very different issues left unresolved by the founders. First, how could stable electoral majorities be assembled from the conflicting preferences of a polity that was historically the first large, very heterogeneous, and militantly democratic polity? The humanist liberal Jacksonians offered several answers, most interestingly Martin Van Buren's theory of party, which was implicitly a rational choice theory. Second, how could the claims of morality be reconciled with the necessary compromises of pluralistic politics? The most revealing of the answers of the reform liberals to this question was the effort by John Quincy Adams to combine hostility to slavery with devotion to the Union. The existence of a liberal polarity, then, accounts for the *different questions* taken up under the humanist and the reform outlooks. Each outlook, when confronted with the problem of slavery, provided answers that were only partially successful. The Lincoln persuasion, however, was a very successful synthesis of both outlooks; and it provided the North with a politically viable and intellectually coherent stand on slavery, because it added humanist features to a more complex and subtle reform liberal understanding of the issue.

The Lincoln persuasion, like any other human perspective, of course, had its own distinctive shortcomings. Even if it offered the best available approach to the slavery issue, as I believe it did, it required compromise on the timing of emancipation, a compromise understandably scorned by committed abolitionists; and it helped bring on a civil war and the almost unimaginable human suffering that haunted Lincoln throughout his presidency. As Hofstadter has so memorably observed, Lincoln's own social vision failed almost entirely to anticipate the wrenching social transformations that his nation would begin to experience within a generation after his death. Nor did Lincoln perceive the way in which his own party and its free labor ideology would contribute to that transformation and to the difficulties and the often sheer human misery that these transformations brought with them. In the end, however, Lincoln's achievement must be understood and, to a degree, judged in terms of its own time and place. With respect to place, I shall try to show its connections to the enduring patterns of liberal thought and practice that constitute American politics. With respect to time, I shall argue that the persuasion that Lincoln developed offered a set of remarkably subtle responses—and solutions—to some of the most serious problems of American republican politics, problems that had already preoccupied both the founders and their antebellum successors.

One of the basic concerns of the present work is with understanding the development of American political history from Lincoln's viewpoint, primarily by exploring the philosophic as well as the cultural sources of his outlook. In this way, I think, we can understand his achievement as an achievement that amounted to a refounding of the Union. The present account, then, is concerned with explanation, although the explanation offered will be cultural rather than causal, and intentional rather than reductionist. As chapter one makes clear, my chief concern is not with the interests or motives—as important as they are—that caused Lincoln or any of his contemporaries or predecessors to adopt this or that political position. Rather my analysis will emphasize the perspectives of the actors themselves—their responses to those problems with the American republican experiment that they found most troubling. I shall, thereby, try to emulate Meyers's achievement by offering fresh readings of often familiar materials. My concern is with the cultural, and ultimately the philosophical, tools the actors used and improved in fashioning solutions to the political problems they encountered; my concern is also with the question of why and especially how Lincoln and his political allies devised solutions that built upon and surpassed the solutions of his predecessors. To answer these questions, the present work focuses on the particular features of Lincoln's culture and political tradition that shaped his outlook. Some of these he was explicitly aware of; others he may simply have taken for granted. It is only by understanding these features that we can see fully the strengths, as well as the limits, of Lincoln's complex persuasion.

ONE

THE LINCOLN MYTH RECONSIDERED

MEMORIAL DAY, as W. Lloyd Warner wrote in his study of a small New England city, "is a cult of the dead which organizes and integrates the [community] . . . into a sacred unity." In that cult, Abraham Lincoln functioned as a "martyred" saint. Revered as a prophet, his words "intoned . . . as if they were a religious chant," he "loomed over the memorial rituals like some great demigod over the rites of classical antiquity."[1] Warner's overt claim was that Lincoln occupies a mythic place in American political culture. Warner suggested, moreover, that understanding the significance of Lincoln—and, more broadly, the significance of the Lincoln persuasion—for American politics requires an analysis based on American culture.

According to the myth, Lincoln was truly the Great Emancipator, who spoke and acted on his culture's profound commitment to human freedom.[2] From 1854 on, Lincoln repeatedly denounced slavery as so thoroughly immoral that it must never be allowed to expand. After his election as president, his position on slavery made secession and civil war virtually unavoidable. During the war, Lincoln proclaimed most of the slaves to be "forever free," he gave crucial support to the Thirteenth Amendment, which freed the rest, and he saw his armies devastate the rebellious slave states. The myth also depicts Lincoln as the wise and principled visionary. He is Father Abraham, who correctly predicted the eventual demise of the peculiar institution and led the North in a terrible war to uproot it. Whereas his contemporaries seemed caught up by the bewildering events that began in 1850, Lincoln drew on the resources of his culture, notably on the rhetoric of liberty and union, in order to illuminate the consuming crisis of their era. In liberating the slaves, he led his generation to free itself from a national sin.

By assigning an important place in American politics to moral issues and to a concern for the community, the Lincoln myth draws on pivotal cultural themes. The myth reasserts, in its own idiom, the seventeenth-century Puritan ideal of the saints' godly errand and the eighteenth-century republican vision of citizen virtue; it prefigures as well the Progressive party's commitment to the public interest a century later. From the mythic perspective, treating Lincoln as if he were just another self-serving politician would be vulgar reductionism—but myths invite demystification.

[1] Warner 1961, 217, 234, 247.
[2] Jaffa 1965, 140–41; Oates 1977.

One kind of demystification was offered by Marx. In "On the Jewish Question," Marx drew an important distinction between, on the one hand, the egoism of civil society that is capitalist economic life, and, on the other, the belief of the bourgeois political community in its own idealism and political morality:

> All the presuppositions of . . . egoistic life continue to exist in *civil society outside* the political sphere. . . . [By contrast, w]here the political state has attained to its full development, man lives . . . in the *political community*, where he regards himself as a *communal being*. . . . The political state . . . stands in the same opposition to civil society . . . as religion [stands] . . . to the narrowness of the profane world; i.e., it has always to acknowledge [the profane world] . . . and allow itself to be dominated by it.[3]

Marx's account is dualistic, causal, and reductionist. First, it describes two quite different realms, the egoistic economy and the moral polity. Second, it assigns causal priority to the former. Finally, it argues that liberal politics functions to sustain capitalist economic relations, within which self-regarding motives have a certain primacy.

From Marx's perspective, the Lincoln myth epitomizes the bourgeois moralism that masks the underlying but dominant selfishness of bourgeois culture. In Lincoln's case, accounts that attempt to reduce explanations of his actions to one or more of his self-regarding motives have a wealth of evidence to draw upon. In the decade after its passage, Lincoln accepted the Fugitive Slave Act of 1850, despite its flagrant bias in favor of the slave owners.[4] In the years before the Civil War, he called only for a "gradual" process of emancipation, which might well take no "less than a hundred years," and he disclaimed any support for the social or political equality of free blacks.[5] This celebrated moderation helped him to win the Republican nomination for president in 1860, and it characterized his presidency. In a famous letter to Horace Greeley in 1862, Lincoln wrote that he intended to free only that number of slaves most likely to preserve the Union.[6] Indeed, the Emancipation Proclamation left unfreed all those slaves whose masters resided in areas then under Union control. The result, Hofstadter wrote, achieved "all the moral grandeur of a bill of lading."[7] Although Lincoln obviously took a leading part in the events that freed the slaves, he confessed quite movingly in his Second Inaugural that he had neither foreseen nor controlled those events.

[3] Marx 1843, in Tucker 1978, 34.
[4] Johannsen 1965, 76–77.
[5] Basler 1953–1955, 2:256, 370, 407–9; 3:16ff.
[6] Ibid., 5:388.
[7] Hofstadter 1974, 169.

According to accounts that stress Lincoln's self-regarding motives, the Lincoln myth is a case of hagiography as well as of mystification, because the celebration of the role of beliefs obscures the decisive importance of the self-regarding motives. Whether or not Lincoln was moved by a principled opposition to slavery, he almost certainly reasoned and acted instrumentally to satisfy one or more of those motives. Furthermore, his positions on slavery and union were means that could be adopted, dropped, or changed as the pursuit of his self-regarding goals required. And, if Lincoln's self-regarding motives were decisive, cultural considerations could count only in the relatively trivial sense that for social action to proceed smoothly, there must be some agreement on fundamentals—for example, a shared understanding of basic legal rules.

We have, then, two competing views of Lincoln, each resting on empirically supported intuitions: the view of Lincoln as acting on principle and the view of Lincoln as acting on self-regarding motives. The two may appear to be incompatible and thus "essentially contested,"[8] but it is not entirely clear that we must choose between them. Lincoln's conduct, after all, was not a single act but an extended series of actions that can validly be described in a number of different ways. As I will show, Lincoln himself developed a persuasion that effectively appealed to both the idealism and the self-interest of his political allies. He relentlessly pursued political success, yet he also had penetrating, at times profound, moral insights that resonated among his compatriots, presumably because he shared with those compatriots certain fundamental commitments. Moreover, once he had come to prominence during the sectional crisis of the 1850s, his pursuit of success and his moral insights seem to have developed in tandem.

The wisest course for the interpreter, then, may not be to attempt to vindicate one view of Lincoln at the expense of the other but, rather, to ask how his self-regarding motives were connected to the principle at the heart of the myth. In addressing these questions, this chapter first considers Lincoln's political, economic, and social-psychological motives. It next examines what he himself called his "principle of action" with regard to the issues of liberty and union—the principle, that is, that formed the core of his political persuasion. The chapter then analyzes the general differences between motive and principle. Finally, it identifies three important connections between Lincoln's own motives and his principle. Two of these connections are consistent with Marx's reductionist view. First, the principle helped Lincoln pursue his self-regarding aims more effectively, and, second, the principle committed him to supporting the social order in which his ambitions could be pursued effectively. The third connection is contrary to

[8] Gallie 1964.

Marx's basic account: there were certain respects in which Lincoln's principle committed him to changing his social and political order—to solving certain fundamental political problems—in ways that *limited*, rather than served, his ulterior motives. It is at this point, after granting as much credence as possible to the reductionist, ulterior-motive accounts, that we will be able to see the ultimate importance of Lincoln's principle and of his broader persuasion. In so far as the Lincoln persuasion offered solutions to the problems of Lincoln's polity, in so far as it was a genuine cultural achievement, we must understand fully the cultural sources of the political as well as the intellectual success of the persuasion.

Lincoln's Ulterior Motives

Lincoln readily acknowledged the importance of his own and other people's self-regarding, ulterior motives. For himself, he put the case with typical wit in his 1858 debate with Stephen A. Douglas at Alton: "The Bible says somewhere that we are desperately selfish. I think we would have discovered that fact without the Bible. I do not claim that I am any less so than the average of men, but I do claim that I am not more selfish than Judge Douglas [roars of laughter and applause]."[9] Different sets of scholars have emphasized three motives in particular: Lincoln's ambition for political office, his ambition for economic success, and his desire for social-psychological independence from the founding generation.

Political Ambition

Lincoln's political ambition is notorious. He loved politics from his youth. He talked about it incessantly, read about it voraciously, and played it for keeps. Bound by the Whigs of his county to vote for another candidate at a congressional district convention, for example, Lincoln still sought votes for himself elsewhere in the district.[10] After finally serving a term in Congress, he "frantically" but unsuccessfully sought an appointment as commissioner of the United States General Land Office, even though he had promised to support a political associate for the position.[11] Depressed by this failure, Lincoln was disappointed once again in 1855, when the Illinois legislature chose Lyman Trumbull for the U.S. Senate.[12] Yet, in the words of his law partner, Lincoln's ambition was "a little engine that knew no rest."

[9] Basler 1953–1955, 3:310.
[10] B. P. Thomas 1952, 102–3.
[11] Ibid., 128–29; cf. Oates 1977, 96.
[12] Oates 1977, 131; B. P. Thomas 1952, 155.

Driven by it, Lincoln became a leader among Illinois Whigs and later among the state's Republicans.[13]

In advancing his career, Lincoln carefully calculated his positions on prominent issues. As a state legislator in the 1830s, his chief goal was to move the capital of Illinois to Springfield, and, although he dissented publicly from the legislature's proslavery resolutions, he waited until the decision to move the capital had been made before doing so. "Young Lincoln," one biographer has observed, "had elected to work within the system, and was not about to ruin his career" on behalf of blacks.[14] Lincoln scorned the nativist movement during the 1850s, for example, but he muted his disapproval, because he and his party needed the movement's supporters.[15] During this same period, in contrast, some Republicans were consciously using the slavery issue to arouse their own loyalists,[16] and few did so to more effect than Lincoln.

His eloquent attack on the Kansas-Nebraska Act in 1854 revived a career that was in partial eclipse after his opposition in Congress to the Mexican War.[17] In 1858, Lincoln distinguished himself from Douglas by emphasizing his own belief in slavery's immorality, while at the same time playing down his and Douglas's specific agreement on the institution's fate in Kansas and their partial agreement on the broader question of its expansion.[18] Once the campaign began, however, Lincoln also made an appeal to more conservative voters by disclaiming the idea of social and political equality for blacks. Moreover, his policy of excluding slavery from the territories would have protected white settlers from having to associate or compete with blacks whether they were slave or free. "Irrespective of the moral aspect of this question," as he carefully put it, "I am still in favor of our new Territories being in such a condition that [they will be] . . . an outlet for *free white people everywhere*."[19] During the war, the same penchant for political calculation continued. Most notably, the complex terms of the Emancipation Proclamation, for example, were explicitly designed to appeal to the border states as well as to Republican strongholds in the North; the proclamation was adopted "only after all his other policies [compensated emancipation in the border states, for example] had failed."[20]

[13] Oates 1977, 106, 161; cf. 26; cf. Basler 1953–1955, 3:310.

[14] Oates 1977, 40–41.

[15] Fehrenbacher 1962, 14; Basler 1953–1955, 2:323, 333, 373.

[16] Holt 1978, 13.

[17] Fehrenbacher 1962, 20–21.

[18] Potter 1976, 338–39; Fehrenbacher 1962, 38–39; Craven 1971, 391; see also Wells 1971.

[19] Johannsen 1965, 316. See Oates 1977, 171; Jaffa 1959, 61. Despite his denials, Lincoln even appears to have formed a tacit alliance with prosouthern Buchanan Democrats (Fehrenbacher 1962, 113).

[20] Hofstadter 1974, 168.

Capitalist Loyalties

Lincoln was also enthusiastic about the capitalist pursuit of wealth and profit. The son-in-law of a prosperous banker, he joined in promoting Illinois railroads, and he represented many of them in court for sizable fees.[21] In 1840, "he helped renew the charter of the Springfield state bank . . . partly out of loyalty to Whig chums who were indebted to that institution." Over the next twenty years, Lincoln himself accumulated substantial financial equity.[22]

As a member of the Illinois legislature and later of Congress, Lincoln was "sound" on those issues that tied most northern business interests first to the Whig and then to the Republican party.[23] In 1860 he readily accepted a platform that "spoke in timid and faltering accents about slavery . . . but on [the] economic questions . . . its voice rang out loud and clear."[24] Once in office, Lincoln approved tariff, homestead, banking, and railroad legislation, as well as a liberal immigration policy that was intended to hold down wages by replenishing a labor force already drained by western settlement. During his administration, Charles and Mary Beard concluded, "the Republicans had accomplished amid the crash of arms what neither the Federalists nor the Whigs had been able to achieve in time of peace."[25]

Until then, slave-owning interests had resourcefully opposed essentially all of this program. According to this familiar economic account, therefore, Lincoln opposed slavery because the planter class was the chief political enemy of his business allies. The proclamation, to be sure, respected bourgeois property rights by exempting the slaves belonging to loyal border-state slave owners; however, in freeing all other slaves without compensation, it effectively destroyed the economic base of the southern planters.

Social Status and Problems of Parental Authority

Although a sometime leader in his church and village community, Lincoln's father Thomas was an illiterate and a failure in the eyes of his more obviously successful son.[26] Troubled by his inferior social background, the son, according to a sympathetic biographer, harbored "considerable hostility" toward his father, "all mixed up with love, rivalry, and ambition." Lincoln, for example, invited none of his relatives to his wedding, and he told his parents about it only months later when he happened to visit the family

---

21 Oates 1977, 58; B. P. Thomas 1952, 111.
22 Oates 1977, 54, 107.
23 Ibid., 23–24, 195, 215; B. P. Thomas 1952, 58, 62, 77–78.
24 Hacker, in Stampp 1959, 64.
25 Beard and Beard 1936, 2:104; see also 2:106–11, 128.
26 Oates 1977, 6–7.

farm.[27] In 1851, when his father was dying, Lincoln could manage only to write a stilted letter.[28] When he was "repeatedly . . . urged to make a parting visit, he first ignored the letters from his family and then finally wrote to his stepbrother saying that he would not come. The press of business was one excuse; the minor illness of his wife was another. . . . Thomas Lincoln died a few days later. His son did not go to the funeral."[29] Thomas Lincoln was neither a model of success nor a source of encouragement for an ambitious son; he could never really have been a worthy rival in his son's eyes.[30] Lincoln's actions, interpreted psychoanalytically, thus suggest Oedipal feelings that were never fully developed, or resolved, by identification with his father.

Lincoln's rivalrous feelings, however, could be shifted from his personal conflicts with his father to a public conflict with the founders of his country. Having won independence and launched the great republican experiment, the "fathers," especially Washington, were painted in mythic terms that captured the imagination of Lincoln and his peers.[31] How then, as Lincoln himself asked in his 1838 Lyceum Address, could the new generation equal these accomplishments, unless it either tore down the republic or preserved it in a way that outshone the achievements of the fathers? After dutifully praising the fathers in the Lyceum Address, Lincoln subtly disparaged them by suggesting that they benefited from good fortune and acted out of passion.[32] Still, Lincoln conceded that his own generation could try only to preserve its republican inheritance—a role so modest it would never satisfy an ambitious Caesar, who "thirsts and burns for distinction" and "*scorns* to tread in the footsteps of *any* predecessor." So great would be the usurper's ambition that he would violate the fathers' "temple of liberty"—whether his cause be "emancipating slaves or enslaving freemen."[33]

The achievements of the revolutionary generation provided Lincoln with a worthy rival and the opportunity to transfer both identification and rivalry from his own father to the founding patriarchs. From the psychoanalytic perspective, in other words, Lincoln sought to resolve his Oedipal feelings first by identifying with the fathers of the prior generation and their cause of republican freedom, and then by surpassing their achievements with his own. He was able to move "beyond the fathers while being true to them"[34] by attacking the institution of slavery, which the fathers had, however

---

[27] Ibid., 14, 69; cf. Strozier 1982, 51.
[28] B. P. Thomas 1952, 134; Oates 1977, 103.
[29] Forgie 1979, 34.
[30] B. P. Thomas 1952, 134–35.
[31] Forgie 1979, 19, 35ff.; cf. Strozier 1982, 61ff.
[32] Basler 1953–1955, 1:113–14; see also Forgie 1979, 62–65.
[33] Basler 1953–1955, 1:114–15.
[34] Forgie 1979, 241.

grudgingly, accepted.[35] A crucial step for Lincoln, George Forgie has argued, was to secure his own identification with the fathers by depicting Stephen A. Douglas—the Democrat with whom he had competed for many years—as the disloyal son who was responsible for the repeal of the fathers' venerated Missouri Compromise. In contrast, Lincoln portrayed himself as the faithful son who would defend the fathers' commitment to freedom. To Forgie, for example, the deepest source of Lincoln's motivation was therefore psychological, and Lincoln's object was not "to solve the problem of slavery for the slave or for the slave-holder, but to solve it for Northern whites in psychological terms."[36] Thus a case can be made that Lincoln's rivalrous feelings toward the revolutionary fathers fueled a towering ambition that, through his attack on slavery, led him to the White House and to the bloodshed, the authoritarianism, and the tragedy of the Civil War.[37]

The psychoanalytic account can be restated sociologically. Committed to rising from his lower-class origins, Lincoln was preoccupied with issues of social mobility and recognition. Painfully ill-at-ease with the opposite sex, he was still attracted to women from families much more cultured than his own, and he was hurt when his future wife's family thought him a socially unsuitable match.[38] These feelings about his own social inferiority were reinforced by his generation's widely recognized preoccupation with the achievements of the founders. The slavery crisis offered him and his peers a route to comparable fame and glory. As Lincoln himself put it in a presidential message, "this fiery trial" would, if fully endured, "light us down, in honor or dishonor, to the latest generation."[39]

Lincoln's Devotion to Liberty and Union

These ulterior-motive explanations demonstrate Lincoln's extraordinary ambition. Yet the myth is indisputably correct on one crucial point: in both word and deed, he demonstrated a consistent devotion to the values of liberty and union that were central to his political culture. In David Potter's words, Lincoln was a romantic nationalist, "a devotee of the cult of Union as preached by [Daniel] Webster and [Henry] Clay." In his eulogy of Clay in 1852, Lincoln praised the Kentuckian for carefully avoiding "all sectional ground. Whatever he did, he did for the whole country."[40] Lincoln himself considered the Union to be "perpetual," based on "mystic chords of mem-

---

[35] Basler 1953–1955, 3:534–35.
[36] Forgie 1979, 275.
[37] Rogin 1982, 79–80.
[38] Oates 1977, 60.
[39] Basler 1953–1955, 5:537.
[40] Potter 1976, 343; Basler 1953–1955, 2:126.

ory," on the people's "pride in, and reverence for, the history, and government, of their common country."[41] He had as little use for southern secessionists as for abolitionists, who would, in his words, "shiver into fragments the Union . . . [and] tear to tatters its now venerated constitution."[42]

Lincoln's unionism reflected more than patriotic sentiment. To some scholars, it had an aristocratic element. As early as 1838, Jaffa has written, Lincoln called for virtuous "great souled" leaders devoted to the rule of reason, because successful popular governments had to resolve "the eternal antagonism within the human soul of reason and passion." Moreover, justice required "the discretionary judgment of wise men."[43] Lincoln himself remarked that Henry Clay "loved his country partly because it was his own country, but mostly because it was a free country."[44] More particularly, Lincoln held that the American nation rested on the universal "moral principles" of the Declaration of Independence.[45] Especially after the failure of Europe's republican revolutions in 1848, the survival of the Union could demonstrate that popular government was not an absurdity—a theme he repeated at Gettysburg.[46] As he told a group of abolitionist clergy from Chicago just before he issued the Emancipation Proclamation, "We already have an important principle to rally and unite the people in the fact that constitutional government is at stake. [That] fundamental idea . . . [goes] about as deep as anything."[47] As late as 1864 Lincoln insisted that the essence of the Civil War was saving the Union: "The issue is distinct, simple, and inflexible."[48]

According to a number of scholars, Lincoln's unionism was so important to him that he was willing to limit or even abandon his opposition to slavery. For other scholars, Lincoln opposed the slave interest less in order to eliminate the institution than to preserve the national status quo.[49] In Holt's words, Lincoln "raised the . . . issue [of slavery's immorality] less to [evoke] . . . humanitarian sympathy for black slaves than to supplement his primary theme . . . [of] a pro-slavery plot" against the republic.[50] According to Jaffa, Lincoln regarded disunionism as the main enemy; he thought that "the human condition is full of evils of which slavery is only one," and "political societies are not obliged to practice suicide."[51]

[41] Basler 1953–1955, 4:264, 271, 432.
[42] Ibid., 2:130; cf. 253.
[43] Jaffa 1959, 195, 203, 218. [Thanks to Nathan Tarcov for this citation.]
[44] Basler 1953–1955, 2:126.
[45] Ibid., 2:499–500.
[46] Ibid., 7:23; cf. B. P. Thomas 1952, 268–69.
[47] Basler 1953–1955, 5:424; cf. Jaffa 1965, 144.
[48] Basler 1953–1955, 8:151.
[49] Cf. ibid., 2:461–68; Holt 1978, x.
[50] Holt 1978, 210.
[51] Jaffa 1965, 149–50.

If Lincoln loved the Union, however, he also despised slavery. As a child he had been exposed to the antislavery creed of his parents' church. As an adult, he wrote to an old friend that he hated "to see the poor creatures hunted down"; slave holders must appreciate "how much the great body of Northern people do crucify their feelings, in order to maintain their loyalty to the constitution and the Union."[52] Just before Lincoln took office, one North Carolinian perceptively remarked that the new president "is regarded [by Southerners] as neither a dangerous or bad man. . . . We rather suppose his purpose will be to conciliate. But . . . the *fundamental idea* . . . of his nomination and canvass & his election . . . is the declaration of unceasing war against slavery as an institution."[53] As Lincoln himself put it in one celebrated fragment, no criterion, be it color, intellect, or interest, could justify one person's enslaving a second without justifying the enslavement of the first person by a third of still lighter skin, greater intellect, or more compelling interests.[54] In another reflection Lincoln wondered if God had decreed that "Sambo," the slave of a Dr. Ross, should be freed. Because the divine judgment remained inscrutable, and nobody

> thinks of asking Sambo's opinion. . . . At last, it comes to this, that *Dr. Ross* is to decide the question. And while he consider[s] it, he sits in the shade, with gloves on his hands, and subsists on the bread that Sambo is earning in the burning sun. . . . Will Dr. Ross be actuated by that perfect impartiality, which has ever been considered most favorable to correct decisions? As a *good* thing, slavery is strikingly peculiar, in this, that it is the only good thing which no man ever seeks the good of, *for himself*.[55]

"If slavery is not wrong," Lincoln said near the end of his first presidential term, "nothing is wrong. I can not remember when I did not so think, and feel."[56] During his presidency, he expressed the belief, shared by many northern Protestants, that the war was a deserved punishment for the nation's sins—particularly for slavery.[57]

Lincoln's Principle of Action

Lincoln's devotion to liberty and union obviously drew upon a political culture that he shared with his fellow Northerners. How did he reconcile these two sentiments, when to embrace antislavery was to endanger union

[52] Basler 1953–1955, 2:320.
[53] B. P. Thomas 1952, 228.
[54] Basler 1953–1955, 2:222–23.
[55] Ibid., 3:204–5.
[56] Ibid., 7:281; 2:281; 3:368.
[57] Ibid., 4:482; 8:332–33.

by provoking a southern secession? Given the tension between liberty and union, how do these values actually undermine an ulterior motive account—especially since it could be argued plausibly that Lincoln had the flexibility to take either prounionist or antislavery actions, depending on what his ulterior motives dictated?

The difficulty with this view is that it overlooks the real intuition on which the Lincoln myth, and any analysis of the Lincoln persuasion, rests: Lincoln's actions were determined by what he called a "right principle of action" on the issues of slavery and union.[58] This principle had two sides. In order to promote national unity, the Union had to "faithfully observe" all the constitutional guarantees that protected slavery in the slave states and had to accept even the Fugitive Slave Act of 1850. But the principle also imposed a strict condition: the national government had to stigmatize the institution—to declare it immoral—by "treating it as a wrong, with the fixed idea that it must *and will* come to an end."[59] Moreover, this stigmatization required deeds as well as words. The national government must adopt policies that would eventually end slavery, primarily by preventing the institution's territorial expansion.[60]

All of Lincoln's key stands on slavery can easily be depicted as consistent with this standard. As a member of Congress from 1847 to 1849, Lincoln could and did pursue this goal by supporting the Wilmot Proviso, which would have barred slavery from the areas won during the Mexican War. He was able to avoid extensive public pronouncements on the issue before 1854, because the nation's prevailing policy, the Missouri Compromise of

[58] Ibid., 4:445.

[59] Ibid., 3:370, 368, emphasis added. I am indebted to Nathan Tarcov for this formulation of Lincoln's position.

[60] The House Divided speech, to be sure, called for placing slavery "where the public mind shall rest in the belief that it is in the course of ultimate extinction," and some commentators have asked if the real goal was simply to reassure the public (cf. Basler 1953–1955, 2:461). Yet Lincoln typically insisted that the belief in slavery's demise must be well-founded (cf. Forgie 1979, 275, 270–71; Basler 1953–1955, 2:514). "If we could arrest the spread" of slavery, he remarked later in 1858, "it *would be* in the course of ultimate extinction" (Basler 1953–1955, 3:18, quoted by Fehrenbacher 1962, 77; see also Basler 1953–1955, 3:180–81). This position was at least plausible on the merits. For one thing, Genovese has argued that by exhausting the soil in the lower South, the plantation system threatened slavery's long-run viability (Genovese 1965, 26 and ch. 4; cf. B. P. Thomas 1952, 223). Without new areas for expansion, the slave breeders in the upper South would lose an essential market, thus eroding the institution's economic viability in their own states. Moreover, the Republican plan to treat slavery as an evil—to make "freedom national"—threatened slavery in other ways. Lincoln came to support procedural protections for blacks accused of being runaways, notably jury trials, that would have seriously undermined enforcement of the Fugitive Slave Act of 1850 (Basler 1953–1955, 4:264). It was widely thought that Republican presidents would eventually appoint antislavery federal officials in the South, end proslavery censorship of the mails, and perhaps encourage agitation among the slaves and hostility among poor whites toward rich slave owners (Potter 1976, 398).

1820, did brand slavery as a wrong by excluding it from the northern Louisiana Purchase.[61] The Kansas-Nebraska Act repealed this exclusion and removed the stigma. After that, slavery might go any place where the climate and economic conditions were favorable, including to any newly acquired territories in the Caribbean.

Just as his principle required, Lincoln responded with unremitting protest. During the Civil War, Lincoln's policies and speeches continued to treat slavery itself as a wrong, and he joined with the Republican Congress in outlawing the institution throughout the federal territories.[62] Similarly, although the Emancipation Proclamation respected slavery's constitutional protections by exempting the slave owners still in the Union, it freed all other slaves because the masters who had left the Union were beyond the protection of the Constitution. In the end, Lincoln moved against slavery in the loyal border states in the one way his principle permitted: by amending the Constitution.

It might be objected, once again, that reference to Lincoln's principle of action does not really count against ulterior-motive arguments. Because the principle combined such very different values, because it required him both to denounce slavery and to defend union, it might seem flexible or capacious enough to justify almost any action, even if the action were actually self-serving. However, this argument confounds flexibility with indeterminacy. Lincoln could both reject slavery as immoral and yet try to preserve union, even though that union included the slave states, because, as a good Whig, he relied on time to provide a solution. He did not, in other words, specify a determinate date for slavery's demise. Instead, he insisted, as we have seen, on three strict conditions: first, the national government must brand slavery as a wrong; second, it must act on that judgment by restricting the institution to the existing slave states where it could be expected—in time—to die; and, finally, the government must ensure the outcome by precluding any retrogression. Once a step forward was taken, no backward step would be allowed.

---

[61] The Compromise of 1850 did permit the territorial organization of Utah and New Mexico without explicit restriction of slavery. Yet "[u]nder all the circumstances," Lincoln said in a lawyer-like remark at Peoria, "perhaps . . . [the compromise] was not wrong" (Basler 1953–1955, 2:235). For one thing, as he pointed out in 1858, the prevailing Mexican law in Utah and New Mexico would still preclude slavery. Moreover, the laws of 1850 created a free-state majority in the Senate by admitting California, rejected Texas's territorial claims against New Mexico, and abolished the slave trade in the District of Columbia (Basler 1953–1955, 2:259). In return, as Potter noted, the new Fugitive Slave Act returned to Southerners only about three hundred slaves up to 1860 (two slaves per slave state per year), while almost no slaves actually reached Utah or New Mexico (Potter 1976, 119). Perhaps most importantly, the laws of 1850 left the stigma of slavery unchanged by continuing to exclude slavery from the northern part of the purchase.

[62] Jaffa 1965, 153, 163.

The essential point for Lincoln, then, was not an immediate, determinate result, but the observable and morally meaningful *direction* in which policies moved and the way in which one's actions reaffirmed this goal. The universal equality asserted in the declaration, he said, must be "a standard maxim for free society . . . constantly looked to, constantly *labored for*, and even though never perfectly attained, *constantly approximated*, and thereby constantly spreading and deepening its influence . . . [on behalf] of all people of all colors everywhere."[63] What was absolute about liberty was not the need to achieve it immediately, but the commitment to realizing it eventually—by deeds as well as words—while never tolerating a backward step. At the policy level, therefore, it was necessary to brand slavery as immoral and take the concrete step of restricting it to the South. In this way, Lincoln's principle controlled his actions, without regard to the dictates of his ulterior motives. Indeed, it would seem to have been this stand—his demand that the national government delegitimate slavery—that made his election unacceptable to the South and provoked secession. In any case, he stood by these conditions during the secession crisis despite pleas from northern moderates to abandon the conditions.

Lincoln's Motives and Principle

The discussion to this point has made clear how Lincoln's principle of action could account for his conduct, for *why* he took certain actions. Having adopted the principle, Lincoln was committed to acting according to its terms, to regarding certain deeds as intrinsically right because their features were consistent with the principle. A practical syllogism suggests the way in which Lincoln's principle, for example, called for the Emancipation Proclamation:

(a) The Union's commitment to liberty for all required ending or prohibiting slavery wherever it was not protected by the Constitution.

(b) During the Civil War, slavery was not protected by the Constitution in rebel areas.

(c) Therefore, slavery could and should be ended in rebel areas by the proclamation, even though it must be abolished elsewhere by constitutional amendment.

Weber's distinction between instrumental reasoning and principled reasoning is useful here. According to the motives explanation, individuals take the actions that appear most instrumentally effective in securing the end they seek (e.g., Lincoln's machinations to secure public office). Principled

[63] Basler 1953–1955, 2:406, emphasis added; cf. 2:385.

reasoning, in contrast, identifies actions that deserve to be taken because their features are consistent with some moral or ethical principle. If I adopt a principle, I am constrained to take actions that conform to it.[64]

In what sense, then, is an explanation based on principles truly valid? And how are we to choose between it and an explanation based on ulterior motives, if each seems plausible but they are "essentially contested"? On the one side, Lincoln's ulterior motives were obviously important. He thought his life meaningful and his society valuable because he and others like him could pursue success freely. On the other side, Lincoln's principle of action expressed his and his section's deepest ethical concerns. Lincoln himself certainly acknowledged the importance of both motives and principle. As he observed in 1863, many "motives" encouraged enlistments in the Union army, including "patriotism, political bias, ambition, personal courage, love of adventure, want of employment, and convenience, or the opposite of some of these."[65] Yet Lincoln also stressed "principles of action." As he said in 1858, the difference between him and Douglas was not that they had different "motives"; rather, he insisted, until we "can come together on *principle*," Douglas "is not now with us . . . [and] does not *promise* to *ever* be."[66]

One promising approach to the dilemma of choosing between principled and self-regarding motive explanations is to set aside the idea that these alternatives are mutually exclusive and to entertain instead the possibility that *principle* and *motive* refer to complementary features of a person's psyche, to different components of human action and, further, to different phenomena whose relationships vary according to circumstances. In Lincoln's case, for example, ulterior-motive explanations specify his goals but leave open the question of his choice of actions to reach those goals; that is, such explanations expect Lincoln to have chosen whatever means were most causally effective. In contrast, discussions of principles often concentrate on the moral features of an action without specifying definite or immediate results. Lincoln's principle, therefore, would have specified what actions were morally permissible and impermissible according to their ethical meaning—according to whether, for example, they condemned or condoned slavery—but the principle did not require a particular outcome at a particular time.[67] The focus here is *not* on the *strength of an actor's desires or motives* or on their likely effects on that individual's actions; it is rather on the *consistency of meaning* between the features of an act and the principle the actor has adopted. An individual, that is, would be willing to take any action

---

[64] Weber 1978, 24–26, 339, 1376.
[65] Basler 1953–1955, 6:445.
[66] Ibid., 2:468; cf. 3:310.
[67] Cf. Lawrence 1972, 3–12.

whose features are consistent with the principle adopted, no matter what motive causes the individual to take it.

No logical operation, that is, can reduce principle to motive, or motive to principle. We cannot logically, for example, begin with the premise that Lincoln acted on ulterior motives and then conclude that he was not constrained by a moral principle. Such an argument is defective, because the premise refers to motives while the conclusion refers to a principle. By the same token, we cannot reason from the importance of Lincoln's principle to the conclusion that his motives were unimportant. This argument brings us to a paradoxical possibility. If we assume that motives and principle point to identifiably different features of Lincoln's outlook, no complete account of Lincoln's actions can ignore one or the other. If motives and principle are separate in this way, then they may be causally related, and perhaps in just the way Marx suggested in the passage quoted above. However important Lincoln's principle was in shaping his conduct, that is, he may still have adopted it because it was instrumentally useful in pursuing his ulterior motives. In such a case, the motives would remain decisive in accounting for his actions. It is to that possibility that we now turn.

The Instrumental Dimension of Lincoln's Principle: The Advantage of Consistency

The ulterior-motive explanations to be considered here are not entirely consistent with each other. In pursuing a glory to rival that of the founders, Lincoln adopted a rigid, negative position on the question of extending slavery to the territories. Such a stance was disruptive of the nation's economy taken as a whole, and it antagonized many eastern capitalists.[68] Lincoln himself, of course, took a moderate position on other issues such as the Fugitive Slave Act, but a calculated mixture of moderation and rigidity was not the most effective way to compete with the towering achievements of the founders, a competition on which the psychological account depends.

As Lincoln saw it, such diverse economic, political, and psychological objectives created a problem for any political actor. As a case in point, in 1859 Lincoln warned his fellow Republicans in the new party not to take policy positions on behalf of one region that would harm another region.[69] As he had said in the House Divided speech, the Republicans had to concert the actions of *"strange, discordant*, and even, *hostile* elements."[70] To maintain its own unity and effectiveness, the party had to adopt an appropriate guide to action that would generally be accepted because it partially, even if only

[68] Stampp 1959; Potter 1976, 525ff., esp. n. 18.
[69] Oates 1977, 176.
[70] Basler 1953–1955, 2:468; cf. B. P. Thomas 1952; Fehrenbacher 1962; Forgie 1979, 251.

partially, satisfied the demands of each faction. Because all wings of the party shared a "principle"—opposition to slavery's expansion—the party as a whole could pursue a consistent policy on slavery.

Lincoln faced a problem analogous to the one his party faced. If he had simply moved with the ebb and flow of his particular ambitions—if he had first tried to implement his economic objectives, then his careerist desire for office, and finally his drive to surpass the founders—his erratic conduct might well have cost him both his credibility and his allies. Much as the party needed to unite around a generally acceptable program, Lincoln needed to follow a consistent course of conduct, a course that was possible only if he could reconcile his own somewhat incompatible motives. In this situation, his principle was important precisely because it prescribed a course of conduct that partially satisfied each motive but satisfied none of them completely. His obligation was to obey the principle, whatever the immediate effect on his specific ulterior goals, because obeying the principle was the most effective overall way to pursue his ambitions. Thus, on the one hand, Lincoln's principle, for example, required him to oppose the expansion of slavery regardless of other considerations, even though his stand cost him politically by exposing him to Douglas's race-baiting in 1858 and hurt his economic interests by contributing to the country's economic disruption in 1860–1861. Nevertheless, those actions helped him pursue a glory to equal that of the founders. On the other hand, the principle also demanded of him respect for the legality of slavery in the slave states, a demand that made competing with the revolutionary generation more difficult, even though that same position advanced some of his more immediate political and economic interests.

In functionalist language, the claim would be that Lincoln's principle served to help him achieve a satisfactory balance among the pursuits of his self-regarding objectives. Valid functionalist claims can become causal ones;[71] therefore, if Lincoln knew that the principle would best help him satisfy his ulterior motives, he would adopt the principle *because* of these motives. In that case, the motives would account causally for his principle; they would be the real explanation for his behavior.

The Contextual Dimensions of Lincoln's Principle

As stated so far, however, a purely instrumental account of Lincoln's actions has a major flaw. If such an account were entirely correct, Lincoln would have been willing to alter or abandon the principle in any case in which acting on it would harm his motives taken altogether; yet Lincoln stated

[71] Elster 1982.

that he was not prepared to act in this way. In his last public speech, he insisted that on major questions of principle one had to be "inflexible."[72] Even though he changed the tone and emphasis of his remarks on the race question as he moved across Illinois in the 1858 Senate race, he kept to his fundamental position. Lincoln demonstrated the same fixed determination throughout the struggle that began in 1854. No means-ends considerations, no issues of glory, economic gain, or political ambition would lead him to agree to the expansion of slavery. He maintained that position during the secession crisis after his election, just as he later refused to re-enslave those freed by the Emancipation Proclamation.[73] Again, in each case, once a forward step had been taken, a step backward—for any reason—was unacceptable.

Lincoln was equally unyielding in his devotion to union, whether secession was demanded by abolitionists or by southern fire-eaters, provided only that the Union be committed to policies that stigmatized slavery. As Potter has noted, once the secession crisis began, "Lincoln, who had been clearly less radical than Chase on the subject of slavery, was emphatically the more militant of the two on the subject of preserving the union."[74] There were certain points, then, at which Lincoln would not subordinate his principle to the instrumental considerations rooted in his self-regarding motives.

Nevertheless, it is possible to specify another causal link between Lincoln's motives and his principle. This connection can be explicated in terms of the rules that constitute certain games and social practices by designating and defining their essential activities. (Here, and later in this chapter, my approach will differ somewhat from that of conventional contemporary game theory.) To invoke a familiar example, constitutive rules indicate what counts as a walk in baseball or how one moves the knight in chess; moving a knight three spaces diagonally on the board, for example, does not count as a move in the game. The rules specify appropriate behavior in a context. Furthermore, individuals cannot participate in these practices unless they follow the principle that the constitutive rules are right or appropriate in and of themselves; the rules, that is, make it possible to play. In many cases, however, observing the rules means forgoing some actions that might gain the player a competitive advantage—it means not cheating in a game, for example, or not flouting basic social norms. Self-regarding actors value the rules because such rules make it possible for the actors to pursue their interests, for example by playing and winning a game they enjoy, or even by profiting from it materially.

[72] Basler 1953–1955, 8:405.
[73] Ibid., 6:48; 7:51; 8:152.
[74] Potter 1976, 558; cf. 527.

Lincoln's principled devotion to liberty and union can certainly be interpreted as a commitment to certain rules. Both his unionism and his Whiggish politics had a deeply conservative side.[75] He denounced Douglas, for example, for supporting the repeal of the Missouri Compromise, which had been forged by an earlier generation. As president, Lincoln described the Constitution as a compact that did not provide for its own dissolution—indeed, it presupposed obedience to its provisions—"it being impossible to destroy it, except by some action not provided for in the [Constitution] . . . itself."[76] Thus, his very drive for personal success committed him, at least implicitly, to sustain the values of liberty and union, even though this commitment limited Lincoln's pursuit of his ulterior ambitions. It is possible to seek to be a successful capitalist, for example, only in an economic system whose participants respect certain rules of private property and the operations of a free market. Nor could Lincoln have pursued his ambition for political office if there had been no widely accepted rules that defined the offices and indicated the appropriate ways to seek them. A principled devotion to liberty and union, therefore, was a commitment to satisfying the *preconditions* that were essential for the pursuit of ambition—his own or that of anyone else. (There were of course ambitious politicians of Lincoln's time who did not accept his view of the preconditions.)

Conceptually, then, Lincoln's principle, and the rules it endorsed, were prior to his self-regarding motives. His motives, in turn, presupposed both the social practices in which he participated and the constitutive rules that regulated participation. Such a conclusion does not undermine Marx's claim that self-interested capitalist economics controls moralistic liberal politics. Marx's analysis was basically causal, not conceptual, and the present account can still assign causal priority to Lincoln's ulterior motives. Lincoln was inflexible, by the present account, because he recognized that he and others could seek success only if their society retained its integrity. As Tocqueville might have put it, Lincoln followed the dictates of an enlightened self-interest. From this point of view, Lincoln's principle reflected loyalty to his society, which he valued *because* it permitted and encouraged him to pursue his various self-regarding motives.

The Problem of Political Conflict:
Lincoln vs. Douglas

To sum up the foregoing discussion, Lincoln's principle can be accounted for by a sufficiently sophisticated ulterior-motive analysis, one that empha-

[75] Cf. Basler 1953–1955, 1:108–15.
[76] Ibid., 3:302.

sizes constitutive social and political rules, (i.e., by an approach in explanatory discourse analogous to rule utilitarianism in ethics). At this point, however, the argument for a reductionist, ulterior-motive explanation takes a paradoxical turn. The focus has now been shifted from Lincoln's entirely self-regarding motives to a devotion to the social order that he shared with most other Americans, or, at least, with most other Northerners. However, if his principle expressed a *shared* devotion to *common* practices and institutions, how are we to account for the *conflicts* of the 1850s between the North and the South, or within the North between antislavery elements and those who sought to accommodate the South?

Consider, for example, Lincoln's lifelong rival, Stephen A. Douglas. Douglas's actions, taken by themselves, can be readily accounted for in much the same way as Lincoln's. Douglas too was a quintessential version of the American self-made man. For him too, social status was almost as important as political office, and it was his desire for financial success—in particular, in his financial stake in the western railroads—that pushed him to propose the Kansas-Nebraska Act and, in consequence, the fateful repeal of the Missouri Compromise. Furthermore, Douglas, like Lincoln, asserted and followed a principle of action. During the 1850s, Douglas helped recast the Democrats' traditional commitment to states' rights in the language of the doctrine of popular sovereignty—the doctrine that each state or territory must decide the slavery question for itself. Moreover, this doctrine as a principle of action also served Douglas's self-regarding motives. It attracted moderates throughout the country to the party, for example, making Douglas a leading spokesman for sectional accommodation—for a time, he was one of the few northern politicians who had a national appeal. The doctrine also proved useful in Douglas's efforts to advance railroad development in the west. Popular sovereignty, from this perspective, was much more than a tool with which to pursue his economic and political ambitions. It reflected, in fact, Douglas's commitment to his social order and its constitutive rules in three crucial ways.

First, Douglas hoped his policy of local control would end the threat of national divisions over slavery by removing the issue from national politics. Second, the policy was intended to let the dominant group in each section settle the issue as it wished, allowing each to retain its prevailing social order. Third, popular sovereignty envisioned a polity whose decisions would be shaped by the lived experiences and existing preferences of the largest possible number of whites. As a good Jacksonian Democrat, Douglas wished to have local majorities pursue their own goals free of government interference. Ultimately, when the principle of popular sovereignty was at stake, when loyalty to society and polity demanded, Douglas was quite willing to forgo the quest for immediate personal advantage. During the last year of his life, he saw disunion as a mortal danger and, at the risk of his health, turned his failing race for the presidency into a campaign for national unity, a campaign he continued after the election.

If Douglas's ulterior motives were very similar to Lincoln's, and if the two men were loyal to the same social order, why was each man troubled by the other's politics, and why were their principles so different? The immediate difference, of course, was over slavery. Lincoln moralistically denounced it, whereas Douglas scorned such denunciations as threatening to the Union and its political life. This disagreement is precisely what ulterior-motive explanations should account for—yet the motives of the two men were very similar, though not, of course, identical. Lincoln and Douglas had ties to somewhat different business groups, but economic differences of this sort seem much too slight to account for so portentous a difference on slavery. It is because their motives are not sufficient explanation of this difference that their attitudes toward liberty and slavery on the one hand and union on the other become relevant. Douglas was much more racist in his attitudes than Lincoln, and he thought much more about the Union as a nation for whites than Lincoln, even though Douglas had been raised in Yankee Vermont and Lincoln's family had come from a slave state.

The differences in attitudes were evident in the very different principles of action of the two men. Like Lincoln, Douglas was committed to supporting a set of constitutive social rules that permitted self-regarding ambition. It was the disagreement over slavery that seems to have directed their otherwise similar ambitions into politically different channels. The point of Douglas's principle was to encourage the people in each locale to act on their preferences—notably, their preferences about slavery. For Lincoln, in contrast, slavery was not a matter of preference but of evil, because it denied the opportunity for "the weak to grow stronger, the ignorant wiser; and all better, and happier together."[77] Lincoln's position, thus, did not simply affirm the existing competitive rules of his capitalist society—it committed him to changing them.

A return to the analogy between competitive games and social life will help in specifying two important similarities between Lincoln and Douglas. First, the quest for victory in a game is analogous to their shared pursuit of success in their intensely competitive social world. Second, just as players recognize that the rules of a game impose limits on the pursuit of victory (e.g., by proscribing cheating), so both men recognized constitutive political and economic rules that limited the scope of individual ambition and required loyalty to the Union.

The analogy also serves to clarify the basic division between Lincoln and Douglas. Even in competitive games, it is possible for the players to be

[77] Ibid., 2:222.

concerned not just with victory but with the quality of their performance as well. The two goals are obviously different. First, if one runner wins a race, the other contestants typically cannot. If improvement rather than only victory is the major objective, however, there is no such stark conflict of interest. One player's improvement may actually stimulate and encourage an opponent to improve as well. Second, if a player concentrates on winning, there is no great need to be concerned with the welfare of others; if a player seeks to improve the overall level of play, however, that player cannot be indifferent to the performance of other players. Finally, if the only goal of a player is victory, and that player continues to win, he or she may well be perfectly satisfied with maintaining the existing standard of performance; a concern with winning does not necessarily entail a critical attitude toward the game itself. To make performance the primary concern implies a commitment to improving and therefore changing the game; that is, it entails a critical attitude toward the game itself. In all three instances, then, there is often a basic tension between an instrumental concern with winning the game and what might be called an aesthetic devotion to improving the game.

These three differences illuminate Lincoln's basic conflict with Douglas. Douglas's prime objective was to offer his fellow whites a route to success without trying to impose his own moral standards on them. By favoring local control, he sought to maximize the extent to which they could look out for their own interests (i.e., satisfy preferences they had adopted freely). Douglas looked to the Declaration of Independence as a standard, for example, but he interpreted its assertion of human equality in terms of the practices of the 1770s. The enslavement of Africans was generally accepted at the time of the Declaration of Independence, from which circumstance Douglas inferred that the rights asserted in the declaration applied only to whites.[78] Although he thought slavery an unfortunate institution, he favored tolerating it where local majorities desired it. Because, for Douglas, preferences mattered above all, the issue of self-improvement—for either slaves or slave owners—was, finally, irrelevant. Only when the Union itself was threatened, as it was by southern secession, could the right of local self-government be restricted legitimately.

Lincoln, of course, was neither a revolutionary nor a selfless altruist; he shared Douglas's enthusiasm for their competitive, capitalist society. Unlike the Quakers and abolitionists, who saw American politics (though not the American economy) as irredeemably compromised, Lincoln was committed to defending the Union as the framework within which he and others could compete in pursuit of their self-regarding goals. Much in the way that some players value a competitive game partly because it permits improved

---

[78] See Lincoln and Douglas 1958, 294.

performance, Lincoln revered the Union for the opportunities it offered for self-development. For him, a "right principle of action" had to be devoted to improvement—of himself, others, and the whole society. Slavery was intolerable to Lincoln precisely because it blocked completely the slaves' prospects for self-improvement and advancement; it denied them that opportunity to "grow stronger, wiser, better, and happier." For Lincoln, the Declaration of Independence laid down a standard that required the moral improvement of the community and the self-development of the individual.

At its core, then, Lincoln's position rested on a dynamic aesthetic, a belief in continued improvement that was deeply at odds with Douglas's determination to reproduce his own and others' lived experiences as they had already taken shape. In the case of slavery, Lincoln held that the future of the territories had to be decided without regard to the actual motives or experiences of the settlers. Procedurally, his position implied the continuous pursuit of a new social order that would satisfy the standards of the declaration by excluding slavery. Substantively it meant restricting the competitive drive to win, by requiring that everyone, regardless of color or condition, have an opportunity for self-development.

Furthermore, however closely Lincoln's own ambition matched Douglas's, the two men differed decisively over what the concepts of "ambition" and "success" could properly mean. For Douglas, the criteria for success were relatively straightforward. In antebellum America, these criteria were to be found in a system of offices to which politicians could aspire, in an economy in which the winners could become rich, and in a social system that prized upward mobility. Moreover, the specific content of these criteria was exhibited through local practices. As a result, Douglas was compelled to recognize the ownership of slaves among southern whites as a sign of social status and success.

For Lincoln, these criteria for success offered necessary but not sufficient guidance. In the case of slavery, the paramount issue was the ethical standing of the institution rather than its economic importance. Southern planters might be rich and socially prominent, but holding slaves (like acquiring wealth by fraud) signaled failure rather than success and revealed a defect of character or a flawed vision in the holder. One reason Lincoln hated slavery, he said in 1854, was that it forced "so many good men" to insist "that there is no right principle of action but self-interest."[79] In the end, then, Lincoln's principle directed his self-regarding behavior by subjecting it, and the actions of others, to certain limiting ethical standards that Douglas simply did not share.

[79] Johannsen 1965, 50–51.

Lincoln's Principle as a Political Solution

How does the consideration of Lincoln's principle lead to a cultural account of Lincoln's politics, or of Douglas's? The essential answer is that human beings use culture to render their experiences meaningful.[80] Such patterns of meaning not only help human beings to act effectively to satisfy their preferences (accomplish their goals), but also help them to set their goals and to make sense of the events that shape their lives. In the case at hand, both Lincoln and Douglas affirmed their respective principles not only in order to advance their careers but *also* to help solve the crisis that afflicted their society's political culture. More particularly, they sought to resolve conflict and change the direction in which events were moving. A cultural explanation, thus, has two key elements. First, it indicates what resources or cultural tools are available to a group of individuals for devising and adopting solutions to the issue in question; and, second, it highlights those features of a principle of action that resolve conflict and change the direction of events.

Here, once again, a comparison is revealing. Whereas Douglas's solution emphasized the desire of his compatriots for success or satisfaction of their preferences, Lincoln's had a dual aim: it celebrated the belief of his fellow Northerners in a society dedicated to individual advancement, and it articulated the distaste many of them felt for slavery or the slave owners, or both. Intellectually, that is, Lincoln's position was richer, more complex, and more comprehensive than Douglas's. Politically as well, Lincoln's position was more comprehensive, and it spoke for a more diverse set of feelings. It thus became the core of a politically compelling, electorally successful persuasion.

It follows that a cultural analysis of the Lincoln persuasion must be both interpretive and historical. It must specify through interpretation, as we have tried to do in this chapter, the particular respects in which Lincoln's approach to political issues was more complex and comprehensive than that of his political foes. In addition, a cultural analysis must indicate historically what resources, what cultural tools, were available to Lincoln. The following is a sketch of such a cultural account with respect to his belief in individual improvement; other issues are considered in later chapters.

Until the party died in the 1850s, Lincoln was a good Whig, and his stand on slavery can be understood as one expression of the moral earnestness of northern Whiggery and its Protestant culture.[81] In the seventeenth century, New England Calvinism had interpreted worldly—economic—

[80] Geertz 1973.
[81] Cf. D. W. Howe 1979.

success as a sign of grace, that is, of God's gifts of intelligence and morality. One consequence of this interpretation was the celebration of hard work and of the self-discipline of the successful, ambitious capitalist. By the nineteenth century, as Weber pointed out, this Protestant ethic had in many instances been secularized into the capitalist spirit of a dynamic entrepreneurial class.[82] For many antebellum Southerners the transformation had been all too complete, and they flayed northern society for its greed, materialism, and ruthless pursuit of profit.[83] By the 1830s and 1840s, many Northerners conceded that their economy and culture had become increasingly acquisitive.[84] Some of the critics, however—including those northern Whigs who were sympathetic to moral reform and the antislavery movement—invoked their Calvinist heritage in defence of the North. In the Puritan tradition, economic prosperity had been only one sign of sainthood. Intellectual and cultural development, ethical purity, and religious piety had been other signs. As a result, at the same time that the New England Way celebrated individual success, it also sought to discipline and in some ways redefine the course of that success. In the view of the New England Way, the truly conscientious individual was simultaneously self-interested and principled, economically motivated and culturally committed, rather than one or the other exclusively.

Lincoln preached this Whig gospel, but he also reinterpreted it in three important ways. One way involved linking a concern for individual development and morality to the obligations of citizenship; such obligations included devotion to union, itself also a part of the Yankee-Whig tradition. A second way involved mastering the political realities of the highly partisan world that had been created by Douglas's fellow Jacksonian Democrats, a world in which the Whigs had never been fully comfortable. The third way in which Lincoln reinterpreted the Whig gospel, the way on which this chapter has focused, was to link individual ambition and its rational calculation of means and ends to the Whig tradition of moral commitment. Lincoln's goal was quite familiar to other Whigs: to mold and enrich—rather than to resist—the drive for success that he saw around him and within himself. The question was not only who won the game, or how to win it, but also who was allowed to play and how the game itself might be better played. Lincoln's answer to this complex question was that for each and every American the opportunity must be secured to seek cultural and moral as well as economic improvement. For that reason he spoke out equally for hard work and "cultivated thought."[85]

[82] Weber 1987.
[83] Taylor 1961; Norton 1986.
[84] Meyers 1960, ch. 6; Somkin 1967.
[85] Basler 1953–1955, 3:481.

For Lincoln, the slavery struggle was an occasion to reexamine and reformulate the intimate connection between ambition and moral aspiration. Specifically, he sought to locate these self-regarding goals within a new framework, under a new rubric. The competition with the founding fathers, therefore, became dedication to a new birth of freedom; capitalist loyalties sustained an attack on the aristocratic social order of the slave owners; and political ambition was harnessed to the moral crusade of his party and his section. It was by thus connecting motives and principle that Lincoln was able to organize important materials of his culture into a politically compelling description of reality. By clarifying and structuring his section's available options in a way that Douglas could not, Lincoln helped his section respond more purposefully to the slavery crisis. Here, indeed, was a cultural achievement—one that Geertz might well call ideological—at the core of the Lincoln myth.[86]

None of these considerations, of course, refutes Marx's dualistic claims about the tension between egoism and the ulterior motives of a capitalist society, on the one hand, and the moral pretensions of bourgeois politics on the other. Marx's analysis, however, can account only for those features of Lincoln's conduct that resemble those of Douglas's conduct. Importantly, Lincoln and his allies modified the meaning of success, and thus of personal ambition, by insisting on self-improvement as a universal political norm. More importantly, Lincoln's attack on slavery articulated a social as well as a political vision. Unlike Douglas, he had a vision of a good society in which slavery had no place, in which a satisfactory political ethic must be concerned with social and economic life.

In the American case, then, Marx may have identified the wrong dualism. Rather than a split between economic egoism and political idealism, American political culture exhibits an equally fundamental division between two outlooks, each of which is both social and political. One view of American political culture, which is ordinarily the dominant view, has emphasized the satisfaction of human preferences, of individual and group interests. The other view, in the "dissenting" tradition, has focused on the development of human faculties, and thus on the intimate link between success and improvement.[87] Moreover, the tension between these two perspectives occurs *both in political discourse and at the level of civil society*. As an advocate of the dissenting view, Lincoln himself spoke for many antislavery Whigs and Republicans in the conflict with Democrats such as Douglas. Lincoln's message has since been carried forward by, among others, the settlement house movement, many New Dealers, and several of the protest movements of more recent decades.

---

[86] Geertz 1973.
[87] Greenstone 1982b.

This conclusion by no means wholly vindicates the Lincoln myth. The valid insight of the myth surely is not that Lincoln was simply a political saint or far-seeing patriarch who anticipated later social developments, because clearly neither claim is true. The myth is intellectually revealing, as well as politically and culturally important, rather, because it points out Lincoln's place in a reform liberal tradition. The myth rings true, in other words, in its implicit claim that, in a sharply divided American culture, one important theme has been a belief in self-improvement as an individual and collective project. There has been a division in American liberalism, in fact, that has meant that the actions of individuals based on roughly the same ulterior motives would have different effects, depending on which outlook—or principle, or persuasion—an individual espoused. Each outlook, that is, *imposed a limit* on the ways in which individuals, affiliated by sharing the outlook, might react to changes in their situations. Here, then, is an approach, a way of understanding the role of culture in political life that raises questions not only about the cultural but ultimately about the philosophical foundations of American politics—and, indeed, about those matters on which there has been philosophical division rather than agreement. We will take up this approach by turning to an examination of liberalism in American political culture as a whole.

TWO

AMERICAN POLITICAL CULTURE

LIBERAL CONSENSUS OR
LIBERAL POLARITY?

ANY ACCOUNT of the course of American political development
must confront the issue of American exceptionalism. As citizens of
the first extended republic, white American men were the first to
enjoy nearly universal suffrage and the first to form mass political parties;
yet, after the Civil War, massive industrialization and a continuing ideological devotion to political equality had relatively little impact on society and
politics. Compared to working classes of other countries, for example, the
American working class has been politically cautious—when it has not been
positively quiescent—and the scope of the country's social welfare programs has been distinctly limited. The United States thus has presented a
paradox of change and continuity: on the one hand, rapid political and
economic development; on the other, profound resistance to the social
movements and policies that were typically elicited elsewhere by a dynamic
capitalist economy.

The most persuasive explanation for this pattern of development and
resistance has been one founded on the idea of a constraining cultural
consensus. This consensus—a belief in individual freedom, private enterprise, and republican institutions founded on popular consent—has made it
difficult for competing collectivist movements or policies to take hold. In
chapter one, I suggested a difficulty: Lincoln and Douglas both subscribed
to these general liberal values, but they differed on such issues as ethical
obligation and the rules for pursuing personal success, and these differences
had philosophical and political importance. The agreement of Lincoln and
Douglas over motives suggests that American liberalism has indeed been
pervasive, but their disagreement over principle suggests equally that American liberalism has not been entirely consensual—that Americans have
shared some basic liberal beliefs but have disagreed fundamentally on the
interpretations of these beliefs.

The present chapter assesses the strengths and weaknesses of the consensus thesis. First, the chapter offers both a philosophical defense of the
basic logic and argument of the thesis and a philosophical critique of its
more sweeping claims about the kinds and degree of agreement that exist on

all important political issues. Second, it identifies three kinds of American liberalism—republican, humanist, and reform. I have suggested that most, if not all, Americans share what I have called "republican" or "genus" liberalism; but they differ in the species of their liberalism, which I have called humanist liberalism and reform liberalism and which exhibit politically and philosophically important differences.[1] Chapter one laid out a prima facie case for a polarity between the humanist and reform liberal outlooks; here we focus more explicitly on the differences between them.

A preliminary note about terminology: throughout this discussion, the words *cause* and *causal* refer only to patterns of concomitant *variation*, that is, to relationships in which there are changes in the values of both independent and dependent variables. In this usage, a causal relationship refers to a change in the cause that is followed by (or is coincident with) a change in the effect. In a different usage, in ordinary discourse, we also speak about a stable feature of some particular context producing some effect, where the effect is the preservation of the status quo. Indeed, this latter type of relationship is central to the analysis developed here, but, to be clear about the difference between the two usages, I shall refer to the latter type by the term *boundary condition* and explicate that concept at an appropriate point.

American Exceptionalism: The Consensus Thesis

The liberal consensus thesis is rooted in Tocqueville's classic discussion of American social relations. It is not only fortunes that are equal in America; Tocqueville wrote, "I think there is no other country in the world where . . .

---

[1] [Throughout the present work, the terms *republican liberalism, consensus liberalism,* and *genus liberalism* all refer to the collective, traditional American beliefs in individual rights, in private property, and in government by consent. Following Hartz, these shared beliefs constitute the basis of the American liberal consensus. In addition to sharing these three beliefs, however, liberals differ on other important tenets. On the basis of those differences, liberalism can be divided into two distinctly different traditions, described by JDG as *reform* and *humanist*, that developed within the (still) republican liberal framework. *Humanist liberalism* refers to a set of beliefs that place primary emphasis on "equitably satisfying individual desires and preferences," and on achieving "the welfare of each human being as she or he defines it" (Greenstone 1988, 442). Humanist liberals value negative liberty, that is, "the freedom of individuals to determine their goals and to consider how best to achieve those goals with a minimum of external constraint" (ibid., 442). In this form of liberalism, the term *humanist* emphasizes the central place in everyday life of humans rather than of God and emphasizes happiness in the world rather than salvation. *Reform liberalism,* in contrast, emphasizes not the satisfying of individual preferences (although it does not deny the importance of preferences altogether) but the setting of social goals. Reform liberals value positive liberty and

there are so few ignorant and so few learned individuals."[2] Special material conditions, he thought, helped to produce this result. Even though a few "great lords" migrated to the thirteen colonies, "the soil of America absolutely rejected a territorial aristocracy," largely because the "untamed land" required "the constant and committed labor of the landlord himself."[3] But social relations and conditions were crucial factors. Even the southern planters lacked the traditional—and inherited—privileges that distinguished aristocrats from commoners, and, because their workers were black slaves, the slave masters lacked the usual patronage relations that aristocrats had with ordinary citizens in Europe.

Nor was there room for the honor, to use Weber's term, that most European peoples accorded their social superiors. Especially in the western American states, Tocqueville continued, the inhabitants "hardly know one another, and each man is ignorant of his nearest neighbor's history. . . . No man there enjoys the influence and respect due to a whole life spent publicly in doing good."[4] By the same token, there also were no real "proletarians" in Jacksonian America. "Wealth circulates . . . with incredible rapidity, and experience shows that two successive generations seldom enjoy its favors." Everyone, having some possession to defend, recognizes the right to property in principle.[5]

Partly as a result of these factors, the Americans enjoyed bourgeois liberty, "not the aristocratic freedom of their motherland, but a middle-class and democratic freedom."[6] Trained to govern themselves through participation in voluntary associations, they had learned how to combine democracy and liberty as the French had not.[7] Most important of all, the Americans did not suffer the disease of what Tocqueville called a "democratic revolution." Because they almost all belonged to the same middle class, they did not experience the "implacable hatreds" caused by a "prolonged struggle" to bring down an aristocracy. In Tocqueville's words, "The Americans have this great advantage, that they attained democracy without the sufferings of a democratic revolution and that they were born equal instead of becoming so."[8]

---

insist on "the obligation, not just the option," of individuals "to cultivate and develop their physical, intellectual, esthetic, and moral faculties," as well as to help others do so, in order "to achieve mastery . . . in activities of importance to one's community" (ibid., 445).]

[2] Tocqueville 1969, 55.

[3] Ibid., 33.

[4] Ibid., 55.

[5] Ibid., 54.

[6] Ibid., 34.

[7] Ibid., 61–98.

[8] Ibid., 509.

In this century's most important version of the consensus thesis, Louis Hartz extended Tocqueville's analysis in two directions. First, Hartz employed the French aristocrat's insights to explain the striking absence of an American socialist or militant working-class tradition.[9] Tocqueville himself had anticipated the great division between workers and employers that would soon dominate most capitalist societies.[10] In Hartz's formulation, America's white immigrants, unencumbered by a feudal tradition or Europe's class antagonisms, could pursue their middle-class goals freely; and, because social homogeneity kept most Americans from thinking systematically about class differences, American political culture lacked the European social categories necessary to the expression of antagonism. As meaningful as the ideas of class differences and antagonisms were elsewhere, they had no practical application in the United States. Whereas a European socialist might see class confrontation, most Americans saw only a pluralist conflict among narrowly defined interests, and they behaved accordingly, by shunning class-based policies. As a result, policy debates have often focused on technical issues of distribution, administrative efficiency, and economic management.[11]

Hartz's account applies to liberal reformers as well as to the working class and the socialist left. In Marxist terms, Hartz argued that the failure of the bourgeoisie to develop class consciousness, that is, to be a class "for itself," left American workers ideologically crippled. Expanding on Tocqueville's point about the absence of an antiaristocratic revolution, Hartz wrote:

> A triumphant middle class . . . can take itself for granted. This point, curiously enough, is practically never discussed, though the failure of the American working class to become class conscious has been . . . of endless interest. And yet the relationship between the two suggests itself at once. Marx himself used to say that the bourgeoisie was the great teacher of the proletariat.[12]

Nor did bourgeois intellectuals in America offer aid and encouragement to the left, as they did in Europe, by supporting programs of a collectivist welfare state. Most progressive reformers in the United States looked backward for inspiration to an individualist economy of independent entrepreneurs and an individualist program of "trust-busting and boss-busting."[13] Thus, left-wing politics was constrained further by the way liberal individualism mesmerized the potential allies of militant workers.

---

[9] For other influential statements of the consensus thesis, see Huntington 1981, 7; Boorstin 1953; Hofstadter 1974; Potter 1954; and Bercovitch 1978.

[10] See Tocqueville 1969, 555–58.

[11] Hartz 1955, 7ff., ch. 8, esp. 211ff., 30; 141.

[12] Ibid., 52.

[13] Ibid., 229–30.

Hartz also applied Tocqueville's argument to American political thought. Because American political ideas were thoroughly liberal, Hartz argued that they began with Locke and "stay with [him] . . . by virtue of an absolute and irrational attachment." This was the liberal consensus that made America as uniquely "indifferent to the challenge of socialism" as it had earlier been "unfamiliar with the heritage of feudalism."[14] At the same time, Hartz continued, because there were no feudal institutions to attack, American liberals, unlike either their European counterparts or Locke himself, could reject entirely the idea of a powerful government. They did not need it as a weapon to use against an old order.[15]

In conjunction with an insensitivity to class differences, this fear of government power has consistently weakened every subsequent movement in the United States for large-scale welfare programs or economic regulation, to say nothing of socialism itself. Fear of the state, however, has constrained the political right as well as the left. The most militant American conservatives since Tocqueville's time, including the contemporary Christian right, have been too devoted to individualism and economic freedom to embrace an authoritarian government, much less to appeal to traditions of upperclass rule.

Because American industrial development has generally resembled Europe's, Hartz cast the thesis of exceptionalism in strongly political and cultural terms. His point was not to deny the importance of economic motives. On the contrary, the consensus thesis emphasized the place of material interests in American politics.[16] In much the same way that Lenin distinguished between trade unions and class consciousness, however, Hartz's thesis also distinguished between the workers' pursuit of immediate economic gains and their broader, more revolutionary goals; and the thesis added that these interests have been defined narrowly in the United States because American political culture has been thoroughly liberal.[17]

What has differentiated politics in the United States from politics elsewhere, then, are the limits that have been imposed on economically induced political change by the agreement on liberal beliefs and practices. Many theorists, of course, have asked how a democratic regime can maintain itself without resorting repeatedly to coercion, but the claims of the consensus thesis are particularly far-reaching. According to theories of social hegemony, for example, capitalist social orders are typically legitimated by a compromise among openly contending social classes.[18] In the United States, however, the constraints are more than simply hegemonic; few Americans

[14] Ibid., 6.
[15] Ibid., 59–61. See Tocqueville's very similar point, 1969, 674–79.
[16] Cf. Przeworski 1985; Hartz 1955, 250; Tocqueville 1969, 561ff.
[17] Lenin 1908, 75–168; Hartz 1955, 277–83.
[18] Gramsci 1971.

have ever witnessed firsthand any alternative to a capitalist economy, and their perceptions of class distinctions are dim. Because there is no open conflict over fundamentals, no hegemonic compromise has been needed.

Standard Critiques of the Liberal Consensus Thesis

The thesis of liberal consensus is certainly open to some plausible criticism. Hartz's account, for example, is notorious for not defining "Lockeanism" with any great precision; by linking American liberalism to Locke's political theory, Hartz followed Tocqueville in painting the consensus in very broad terms. After all, as Dave Ericson has pointed out, Locke offered the classic philosophic statement of republican liberalism, what we shall call genus liberalism.[19] Locke, that is, advanced the points that are shared by all liberal thought: government based on popular consent, and devotion to individual liberty and property. It turns out, however, that by depicting American political culture in terms of this broadly defined genus liberalism, Hartz effectively armed the consensus thesis against many familiar criticisms.

According to the most common of these criticisms, the thesis seriously understated the extent and variability of class conflict and government interventions in the economy. Hartz himself conceded that political leaders, from Federalists to Whigs to advocates of the New Deal, went beyond the dictates of laissez-faire, sometimes to provide aid to low-income groups. Furthermore, the Socialist party showed creditably in the presidential campaigns of 1912 and 1924 and in a variety of local races. The simple breadth of the thesis, however, deflects much of this critique. Whatever their differences, for example, Clay, Webster, and Franklin Roosevelt all espoused the basic beliefs of genus liberalism. It was not necessary for the thesis to deny the presence of all socialist politics or welfare state programs. The basic point of the thesis was to compare the United States with Europe and, secondarily, with other "fragmented" societies, such as Australia and Canada.[20] From that perspective, then, the liberal consensus in the United States has sharply limited the extent of socialist success, markedly softened class antagonisms, and restricted the advance of the welfare state. Hartz was correct on these points when he wrote in the 1950s, and his argument is equally on the mark as the century nears its end.[21]

A related criticism of the consensus thesis has acknowledged the weakness of the American political left but has rejected explanations that em-

---

[19] Ericson 1987.
[20] Hartz 1964.
[21] Hartz 1955, 100, 259; see Skocpol 1985, cited in Sparrow 1991, 41, 42.

phasize liberal values and nonfeudal patterns of settlement. It has been argued, for example, that the early onset of white male suffrage in the nineteenth century limited the political grievances of workers; that a pattern of social pluralism—from colonial times through at least the period of nineteenth-century immigration—divided the lower classes; that the country's unparalleled natural riches immunized workers against social appeals; that the development of working-class consciousness was disrupted by the separation of residence and workplace; or, finally, that both the socialists and militant unions were the victims of often violent repression.[22]

Once again, however, the liberal consensus has been defined so broadly that such factors cannot adequately be differentiated within it. Hartz and Tocqueville both recognized the role of widespread economic wealth in sustaining the liberal character of American political thought. Early white male suffrage, for example, reflected the lack of social class distinctions. Similarly, social pluralism and separation of residence and workplace can be attributed at least in part to the openness and fluidity of a liberal society, that is, to a liberal distaste for subordinating some religious or ethnic groups to others, or for prescribing where the lower classes should live or work. Finally, the effective attacks on strikers and union organizers reflected in part the power of a capitalist class whose status and aspirations are highly valued by a thoroughly liberal culture.[23]

Why is this breadth itself not a defect? A well-constructed causal explanation can be tested against competing accounts. Hartz's sweeping thesis, however, seems to absorb likely alternatives. The short answer to this objection is that Hartz's explanation is not really causal—it does not account for a change in some feature or element of the situation by a prior or coincident change in some other feature or element. The very breadth of the thesis thus makes it difficult to distinguish it readily from likely alternatives and to refute the thesis. To develop this point and determine the type of explanation that Hartz and Tocqueville did offer, we must look beyond their explicit theory about American liberalism and turn to their metatheory, that is, to their implicit view of the characteristics that exceptionalist theories must exhibit. Three characteristics appear to be essential. First, the explanation must identify a *boundary condition* that has distinctively, and enduringly, constrained the course of American political development. Second, that boundary condition must be simultaneously *behavioral* and *ideological*. Finally, the explanation must be itself a *theoretic description*. It

[22] Katznelson 1980; Kammen 1972; Potter 1954; Goldstein 1978; Lorwin 1933; Greenstone 1977.

[23] Hartz 1955, 17–18; Meyers 1960, 235–53.

must describe those rules, or standards of correct performance, that make the boundary condition operative—in this case, by excluding alternatives.

The Implicit Metatheory of the Consensus Thesis

By a *boundary condition* I mean a set of relatively permanent features of a particular context that affect causal relationships within it. By way of illustration, let us compare the effect of economic prosperity on rural and urban support for incumbent political parties. Assume that on the average, over a series of elections, equal proportions of rural and urban voters support incumbent parties. Also assume that when the economy does well, rural voters are more pro-incumbent than urban voters, but that they are less pro-incumbent in hard times. There is, in other words, greater variation in voting in rural areas; there, economic performance has greater causal impact. However, if economic performance is the cause, and party voting the effect, then the rural-urban difference is a boundary condition. Because the rural-urban difference is a stable condition, a constant feature of the situation, it does not causally explain varying levels of support for the incumbent party. Over time, indeed, the *average* pro-incumbent vote is the same in *both* rural and urban areas, but this difference does determine how economic performance affects pro-incumbent voting.

The consensus thesis offers an account of the following general sort: a liberal culture is too stable a feature of American politics to be a cause of changes in other features; however, among other things, it has reduced the causal impact of economic changes. In Europe, a changing process of capitalist industrialization has strongly promoted the emergence of a politically militant proletariat and an effective socialist movement. Similar economic developments in the United States, however, have had less effect, in part because of that liberal culture. The consensus thesis, therefore, is not a causal explanation, but it does account for the limited impact of economic change.

To be sure, the consensus thesis does emphasize the causal effects of one historical change: the liberal migration to the thirteen colonies that set American political development on its unique path.[24] Perhaps for that reason Hartz described his thesis as a "scientific analysis" that would "account" for as much of the "historical process" as possible.[25] Similarly, Tocqueville referred to the "social state" of the Americans as a "prime cause" of the situation he observed on his visit.[26] The consensus thesis is concerned primarily with the years *after* the original settlement, however, and there are

[24] Hartz 1955, 20–21.
[25] Ibid., 20ff.
[26] Tocqueville 1969, 50.

three reasons why the thesis is not and cannot be a causal explanation over the more extensive period.

First, the decisive causal factors just referred to took place in Europe, and the consensus thesis itself has little to say about these events or the causes that brought them about. Second, the thesis emphasizes continuity—the unflagging devotion of Americans to liberalism in word and deed. As Tocqueville put it in stressing the importance of America's origin, "Go back; look at the baby in his mother's arms. . . . The whole man is there, if one may put it so, in the cradle."[27] In other words, the consensus thesis does not seek to explain American political *development*—it is clearly not concerned with the way one set of changes produced another set of changes. Leaving that issue to other perspectives, the consensus thesis aims instead to show how a political tradition limited the rate and extent of political and social change. Third, causal explanations must clearly distinguish between dependent and independent variables. Otherwise, even if there is a change, we have observed only one event, not the changes in both cause and effect necessary for a causal relationship. The consensus thesis attributes America's persisting liberal *culture* to the liberal *beliefs and practices* of the original settlers. Beliefs and practices make up a culture, and the original liberalism of the culture cannot be a cause of its liberalism later on.

It is possible, to be sure, to try to find causality in the liberal consensus thesis by asserting that the political culture of Americans causally determined their political *behavior*. This interpretation, however, founders on a difficulty that indicates a second major feature of the metatheory. Hartz, for instance, pointed out that socialist intellectuals and progressive historians could depict a class-based conflict only by applying misleading labels:

> Whiggery became for the Progressives a frightful "conservatism," whereas [Progressivism] itself became "progressive" or "radical," a set of terms which meant nothing insofar as Western history of Western political alignments as a whole went. . . . Beard and Smith went back to the origins of American history . . . discovering a "social revolution" in the eighteenth century, and in general making it impossible to understand the American liberal community.[28]

In chapter nine of *The Liberal Tradition*, Hartz added that "the social science of both Progressivism and American socialism failed in its analysis of America," because the practitioners succumbed to "word worship."[29]

Hartz's point was not to reject all efforts at classification but to insist that terms useful in Europe could not be applied to American life. Specifically, the radical intellectuals whom Hartz criticized overestimated the causal importance of their own attempts to describe important social forces. These

[27] Ibid., 31.
[28] Hartz 1955, 29.
[29] Ibid., 248.

intellectuals assumed that labeling the masses an exploited proletariat would help the workers recognize and act on their true interests. These intellectuals also made the opposite mistake by assuming that an economic process could by itself change the social consciousness of the workers. In fact, the process of capitalist industrialization in America did not lead the workers to see any fundamental contradiction between their own and their employers' interests.[30]

Hartz certainly insisted that the liberal creed was more powerful than the left-wing intelligentsia, than capitalist economic development, or even than the two together; furthermore, both the socialist and the Progressive analyses also violated an important condition of the metatheory of the consensus thesis. The root error of those analysts was to assume any causal relationship at all between the consciousness of the workers and their behavior—or between words and deeds of any sort. In the analyses of both Tocqueville and Hartz, to be sure, the focus was cultural rather than economic: because of the liberal consensus, industrialization failed to create a militant working class. The real issue, however, is what the Tocqueville-Hartz approach implies about the meaning of *culture*—and each of them was more concerned with political and social conduct than with political ideas by themselves. As Meyers perceptively observed,

> The remarkable feature of [Hartz's] . . . book on political thought is the regular substitution of non-intellectual categories for ideas. It is basically, I think, a study of the *un*conscious mind of America, conditioned by peculiar historical and social experience. . . . The substance of American political thought . . . lies in the unarticulated premises of the society and culture rather than the logic of books.[31]

Tocqueville made a similar move. In his remarks on New England, he noted the importance of "the participation of the people in public affairs, the free voting of taxes, the responsibility of government officials, individual freedom, and trial by jury." He also promptly referred to these features of Yankee life as "principles" that "spread first to the neighboring states and then in due course . . . everywhere throughout the confederation."[32]

The consensus thesis, then, focuses on what Hartz called a people's political tradition and Tocqueville called a social state—that is, the total complex of beliefs and actions, of values and institutions, that make up American liberal culture. The crucial suggestion, though it is not explicitly developed, is that these patterns remain stable for very long periods, because they closely interweave words and deeds, actions and beliefs. The American liberal tradition, in other words, has been very effective in limiting Ameri-

[30] Ibid., 29, 248.
[31] Meyers 1963, 264.
[32] Tocqueville 1969, 35.

can political development, precisely because ideas and behavior, words and deeds, have mutually constrained each other.

How then, exactly, does a political tradition operate as a boundary condition? How, that is, do our basic concepts and practices impose these limits on each other? A satisfactory answer begins with the fact that both social practices and modes of discourse are based on norms of correct performance.[33] As Tocqueville noted, "Circumstances, origin, education, and *above all* mores allowed . . . [the Americans] to establish and maintain the sovereignty of the people."[34] Certainly, our use of words can remain intelligible only if this use is governed by appropriate norms, but it is also true that to act consistently we must follow appropriate verbal rules. Even these statements, however, suggest an untenably sharp distinction between words and deeds. In fact, our norms of speech and action work together to preclude the acceptability of both certain combinations of words and certain events. Together our use of the concept "chess" *and* the way we actually play the game mean that throwing a piece of wood in the air does not count as a move in the game. So, too, shooting a bullet at a voting machine does not count as a vote in an election.[35]

The American liberal tradition has operated as a boundary condition, because it embodies certain norms of speech and action that preclude nonliberal politics. Identification of the rules of this tradition provides an interpretive explanation of America's limited political development. These rules serve as the enduring liberal *reasons* Americans find compelling when they decide to take certain actions and not others. A real concern of this book, however, is to go beyond the consciously adopted reasons Americans give for their actions, and to identify the more fundamental criteria Americans employ less consciously in interpreting their experiences and choosing among alternative courses of action. As Hartz argued, these criteria have been important precisely because they have operated silently, because they were taken for granted rather than examined critically and evaluated. By identifying these reasons and criteria and by spelling out their content, the consensus thesis offers a description that is theoretic and therefore explanatory, because it makes clear just how the liberal consensus has constrained American political life.

Before proceeding, however, we must answer two sets of questions that Tocqueville and Hartz did not answer: (1) What warrants are there for rejecting a causal analysis of the relationship between words and deeds? How, in other words, can one justify an interpretive explanation that employs a theoretic description? (2) Does this emphasis on standards of correct

---

[33] Wittgenstein 1958, 56, 186, 27; cf. 393, 520, 592. References to the *Philosophical Investigations* are to paragraph numbers, unless otherwise specified.

[34] Tocqueville 1969, 57, emphasis added.

[35] See Cavell 1969, 25.

performance necessarily imply a consensual interpretation of political culture? If not, how can American political culture be thoroughly liberal while still harboring important disagreements?

In answering these questions, the next two sections draw on developments in the philosophy of meaning and action that became influential in the years after Hartz completed *The Liberal Tradition*. In particular, I shall rely on Wittgenstein's *Philosophical Investigations*. I must emphasize that the present account of the liberal tradition represents my application of Wittgenstein's often elusive remarks to a set of social and political issues that he did not address. Moreover, although references will be made at different points in this discussion to relevant passages in the *Investigations*, my object has *not* been to interpret or construe Wittgenstein's own philosophical position.

The Metatheory of Tocqueville and Hartz: A Philosophical Restatement

Claims that behaviors determine how we speak, or that ideas determine conduct, can appear very attractive. Our interests, the way particular economic or social activities benefit us, seem to determine our preferences, and our preferences determine what we say. According to another, similar perspective, a society's dominant material forces, its patterns of basic economic transactions, account for its worldviews and concepts. A bourgeois society, for example, proclaims the value of at least some forms of liberty, because liberty is essential to the existence of a free market.[36] This causal argument can easily be reversed. We rank one form of activity over another only because our beliefs and values tell us to do so. Whereas one belief system may put reinvestment and self-denial ahead of immediate consumption, another may rank social prestige or holding political office ahead of material wealth.

For all their obvious conflicts, these causal accounts share one major feature: they assume that words can be clearly distinguished from the objects or actions to which they refer.[37] On this view, political actors might introduce new words and then reshape social relationships to conform to the new vocabulary. Alternatively, changing patterns of behavior might require new names or verbal labels. In either case, it is this separation between words and their referents that permits us to speak about the causal relationships argued for by the Progressive and Marxist intellectuals criticized by Hartz.

[36] See, for example, Marx and Engels 1958.
[37] Pitkin 1972, 30–35.

Although Tocqueville and Hartz offered no explicit theory of meaning, their basic position suggests another, very different account, which can be elaborated with reference to Wittgenstein: our words and deeds *constitute* each other; together they form human practices or life forms.[38] Wittgenstein described words as a diverse set of "tools in a tool-box" that have widely differing uses in human life. Words thus constitute actions because they are an inseparable feature of complex human enterprises. Neither calculus nor modern chemistry would be possible without the concepts that organize the activities of their practitioners. Such concepts, in fact, enable us to classify objects in ways that in turn permit us to look for genuine causal relationships, not between words and actions, but between different sets of verbally structured activities. We cannot, for example, assert that class or religion affects voting behavior without concepts such as *class*, *religion*, and *voting*. We cannot even meaningfully wish for Congress to enact a certain law without such concepts as *Congress*, *negotiation*, and *law* that enable us, for example, to distinguish between legislative maneuvering and electoral campaigning.[39]

The converse, the claim that actions constitute words, depends on unavoidable ambiguities of meaning. To understand what a complex word means in any particular case, we must resolve the ambiguities that cloud its usage; that is, we must follow the relevant rules of interpretation. If these rules are entirely verbal, the initial word is understood in terms of still other words, and these defining words must be defined in their turn; the new definitions also involve ambiguous words, and so on indefinitely. In sum, because verbal interpretations are themselves ambiguous, they do not definitively determine the meaning of the original word.[40]

The way out of this problem is to know how the rules are interpreted *by the actions* of the people who use the word; unlike in the case of a single-authored text, in ordinary language there is a community of actors whose behaviors provide interpretations that resist deconstruction.[41] As Wittgenstein put it, "To obey a rule, to make a report, to give an order . . . are *customs* (uses, institutions)."[42] Whatever the rule book says, in practice it is usually clear [to both spectators and players] whether a runner in baseball is safe or out, even without an umpire's decision. In other words, ambiguity is eliminated by the actions undertaken by all the participants. For this reason, changing practices change what concepts mean. The term *constitution* originally referred to the king-in-parliament, for example, but it came in time to mean the complex system of checks and balances in the

---

[38] Wittgenstein 1958, 7, 19.
[39] Ibid., 18; Cavell 1969, 19–20.
[40] Wittgenstein 1958, 29, 198.
[41] Greenstone 1988.
[42] Wittgenstein 1958, 199.

United States, a system that evolved steadily before, during, and after the revolution.[43]

The observation that words and deeds mutually constitute each other illuminates the cultural dimension of American political development. Because our concepts and practices are very closely interwoven, important social changes can occur, and be institutionalized, only through a change in *both* practices and meanings.[44] On one side, the stability of our speech helps make our experiences intelligible and familiar because the meanings of our experiences are relatively constant. We "know our way about" in a legislature only because we have stable concepts such as *amendment* and *bargain* that render events intelligible from one issue or legislative session to the next. On the other side, these very terms mean the same thing in different cases only because we interpret and act on them in the same way in case after case. Without such continuity in conduct, there could not be continuity in meaning.

A Wittgensteinian, then, might well refer to the *grammatical limits* on what we can meaningfully say, think—and do. When we go beyond these limits, there are contexts in which some words and actions have no meaning,[45] but causal explanations cannot readily account for such cases. Certain options are ruled out by very stable patterns of behavior and usage that determine a people's feasible options.[46] As Tocqueville pointed out, certain notions of social deference had no application for Americans, given their mores and circumstances. Americans, that is, did not have words and actions for class distinctions—did not experience class distinctions—as Europeans did. Such grammatical limits can be identified by offering a theoretic description of boundary conditions.

A Philosophical Critique: Multiple Meanings and Descriptions

The liberal consensus thesis holds that Americans are committed to genus liberalism, that is, to the basic values of private property, individual freedom, and government based on popular consent. The thesis, however, allows for the possibility of disagreements only on specific questions. This more sweeping assertion is far less defensible than the rather modest claims about genus liberalism. It implies an important corollary: not just that all American liberals affirm the same beliefs, but that they understand these

[43] Ibid.; cf. 29 and Kripke 1982; Wood 1969.
[44] Cf. Wittgenstein 1958, 18, 354.
[45] Ibid., 520, 418; cf. 390, 417.
[46] Ibid., 109.

beliefs in the same way, and thus that their key political concepts have clear, singular, and unequivocal meanings.

Such a corollary is manifestly inconsistent with Wittgenstein's emphasis on the open-textured, sometimes indefinite character of human speech and action. In one of his most striking images, Wittgenstein compared natural languages to an ancient but still vigorous and growing city.[47] In the newer regions of the language we find technical words or technical senses of old words that have precise, well-defined uses. These uses parallel the regular streets and well-defined boundaries of the city's newer suburbs; but other regions of the language correspond to the crooked streets and irregularly defined districts of the city's first neighborhoods, because the rules that govern the oldest words of a language are complex and not always consistent.

The comparison suggests that neither natural languages nor social practices have permanent limits but that their boundaries are all subject to continual change. It also suggests that language games and life forms differ within societies as well as between them; and, further, that the rules can be indeterminate on certain crucial issues. As Wittgenstein pointed out, some features of apparently well-regulated activities are not rule-bound at all, that rules simply do not provide for every contingency.[48] There is no rule in tennis, for example, about how high a ball may bounce, so long as it bounces first within the bounds of the court. So too, a particular word may apply to a highly diverse set of objects or activities, depending in each case on the specific way in which the word is used. As Wittgenstein put it in a now well-known phrase, the diverse objects to which a single word refers often bear "a family resemblance" to each other. There is no single feature or trait common to all objects or activities with the same name; rather, for example, each of the "proceedings we call games" resembles some or even many of the others, so that each shares a number of features with *some* of the others.[49]

In part two of the *Investigations*, Wittgenstein emphasized a different linguistic fact: we often have diverse descriptions for a single object or action. In Frege's example, the phrases *morning star* and *evening star* have the same *referent*, the planet Venus. At the same time, *morning star* and *evening star* are obviously different *descriptions*; they provide different ways to identify and recognize the planet.[50] Wittgenstein emphasized the point that as our experience increases, so do the complexity and number of our descriptions for a particular object. A streetwise urban resident can de-

---

[47] Ibid., 18.
[48] Ibid., 68; cf. 80.
[49] Ibid., 66, 67.
[50] Frege 1975.

scribe city life in many ways, whereas a lifelong farmer will have fewer and different descriptions of city life; the reverse is true with respect to country life.

What relevance, then, do these considerations have for politics? In the *Investigations*, Wittgenstein did not address this question but focused instead on the ambiguities and multiple meanings that the speakers of a natural language typically recognize and cope with together. Geertz similarly depicted cultural systems as sets of tools—basic beliefs, cognitive categories, affective attitudes, and prescriptions for action.[51] By providing the framework within which even unexpected experiences can be rendered meaningful, such systems help the members of a community react together to those major and often unexpected changes that all societies periodically encounter.

The difficulty here is that in some cases some of the multiple meanings are clearly conflicted, and the conflicts often have political implications. Some of our familiar gender terms, for example, are now subject to competing interpretations.[52] Also, for example, in the language of both ethics and our ordinary discourse, the word *equality* has numerous meanings, including "equality of result," "equality of burden," and "equality of opportunity," and we can always go on to ask "equality [of result, etc.] with respect to what?"

So, too, the criterion of cognitive use that Geertz has advanced by no means requires consistency of meaning among all the major elements of a society's belief system. The key point is how such beliefs or linguistic usages help the members of a community cope with their experiences by making important ranges of experience intelligible. If conflicting elements of a culture have this effect, if one set of beliefs or usages appeals to one group and a second set appeals to another group, then any contradictions or tensions among them are likely to be left unresolved. A society, therefore, whose members share some important values may still harbor politically and philosophically important conflicts. In chapter one, in fact, I suggested that American liberals have differed since Lincoln's time, and before, over the meaning of such key political concepts as *union* and *liberty*.

The Bipolarity in American Liberalism

The discussion to this point has maintained that a pervasively liberal culture need not be monolithically consensual. This claim can be illustrated by further consideration of the three forms of American liberalism noted above: republican, humanist, and reform. The first of these, republican

[51] Geertz 1973.
[52] Wittgenstein 1958, 68; see 80.

liberalism, has been broadly accepted in American culture; the other two have divided the culture, forming a politically and philosophically significant polarity. The remainder of this chapter provides an overview and a more complete development of the relationships among the three.

Republicanism

The study of colonial history has been transformed by scholars who have questioned the characterization of early American political beliefs as monolithically liberal. Eighteenth-century Americans, they have argued, looked not to Locke but to such republican writers as Harrington, Bolingbroke, and Trenchard and Gordon. The major political themes of these latter included an independent, virtuous, participatory citizenry, chastened and uplifted by honest labor; virtue itself understood as devotion to the general good of the community; the beneficent effect of landed property in contrast to artificial paper or financial wealth; honest legislators threatened by a corrupt executive's patronage and other blandishments; the danger of standing armies and, more generally, of all political power; and remedies of short terms in office and a system of institutional checks and balances.[53]

These republican themes echo important strains in ancient political thought, especially those of virtue and the common good. Yet Ericson is surely right in locating republicanism within the family of beliefs that make up genus liberalism.[54] Certainly, Anglo-American republicanism did not prescribe a comprehensive vision of human well-being, nor did it assign the function of prescribing such a vision to any official body or collectivity such as church, tribe, or polis.[55] This republicanism, in fact, imposed such severe limits on the state and its officials that broader questions of individual and social good were necessarily left to the citizens themselves.

Nor is there any difficulty in reconciling a fear of government corruption and executive power and the celebration of an independent citizenry with the liberal creed Hartz described. Not surprisingly, then, a number of English republicans had no trouble embracing liberal doctrines.[56] The Declaration of Independence itself joined a strongly Lockean opening to the litany of republican complaints that appeared in the later sections. Moreover, by stressing public-spiritedness—by proscribing selfish behavior among either ruled or rulers, and by limiting strictly the government's power—republicanism addressed directly the characteristically liberal problem of coordinating autonomous, often competitive individuals. As the popularity of the colonial jeremiads suggests, many Americans found

[53] Pocock 1975; Banning 1978; Bailyn 1967; Wood 1969; Diggins 1984; Appleby 1984.
[54] Ericson 1987.
[55] Yarbrough 1979.
[56] See Banning 1978, 47, esp. n. 18.

the liberal ideal of individual freedom threatening as well as exhilarating.[57] Their republicanism thus reflected the ambivalence of committed liberals toward the ever more individualist social order that they themselves were building.[58]

There is, to be sure, a continuing dispute over republicanism's role in the founding period and later.[59] Yet the literature suggests an overall trend. Although dominant in the early eighteenth century, republican thought was partially replaced by about 1750 by a more specifically Lockean concern with the social contract and natural rights.[60] The decline of republican influence continued after the founding, especially as utilitarian and populist ideas gained ground during the nineteenth century, but the decline has been quite gradual. In the late eighteenth century, Jefferson and Adams respected both Locke and the republican writers as authorities. Later, during the antebellum period, both the Jacksonians and the Whigs plausibly affirmed their attachment to some features of the republican outlook.[61] Even today, republican norms remain part of American political culture, notably the belief in the vigilance of the citizenry and the legislature against corrupt or usurpatious officials.

In the long run, the most important republican legacy has been institutional. As important as the independence of the judiciary in America has been, the most significant contribution of the legacy may be the independence of American legislatures. Taken together, the system of fixed and different terms for executive and legislative officials—along with the quintessentially republican ban against executive officials serving as legislators—has precluded the legislative subservience to the executive so detested by eighteenth-century republicans. In turn, the independence of legislators has encouraged legislative initiatives and, further, has made it extremely difficult to maintain the unduly extended deliberations characteristic of governments in which cabinets dominate parliamentary bodies.[62]

American republicanism, then, has come to focus on the essentially political relations between individuals and their government, and among the branches of the government itself. Even in colonial times, this republicanism did not clearly delineate a vision of the fully developed personality or the place of the individual in the good society. In this century, there are only

---

[57] Bercovitch 1978.

[58] See Meyers 1960, 121–41; Somkin 1967.

[59] Diggins 1984; Pocock 1975.

[60] Kramnick 1982.

[61] Meyers 1960; D. W. Howe 1979; Ericson 1987.

[62] I am grateful to Harry Hirsch, Arthur Maas, David Mayhew, Benjamin Page, and Richard Pious for making these points, among others, at a panel on the continuing political importance of the Constitution, at the annual meeting of the American Political Science Association, Chicago, Illinois, 1987.

traces of the earlier republican sociology that celebrated yeoman farming as the guarantor of an independent citizenry. What offends contemporary republicanism is less the private ambition of individuals to get ahead than the negative impact this ambition may have on public life. To employ a distinction recently advanced by John Rawls,[63] republicanism, together with a traditional American concern for individual rights, is now a specifically political rather than a comprehensive social theory.

By narrowing its scope in this way, republican doctrine retained a grip on the American mind. Almost all currents of American thought still accept the ideals of limited government, institutional checks and balances, citizen virtue, and suspicion of official corruption. These ideals, then, are evidence of an American liberal consensus. The consensus is limited, however, to specifically republican doctrines, notably institutional norms, together with the commitment of genus liberalism to consent, liberty, and property. What remains in dispute are those broader social and philosophical questions— the nature of the human personality and a good society—that are addressed by what Rawls has called comprehensive theories. It is over these broader questions, indeed, that humanist and reform liberals differ sharply.

Humanist Liberalism

Tocqueville and Hartz did not simply focus on the values that all American liberals share.[64] Tocqueville reported that the Americans were animated not by a disinterested, aristocratic devotion to the public good, but by a bourgeois self-interest, enlightened by participation in voluntary associations. As a result, American life was marked by its limited patronage of the fine arts and by a relatively small number of truly outstanding individuals. In sum, he described a stable, sober, materialistic, and shrewdly calculating—in a word, bourgeois—culture.[65]

Hartz agreed. In his account, basically self-regarding individuals and groups pursue their own interests. Accordingly, the "master assumption of American political thought" is "atomistic social freedom," that is, a devotion to negative liberty, or the absence of constraint. Hartz's account of Locke is unbalanced, because it often emphasized the empiricist, hedonistic features of Locke's philosophy, including Locke's emphasis on sense experience and on pleasure and pain as criteria for human well being.[66] For both Tocqueville and Hartz, American liberalism assumed a specifically humanist form.

---

[63] Rawls 1987.
[64] [See note 1 above.]
[65] Tocqueville 1969, 525–28.
[66] Hartz 1955, 62; Tarcov 1984; Greenstone 1982b, 12–13.

For humanist liberals, the satisfaction of self-determined preferences is central to human well-being. Considerations of equity do require the government to act as an umpire in certain instances in which some individuals pursue their goals too aggressively. There are also instances of "market failure," in which individuals acting independently cannot supply certain essential collective goods. In these instances, coercion and individualized incentives may well be appropriate. Yet for the humanist liberal, even when these incursions on individual freedom are necessary, *liberty* still refers to *negative* liberty; it refers to the absence of external constraint on individuals acting on their preferences.

The concern with satisfying preferences also implies a commitment to instrumental reasoning. Others cannot legitimately question one person's self-determined goals; they can assess that individual's rationality, therefore, only with regard to her or his choice of means. They can legitimately question, that is, only whether or not a particular set of strategies and tactics, policies, organizations, and institutions is the most effective way to pursue the chosen goals. The humanist liberal outlook can be expressed in the form of the following practical syllogism:

The Humanist Liberal Syllogism: Instrumental Rationality

Major Premise:
I (or others) wish to achieve goal X.

Minor Premise:
Action Y will most effectively secure X.

Conclusion:
It is in my (or their) *interest* to undertake action Y.

Humanist liberalism has generally dominated American political life. Key political actors have continually sought to increase their effectiveness by altering key institutions and practices—whether by the development of national parties in the nineteenth century; by the more recent formation of alliances or "iron triangles" among executive agencies, interest groups and congressional committees; or by a shift in the focus of presidential rhetoric from Congress to the electorate.[67]

The instrumental concern with selecting the most effective means to an end is a feature of almost all societies and cultures. To that extent, the cultural dimension of humanist liberalism may appear to be rather "thin." Such a conclusion is somewhat misleading, however. In the United States, instrumentalism has been bolstered by a humanist liberal commitment to negative liberty and by the belief that preferences are the most ethically relevant features of the human personality. According to Tocqueville and Hartz, it is a broad agreement on just these beliefs—over and above the

[67] See note 62 above.

tenets of genus liberalism—that has characterized America's political culture. Such a sweeping statement of the consensus, however, raises a question. If all major issues are merely instrumental, how can we account for
those periods in which American politics has turned highly and passionately
conflictual?

Moral Reform and the Problem of Conflict

One obvious problem with arguments about broad consensus in American
political culture is raised by the Civil War. As Hartz himself emphasized,
human slavery was a profoundly illiberal institution,[68] and many of its
southern apologists defended it in hierarchical and even collectivist terms.
Accordingly, Hartz treated the conflict as a struggle between a consensually
liberal North and a South whose neo-feudal arguments in favor of slavery
were forgotten as soon as the war ended.[69] At least with respect to the Civil
War, then, Hartz's version of the consensus thesis applied only to northern
politics and political thought, although, as we will see, it was not entirely
adequate. Following Hartz's lead, the present discussion will exclude the
South's antebellum apologetics for slavery and focus on northern politics
and thought.

Under examination, even Hartz's move to exclude the southern apologia
is not entirely adequate. For him, the North's advocates in the sectional
controversy included Ralph Waldo Emerson, William Lloyd Garrison, William Ellery Channing, and Theodore Parker, whom Hartz described as
"romantics."[70] Despite their heterodox theology, these Yankee intellectuals
exemplified the crusading style and much of the outlook of New England
Protestantism. Moreover, major studies of other reform movements of the
1830s and studies of the antislavery Whigs and the young Republican party
suggest they all espoused a moderated version of the Protestant religiosity
and ethical outlook of the abolitionists.[71] Hartz, however, had little if
anything to say about abolitionism or, indeed, about New England's role in
American culture, beyond acknowledging the region's Puritan origins and
the Protestant clergy's support for the revolution.[72]

Although he came to America in the same year in which Garrison founded *The Liberator*, Tocqueville also ignored the abolitionists. While he recognized the importance of New England Calvinism, he preserved the basic
consensus argument by viewing American religion in essentially functional
terms. As Tocqueville saw it, religion contributed to the development of a

[68] Hartz 1955, 147.
[69] Ibid., 172ff.
[70] Ibid., 186.
[71] D. W. Howe 1979; Foner 1970, 106ff.
[72] Hartz 1955, 4, 40–43.

liberal secular culture devoted to individual liberty and material acquisition: "Religion regards civil liberty as a noble exercise of men's faculties, the world of politics being a sphere intended by the Creator for the free play of intelligence. . . . Freedom sees religion as the companion of its struggles and triumphs, the cradle of its infancy, and the divine source of its rights."[73]

That Tocqueville overlooked the connection between New England religion and the antislavery reform impulse may be due less to Tocqueville's Catholic background than to his commitments as a French liberal. For him, America had solved the problem posed by the inevitable spread of social equality, which, he feared, would doom the cause of liberty in Europe. In Tocqueville's view, America was a sober world in which the perpetuation of revolutionary sentiments, or any political passion, had somehow been avoided.

If Tocqueville and Hartz paid too little attention to the political implications of New England Puritanism, however, the connection between liberalism and American Calvinism has been explored thoroughly elsewhere. Locke himself is now viewed as having had real affinities with the seventeenth-century English Protestants.[74] One important topic has been the tension between Yankee Protestants and other cultural groups. Some of these accounts typically have emphasized cultural and social differences rather than, or more explicitly than, political issues or fundamental philosophical differences.[75] Sacvan Bercovitch has argued cogently that the New England Calvinist jeremiad made a signal contribution to the dominance of a liberal consensus. The jeremiad overtly pointed out New England's and, later, America's failings and the sins of its people. The more often the preachers named the nation's sin and appropriate punishment, the more strongly they asserted the nation's special mission as God's chosen instrument.[76] Following Weber, Bercovitch has argued that this mission was essentially individualist and capitalist—in a word, liberal. "New England was from the start an outpost of the modern world. It evolved . . . into a middle-class culture—a commercially oriented economy . . . sustained by the prospect (if not always the fact) of personal advancement." Accordingly, social criticism always carries with it reaffirmation. Because the jeremiad consistently invoked the society's basic values and historic mission, its persistent reassertion precluded the "possibility of fundamental social change." Even the most radical feminists of the time, for example, appealed to their culture's shared stock of values and ideals.[77]

---

[73] Tocqueville 1969, 31–46, and esp. p. 47.

[74] See, for example, Dunn 1969. [Thanks to Nathan Tarcov for this citation.]

[75] See, for example, Kleppner 1970 and Kelley 1979; see also Greenstone 1988, 24–25.

[76] See, for example, Bercovitch 1978, 60, 120.

[77] Ibid., 20, 179, 158.

Bercovitch's account powerfully reinforces the arguments of Tocqueville and Hartz. Here is a cultural foundation—the "spiritual cohesion" that comes only from a "social ideal"—for the American social order that a purely secular concern with "personal aggrandizement" could not provide. The ritual of the jeremiad, Bercovitch has written, "bespeaks an ideological consensus [that is] . . . moral, religious, economic, social, and intellectual" and that even "gave . . . free enterprise the halo of grace."[78]

Ultimately, however, the accounts of both Bercovitch and Hartz remain troubled by the slavery crisis. In the case of the jeremiad, if every critique was simultaneously a reaffirmation, from what sources did the disagreements emerge that led to the Civil War? Persuasively describing Lincoln's speeches as jeremiads tells us little about the cause to which Lincoln was devoted and for which he was willing to rend the Union.[79] It also largely ignores those issues, raised in chapter one, on which Lincoln disagreed with his northern political foes. For his part, Hartz failed to note that each of the "romantics" who had defended the North against the South was either an abolitionist, a Transcendentalist, or a sympathizer with one or the other. Although these romantics embraced genus liberalism, they rejected the humanist, hedonistic side of Locke's philosophy. On epistemological issues, they rejected Locke's empiricist belief in the primacy of sense impressions in cognition. In ethics, they emphasized the commands of duty and the overriding role of conscience, rather than the sober concern with utility or the enlightened self-interest emphasized by Tocqueville.[80] On the slavery question, most of the romantics assailed the accommodating stance of northern politicians such as Douglas, against whom Lincoln was to mount a partisan political assault in the 1850s.

In his study of disharmony in American politics, Samuel Huntington has tried to resolve these difficulties by generalizing from Myrdal's classic argument about American racial attitudes. Although Huntington has endorsed Hartz's claims about an ideological consensus, he has argued that this broad agreement actually promotes social tensions.[81] Morality and political life are in constant tension, producing a permanent gap "between American political ideals and American political institutions and practice." As well, a radical Puritan preoccupation with "purification and a return to first principles," which emerged in English Puritanism in the 1630s, took root in

[78] Ibid., 140, 176, 141.

[79] Ibid., 174.

[80] Greenstone 1982b; Hartz 1955, 155, 165, 182–83, 186. Among the post-1960 studies of the Protestant roots of the abolitionists (apart from biographies of William Lloyd Garrison) are Mathews 1965; J. L. Thomas 1965b; Wyatt-Brown 1971; Walters 1976, esp. ch. 3; Friedman 1982; and Perry 1973.

[81] Myrdal 1964; Huntington 1981, 4; see also 19–20, 33, 36, 40.

Calvinist New England and then spread through the whole United States. Amending Tocqueville's remark that Americans were "born equal," Huntington has added that they were "born Protestant." The result has been recurrent moralistic attacks on "the legitimacy of the dominant institutions" and "more sociopolitical conflict and violence than [in] many European countries."[82]

Huntington's analysis can account for four periods of creedal passion: the revolutionary 1770s; the Jacksonian reforms of the 1820s and 1830s; the Progressive era of the 1890s and 1900s; and the protests of the late 1960s and early 1970s.[83] Huntington has maintained that other eventful periods, including the 1850s and especially the New Deal era, were marked by "pragmatism . . . rather than the passionate affirmation of moral values."[84] Such a view, however, emphasizes style at the expense of substance. The social vision of the New Deal, for example, is linked closely to the eras immediately before and after, eras Huntington has characterized as moralistic. Many of the policy objectives of the New Deal were advanced first by the social reform wing of the Progressive movement; others were achieved only during the 1960s, yet Huntington has ignored the social reforms of the Great Society in his extensive discussion of the 1960s. Similarly, the 1850s were preoccupied with the greatest moral issue in American history. Indeed, as chapter one has suggested, if the style of Lincoln's Republicans was often that of sober practical politicians, their denunciation of the Democrats for an entirely immoral stand on slavery was quite passionate.

Later chapters will explore these issues in detail, but the preliminary conclusion is that even though humanist liberalism has been the dominant strain in American political culture, its dominance has never been complete. In colonial times, as James Kloppenberg has pointed out, all versions of colonial liberalism included belief in some restraints on individual ambition.[85] As good genus liberals, republican theorists honored the autonomy of the citizens vis-à-vis government, and even each other, but they condemned the extremes of greed and wealth produced by unchecked ambition in the pursuit of individual preferences. Over time, however, as republicanism evolved into a set of widely accepted institutional norms, the operative polarity in American political culture came to be defined by the humanist and the reform variants of liberalism.

[82] Huntington 1981, 4, 115, 154, 8.
[83] Ibid., 8, 4.
[84] Ibid., 90.
[85] Kloppenberg 1982.

Reform Liberalism

The humanist-reform polarity reflects a deep ambiguity in liberal thought about whether or not human beings are in fact equipped to determine their own basic *goals*, or only to determine the *means* with which to pursue set goals. For humanist liberals, individuals must be free to choose the goals as well as the means, provided those individuals respect the rights and abilities of others to set and meet their own goals. Reform liberals, in contrast, profess a broadly Kantian ethic that is rooted in the New England Puritan tradition and according to which individuals have an obligation—not just the option—to cultivate and develop their physical, intellectual, aesthetic, and moral faculties. Importantly, the obligation extends to helping others to do the same. These faculties range from competence in language and arithmetic to the command of practical and moral knowledge vital for daily living as well as to excellence in the arts and sciences. The exercise of their abilities allows individuals to become full human beings and fully participating members of particular communities. Taken together, these activities are the distinctive, cultural achievements of the human species. For humanist liberals, then, the emphasis is on the freedom of the individual in forming and attaining individual goals; for reform liberals, the emphasis is on meeting shared standards of practice to the best of one's abilities and encouraging others to do so as well.

The issue, however, is not one of choosing between individual and community. Liberals of all views regard the individual as primary, while also recognizing the community's indispensable role in the pursuit of individual goals. For humanist liberals, the role of the political community is to provide collective goods and satisfy individual preferences equitably. For reform liberals, the role of the community is to set standards of mastery and excellence. Without such communally, interpersonally established norms, the serious cultivation of one's faculties faces a basic difficulty: the lack of a test of an individual's performance that is independent of the individual's own personal inclinations or whims. In other words, if the person whose achievements are to be measured is also the one who sets the terms of evaluation, and if the person who defines the standards of performance for herself or himself is free to alter them whenever it is convenient to do so, the whole idea of developing or improving one's skills loses much of its meaning for reform liberals. For them, the point of achieving mastery or excellence is to meet standards that are set by a community rather than by the individual alone.[86]

---

[86] Greenstone 1982b; Wittgenstein 1958, 269ff.; see esp. Wittgenstein's arguments against private language.

This reform outlook, in turn, encourages a different view of rationality. Where appropriate, of course, reform liberals certainly reason instrumentally in order better to pursue their goals, but the activities prescribed by their ethic are, in principle, obligatory. Reform liberals, therefore, recognize a duty to develop their own faculties, and the development of their own moral capacities entails an obligation to help others do so. As the following practical syllogism suggests, this form of reasoning is not instrumental but principled. Accordingly, reform liberals seek not the most effective means to achieve an end but rather those actions that affirm their moral commitments.

The Reform Liberal Syllogism: Logical Consistency

Major Premise:
My duty is to take actions that affirm a commitment to developing human faculties.

Minor Premise:
Action Y satisfies this criterion.

Conclusion:
My *duty* is to undertake action Y.

This ethic, in turn, entails a view of liberty more positive than that of humanist liberals, who favor the absence of restraint. Full human freedom requires the developed abilities, of body and mind, that come with mastery or excellence in important human practices. One truly has the freedom to read a text—one can choose to do so—only if one is literate, and the freedom to read a complex text depends on one's ability to read with discernment.

The disagreements between humanist and reform liberals thus occur entirely within the framework of genus liberalism. The issue is what place autonomous individuals should have in a viable political community. American politics may be exceptional, therefore, not simply because Americans agree on certain liberal values but also because their most basic cultural opposition turns on classically liberal questions. By dominating the political agenda, in fact, these issues may have inhibited the emergence of class antagonisms and collectivist politics. Admittedly, no set of criteria can distinguish definitively between vital and trivial differences, yet we do have as criteria competing stands on the nature of the individual personality, on the character of human rationality and freedom, and on the obligations individuals and communities owe each other—as well as competing stands on epistemology and ontology, as we shall see in chapter four. Here, then, is the basis for a fundamental polarity, unless we simply state that there can be no basic conflicts between two liberal or bourgeois social philosophies.

Is reform liberalism genuinely liberal? Its advocates, including contemporary fundamentalists, share the devotion of their culture to republican institutional norms and the belief of genus liberalism in individual liberty, private property, and political consent. Typically, they insist that individuals take responsibility for their own actions, but it is also true that the impulse of Protestant reform, which spawned the Lincoln persuasion, looked to constraint and conformity as well as to liberation. To be sure, the antebellum moral reformers worked for positive liberty—for the opportunity for individuals to develop their faculties freely—by supporting public education, decent treatment for the indigent insane, and the antislavery cause.[87] Yet these objectives imposed restraints on those the reformers believed to be less worthy than themselves; the objectives, for example, called for depriving slave owners of their property and imposing on the children of illiterate immigrants an education that sometimes conflicted with the beliefs of the parents. The reformers also had more overtly conformist goals; goals that required obedience to certain behavioral norms: those of the temperance movement, for example, and of nativists whose efforts were directed toward the exclusion of immigrants judged to be unruly. Yet such goals were viewed by reformers as liberating. To the nativists, for example, Catholic immigrants belonged to a hierarchical, authoritarian church from which the immigrants should be freed. Similarly, temperance advocates saw drunkenness as the enslavement of individuals to passion and as the constraint of the exercise of individual free will.

The foregoing comparison of humanist and reform liberalism misstates matters to some extent. All liberal theories rely on some constraint. Humanist liberals, for example, also resort to coercion when it is necessary to resolve conflicting preferences. The significant feature of the difference between humanist and reform liberals is the insistence of reform liberalism on the importance of the cultivation of faculties according to communally or socially rather than individually determined standards. Armed with such standards, even those reform liberals who stress freedom and individual development rank some individually determined goals and preferences ahead of other such goals and preferences; that is, those occupations and activities that encourage individual development are intrinsically more worthy than those that do not. As illiberal as the position may seem, however, three considerations argue in favor of the genuinely liberal status of reform liberalism.

First, like other liberal theories, the reform version focuses on individual development. Not every political or ethical theory committed to such development can be considered liberal, of course, but the reform position insists that the cultivation of faculties is an intrinsically individual enterprise.

[87] Greenstone and Peterson 1983; Greenstone 1979.

Second, these individuals must practice *self*-development; they must acquire the skills for themselves. Accordingly, each individual—and not some religious, social, or political authority—must determine just how this project should be undertaken; and each person must decide which activities, occupations, sports, or hobbies to pursue, in order to secure the recognition of others or the intrinsic satisfaction that these achievements bring. The individuals remain sovereign, that is, with respect to this choice of means (broadly defined) for developing their faculties, even though their goals may have been shaped by widely accepted social or cultural understandings.

Third, the real animus of liberal theory is directed against illicit forms of interpersonal domination, that is, against the subjugation of one person by another. As the liberal republican theorist, Algernon Sidney, put it, "Liberty solely consists in an independency upon the will of another."[88] Can it be argued, then, that the standards important to reform liberals are *imposed* by some people on others? The short answer is that such a claim ignores the foundations on which a culture must be erected. These standards are too important to be seen as merely satisfying some particular preference or interest. It is not sufficient to argue, for example, that each individual benefits if all members of a society master the rules essential for complex human communication. The point is that a culture can remain viable only if basic features of this sort in a culture are rarely, if ever, seriously challenged. If the capacity to meet these standards were not almost universally distributed, the result would be more than social chaos; it would mean the unraveling of civilized life itself. Rousseau's *Discourses* aside, then, almost all critics who attack existing cultures typically call for the development of a cultural alternative rather than assailing the acquisition of all cultural competence. In this situation there is little point in talking about one particular set of individuals imposing cultural standards on another.

To use a somewhat different idiom, Locke's classically liberal notion of tacit consent must have a cultural as well as a political dimension. Whereas humanist liberals stress consent to institutions that resolve disputes over preferences, reform liberals emphasize consent to a culture's fundamental practices. These practices are adopted not as a matter of deliberate choice but simply because (and to the extent that) the individuals concerned participate in that culture—the question of the subjugation of some individuals by others simply does not arise. As Wittgenstein suggested in a related situation, the issue is not whether particular individuals are free to accept or reject this or that opinion as propounded by another; rather, as long as an individual continues to practice a particular form of life, it is impossible, or

---

[88] Sidney 1751, 12, cited in Banning 1978, 47, n. 18.

at least infeasible, to reject the central practices and norms that make up that life form.[89]

The Liberal Polarity:
Conflicting Dispositions

It is possible, of course, to believe in both satisfying preferences and developing faculties, but the ability of some individuals to internalize the two has by no means eliminated all conflict. Reform liberalism has had a major impact on American politics *because* it offers a far-reaching idea of a common life and culture. The appeal of reform liberalism goes beyond republicanism, because, in Rawls's terms, the concerns of reform liberalism are widely social and cultural and not narrowly political. It also directly challenges the neutral stance of humanist liberalism with regard to individual preferences. The civil rights and feminist movements of recent decades, for example, reasoning from reform liberal premises, have dismissed as unworthy the preferences of their opponents. To these reformers, invidious distinctions of race and gender have done much more than deny equal opportunity to some citizens. The opponents of reform liberalism, by countenancing discrimination based on physical differences, have ignored the ethically decisive fact that blacks and women have both the abilities and the obligation to develop their distinctively human capacities. In terms of policies, reform liberalism supports government aid to education, cultural development through agencies such as the National Endowments for the Arts and the Humanities, and scientific progress through the National Science Foundation. In each case, political considerations, including the balance of conflicting preferences, have been relevant to questions of implementation. Nevertheless, the goals themselves reflect the priority accorded to the development of individual faculties and the importance of extending opportunity for such development to every member of the political community.

The antebellum era offers a striking case in point. Most Yankee reformers of the period valued the petty bourgeois capitalism of their time, because it rewarded those who exercised self-discipline and reinvested their earnings to make their enterprises more efficient.[90] These reformers also treasured other features of a liberal society that encouraged self-development, and they assailed every institution or practice—most particularly human slavery—that stifled it. In this sense, reform liberalism has supported a critique of bourgeois society that is *internal* to the liberal

[89] Wittgenstein 1958, 241.
[90] Greenstone 1982b, 7–8.

enterprise, because its criticisms stem from liberal rather than radical premises.

If the reform and humanist outlooks had such influence, then we may ask what form this influence has taken. Certainly the influence cannot have been causal, as long as that term refers to a *change* in one feature of a situation that leads to or produces a change in another feature. Because basic beliefs of this sort are stable rather than transitory elements of an individual's or group's outlook, a causal analysis must look elsewhere—for example, to economic or social changes such as the accelerated growth of slavery after the invention of the cotton gin. Nor can the influence be explained by a boundary condition, because neither the humanist nor the reform perspective alone constitutes a boundary condition. The disagreement between the two perspectives meant that neither perspective alone could completely or distinctively characterize the American context.

Accordingly, I shall treat the humanist and reform liberalisms as dispositions, that is, as combinations of concepts and attitudes—with rules for correct performance—that encourage certain types of actions and discourage others. To believe an action is right is to be disposed to perform that act in the appropriate circumstances. Thus, to say that two groups have opposing dispositions is to say that they are disposed to react differently, because they have different sets of criteria for evaluating, interpreting, and reacting to particular events. In this situation, the cause of a particular action remains the event or other change that brought the reaction about. A full explanation of the reaction in question—why groups reacted to the same event in different ways—must include consideration of dispositions such as reform and humanist beliefs.

In the end, however, it is one thing to assert the philosophic and political importance to the culture of this conflict between opposing dispositions. It is another thing entirely to demonstrate the political centrality of that conflict; to show, that is, the influence of that conflict on the course of American political development, as well as to show the ways in which that influence was exerted. Before returning to Lincoln, therefore, we will examine the thought and politics of six leading figures of the period from the founding to the Civil War. The analysis begins with two of the founders, John Adams and Thomas Jefferson, whose complex relationship exhibited the basic split between reform and humanist liberalism in its most explicitly philosophic form and suggested the eventual connection between that split and the slavery issue. The discussion then turns to the Jacksonian era, in which this philosophic opposition became political, and considers, first, three Jacksonians: William Leggett, Stephen A. Douglas, and Martin Van Buren; and then a Yankee Whig, John Quincy Adams.

For the most part, these figures are *revealing* rather than either merely representative or fundamentally innovative intellectual figures. They were more than simply representative of their culture, because they critically explored and examined, rather than merely reproducing, the conventional political views of their time and place. Unlike the great philosophers, they were less than fundamentally innovative, since they did not formulate new political principles or break with or reorder the culture's basic beliefs.[91] Nevertheless, these figures are revealing, because they identified certain crucial ideas, assumptions, and beliefs that have a central place in American political culture. By delineating the available conceptual and normative resources in their humanist and reform beliefs, these individuals illuminated the ground on which the battle over slavery would be fought. Indeed, it is in terms of the intellectual and political achievements—and failings—of these figures, and in terms of the differences between them, that we can best understand the Lincoln persuasion. The Lincoln persuasion was an authentic variant of reform liberalism that nevertheless made important use of its humanist counterpart.

[91] Again, I am indebted to Dave Ericson for this formulation.

PART TWO

INTRODUCTION TO PART TWO

FOR ALL its virtues, Hartz's version of the consensus thesis had a manifestly static character. The problem is not that the thesis ignored all change. In his narrative, in fact, Hartz often noted the effects of social and economic developments. The problem, rather, is that in Hartz's account these developments affected political life from the outside while leaving its fundamental Lockean commitments undisturbed. But what of those essentially political developments such as the rise of political parties, the transformation of the presidency, and the constitutional supremacy of the federal government? Together, these developments profoundly separate contemporary politics from the world the founders knew or even envisioned. For Hartz, these mainly institutional changes could not have any theoretical significance, because they do not signal a deviation from Lockean values.

Nevertheless, in the event, American political culture did have to confront the problems—political, moral, and philosophical—posed by the unprecedented formation of a large democratic republic. In responding to the challenges, the culture did adopt new, though still liberal, rules for correct performance. Certainly, the rise of parties had obvious implications for American democracy. And the predominance of the federal government was one result of the struggle over basic political commitments that Lincoln waged with Douglas's Democrats as well as with the South.

Nor was this struggle only over slavery. It took place, in fact, in a particular historical and social-psychological context. Lincoln's society, after all, did more than celebrate individual striving for success. His society also assumed that the members of each generation would understand, better than either their parents or grandparents, the new world into which they had been born, and they would therefore be able to surpass the achievements of both their parents and grandparents. The founding, however, presented the profound complication of seemingly matchless accomplishments. How could the second generation of the republic match its predecessors, whose success combined the winning of independence and the establishment of a new constitutional order?

As we noted in chapter one, in 1838, at the age of twenty-nine, Lincoln graphically captured these tensions in his first major speech, to the Young Men's Lyceum in Springfield. In his words, the "experiment" of the founders in establishing a genuinely popular, self-governing republic was obviously "successful; and thousands have won their deathless names in making it so. But the game is caught. . . . This field of glory is harvested, and the crop is already appropriated." Lincoln's concern was that "men of ambition and talents" would continue to "spring up," men who would not be satisfied with merely "supporting and maintaining an edifice that has been erected by others."[1]

According to the prevailing, and perhaps most obvious, interpretation, the Lyceum Address voiced Lincoln's own frustrations, as well as those of his contemporaries. According to Forgie's arresting psychoanalytic account, Lincoln's politics exhibited the inevitable ambivalence with which the founding generation was regarded by its successors. The intensity of Lincoln's own ambition made him particularly sensitive to the fact that the achievements of the founders were too extensive to be equaled by later generations.

Was Lincoln really a second-generation figure? The leading figures in Jacksonian politics clearly include John Quincy Adams, the son of a leading founder; two other presidents, Andrew Jackson himself and Martin Van Buren; and the triumvirs of the Senate, John C. Calhoun, Henry Clay, and Daniel Webster. The oldest of these, Adams and Jackson, were born in 1767, and the youngest, Calhoun, was born in 1787; all were dead by 1852, except Van Buren, whose public career had ended in 1848. Lincoln was born in 1809 and emerged as a major political figure only in 1854, at the time of his attacks on the Kansas-Nebraska Act. Lincoln, then, was a man of the third generation, not the second, both chronologically and politically. In contrast, Lincoln's great political antagonist, Stephen A. Douglas, was politically aligned with Jackson and Van Buren, although Douglas was four years younger than Lincoln. Douglas personally saw himself as a loyal Jacksonian Democrat. As late as 1858, he correctly asserted that Lincoln was trying to supplant the familiar economic divisions of the Jacksonian era with a new, moralistic, and profoundly divisive politics based on the slavery issue.[2]

As the chapters that follow maintain, the second generation confronted, but by no means resolved, a set of questions originally posed by the founders when they established this large, diverse, popular regime. The aim of Lincoln's politics, the essential point of his persuasion, was to build on, and go beyond, these second-generation solutions. Moreover, his success in doing so can be understood only in terms of the American liberal polarity. That polarity shaped both the problems Lincoln addressed and the solutions on which he built. To explicate this argument, we will begin with two of the founders—Thomas Jefferson and John Adams—whose achievements helped create the challenges that confronted their successors.

[1] Basler 1953–1955, 1:114.
[2] Johannsen 1965, 37–38.

THREE

ADAMS AND JEFFERSON

A SHARED LIBERALISM

DISPOSITIONS vary in importance over time. Apart perhaps from the painful case of the Alien and Sedition Acts, the first political struggles of the American regime did not reflect the reform-humanist polarity. The central concerns were, first, for securing independence and establishing the new regime and, then, for determining the proper powers of the federal government and addressing the conflicts among economic and regional interests. There was, to be sure, a continuing interest in the perspectives advanced by Lockean theory, by republicanism, by the continental and Scottish Enlightenments, and by Protestant morality. During this period, however, American political culture was marked by a complex *founding synthesis* rather than by the polarity that surfaced in response to the slavery issue.

The pattern of synthesis and then polarity accounts for the present focus on John Adams and Thomas Jefferson rather than on the more centrist James Madison. The basic philosophical disagreements to be discussed in chapter four will suggest the extent to which this liberal polarity was present in American culture, even before it began to structure political life. As the present chapter will show, the commitment of these two men to the founding synthesis—despite sometimes bitter personal and political antagonisms—emphasized the quiescence of the reform-humanist polarity during their lifetimes, except perhaps with regard to the complex issue of equality.

Friendship, Rivalry, Friendship

The bitter campaign between Adams and Jefferson for the presidency in 1800 ended with the decisive election of their era. Although Adams had been Washington's vice president and Jefferson his first secretary of state, Adams and Jefferson were at odds with each other on both foreign and domestic issues, notably on the proper attitude of the United States toward the French Revolution and on Hamilton's program for the control by the federal government of the course of the country's economic development.[1] By 1796, the year in which Adams narrowly defeated Jefferson for president, the two men had become partisan enemies. In 1800, when Jefferson defeated Adams, Jefferson's running mate, Aaron Burr, tried to exploit a procedural defect in the election process to secure the presidency for himself. Hurt and angry over his own defeat, Adams did little to help resolve the impasse,[2] and he went home to Massachusetts before Jefferson's inauguration. The two men would not meet again.

In the end, however, through the friendship they developed in correspondence over a number of years, Adams and Jefferson overcame many personal and political differences. Before the revolution they shared very similar views of the status of the American colonies in the British Empire.[3] As members of the Continental Congress, they found, in Jefferson's words, a "perfect coincidence of principle and of action";[4] they personally hit it off at once;[5] and they collaborated closely on the Declaration of Independence. A close friendship followed. In the 1780s, as ambassadors to Great Britain and France respectively, Adams and Jefferson consulted each other regularly—Jefferson often looking to his older friend for "counsel" and "advice."[6] Their personal ties deepened after Jefferson's daughter Polly stayed with Adams and his wife Abigail on her way from Virginia to Paris.[7] When the Adamses returned to the United States in 1788, Jefferson, still in France, pronounced himself "bewidowed."[8] Even through their conflicts, the two men continued to respect each other's abilities and character.[9] Jefferson thought that "Mr. Adams was honest as a politician, as well as a man."[10] "He is an old friend," Adams wrote of Jefferson, "whose abilities and steadiness I always found great cause to confide."[11]

---

[1] Peterson 1976, 58–61. The following abbreviations are used in the notes of chapters three and four: JA for John Adams; AA for Abigail Adams; TJ for Thomas Jefferson; JQA for John Quincy Adams.

[2] Chinard 1933, 309.

[3] J. Adams 1850–1856, 4:99–121; Peterson 1987, 21.

[4] Koch and Peden 1944, 608, TJ to Dr. Benjamin Rush 16 Jan. 1811.

[5] Padover 1942, 44.

[6] Cappon 1959, 224, TJ to JA 6 Feb. 1788; Koch and Peden 1944, 539, TJ to James Madison 1 Jan. 1797; Cappon 1959, 271, TJ to AA 13 June 1804.

[7] Cappon 1959, 159, TJ to AA 21 Dec. 1786; 165; 178, AA to TJ 26 June 1787; 179, AA to TJ 27 June 1787; 183–87, AA to TJ 6 July 1787, TJ to AA 10 July 1787, AA to TJ 10 July 1787; 197, AA to TJ 10 Sept. 1787; 201, TJ to AA 4 Oct. 1787.

[8] Ibid., 172, TJ to JA 20 Feb. 1787; see also 222, TJ to AA 2 Feb. 1788.

[9] Koch and Peden 1944, 609, TJ to Benj. Rush 16 Jan. 1811; Padover 1942, 132 n. 5; J. Adams 1850–1856, 8:153–54, JA to James Lloyd 31 Mar. 1815.

[10] Koch and Peden 1944, 609.

[11] Padover 1942, 132, n. 5; see also J. Adams 1850–1856, 8:154–55, JA to James Lloyd 31 Mar. 1815.

Even their policy disagreements proved somewhat transitory. On his side, Jefferson was willing for his followers to deviate from principle when the need seemed pressing. Indeed, he and his two immediate successors to the presidency eventually adopted the more moderate parts of the Federalist economic program. On his side, Adams appealed to those mainly agrarian Federalists who rejected Hamilton's more ambitious proposals. In fact, Adams and Jefferson shared an essentially rural perspective that looked with suspicion on the development of an urban commercial economy, and they both rejected doctrinaire opposition to government assistance for the economy.[12] By 1808, Adams's son and confidante, John Quincy Adams, had joined Jefferson's Republicans, and Adams himself had effectively left the Federalist party. By 1812 Adams and Jefferson had resumed their friendship through a memorable correspondence, in which they considered all the major intellectual issues of their era, and whose topics ranged from the heroic achievements of their generation to concerns about old age, declining health and approaching death, and the loss of loved ones. The end of their exchange stunned contemporaries and has intrigued scholars ever since: both men died on the fiftieth anniversary of the Declaration of Independence, July 4, 1826.

The Problem of Adams's Liberalism

If the disagreements of Adams and Jefferson on policies and parties proved temporary, other differences were more enduring. Jefferson was the quintessential enlightenment rationalist and egalitarian liberal democrat. In his view, almost all human beings could use their reasoning powers to contribute to the progress of their species. There was, indeed, no definite limit on human improvability. As he wrote to Benjamin Waterhouse in 1818, "When I contemplate the immense advances in science and discoveries in the arts [during] . . . my life, I look forward with confidence to equal advances by the present generation, and have no doubt they will consequently be as much wiser than we have been as we than our fathers were, and they than the burners of witches."[13] Here, in Jefferson's view, was the source of his differences with Adams. As he pointedly wrote to his Yankee friend, "The enemies of reform [that is, Adams's party] . . . denied improvement, and advocated steady adherence to the principles, practices, and institutions of our fathers, which they represented as [an] . . . akmé of excellence, beyond which the human mind could never advance."[14] Although Jefferson

---

[12] See Dauer 1968.

[13] Koch and Peden 1944, 687, TJ to Waterhouse 3 Mar. 1818.

[14] Cappon 1959, 332, TJ to JA 15 June 1813; see also Koch and Peden 1944, 687, TJ to Benj. Waterhouse 3 Mar. 1818; 729–30, TJ to C. Weightman, 24 June 1826.

recognized the existence of a natural aristocracy distinguished by unusual talents, he assigned to it a mainly political role: to provide leadership for the polity. If leaders and citizens alike were freed from the sway of ignorance, prejudice, and passion, including unsubstantiated religious dogma, they were likely to arrive at the truth.

Adams, by contrast, became increasingly skeptical—about human nature and the ability of human reason to control passion—and thus conservative as time went on. Even in the revolutionary era, when Adams had thought the American people were particularly virtuous, he distinguished between the rabble and the people's "greater and more judicious part." Later, even this qualified faith weakened.[15] As social order and morality seemed to decline, Adams treated disorders such as Shays' Rebellion as serious threats, undertaken, in his wife's words, by "[i]gnorant, wrestless desperadoes, without conscience or principals" and desirous of "an equal distribution of property . . . [and the] annhiliati[on of] all debts."[16]

Not surprisingly, then, as he wrote Jefferson, the first major issue on which they disagreed was the French Revolution.

> You was well persuaded in your own mind that the Nation would succeed in establishing a free Republican Government: I was as well persuaded, in mine, that a project of such a Government, over five and twenty millions people, when four and twenty millions and five hundred thousands of them could neither write nor read: was . . . unnatural, irrational and impracticable.[17]

Almost from the beginning, Adams thought revolution epitomized the dangers of mob violence and of the democratic passion for innovation to which democratic regimes were liable. Adams concluded that the republic's later excesses fully vindicated his initial fears.[18]

This quite general suspicion of the people encouraged Adams's acquiescence in the lamentable Alien and Sedition Acts and thus in the prosecution of Jeffersonian editors and activists. Adams had not, to be sure, initiated the legislation, and on occasion he tried to moderate the enforcement of the acts.[19] Once out of office, understandably, he took little pride in the episode.[20] Yet Adams's doubts about the ability of unaided reason to control the passions led him to turn more and more to support of the constraints imposed by government, including the prosecution of Republican editors and activists under the acts. During his presidency, Adams had been trou-

---

[15] J. R. Howe 1966, 106; J. Adams 1850–1856, 4:82; Handler 1964, 94–95.

[16] J. R. Howe 1966, 130, 107; Cappon 1959, 168, AA to TJ 29 Jan. 1787.

[17] Cappon 1959, 355, JA to TJ 13 July 1813.

[18] See Haraszti 1952, 21–22; Chinard 1933, 122.

[19] See, for example, Dauer 1968, 242; J. R. Howe 1966, 198–99; Chinard 1933, 275–76, TJ to AA 24 July 1804; and Shaw 1976, 257.

[20] Cappon 1959, 329, JA to TJ 14 June 1813.

bled by the threat of sedition and disloyalty, rumors of armed insurrections, and even the increasing opposition to his administration, which he regarded as partisan and therefore unrepublican. Indeed, his harsh response to opposition contributed to the climate of partisan distrust in which the acts were adopted.[21] Adams's views, his own political ineptitude, and the Federalists' use of the Alien and Sedition Acts all contributed to his defeat in 1800 and to the collapse of his party. From that point, it was the egalitarian, secular, optimistic Jefferson, rather than Adams, who became the admired sage and whose disciples went from victory to victory.

There is a question, then, about whether or not Adams really shared the basic premises of a pervasively liberal order. Hartz noted at the outset of *The Liberal Tradition* that "aspects of our original life in the Puritan colonies" as well as in the South "hardly fit" a Lockean politics.[22] Hartz implied that these Puritan elements of colonial culture had been extirpated before the revolutionary era and that slavery's neo-feudal apologists were not taken seriously outside their own region before the Civil War or anywhere after it.

In a justly celebrated discussion, Gordon Wood has taken up this issue directly. Wood's argument rests on a shift in the republican doctrine of the separation of powers. Traditionally, republican theory had linked each major institution of goverment to a different social group. The English people were represented in the House of Commons, the aristocracy in the House of Lords, and, at the pinnacle of the social pyramid, the monarch exercised the powers of the executive. After the revolution, however, almost all Americans rejected the elitist features of this arrangement. The Constitution, in response to this rejection, provided for the separation of the three branches of government and for a bicameral legislature, and the people were declared to be the source of authority for the separate parts. Senators, for example, even though they were not elected directly, were chosen by the people's elected representatives in state legislatures. Adams, however, found the arrangement wanting. Faithful to the classical republican view, he repeatedly praised constitutional arrangements that based particular institutions in specific social strata. In consequence, Wood has concluded, Adams became politically irrelevant.

Wood's conclusion is clearly correct up to a point. Adams did lose the presidency in 1800, in part because he was politically out of step, but there are two problems with Wood's thesis. First, Adams's untimely traditionalism was only one of several instances in which the moralist and elitist features of New England culture proved untenable in an increasingly secular and egalitarian political world. There is a question about why this pattern kept repeating itself. Second, granted Adams's political conservatism and

21 Dauer 1968, 159–60; J. R. Howe 1966, 195–96; Peterson 1976, 80–81.
22 Hartz 1955, 4.

his complicity in the Alien and Sedition Acts and their aftermath, Wood's account obscures Adams's liberalism, the complex founding synthesis that he shared with Jefferson and that helped sustain their generation during both the revolution and the first crucial decades of the fledgling regime.[23]

The Multiple Declensions of New England Culture

Although Hartz said little about the way in which New England's elitist and moralistic beliefs were driven out of the American liberal world, other scholars have offered persuasive accounts. To Richard L. Bushman, for example, much of the New England colonial experience was of the transition from Puritan to Yankee, that is, from a theocracy to a secular, individualist—indeed, liberal—society.[24] New England's founders had denounced materialism, they had insisted on rigorous self-denial, and they had acknowledged their sins to a distant and angry god. Their descendants, however, began to appreciate an enjoyment of wealth as well as its pursuit, and to be repelled by illiberal beliefs such as those in predestination, infant damnation, and the election of only a few chosen saints.

Bushman's account focused primarily on the first two-thirds of the eighteenth century. In his own, now classic discussion, however, Perry Miller discerned an earlier beginning for the process:

> The real . . . story of late seventeenth-century New England becomes . . . a shedding of the religious conception of the universe, [and] a turning toward . . . secular [politics] . . . by translating Christian liberty into those liberties guaranteed by statute. Which is another way of saying that religion became the support . . . of property. . . . Soon afterward, the philosophy of social status yielded to the ethic of success, and merchants . . . learned to control congregations despite the clerics.[25]

Although the issues and factional alignments were clearly different in the period Hartz treated, Hartz argued that a similar process occurred a century and a half later. According to his account, it was obvious—at least to many of the eastern, urban Whigs—that the wise, self-disciplined, economically successful, and therefore morally worthy among the citizenry should run the government and supervise the course of capitalist development. Also according to Hartz, however, the price for clinging to such an elitist, moralistic politics, in the democratic atmosphere of the 1820s and 1830s, was a series of painful political defeats. These reversals began in 1828 when John Quincy

---

[23] Wood 1969, 568.
[24] Bushman 1967.
[25] P. Miller 1961b, 171.

Adams was driven from the White House by a southern populist, just as his father had been twenty-eight years before. The reversals stopped only in 1840, by which time the Whigs had learned to adopt much of the democratic, exuberant, and culturally tolerant style of their Jacksonian opponents.

It goes almost without saying that the elitist, moralistic Whigs of the 1830s lived in a cultural and political world very different from that of New England's seventeenth-century clerical elites; in addition, the politics of each of those periods differed from the traditional republicanism of John Adams's time. Yet accounts of these groups suggest an important continuity in American political history: in each case, the major leaders of New England proved fatally at odds with a new, more tolerant, social order. The pattern is strikingly consistent.

As insightful as each of these accounts is when taken by itself, taken together they raise troubling questions. If, as Miller argued, the outlook of the colonial clerics was very much at odds with the trend toward a dominant, secular liberalism, why did similar episodes occur and reoccur in later decades? How, indeed, was it possible for John Adams to live to see his son become president, and for John Quincy Adams, after his own defeat in 1828, to go on to a memorable career in the House of Representatives as the great antislavery tribune? And how in turn could *his* son, Charles Frances Adams, play an important role in the rise and triumph of the new Republican party? In these cases, at any rate, neither the traditional politics nor the cultural styles of the figures denied them a place in the political mainstream.

If John Adams was at all typical, the most plausible inference is that New England culture was much too complex to have simply declined or prospered as a whole. What did very gradually "decline" in the New England tradition was, first, a belief that success in the world must be subordinated to the demands of one's religious community, and, second, an elitism that was both religious and secular. What survived among many Yankees was a devotion to the reform variant of liberalism. John Adams neither abandoned his Protestant outlook nor transformed it into a purely secular concern with individual success. Instead, he asserted a perspective on morality and politics—a disposition—that others would fashion into an attack on slavery.

There is no need to deny the very real differences between the second and third presidents—they differed not only over specific policies but also over basic cultural loyalties. Adams, for example, proudly acknowledged his Puritan background and viewed human nature moralistically and pessimistically; Jefferson serenely affirmed the secular, libertarian values of the Enlightenment. For all their differences, however, both men embraced not only genus liberalism and republicanism, but also a belief in rationality and sentiment as social restraints and in a clearly Protestant ethic. They thus exhibited a complex convergence, a founding synthesis, that for most of their lives was more important than their nevertheless real and persisting differences.

The Founding Synthesis

Genus Liberalism

Jefferson and Adams articulated the core of their genus liberal beliefs in 1776. The Declaration of Independence—which the Virginian drafted and the Yankee defended "fearlessly" (as Jefferson put it) on the floor of Congress—began by balancing the claims of individual and community. As its most celebrated passage asserted, legitimate governments must recognize each individual's "inalienable rights" to "life, liberty, and the pursuit of happiness," rights that can be secured only when governments are "instituted" through the exercise of popular consent.[26] It is the condition of consent that creates particular peoples, and thus it was by collectively withdrawing their consent that the Americans dissolved their "political bands" with their "British brethren."

Jefferson spent much of his career elaborating the principles of the Declaration. Beginning with *A Summary of the Rights of British America* in 1774, his writings are replete with individualist, Lockean themes such as natural rights, consent, freedom of conscience, and the sufficiency of each individual's natural reason.[27] Accordingly, he disliked energetic, meddlesome government, describing it as "always oppressive," and he asserted a natural right of expatriation if government became too oppresive.[28] Sovereignty, he insisted, must reside in the living rather than the dead, because a particular generation had no right to bind its successors, and the "earth belongs always to the living generation."[29] He regarded as essential liberties the traditional British rights of representation in the legislature, trial by jury, and habeas corpus.[30]

This individualism sustained a deeply processual approach to both intellectual and social life. As an admirer of Adam Smith, Francois Quesnay, and Count Destutt de Tracy,[31] Jefferson opposed controls on the free market. He also affirmed the individual's absolute freedom of opinion. No sect could acquire oppressive power if all citizens had their say, and no government could find its true course without the criticism and open debate of its citizens. To further the course of progress, Jefferson fought for freedom of

---

[26] Koch and Peden 1944, 22.
[27] Ibid., 293ff.; 490, TJ to James Madison 6 Sept. 1789; 217; 275; Peterson 1987, 323.
[28] Koch and Peden 1944, 440, TJ to James Madison 20 Dec. 1787; 42.
[29] Ibid., 491, TJ to James Madison 6 Sept. 1789.
[30] Chinard 1946, 497.
[31] Cappon 1959, 491, TJ to JA 14 Oct. 1816; Chinard 1946, 328.

press and religion throughout his career, and he viewed the patent laws with suspicion lest they impede that course.[32] In effect he held that the intellectual market would "clear"—truth would triumph over error, as he said in his Second Inaugural—if the individual participants could act freely.[33] In that spirit he swore "eternal hostility against every form of tyranny over the mind of man."[34]

Yet Jefferson was equally devoted to the welfare of his liberal polity. He accepted, for example, Locke's assertion of the responsibility of government to umpire the unavoidable conflicts between individuals; and, however much he cherished freedom of conscience, he denied any such absolute right in the realm of action.[35] Some rights were inalienable, that is, but others must be partly abridged in order to establish a secure polity.[36] Though Jefferson rejected censorship, he accepted the eighteenth-century restrictions on license where it threatened the public order, including the prosecution of offending newspaper editors by state governments, though never by the federal authorities.[37]

These sentiments partly reflected the nationalist loyalties that led Jefferson to defend the intellectual and artistic accomplishments of his country and even the size of its native animals.[38] In his eyes, America represented the hope of the future, as a land of social equality and healthy mores. "A just and solid republican government," he wrote, would be a "standing monument and example" for others seeking their own liberty. "The last hope of human liberty in this world," he thought, "rests on us."[39] Thus the new nation required a *national* government.[40] As the political situation seemed to deteriorate during the 1780s, he concluded that central authorities must have the power to act directly with regard to its citizens. With a few important qualifications (most notably the need for a bill of rights), Jefferson therefore welcomed the new Constitution, believing with Madison that a large, diverse polity would be the best protection for republican liberty. Accordingly, Jefferson opposed separatist tendencies and favored westward expansion.[41] When the opportunity arose, Jefferson effectively doubled the nation's territorial expanse by the Louisiana Purchase, his constitutional

---

[32] Koch and Peden 1944, 629–30, TJ to Isaac McPherson 13 Aug. 1813.

[33] Ibid., 343–44.

[34] Ibid., 558, TJ to Benj. Rush 23 Sept. 1800; Peterson 1987, 252–53.

[35] See, for example, Koch and Peden 1944, 323; Chinard 1946, 106–7.

[36] Chinard 1946, viii–ix, 80–81, 85.

[37] Cappon 1959, 279, TJ to AA 11 Sept. 1804.

[38] Koch and Peden 1944, 205–10; Chinard 1946, 216–17.

[39] Koch and Peden 1944, 386–87, TJ to J. Banister 15 Oct. 1785; 561, TJ to John Dickinson 6 Mar. 1801; 613, TJ to William Duane 28 Mar. 1811.

[40] Chinard 1946, 155.

[41] Koch and Peden 1944, 391, TJ to A. Stuart Esq. 25 Jan. 1786; 514, TJ to George Washington 23 May 1792.

scruples notwithstanding. He even favored a program of roads and canals—supported by state governments—in order to foster national unity.[42]

Adams, too, as much as Jefferson, dealt with the tension between individual and polity in broadly liberal, even Lockean terms. Early in his career, in his *Dissertation on Canon and Feudal Law*, Adams wrote, "British liberties are not the grants of princes or parliaments, but original rights, conditions of original contracts, coequal with prerogative, and coeval with government."[43] Even late in the 1780s, Adams wrote to Jefferson that the new Constitution ought to have a declaration of rights.[44] At a minimum, these rights included petition, freedom of speech and press, and a right to property produced in Lockean fashion by mixing one's labor power with the material world.[45] At the same time, any people, in Adams's view, had a natural right to form a political compact.[46] Without such a compact, no individual had the right to govern others.[47] All rightful legislative power must rest on popular consent.[48]

These same beliefs sustained even the pessimistic side of Adams's political thought, the side that seemed so conservative to Jefferson. No matter how popular or democratic, Adams thought, every government must respect those individual rights that ultimately come from God, that are "antecedent to all earthly government" and are designed to protect minority groups.[49] Before the revolution as well as after, Adams feared that the love of power would lead one individual or group to subjugate or dominate another, even in a republican political regime.[50] Indeed, Adams's notorious plan for a separate legislative chamber for aristocrats was designed to isolate them, so they could not corrupt the representatives of the people; it was designed to "set bounds to passions," and thus to protect individuals against an invasion of their rights, which included the vital liberal right to property.[51] As Adams wrote to Jefferson in 1787, "You are afraid of the one [the executive]—I, of the few [in the legislature]."[52] Because in his view the legislature was the more dangerous of the two, Adams favored both dividing it into upper and lower houses and arming the executive with a veto.[53]

---

[42] Ibid., 341, 326.
[43] J. Adams 1850–1856, 3:463.
[44] Cappon 1959, 210, JA to TJ 10 Nov. 1787.
[45] J. Adams 1850–1856, 4:60; 3:457; 8:161.
[46] Peterson 1987, 12.
[47] Butterfield 1961, 2:57.
[48] J. Adams 1850–1856, 4:100–101, 108.
[49] Ibid., 3:449.
[50] Ibid., 3:448.
[51] Peek 1954, 191; cf. 156, 107–12, 115; J. R. Howe 1966, 188.
[52] Cappon 1959, 213, JA to TJ 6 Dec. 1787.
[53] Haraszti 1952, 28; J. R. Howe 1966, 97.

The same liberal concern with curbing legislative abuses led him to oppose the creation of divisions within the executive itself.[54]

Despite these views, Adams was in his own way as nationalistic as Jefferson. Initially, Adams too believed that Americans had a special virtue and destiny.[55] For all his later doubts on this point, Adams never wavered in his basic nationalism, especially in his support for a strong central government. Despite his early admiration for a simple agrarian society, he concluded that only a large, continental union could secure the order essential for true civic liberty and individual rights. Adams therefore welcomed the Constitution of 1787, and, as did other Federalists, he interpreted the powers of the new national government very broadly. Subsequently, he opposed any attempt to favor states' rights, whether it was Jefferson's in the Kentucky Resolutions in 1798, or that of the Yankee separatists at the Hartford Convention in 1814.[56]

Republicanism

Contrary to the scholarly dispute that characterizes the influences on the founding generation as *either* Lockean *or* republican, Adams and Jefferson adopted both outlooks. Although the first paragraphs of the declaration were plainly Lockean and consistent with genus liberalism, subsequent paragraphs went on to arraign the British for abuses that were especially offensive to republican theorists. Among other grievances noted, the king had subverted the operations of the people's "legislative bodies," undermined judicial independence, "erected a multitude of new offices, and sent hither swarms of new officers," "kept among us standing armies in times of peace," and made "the military independent of, and superior to, the civil power."[57]

Jefferson continued to voice these republican themes throughout his career. As a classicist, he admired the devotion of Greek Stoics to duty and patriotism, and thus to the pursuit of the common good.[58] By the same token, he welcomed the new Constitution's "distribution" of the government's powers as a check on self-interested officials, although he regretted the failure to limit the power of the president by forbidding reelection.[59] In the same spirit, Jefferson feared standing armies because they could be used the more readily to impose the government's will on citizens, and he en-

---

[54] J. Adams 1850–1856, 8:560, JA to Thomas Pickering 31 Oct. 1797.
[55] Cf. J. Adams 1876, 405, JA to AA 17 Sept. 1782.
[56] J. R. Howe 1966, 194, 154, 224–25.
[57] Peterson 1987, 235–41.
[58] Chinard 1946, 26; Koch and Peden 1944, 321–22.
[59] Koch and Peden 1944, 438, TJ to James Madison 20 Dec. 1787.

dorsed the independent sovereignty of the states as a further check on federal power, most notably in his attack on the Alien and Sedition Acts.[60]

Institutional arrangements alone, however, were insufficient. Republican regimes also required an independent citizenry who could make dispassionate political judgments. For all his own effectiveness as a party leader in attracting supporters, Jefferson warned against parties that would expect the blind loyalty of supporters. He demanded "a government rigorously frugal and simple," so that it could not corrupt its subjects.[61] Independence also depended on the right social conditions, notably on landed property.[62] As he wrote in his most famous passage in the *Notes*, "Those who labor in the earth are the chosen people of God, if ever He had a chosen people, whose breasts He has made His peculiar deposit for substantial and genuine virtue."[63] Admittedly, Jefferson's ideal of a largely rural society functioned as a normative standard rather than a concrete program of action.[64] He did eventually accept the idea of encouraging some manufacturing in America to foster independence from Europe, yet he sought to preserve the society of yeoman farmers wherever he could, most notably by the purchase of Louisiana to provide additional land for cultivation.[65]

Adams and Jefferson differed on many issues, at least in emphasis and rhetoric, including the vision of an agrarian America. Yet Adams's moralist politics had a strongly republican cast, and even his pessimism had republican origins. Adams explicitly affirmed both the country party tradition and his admiration for the great English republicans such as Harrington and Sidney, and he endorsed their belief in the eventual decline of every political regime.[66] Adams also shared Jefferson's opposition to unlimited arbitrary power in any form, and he reacted with republican suspicion when the Hamiltonians in his cabinet argued for a large standing army.[67] Most importantly, both Adams and Jefferson welcomed the Constitution because it provided those checks and balances that were the real bulwark of republican

---

[60] Peterson 1987, 249; 524, TJ to Destutt de Tracy 26 Jan. 1811; 281–84; Koch and Peden 1944, 286; 545, TJ to Elbridge Gerry 26 Jan. 1799; 84; 463, TJ to James Madison 15 Mar. 1789.

[61] Koch and Peden 1944, 545, TJ to Elbridge Gerry 26 Jan. 1799.

[62] Cappon 1959, 341; Koch and Peden 1944, 578–79, TJ to the Chiefs of the Cherokee Nation.

[63] Koch and Peden 1944, 280.

[64] D. L. Wilson 1981, 340, 342–43.

[65] Ibid., 343; Koch and Peden 1944, 441, TJ to James Madison 20 Dec. 1787; Chinard 1946, 418.

[66] J. Adams 1850–1856, 4:69, 194; J. R. Howe 1966, 32–35.

[67] Cappon 1959, 456, JA to TJ 13 Nov. 1815; J. Adams 1850–1856, 8:613, to James McHenry, Secretary of War 22 Oct. 1798; Dauer 1968, 212; cf. J. Adams 1850–1856, 4:40–41; Peek 1954, 128.

liberty.[68] "Without three divisions of power, stationed to watch each other, and compare each other's conduct with the laws, it will be impossible that the laws should at all times preserve their authority and govern all men."[69]

Adams believed also in an independent citizenry.[70] Early in his career, he warned that an overweening executive might use its patronage to subvert the people's virtue, and he dismissed the foes of the revolution as abject, corrupt hirelings of the crown.[71] He was more worried than Jefferson that factional or partisan loyalties in both the electorate and the legislature might subvert independent, disinterested judgments.[72] Even when he somewhat grudgingly affiliated with the Federalists, in the 1790s, he opposed factional cabals, including the Hamiltonian wing of his own party.[73]

Moreover, John and Abigail Adams both believed that republican independence was safest in a simple rural society free from the cloying sophistications to be found in Europe.[74] Personally, Adams himself returned home to Quincy from his official duties whenever he could, and, although he had a largely urban law practice up to the time of the revolution, from that point on he devoted himself entirely to public service and to farming.[75] Furthermore, he drew his political support from the rural wing of the Federalist party, the wing that eventually made common cause with moderate Jeffersonians. Here, as Dauer has pointed out, were the roots of his reconciliation with Jefferson.[76]

Reason, Sentiment, and Restraint

If Adams and Jefferson were liberals, however, they were also men of the eighteenth century. As such, they valued the civility and restraint that characterized that entire era, and they behaved accordingly. As the nineteenth century wore on, their manners and even their rationalism became increasingly outmoded. The editor of their correspondence observed

> They had lived almost too long. . . . "Yours as ever" had replaced "Your most humble and obedient servant" and "Esquire" was becoming a badge of cour-

---

[68] Cappon 1959, 334, JA to TJ 25 June 1813; 210, JA to TJ 10 Nov. 1787; J. Adams 1850–1856, 8:560; cf. Haraszti 1952, 30.

[69] J. Adams 1850–1856, 4:462; cf. Cappon 1959, 199, TJ to JA 28 Sept. 1787; Koch and Peden 1944, 126–27.

[70] J. Adams 1850–1856, 3:454.

[71] Ibid., 4:43, 56; Butterfield 1961, 1:272, 365.

[72] J. Adams 1876, 405; J. R. Howe 1966, 100, 194–95.

[73] Dauer 1968, 126; J. R. Howe 1966, 205–6.

[74] Cappon 1959, 119, AA to TJ 11 Feb. 1786.

[75] Ibid., 259, JA to TJ 31 Jan. 1796; Dauer 1968, 56.

[76] Dauer 1968, 7.

tesy rather than of gentility. . . . But in the twilight of the Revolutionary era Adams was still occupied with his books and correspondence and Jefferson was building his university on a new plan.[77]

Thus Adams wrote poignantly to Jefferson in 1815

that the Eighteenth Century, notwithstanding all its Errors and Vices has been, of all that are past, the most honourable to human Nature. Knowledge and Virtues were increased and diffused, Arts, Sciences useful to Men, ameliorating their condition, were improved, more than in any former equal Period. But . . . is the Nineteenth Century . . . to extinguish all the Lights of its Predecessor?[78]

Their correspondence, in fact, embodies a devotion to the life of the mind, to a reasoned and philosophically learned discourse that was rare at best among later politicians.

This eighteenth-century rationalism, however, as the Declaration of Independence itself suggested, was linked to the idea of virtuous sentiments. A people should adopt the extreme measure of rebellion, asserted the pivotal second paragraph, only when sanctioned by "prudence," that is, by instrumental reasoning that takes into account the "opinions of mankind."[79] Accordingly, the document offered a detailed brief of the misconduct of the British. It offered also an emotional appeal. The King's mercenaries were engaged in "works of death, desolation, and tyranny." He had used "the merciless Indian savages," against "all ages, sexes, and conditions." Having suffered this "last stab to agonizing affection," asserted the preliminary draft, "manly spirit bids us to renounce forever these unfeeling [English] brethren [and] . . . endeavor to forget our former love for them."[80]

Attention to balance marked the whole of Jefferson's activities and writings. The leading American intellectual of his time, he served for many years as president of the American Philosophical Society and helped to found the Library of Congress. In Jefferson's eyes, the human intellect was a precious gift from God, and, in 1788, he proudly proclaimed that the American government had been "reformed by reason alone."[81] Perhaps, therefore, participation in government or public service should exempt persons of genius from the political obligations of the ordinary citizen.[82] At the same time, Jefferson favored an educational system that would equip the majority of white Virginians to scrutinize their rulers and that would also identify the

[77] Cappon 1959, 1 [Roman *fifty*].
[78] Ibid., 456.
[79] Peterson 1987, 235–36.
[80] Koch and Peden 1944, 25, 27; Peterson 1987, 238, 240.
[81] Koch and Peden 1944, 311; 448, TJ to E. Rutledge 18 July 1788.
[82] Peterson 1987, 362, TJ to David Rittenhouse 19 July 1778.

intellectually gifted, who would become social and political leaders.[83] To that end, Jefferson devoted his last years to planning and launching the University of Virginia.[84]

Rationality, in addition to its virtuous sentiment, had an explicitly practical side. As a good lawyer, Jefferson looked to specific rulings rather than to abstract theories.[85] In trying to make the work of his slaves efficient, he anticipated the techniques of later time and motion studies.[86] He also offered his favorite grandson an elaborate set of "prudential rules for our government in society" that were worthy of Shakespeare's Polonius.[87] Jefferson defended his perspective in the revealing dialogue between the Head and the Heart, which he addressed to an absent, intimate friend, Maria Cosway. In the dialogue, the head warned against emotional entanglements with new acquaintances that might end in painful separations. Because "everything in this world is a matter of calculation," the "art of life is the art of avoiding pain. . . . Hence the inestimable value of intellectual pleasures" that leave us "serene and sublime."[88] Following his own advice, Jefferson in the end spurned Cosway when she tried to renew their friendship.[89]

Instrumentalism also shaped Jefferson's public career.[90] "Circumstances," he wrote to William Short, "sometimes require, that the rights the most unquestionable should be advanced with delicacy."[91] As Alexander Hamilton observed just before Jefferson's election, "Jefferson is [not] zealot enough to do anything in pursuance of his principles, which will contravene his popularity or his interest. He is as likely as any man I know, to temporize; to calculate what will be likely to promote his own reputation and advantage."[92] Hamilton was on the mark. To preserve the nation's economic independence, Jefferson abandoned his famous opposition to industrial development.[93] When the opportunity to purchase Louisiana arose, Jefferson acted despite his usually strict construction of the Constitution.

---

[83] Koch and Peden 1944, 262–63, 265.

[84] Ibid., 695–96, TJ to William Short 31 Oct. 1819; 721, TJ to Ellen W. Coolidge 27 Aug. 1825; 642–49, TJ to Peter Carr 7 Sept. 1814.

[85] Chinard 1946, xiv, 31; see also J. C. Miller 1977, 39–40.

[86] J. C. Miller 1977, 105, 108.

[87] Koch and Peden 1944, 591, TJ to Thomas Jefferson Randolph 24 Nov. 1808.

[88] Ibid., 397–99, 401–2, TJ to Maria Cosway 12 Oct. 1786.

[89] J. C. Miller 1977, 190.

[90] Koch and Peden 1944, 15–20; 384, TJ to Charles Van Hogendorp 13 Oct. 1785; Chinard 1946, 357–58.

[91] Koch and Peden 1944, 508, 28 July 1791.

[92] Padover 1942, 281.

[93] Koch and Peden 1944, 621, TJ to John Melish 13 Jan. 1813; Peterson 1987, 329, TJ to Society of Tammany or Columbian Order No. 1 of the City of New York 16 Feb. 1808.

Nevertheless, this cool intellectuality was tempered by a modulated romanticism.[94] As the Heart wrote to Cosway, if philosophers "ever felt the solid pleasure of one generous spasm of the heart, they would exchange for it all the frigid speculations of their lives."[95] Still, Jefferson was an Epicurean who countenanced the passions as long as they were harnessed to larger republican and rationalist purposes.[96] In the end, the passions too operated as a form of constraint on human conduct.

Most notably perhaps, whereas Jefferson sometimes referred to the individual conscience as a source of moral control, he more often relied on what the Scottish Enlightenment called the moral sense.[97] "To you," the Heart told the Head, "[nature] allotted the field of science; to me, that of morals."[98] That "moral sense of right and wrong," he observed in the *Notes*, is "like the sense of tasting and feeling in every man . . . a part of his nature."[99] Moreover, this moral sense resisted the "errors of reasoning or of speculation."[100] The command of this universal moral sense was clear: "though we cannot relieve all the distressed, we should relieve as many as we can."[101]

For all Adams's devotion to a Puritan tradition that left Jefferson cold, for all his philosophical defenses of his views, the Yankee moralist shared this late eighteenth-century outlook. "The human Understanding," Adams wrote to his Virginian friend, "is a revelation from its Maker which can never be disputed or doubted."[102] Even God himself at Sinai could not credibly deny the truths of mathematics that reason gives us.[103] Contrary to Rousseau, Adams voiced the "humble opinion . . . that knowledge, upon the whole, promotes virtue and happiness."[104] Knowledge, in fact, was a necessary condition for a good society; it could improve a person's capacities, even if it could not overcome one's lack of natural genius.[105] Consequently, he admired the fervent devotion of his own Puritan ancestors to

---

[94] J. C. Miller 1977, 177; cf. Koch and Peden 1944, 197.

[95] Koch and Peden 1944, 403, TJ to Cosway 12 Oct. 1786.

[96] J. C. Miller 1977, 178–79.

[97] Koch and Peden 1944, 318; see Ostrander 1978, 237.

[98] Koch and Peden 1944, 404, TJ to Cosway 12 Oct. 1786.

[99] Koch and Peden 1944, 221; see also 357, TJ to Robert Skipwith 3 Aug. 1771; Cappon 1959, 492, TJ to JA 14 Oct. 1816.

[100] Koch and Peden 1944, 636; 638–39, TJ to Thomas Law 13 June 1814; see J. C. Miller 1977, 91.

[101] Koch and Peden 1944, 404, TJ to Cosway 12 Oct. 1786.

[102] Cappon 1959, 373, JA to TJ 14 Sept. 1813.

[103] Ibid.

[104] Peek 1954, 207, JA to John Taylor.

[105] Butterfield 1961, 1:20; see J. Adams 1850–1856, 4:199.

education and hoped to make it a major priority of his administration, and he admired Jefferson's efforts to found the University of Virginia.[106]

Over time, Adams did conclude that education and rationality alone could not secure human progress and well-being. Human beings were much too often ruled by passion.[107] Even though intellect was sometimes a helpful check, bad individuals could use their education to pursue nefarious ends. Nevertheless, Adams's proposed remedy—elaborate institutional checks to prevent the abuse of power—only testified to his rationalism.[108] Devising an appropriate set of such arrangements manifestly required the exercise of his own and others' rational powers.[109] As Adams remarked, too many people lacked the forethought and failed to take the "prudent precautions" exemplified in a well-ordered regime.[110]

Adams's second remedy was to rely on the passions themselves. In particular, because nature had made men for social life by giving them a passion for distinction or reputation, this desire to be well-regarded could be used to limit men's innate selfishness.[111] Other feelings also had their uses. As John Howe has remarked, Adams was often impetuous; compared to Jefferson, Adams was much warmer, more impulsive, and less calculating.[112] As Adams confessed to a correspondent, "Zeal, and fire, and activity, and enterprise, strike my imagination too much. I am obliged to be constantly on my guard; yet the heat within will burst forth at times."[113] So, too, he wrote in an early remonstrance against the British, "There is a latent spark in the breasts of the people. . . . The love of liberty, . . . resentment of injury and indignation against wrong; a love of truth, and a veneration for virtue. These amiable passions are the 'latent spark.' "[114]

A Protestant Connection

The final element of the founding synthesis was a Protestant morality that powerfully reinforced republican restraints on excessive individual ambition. A proud child of the New England way, Adams joined his early attacks

[106] Peek 1954, 7–8, 11–12; J. Adams 1850–1856, 9:109; Cappon 1959, 532. [Thanks to Nathan Tarcov and Dave Ericson for these citations.]

[107] J. Adams 1850–1856, 4:557, 234; Peek 1954, 181, 184; see also xxi, 2.

[108] J. Adams 1850–1856, 6:64.

[109] Ibid., 4:234. Thanks to Stephen Casmier for this point.

[110] Peek 1954, 148.

[111] J. Adams 1850–1856, 3:448–49; J. R. Howe 1966, 19–20; see J. Adams 1850–1856, 4:234, 237, 240, 245.

[112] J. R. Howe 1966, 25; Cappon 1959, xxxvi–xxxvii.

[113] J. Adams 1850–1856, 9:369, JA to Mercy Warren 25 Nov. 1775; cited in J. R. Howe 1966, 25.

[114] J. Adams 1850–1856, 4:14.

on British usurpations to a celebration of his Puritan forebears.[115] Here was a republicanism whose strongly Protestant cast went beyond purely secular allusions to ancient civic heros and civic virtues. So, too, Adams's Protestant conscience rejected all forms of personal self-indulgence. Fearful of luxury as inimical to civic virtue, he denounced the "extravagance of debauchery."[116] Offended by the seductions of provincial Philadelphia, he hoped the American merchants in Paris would avoid the alluring amusements of the French capital.[117] More positively Adams demanded self-discipline and self-development, in vocation and avocation, through thrift, honesty, and hard work.[118] Exercise, he wrote, "invigorates, and enlivens all the Faculties of Body and of mind," but indolence threatened the future of his young compatriots.[119] Here, as Howe has remarked, was an ethic that conflated Calvinist and republican virtues by embracing the "qualities of industry, frugality, and prudence."[120]

This perspective was to be found beyond Adams's New England as well. As enthusiastic as Jefferson was about Europe's secular enlightenment, his ethics also reflected a biblical morality and devotion to self-improvement, preached to Jefferson in his childhood by his pious father.[121] Like Adams, Jefferson made a point of keeping himself in excellent physical and mental condition after he left the presidency.[122] "Punctual" and "attentive to details," Jefferson exercised a "rigid self-discipline" in answering the stream of letters sent to him both before and during his retirement.[123] Hard work, he believed, had made American society superior to that of its uncivilized Indian neighbors. "Humanity," he wrote, "enjoins us to teach them agriculture and the domestic arts; to encourage them to that industry which . . . to bodily comforts adds the improvement of the mind and morals."[124] Jefferson also contrasted the independent and hard-working yeomen of his own society with the parasites—that is, government officials—who lived off the honest labor of others.[125]

Industriousness, in its turn, depended on two traits espoused by God-fearing Protestants. The first was self-control. Jefferson repeatedly warned about "unbounded licentiousness," favored drinking alcohol only in mod-

[115] Ibid., 3:451–52.
[116] Ibid., 6:96; 3:461; 6:9; cf. 4:28.
[117] Cappon 1959, 109–10, JA to TJ 20 Dec. 1785.
[118] J. R. Howe 1966, 102.
[119] Butterfield 1961, 1:127; Peek 1954, 161–62.
[120] J. R. Howe 1966, 30.
[121] Chinard 1946, vi.
[122] Padover 1942, 364.
[123] Chinard 1946, 113.
[124] Koch and Peden 1944, 341.
[125] Peterson 1987, 583–84, TJ to William Ludlow 6 Sept. 1824.

eration, and cautioned against wasting valuable time—for example, in useless play.[126] He had no use for dissipation or loose morals and saw such attitudes as a threat to "republican virtue."[127] It was better, he wrote his daughter Martha, to be simply rather than "gaily" dressed.[128] He himself shunned pomp and circumstance at his inauguration as president.[129] At one point he even thought about laws to regulate dress.[130]

The second important trait was self-development. As did Adams, Jefferson stressed the need to exercise the mind. As he wrote in the *Notes*, "We hope to avail the State of those talents which nature has sown as liberally among the poor as the rich, but which perish without use, if not sought for and cultivated."[131] He urged his children and nephews to educate themselves in order to serve others better.[132] Jefferson's commitment to ethical precepts of this sort led Philip Greven to count him—along with the Adams family—as an exemplar of the moderate form of the Protestant temperament.[133]

Many scholars, of course, would find this Protestant element in the founding synthesis to be no surprise. In Weber's classic account, Calvinism and related Protestant confessions insisted on ascetic devotion to one's worldly vocation, a devotion that fostered the liberal rationalization of economic life. By denouncing the indulgence of worldly desire at the same time, these creeds provided an ethical impulse toward reinvestment rather than consumption, and they thus fostered dynamic capitalist growth. In this way, the Puritan legacy helped create the economic foundations of capitalist society. Since Weber, Bercovitch's analysis of New England Calvinism, has identified a more specific connection between it and America's liberal politics. Through the jeremiad, Americans came to see a special place for their country in the world, if not in sacred history. As a result, the Puritan rhetoric of social criticism actually reaffirmed a belief in the legitimacy of the American regime by promising to purge it of its defects. Shorn of a specifically New England focus and its elitist theology, American Protestantism thus supported both the political and economic sides of American liberalism.

---

[126] Koch and Peden 1944, 217; 373, TJ to Peter Carr 19 Aug. 1785; Peterson 1987, 305–6, TJ to Brother Handsome Lake 3 Nov. 1802.

[127] J. C. Miller 1977, 183, 33.

[128] Koch and Peden 1944, 366, TJ to Martha Jefferson 12 Dec. 1783; cf. Cappon 1959, 193, TJ to AA 30 Aug. 1787.

[129] Padover 1942, 290.

[130] J. C. Miller 1977, 34.

[131] Koch and Peden 1944, 265.

[132] Ibid., 373, TJ to Peter Carr 19 Aug. 1785.

[133] Greven 1977.

Equality and the Liberal Polarity

The important point for the present discussion, then, is that the founding synthesis of Adams and Jefferson exhibited some elements of each of the liberal variants discussed in chapter two: not only a reform liberal ethic of self-discipline and development, but also genus liberalism and republicanism, and the instrumental rationality vital to humanist liberals. Moreover, both Adams and Jefferson linked these beliefs to a late eighteenth-century emphasis on restraint, which was much less prominent in later generations. Their genus liberal belief in individual rights, for example, was qualified in Adams's case by his complicity in the Alien and Sedition Acts, and in Jefferson's by his willingness to prosecute individuals for the exercise of some forms of speech and writing that would later be constitutionally protected. Again, the republicanism of the two men included an emphasis on citizen virtue and the salutary limits on behavior imposed by rural life, an emphasis that began to weaken in the more acquisitive Jacksonian era. Finally, their beliefs in instrumental rationality and the Protestant conscience were to be supplanted by far less restrained versions of liberalism: by humanist liberalism, on the one hand, with its drive by individuals to maximize utilities or satisfy preferences; by reform liberalism, on the other, with its impulse toward reform that included the crusade against slavery.

If Adams and Jefferson were in considerable agreement on both substance and style in politics and society, on what fundamental issues did they differ? As their conflicts over policies and party affiliations suggest, the place to begin is the issue of equality. Their precise differences on this question turn out to be complex and even paradoxical.

At one level, the issue straightforwardly pitted the egalitarian Jefferson against the more conservative Adams. Throughout his career, the Virginia rationalist opposed all forms of hereditary privilege.[134] The great division in American politics, he wrote, was between those who feared popular ignorance and others who feared elite selfishness—that is, "between the advocates of republican, and those of kingly government."[135] A confirmed democrat, Jefferson believed that "governments are republican only in proportion as they embody the will of their people, and execute it."[136] By the mid-1780s, Jefferson firmly supported extending suffrage to all white males.[137] Abhorring the selfishness of the rich, he favored taxing luxuries to foster broad public purposes such as public education, roads, rivers, and

---

[134] Koch and Peden 1944, 118–19, 125.
[135] Ibid., 117.
[136] Peterson 1987, 553, TJ to Samuel Kercheval 12 July 1816; cf. 269.
[137] Chinard 1946, 141.

canals.[138] Appalled by the divisions and inequality of French society, he hailed the French Revolution for opening a new democratic era, and he loyally defended the First Republic, even when others began to criticize its excesses.[139]

Jefferson's attitudes reflected his optimism about the common people. Under a "government like ours," he wrote in 1785, where "the people are truly the mainspring . . . they are never to be despaired of. When an evil becomes so glaring as to strike them generally, they arouse themselves, and it is redressed."[140] In order to maintain popular control, he thought periodic rebellions were as "good [a] thing . . . in the political world as storms in the physical."[141]

By contrast, Adams could write Jefferson during their retirement that "Election is the grand Brama, the immortal Lama, I had almost said, the Jaggernaught, for Wives are almost ready to burn upon the Pile and Children to be thrown under the Wheel."[142] Adams's scornful stand, to be sure, rested on a liberal conception of rights as an entitlement for individuals against any sovereign power, democratic or not. Adams was concerned not about small New England towns, but about larger polities. In the latter, the people had less information, could not deliberate effectively, and might tend to divide into the rich and poor.[143] An equally serious concern to him was that a large electorate could be more easily corrupted by the aspiring and unscrupulous.

In Adams's view, then, a purely democratic regime did not have the checks and balances necessary to restrain the people's antirepublican—that is, their oppressive—tendencies.[144] One possible form of abuse under such a regime was the expropriation of the rich by the people, even though the rich "have as clear a right and as *sacred* a right to their large property as others have to theirs which is smaller."[145] As the 1780s wore on, Adams came to see the aristocracy, for all its defects, as a force for order and defense of property.[146] At one point, Adams even had qualified praise for the Bourbon despotism in France.[147] Indeed, to him a pure monarchy, deplorable as it was compared to a republican regime with limited powers, seemed less

---

[138] Koch and Peden 1944, 412, TJ to Edward Carrington 16 Jan. 1787; Peterson 1987, 326.

[139] Peterson 1976, 89; Koch and Peden 1944, 522, TJ to Wm. Short 3 Jan. 1793.

[140] Peterson 1987, 372–73, TJ to Richard Price 1 Feb. 1785.

[141] Koch and Peden 1944, 413, TJ to James Madison 30 Jan. 1787.

[142] Cappon 1959, 427, JA to TJ Feb. (i.e., 3 Mar.) 1814.

[143] Chinard 1933, 93; J. R. Howe 1966, 134, 136.

[144] J. Adams 1850–1856, 6:211.

[145] Ibid., 6:65, 89.

[146] J. R. Howe 1966, 174–75.

[147] Peek 1954, 78; cf. 73–79.

dangerous than a pure democracy.[148] Given the danger of factions and popular passions, he also entertained for a time the idea of strengthening the government by awarding aristocratic titles to leading public figures.[149] Whatever the merits of Adams's arguments, it is not surprising that by the mid-1790s Jefferson concluded that his friend had lapsed into antidemocratic heresy.

Adams's basic outlook, however, also had an egalitarian side that persisted long after he had collaborated on the Declaration of Independence. True enough, he thought that inequalities of talents, birth, and wealth were natural and made an aristocracy unavoidable. He therefore turned again and again to thoughts about heredity as the basis for a legislative upper house. This stand, however, was only conditional. It made sense if, but only if, problems such as corrupt elections actually emerged. In that light, his position was political rather than principled, so he could tell Jefferson that he never actually favored such an arrangement in America, because the need never became sufficiently pressing.[150]

Nor did Adams ever fully renounce the democratic beliefs he embraced in the 1770s. At that time he insisted that "the people were universally too enlightened to be imposed on by artifice." He celebrated the fact that the colonies' "thirteen governments . . . [were] founded on the natural authority of the people alone, without a pretence of miracle or mystery."[151] "I appeal to all experience, and to universal history," he went on, "if it has ever been in the power of popular leaders . . . to persuade a large people, for any length of time together, to think themselves wronged, injured, and oppressed, unless they really were."[152]

The young Adams also shared his compatriots' aversion to feudal traditions and to the aristocracy's contempt for commerce.[153] Later, he continued to dislike elites marked out by legal privileges; he disliked, that is, any "*artifical* inequalities of conditions," created by "established marks, as stars, garters, crosses, or ribbons."[154] Throughout his career, Adams voiced alarm at antirepublican cabals of those, such as the Order of the Cincinnati, that claimed hereditary distinctions.[155]

Even Adams's reservations about the democratic principle reflected his egalitarianism, although his was of a rather pessimistic sort. No individual could be trusted entirely, because all were affected—equally—by selfish

---

[148] Ibid., 113, xvii–xviii.
[149] J. R. Howe 1966, 177–78.
[150] Cappon 1959, 356, JA to TJ 13 July 1813; 401, JA to TJ 15 Nov. 1813.
[151] J. Adams 1850–1856, 4:294; cf. 3:352.
[152] Ibid., 4:14.
[153] Ibid., 3:450; 4:395; J. R. Howe 1966, 94; Haraszti 1952, 127.
[154] Peek 1954, 133, emphasis added.
[155] J. Adams 1850–1856, 4:293.

motives. Accordingly, Adams's willingness to give the aristocracy a special political role was both limited and grudging. He favored isolation (his word was "ostracism") of the aristocracy in a chamber of its own, because in a single legislative chamber its members were very likely to dominate their social inferiors,[156] and in a bicameral legislature, the common people would be able to control their own chamber.[157] Adams insisted to Hamilton, among others, that the lower house of the legislature must truly represent the people.[158] Specifically, it ought to be "an exact portrait, in miniature" so that it would "think, feel, act, and reason like the people."[159]

If Jefferson was manifestly more enthusiastic about equality than Adams, there were, nevertheless, enough areas of agreement between them for an egalitarian ideal to figure centrally in their founding synthesis. There were also differences, however, in the ways the two men understood that ideal, and those differences signaled the presence of a nascent liberal polarity in American political culture. For Jefferson, equality was a matter of will and capacity, as well as rights. All individuals, or at least all whites, had the right to determine their goals for themselves and to try to secure them. Just as important, if they had sufficient information and education, they could be expected to exercise that right prudently and effectively. Even a natural aristocracy of talent must be restrained by the common people, who were able to look out for their own interests and to check oppressive tendencies in their rulers.

Adams looked to equality of another sort, one that reflected his greater and more explicit devotion to the Protestant tradition that influenced both him and Jefferson. Pessimistically, he believed all individuals were likely to err, if not sin, in pursuing their self-interests. More positively, he also believed in a moral equality of duties as well as rights. Thus he could write in 1791 that "Nature . . . has ordained that . . . no two objects shall be perfectly alike." Yet in the same passage he went on to assert that "among men, all are subject by nature, to *equal laws* of morality."[160] So, too, while maintaining from 1786 to 1787 that there are "inequalities" that "must be acknowledged," he went on to assert that "in this society of Massachusetensians . . . there is . . . a moral and political equality of rights and duties among all the individuals."[161] Thus, even the conservative Adams of the 1780s and 1790s insisted that however great their differences in ability or situation, all human beings, as moral agents, stood on the same footing.

[156] Peek 1954, 115; J. R. Howe 1966, 231.
[157] Peek 1954, 115, 126–28.
[158] Koch and Peden 1944, 608–9, TJ to Benjamin Rush 16 Jan. 1811.
[159] Cited in J. R. Howe 1966, 95, JA to John Penn January 1776; J. Adams 1850–1856, 4:205.
[160] J. Adams 1850–1856, 6:285.
[161] Peek 1954, 133.

They shared not only rights and duties, but a tendency to succumb to passion and self-interest.

Adams, then, was not only concerned with what individuals already were, that is, with their passions and interests, but with what they could become, for better or worse. Human beings shared a *potential* either for evil or for moral excellence. Stripped of its theological vocabulary and the elitist doctrine that a few were predestined for salvation, here was a traditional Puritan idea: each and every individual had the potential to be a saint or a sinner. Whereas Jefferson's concept of equality pointed to existing individuals and trusted their moral sense to produce reasonable preferences, Adams's pointed to human abilities, including the capacity of humans to answer the commands of duty and obligation. Jefferson, that is, emphasized the existing capacities of humans, and Adams emphasized their potential, and their obligation, to cultivate and improve their capacities.

During their lifetimes, the differences of the two friends on the concept of equality were not decisive. They agreed on the relevant issues that emerged during the revolution, and they shared enough liberal and republican beliefs, despite their different emphases, to reach a second political convergence during their years of retirement. These areas of genuine agreement, however, obscured the fundamental differences on equality that, eventually, in other circumstances, were to rend the founding synthesis.

FOUR

ADAMS, JEFFERSON, AND THE

SLAVERY PARADOX

"I HAVE THUS stated my opinion on a point on which we differ," Thomas Jefferson wrote John Adams in 1813, "not with a view to controversy, for we are both too old to change opinions which are the result of a long life of inquiry and reflection; but [rather] on the suggestion of a former letter of yours, that we ought not to die before we have explained ourselves to each other."[1]

What were the vital points on which Adams and Jefferson disagreed? In the 1770s, they had collaborated on the founding synthesis that guided both the revolution and, in large measure, the framing and ratification of the Constitution. Although they were bitterly divided on policy issues in the 1790s, even these differences faded during their retirement, and Adams's son John Quincy Adams wholeheartedly joined Jefferson's Democratic Republicans. There were, however, two matters on which Adams and Jefferson remained profoundly at odds. One was their basic philosophic commitments, an issue they raised again and again in their later correspondence. The other was human slavery, a subject so painful that they passed over it in their letters in virtually complete silence.

This chapter examines the relationship between their reiterated discussions of philosophy and their almost complete silence on slavery. My claim is, first, that Adams's and Jefferson's stands on slavery were paradoxical, and, second, that this paradox can be resolved and understood only in terms of their basic philosophical disagreements. To state the case in the briefest terms: for all his egalitarianism, Jefferson focused on human interests and preferences and on finding an equitable adjustment when the two clashed. Thus his egalitarianism sustained a devotion to accommodation and compromise that legitimated patience toward slavery. By contrast, Adams insisted on the duties that flowed from a transcendent, moral law of divine rather than human origin, and, for all his political conservatism and even elitism, this stance finally tilted Adams in an antislavery direction. Two sets of ethical and philosophic questions are thus raised: (a) How important is balancing the competing claims, rights, and preferences of different human beings, as opposed simply to doing one's moral duty to develop one's own and others' human faculties? In addressing this question, the two men

[1] Cappon 1959, 391, TJ to JA 28 Oct. 1813.

examined the issue of human happiness and freedom. (b) How ethically important are the observable facts of a social situation, and thus what deference should one accord to the existing social practices and institutions of a free society? Here the two men considered both the character of human rationality in determining social action and the philosophic issues of epistemology and ontology. We begin with the slavery paradox itself.

The Slavery Paradox

Jefferson the Progressive, Adams the Conservative

Given the political differences between Adams and Jefferson, we might expect Jefferson to be the more consistent and outspoken foe of slavery. In waging political war against Adams and the other Federalists, the Virginian consistently celebrated the virtues of the common people and scorned the dead hand of the past. A tribune for all those who insisted on political democracy, Jefferson welcomed the French Revolution as a harbinger of a new age.

Preaching this new gospel, he led the revolution of 1800 against the Federalists, and after his presidency he became a symbol of liberty.[2] Adams, by contrast, insisted on the conservative values of hierarchy and self-discipline, respect for authority, and institutional constraints on popular passions. Encumbered by his elitist and therefore "irrelevant" republicanism and embittered by his defeat in 1800, Adams left the White House for a relatively obscure retirement as a crotchety moralist.[3] His fellow Federalists never won another presidential election.

Yet, although these political conflicts subsided during the 1800s, parallel cultural differences persisted. In Henry Commager's words, Jefferson's commitment to the ideas of the Enlightenment was "tenacious and unqualified."[4] Whereas most Americans in the 1720s attempted to discover and act on the will of God, by the 1770s, the master of Monticello and his intellectual friends saw a world designed for the well-being of ultimately self-reliant human beings. Humankind rather than God was at the center of the universe. Convinced that his species was blessed with impressive abilities and a bright future, Jefferson considered human happiness rather than salvation to be the supreme goal.[5] It is in this fundamental sense that Jefferson's liberalism can be termed *humanist*.

[2] Peterson 1976, 129.
[3] Wood 1969, 574ff., esp. 588–89.
[4] Commager 1975, 73.
[5] Peterson 1976, 6–7; Peterson 1987, 251–53; Commager 1975, 24–27, 150, 93, 108.

An admirer of Locke and Bacon as well as of Newton, Jefferson bolstered his stand with a fervent belief in the scientifically guided progress of his species.[6] Just as Newton had revealed the regularities of the physical world, Jefferson observed the careful accumulation of facts about the social world that enabled rational men to lift the bonds of ignorance.[7] In his celebrated *Notes on the State of Virginia*, Jefferson used the latest scientific theories to organize his many empirical observations.[8] When Adams reopened their correspondence in 1812 by promising to send Jefferson some "local home-spun," Jefferson immediately responded with observations about Virginia textiles—only to receive in reply a set of lectures on rhetoric by Adams's son, John Quincy Adams.[9] As the editor of their correspondence has noted, the letters that followed reveal Jefferson's more practical intellectual interests in the physical sciences, the fine arts, architecture, and medicine.

Adams exhibited much of Jefferson's rationalism, but he embraced little of the Virginian's enlightenment outlook.[10] Whereas Jefferson looked to the contemporary sciences, Adams focused on law, government, and the classics, and he probed more deeply than Jefferson into theology, philosophy, and religion.[11] Whereas Jefferson viewed the Puritans as having exhibited an oppressive religious fanaticism, Adams admired his forebears and saw the revolution as continuing their errand in the New World. Certainly Adams's assessment of human thought and action was closer to Puritan skepticism than to Jefferson's optimistic humanism.

Since Adam's fall, Adams wrote, "avarice and ambition, vanity and pride, jealousy and envy, hatred and revenge" had been all too evident.[12] Particular individuals might sometimes respond to reasoned appeals, but in most cases the rational and moral faculties of humans were insufficient.[13] As Adams saw it, "very few in any nation" always "prefer the public to a private interest, and fewer still are moral, honorable, or religious enough to practice such self-denial."[14] In fact, the best hope for humankind was the self-regarding desire of individuals for reputation or fame. Given the right setting and institutions, this desire for the approval of others might induce many individuals to act on behalf of the public good.[15]

[6] Ferguson 1980, 403; Commager 1975, 53.

[7] Commager 1975, 82–83.

[8] Koch and Peden 1944, 187ff.; see also 153, TJ to Herbert Croft, Esq. 30 Oct. 1798, and 223–24; Cappon 1959, 323, TJ to JA 27 May 1813.

[9] Cappon 1959, 290–91, TJ to JA 21 Jan. 1812.

[10] Ibid., 456, JA to TJ 13 Oct. 1815; 458, TJ to JA 11 Jan. 1816; cf. Peek 1954, 107–8.

[11] Cappon 1959, xlvii.

[12] J. Adams 1850–1856, 6:245.

[13] Chinard 1933, 40.

[14] J. Adams 1850–1856, 6:211.

[15] Ibid., 6:245; J. R. Howe 1966, 182.

In Adams's eyes, the rational and moral faculties of even intellectuals were suspect. Europe's enlightenment philosophes, whom Jefferson admired, were able men, Adams conceded, but they lacked common sense, and they overestimated the power of philosophy to shape human affairs. Rousseau was dangerous; Diderot and Voltaire reminded Adams of his bêtes noires, Robespierre and Napoleon.[16] In fact, the examples of the philosophes led Adams to think favorably about government supervision of potentially subversive learned academies.[17]

By the 1780s, Adams's skepticism had turned against Jefferson's trust in human progress. Improvement was always possible, perhaps even likely.[18] "I am a Believer," he later wrote Jefferson, "in the improvability and Improvement, the Ameliorabi[li]ty and Amelioration in human Affairs."[19] Yet progress was far from certain. It might occur, and it might not; only experience could tell whether or not there would be obstacles and setbacks.[20] Certainly nature did not have any " 'simple plan of perfection in politics' " that human beings could just copy.[21] If anything, Adams once remarked, the progress of anarchy was as notable as the progress of truth.[22] Furthermore, progress in one sphere—economic growth, for example—by no means assured progress elsewhere, because material prosperity might ultimately corrupt even American society.[23]

Jefferson himself saw a connection between these disagreements over progress and his specifically political disputes with his Yankee friend. Adams's unease with the efficacy of human reason and his fear of human passion made him increasingly suspicious of any political movement that harnessed popular enthusiasm in the name of broad social change. Shays' Rebellion confirmed his fears, and the excesses of the French Revolution, which Jefferson loyally supported, were to Adams the classic case in point. In that spirit, as checks on such popular excesses, Adams considered an aristocratic upper legislative chamber to be a possibility and the need for a strong executive to be a certainty. So, too, Adams welcomed most of Hamilton's economic program, even though Jefferson denounced it as elitist. As Peterson has put it, "Adams was a voice from the past, while Jefferson continued to voice the aspirations . . . of American democracy."[24]

---

[16] Haraszti 1952, 81; see Chinard 1933, 206; Cappon 1959, 464, JA to TJ 2 Mar. 1816; 466, JA to TJ 2 Mar. 1816.

[17] J. Adams 1850–1856, 8:596, to T. Pickering 16 Sept. 1798.

[18] Cappon 1959, 357, JA to TJ 15 July 1813; 391, TJ to JA 28 Oct. 1813.

[19] Ibid., 435, 16 July 1814.

[20] Haraszti 1952, 45; cf. Cappon 1959, 358, 15 July 1813.

[21] Handler 1964, 80.

[22] Cappon 1959, 435, JA to TJ 16 July 1814.

[23] J. R. Howe 1966, 136, 144.

[24] Peterson 1976, 115.

Slavery as an Anomaly

On Peterson's very plausible reading, it was the Virginian rather than the Yankee who could be expected to enlist enthusiastically in a campaign against human bondage. Yet as I argued in chapter three, Peterson's general conclusion is overly simple. Adams was surely no European conservative. His skepticism applied to elites and citizens from all social strata, and his concern was always with protecting individual rights (including the right to property). Moreover, Adams's solution was eminently rationalist, that is, it was concerned with constructing—rather than preserving—an appropriate set of institutions that would check all tendencies toward abuse.[25] However, for the present purposes, the important point is that on the issue of slavery itself, Peterson's judgment is simply mistaken.

In the 1770s, the young Jefferson had spoken out more forcefully against slavery than his colleague from Massachusetts. The existence of slavery violated his belief in justice and the universal right to liberty. In addition, in the *Notes*, Jefferson assailed the effects of the institution on the slave holders and their children. Everything that made Jefferson an enlightenment rationalist cried out against the injustice of one human's enslavement of another. Many of his friends among the European philosophes, in fact, joined the society, *Amis des Noirs*, to oppose slavery. Moreover, Jefferson's own humanist faith rejected the unwarranted pretensions of any social elite— witness his attack on the French Old Regime and what he saw as elitist Hamiltonian policies. In the 1780s, Jefferson sought to bar the institution of slavery from all the federal territories, and he succeeded in excluding it from the Northwest Territory. Later, as soon as the Constitution permitted it, he supported prohibition of foreign slave trade.

On Adams's side, however, the issue of slavery aroused just that political caution that made him so conservative on the major issues of the 1790s, despite his belief in liberalism as a political philosophy. Some of his earlier rhetoric, to be sure, seemed to have an antislavery cast:

> Let us see delineated before us the true map of man. Let us hear the dignity of his nature, and the noble rank he holds among the works of God—[so] that consenting to slavery is a sacrilegious breach of trust, as offensive in the sight of God as it is derogatory from our own honor or interest or happiness.[26]

But these words, penned in 1765, referred to the grievances of white colonists against Britain. With regard to chattel slavery itself, Adams's correspondence with his wife Abigail in 1776 was more revealing. As Abigail wrote John:

[25] Casmier 1986.
[26] J. Adams 1850–1856, 3:462–63.

I have sometimes been ready to think that the passion for Liberty cannot be Eaquelly Strong in the Breasts of those [in Virginia] who have been accustomed to deprive their fellow Creatures of theirs. Of this I am certain that it [slavery] is not founded upon that generous and christian principle of doing to others as we would that others should do unto us.[27]

A few paragraphs later, she went directly to the issue of one person's power over another:

Remember the Ladies and be more generous and favourable to them than your ancestors. Do not put such unlimited power in the hands of the Husbands. Remember all Men would be tyrants if they could. . . .

. . . That your Sex are Naturally Tyrannical is a Truth so thoroughly established as to admit of no dispute.[28]

Adams's reply scoffed at his wife's feminism. "In Practice," he wrote, "you know [that] We are the subjects. Rather than . . . subject Us to the Despotism of the Peticoat, I hope General Washington, and all our brave Heroes would fight."[29] On slavery itself, Adams said nothing at all. Indeed, his often repeated fears about the character of human nature made it relatively easy for him to see slavery as a regrettable but useful restraint on a willful population.

Much of Adams's political thought and practice, after all, was devoted to controlling popular passions and, especially, mobs led by demagogues. Moreover, he believed that the natural aristocrats were distinguished in part by the circumstances, such as level of family education and social connections, into which they were born.[30] If these factors gave advantages to the already fortunate, then the capacity of slaves to act responsibly—rather than vengefully—could well have been damaged, a result of their lack of education and experience as free citizens. The most prudent course, then, might be to leave them under the control of their owners, most of whom had enjoyed superior training and education. "Terrified" by a vision of the "Armies of Negroes marching and counter marching in the air," Adams wrote in a letter to Jefferson about the Missouri Crisis of 1820, "I must leave [the subject of slavery] . . . to you. I will vote for forceing no measure against your judgements."[31]

In the end, however, there was a striking anomaly in their respective attitudes. By 1820, Jefferson had clearly adopted a protective attitude toward the institution he had once assailed, whereas Adams's views, privately

---

[27] Butterfield et al. 1975, 120.
[28] Ibid., 121.
[29] Ibid., 123.
[30] See, for example, Cappon 1959, 398, JA to TJ 15 Nov. 1813.
[31] Ibid., 571.

at least, had become unequivocally critical. Jefferson's political deeds, in fact, had not always matched his egalitarian words. In the 1790s, he had abandoned his overt efforts to end or limit the institution, and he had supported the Fugitive Slave Act of 1793. As president, he refused to discuss the issue at all.[32] But Jefferson's shift was most dramatic during the Missouri Crisis of 1820. Northern opposition to admitting Missouri as a slave state, he thought, would promote sectional rancor—and threaten the republic's very survival—without helping the slaves.[33] Most remarkably, Jefferson responded to the controversy by calling for the spread of slavery throughout the Louisiana Purchase. Contrary to the stand he had taken on the Northwest Ordinance of 1787, he now maintained that happiness could be found in areas with slavery, as well as in those without.[34]

Yet the same crisis left the usually conservative Adams relatively unperturbed. In 1776 he had ignored his wife's antislavery sentiments, though he never challenged her fundamental opposition to the despotic domination of one human by another. By the early 1800s, it was clear that political conservatism did not necessarily entail a protective stand on slavery. Many northern Federalists, including the antislavery Alexander Hamilton, saw their economic program as benefiting all races, and they charged their egalitarian but proslavery opponents, including Jefferson, with hypocrisy.[35] During his retirement, Adams himself moved closer to his wife's views, although he avoided the subject with Jefferson. He now believed abolition in the North, where there were few blacks, to be an unmixed blessing, and his view of sectional issues came to be the reverse of Jefferson's. Fearing the power of the South's "aristocratic" slave owners, Adams opposed permitting slavery in Missouri, to say nothing of in the rest of the Louisiana Purchase.[36]

Some of Adams's concerns were prudential. The interests of most Missourians, he thought, would be "against the admission of Slavery."[37] Northern "labouring people" and family farmers, he wrote, "hate to go among slaves because they cannot get employment among them—or if they do—they are considered upon a level with them." The prudential shaded into the ethical, as his concern extended to the slaves themselves: "If the gangrene is not stopped—I can see nothing but Insurrection . . . till at last the Whites will be exasperated to Madness—[and] shall be wicked enough to exterminate the Negroes." Thus the Missourians ought to have been

[32] J. C. Miller 1977, 276–77, 120, 229, 130.

[33] Peterson 1976, 125–26; Koch and Peden 1944, 712, TJ to the Marquis de Lafayette 4 Nov. 1823.

[34] Cappon 1959, 549, TJ to JA 10 Dec. 1819; Koch and Peden 1944, 698–99, TJ to John Holmes 22 Apr. 1820.

[35] Kerber 1980.

[36] J. R. Howe 1966, 223.

[37] J. Adams 1955, reel 124, JA to Louisa Adams 23 Dec. 1819.

moved by "feelings of humanity" in deciding "to exclude slavery sternly from their state."[38]

Their respective shifts, seemingly out of character in the context of the basic beliefs of each man, constitutes the slavery anomaly. To recur to the discussion in chapter two, my point is not that Jefferson's humanist liberalism directly *caused* his proslavery shift, any more than Adams's reform liberalism directly produced his turn against the institution. Once again, the difficulty with such an explanation is that *stable* beliefs cannot cause *changes* in attitude or behavior. Indeed, the strictly causal question would ask what events or changes in American society produced these shifts, and it would lead the discussion in a different direction.

In the case of Jefferson's shift, changing racial attitudes were important. Even the young, antislavery Jefferson asserted the intellectual inferiority of blacks, in the *Notes on Virginia*, although he later made some grudging concessions with regard to their intellectual abilities.[39] More revealingly, however, Jefferson's draft of the declaration treated blacks and whites, as well as the Americans and the British, as different peoples. The slave revolts abroad in Santo Domingo and domestic insurrections such as Nat Turner's rebellion gave a more ominous cast to Jefferson's perception of blacks as a separate and alien people. As he wrote of white Southerners in 1820, "But as it is, we have the wolf by the ears, and we can neither hold him, nor safely let him go. Justice is in one scale, and self-preservation in the other."[40]

Economic and political considerations were also important factors in the shifts in Adams's and Jefferson's attitudes toward slavery. Jefferson, of course, depended for his own income on plantations operated by large numbers of slaves, thus any threat to slavery was also a threat to his own livelihood. More importantly, he was an ambitious and practical politician whose political career ultimately depended on the support of other southern whites. His early opposition to slavery expressed the egalitarian spirit of the time, but the subsequent introduction of the cotton gin made slave labor an increasingly vital part of the southern economy. As the prospect for the gradual demise of slavery thereby receded, it became steadily more difficult for Jefferson, or any other southern leader, to oppose the institution. By 1820, then, the effects of economic change had reinforced the racial fears of Jefferson and his fellow Southerners.

Adams's stand on slavery, however, like his eventual opposition to its expansion, was always more cautious and muted than Jefferson's, and the events that triggered Adams's shift were less direct and dramatic. Adams could freely invoke the "feelings of humanity" in the Missouri crisis, after

[38] Ibid., JA to Louisa Adams 13 Jan. 1819; John Adams also mentions "their own interests as well as feelings."

[39] Peterson 1987, 188; J. C. Miller 1977, 46–59.

[40] Koch and Peden 1944, 698, TJ to John Holmes 22 Apr. 1820.

all, partly because he had no major material interest at stake. Still, over the years, northern unease, already evident in Abigail's letter of 1776, became a more pressing factor. Many of the North's politicians resented the South's right to count three-fifths of its slaves in apportioning representatives in the House of Representatives, and the Northerners' grievance became more urgent with the prospect of territorial expansion and the creation of even more slave states. By the 1820s, there were important economic conflicts between New England and the South over issues such as the tariff and internal improvements. Moreover, with the cotton gin in place, slavery began to seem an ever more important, and permanent, feature of the American economy, quite confounding the hopes of the founding genera-tion that slavery would gradually disappear. These developments obviously affected the climate in which Adams and his fellow Yankees thought and talked about the issue.

Whatever the relative importance of each of these specific changes, how-ever, their collective role seems clear. Jefferson, Adams, and other white Americans altered their positions on the slavery question in response to important changes in their political, economic, and social lives. Is this the whole story? Did Adams's and Jefferson's eventual differences on slavery simply reflect their different circumstances: Jefferson's growing concern, for example, about a servile insurrection, and the different patterns of economic development in their respective sections of the country? As chapter two pointed out, this claim need not ignore Adams's and Jefferson's beliefs, provided it assumes a consensus on fundamental issues and limits the con-flict between them to particular interests and preferences.

This claim does encounter two basic difficulties, however. First, if the conflict over slavery only reflected specific differences in economic and social interests, why could the two sides not have reached a broadly satisfac-tory settlement with relative ease? Few, if any, Northerners at the time condoned slave revolts, and a middle ground can almost always be found on purely economic matters. Barrington Moore asked similar questions with regard to the crisis-ridden 1850s, and it is true that a generally accepted compromise had been adopted in the less heated atmosphere of 1820. But the agreement over Missouri followed a period of bitter sectional divisive-ness, denounced by Jefferson as a profound threat to the very existence of the republic.[41] If a few specific points were all that was at stake, the intensity of the response was clearly disproportionate.

The second difficulty is how Jefferson and Adams each reconciled his position on slavery with his own broader political stand. The answer from one perspective is a matter of intellectual and cognitive consistency. The slavery issue for each man seems paradoxical, after all, because with respect

---

[41] See, for example, Cappon 1959, 548–49, TJ to JA 10 Dec. 1819.

to it each man appeared to depart markedly from his broader commitments. For all Jefferson's egalitarianism and for all Adams's skepticism about popular protest, neither seemed to think that his shift on slavery violated his basic beliefs. Indeed, we may ask whether there was a way in which their fundamental commitments actually encouraged the shifts.

Such considerations alter the focus of the inquiry: the difficulties in question cannot be resolved satisfactorily simply by reiterating that Adams or Jefferson acted in accord with this or that interest, nor indeed by invoking any reductionist account. Whereas such accounts can identify the *content* of an individual's or group's preferences—that is, the goal to which an action is directed—they cannot account for certain *other* attributes. What is at issue here are those other attributes: the skill, plausibility, and consistency with which an action is undertaken. In this case in particular, the issue is whether Adams's or Jefferson's stand was regarded as legitimate by the relevant actors. That legitimacy in turn depended on each man's persuasively reconciling his particular objectives or goals with each other and with his more general principles.

The question of legitimacy is especially pressing if we take into account potential allies and supporters. Consider, for example, those northern whites who regarded themselves as Jeffersonians or, later, Jacksonian Democrats. Many of them not only admired Jefferson personally and shared his commitment to equality and individual liberty, they also followed his lead on slavery. In their view, devotion to union required patience toward the South, not antislavery moralizing. They were not, however, motivated to take their stand on slavery by the same social and economic interests that animated southern whites. Almost none of these Northerners owned slaves, and a few even lived with freed blacks as neighbors. Some Jacksonian artisans and workers, it is true, worried about competition with freed slaves for jobs, but few northern farmers had this concern. Western farmers shared the Southerners' interest in low tariffs, but they tended to favor the internal improvements that most Southerners opposed. There were indeed large numbers of Northerners who wanted to keep freed blacks out of the North.

The important question raised by these factors is a comparative one: why were the Jeffersonian and Jacksonian humanist liberals in the North so much more devoted to social equality and equal rights than were Adams and other reform liberals, and yet so much more prejudiced against blacks than the reform liberals? In this sense, the essential issue is not economic or social, but political; the question is not what goals were adopted, but how a set of quite distinct preferences and attitudes could be fashioned into an authentic and effective outlook, or persuasion.

It is on such issues that the reform liberalism of Adams and the humanist liberalism of Jefferson appear particularly relevant. Their differing stands— their apparently anomalous shifts—on the slavery issue not only did not violate their basic principles, but, taken together, their stands actually exemplified the basic polarity within the American liberal tradition. This polarity was largely latent during the revolutionary and founding periods, but it emerged in the philosophical exchanges of their later correspondence. In the discussion that follows, I shall therefore treat the basic positions of Adams and Jefferson as stable dispositions that determined the reactions of the two men to the crisis of 1820—and shaped the conduct of many others in the troubled decades that followed.

Liberalism and the Issue of Slavery

Jefferson's Humanist Liberalism

Jefferson's philosophical premises were as Lockean as his political theory.[42] Radically amending Descartes, he wrote Adams that " 'I feel: therefore I exist' . . . When once we quit the basis of sensation, all is in the wind." He thus rejected "all organs of information . . . but my senses."[43] Ontologically, Jefferson linked his sensationalism to a philosophic materialism. "I feel bodies which are not myself: there are other existencies then. I call them *matter*. . . . Where there is an absence of matter, I call it *void*, or *nothing*, or *immaterial space*. On the basis of sensation, of matter and motion, we may erect . . . all the certainties we can have or need."[44]

Because human beings were constituted to seek pleasant experiences and shun painful ones, sensory experience was the basis for ethics as well as empirical knowledge. The right object, therefore, was a tranquil happiness based on well-regulated pleasure. Jefferson commended the French for excelling Americans in "the pleasures of the table," and he savored these delights himself.[45] He also disliked pain in himself or others. "For what good end," he asked Adams, could "the sensations of Grief . . . be intended. All our other passions, within proper bounds, have an useful object . . . [but] what is the use of grief?"[46] On this view, each individual had the right to define happiness in terms of his or her own experiences and then pursue it. Because this attitude left little, if any, room for an obligation to obey God or some transcendent moral law, utilitarianism and humanism merged. This utilitarianism had a relativistic side as well. "Nature," he remarked, "has constituted *utility* to man, [as] the standard and test of virtue. Men living . . . under different circumstances . . . may have different utilities; the same

---

42 Koch and Peden 1944, 609, TJ to Dr. Benjamin Rush 16 Jan. 1811; Commager 1975, 53.

43 Cappon 1959, 567–68, TJ to JA 15 Aug. 1820.

44 Ibid., 567, TJ to JA 15 Aug. 1820.

45 Koch and Peden 1944, 383, TJ to Charles Bellini 30 Sept. 1785; J. C. Miller 1977, 99.

46 Cappon 1959, 467, TJ to JA 8 Apr. 1816; see 490, TJ to JA 14 Oct. 1816.

act, therefore, may be useful, and consequently virtuous in one country [even though it] is injurious and vicious in another differently circumstanced."[47]

Fortunately, however, human beings also had a moral sense; Jefferson followed the Scottish Enlightenment, for example, in holding that pleasure came from helping others as well as satisfying oneself.[48] Jefferson, in fact, regarded "self-love" as "the sole antagonist of virtue," and he assailed Hobbes's egoism.[49] As Jefferson wrote Abigail Adams, "I am never happier than when I am performing good offices for good people."[50] His humanism sustained a charitable presumption about individual motives—both in others and himself. When "our duties and interests . . . seem to be at variance," he wrote, "we ought to suspect some fallacy in our reasonings."[51] In Miller's words, the Virginian believed "in original goodness, not in original sin: if man had fallen from grace it was . . . because he had submitted his own free will to the oppressive rule of kings, priests, and nobles."[52] Jefferson was, Peterson has added, "an Epicurean, though of sober mien, to whom emotional torment and self-flagellation were alien. Never [a diarist], . . . he kept records of everything . . . except the state of his soul."[53]

Jefferson recognized, of course, that even well-intentioned individuals might have conflicting goals. Like Locke, however, he thought in terms of rights and thus in terms of striking an appropriate balance among individual claims, a balance in which every individual's claims must be weighed equally. In this connection, Jefferson was deeply ambivalent about demands for his own continued public service. As he wrote to his protege James Monroe, "If we are made in some degree for others, yet, in a greater, are we made for ourselves. . . . [A situation in which] a man had less rights in himself than . . . his neighbors [have in directing his activities] . . . would be slavery."[54] The controlling principle, clearly, was to find a balance between Jefferson's own right to happiness, as he defined it for himself, and the claims on him of his fellow citizens.

Jefferson had a parallel understanding of human freedom. If individuals are free to define happiness for themselves, then they should be as free and unobstructed as possible in pursuing their self-determined goals. As Cooke has remarked, Jefferson's position "was . . . very much in the tradition of what . . . [Isaiah] Berlin has called 'negative' freedom," or exemption from

---

[47] Koch and Peden 1944, 639–40, TJ to Thomas Law 13 June 1814; J. C. Miller 1977, 94.
[48] Robbins 1975, 135.
[49] Koch and Peden 1944, 638, TJ to Thomas Law 13 June 1814; J. C. Miller 1977, 94.
[50] Cappon 1959, 157, TJ to AA Nov. 1786.
[51] Koch and Peden 1944, 575, TJ to Jean Baptiste Say 1 Feb. 1804; cf. Peterson 1987, 323.
[52] J. C. Miller 1977, 44.
[53] Peterson 1976, 9.
[54] Koch and Peden 1944, 364, to James Monroe 20 May 1782.

the coercion of others.[55] This stand, in turn, reinforced Jefferson's fundamental commitment to weighing equitably competing moral claims. If freedom means unobstructed action, and if individuals and groups have conflicting goals, an equitable arrangement will probably subject everyone to some restraint. In Jefferson's words, freedom was rightful only "within the limits drawn around us by the equal rights of others."[56]

This same respect for individual autonomy also supported Jefferson's ethical empiricism. Because individuals are entitled to choose their own goals, others can take note of such choices, but they cannot reasonably criticize them. Rationality thus becomes instrumental and empirical. If the pursuit by an individual of his or her chosen goal will not unduly interfere with the rights of others, the only questions that can be asked legitimately by outsiders are empirical rather than evaluative: are the actions that an individual undertakes the most effective available for reaching the goal? Jefferson himself devoted considerable attention to the matter of practical efficacy. It shaped his view of education, of travel, and the way he ran his plantation. "The study of law," he wrote a nephew, "is useful in a variety of points of view. It qualifies a man to be useful to himself, to his neighbors, and to the public." Fortunately, it is also "the most certain stepping-stone to [political] preferment."[57] This statement illuminates both Jefferson's enthusiasm for collecting facts and his broader humanism. One of the deepest impulses of the Enlightenment was its revolt against everything supernatural and mysterious in medieval and feudal culture, in favor of the natural, the human, the commonplace—and the observable.

Humanist Liberalism and Slavery

Jefferson's philosophical beliefs did not require, and certainly did not logically entail, any particular stand on slavery. Some of Jefferson's northern followers and admirers, such as the Jacksonian William Leggett, came to oppose slavery on the grounds of equality and individual rights. There is, then, a temptation to dismiss Jefferson himself, and other Jeffersonians, as racist. However, for the Virginian, at least, such prejudice clearly ran counter to his profound belief in enlightenment rationalism. I shall argue here that Jefferson's rationalism was not the whole of his fundamental philosophical outlook; nor did that outlook fundamentally support racism, even though some elements of his outlook may have proved comforting to friends of slavery. To anticipate the analysis: Jefferson's humanist liberalism emphasized deference to the experiences and preferences of every individ-

---

[55] Cooke 1973, 575.

[56] Ibid., TJ to Isaac H. Tiffany 4 Apr. 1819.

[57] Koch and Peden 1944, 496, TJ to Thomas Mann Randolph 30 May 1790.

ual. Tolerance was a centerpiece of his creed: he detested every governmentally sponsored religious or cultural orthodoxy. As we shall see, this stance made it easy to emphasize caution, forbearance—tolerance—in dealing with complex, controversial issues like slavery.

Jefferson's emphasis on compromise, then, on striking a balance among competing interests is very important. At times, to be sure, he would not compromise. Recall his support for the revolution and for religious liberty, and his opposition to the Alien and Sedition Acts, each of which demonstrated his hostility to governmental threats to the freedom of the individual. As his political success showed, however, Jefferson mastered the art of compromise and accommodation far more completely than his friend Adams. Consider Jefferson's reluctant agreement to the federal assumption of state debts in exchange for locating the new capital city on the Potomac; his middle position on the notorious Yazoo land frauds; his pragmatic decision to buy Louisiana, despite his strict constitutional principles; his eventual openness to the development of manufacturing in the United States as a response to British threats; and, above all, his skillful management of the Republican party. In every case, his pursuit of his own preferences was conditioned by his assessment of the preferences of other actors.

The issue was ethical as well as political, however. A regime could act fairly only by taking all individual preferences into account. This broadly utilitarian aim of satisfying as many citizens as possible meant, where necessary, some sacrifice of individual rights. The relative freedom or unobstructed action of some—to do as they wished with their own property, for example—would have to be limited somewhat in order to let others pursue conflicting goals. Liberal theory, however, has always been concerned with just such tradeoffs.

From the very first, Jefferson had no difficulty in connecting these concerns with the slavery issue. Even the young Jefferson had seen a conflict between the desires—or utilities—of the two races, suggesting the need for some appropriate balance. The slaves, of course, wanted to be free, and Jefferson's belief in negative freedom would seem to have supported them. Thus his draft of the declaration berated the English king for obtruding the slave trade on the colonists. In the same draft paragraph, Jefferson also assailed the monarch for trying to incite the slaves to revolt. The institution was strongly, and increasingly, supported by many whites in the South, and it was at least tolerated by many others in the North. Emancipation would have limited the freedom (obstructed the actions) of those who favored slavery or owned slaves, and it would have threatened their lives in the pursuit of the liberties of the slaves.

There was also a relativist side to Jefferson's utilitarianism, which emphasized in each particular case the effects of an institution or practice. As immoral as slavery was considered to be generally, slavery in America had obviously flourished. At the same time, Jefferson recognized the fears of southern whites about the violent reprisals they would suffer if their slaves were ever freed.[58] Here was a compelling interest to be balanced against the slaves' claims to freedom.[59] The same point could also be stated in terms of rights. In much the same way that he had argued in his draft of the declaration, Jefferson wrote in 1820 that the right to freedom of the blacks conflicted with the ultimately more important right to life of the whites.[60]

His devotion to freedom had still another consequence. Taken together, Jefferson's empiricism and his humanist belief in social progress meant that observable historical facts could affect moral judgments—provided the society in question was genuinely free. If individuals were free to reason instrumentally about how to implement their preferences, then social conditions, institutions, and practices were likely to improve over time. In economic life, Jefferson embraced the argument of Adam Smith and other political economists that in a free market even self-regarding economic activity would be beneficial generally. So, too, in his First Inaugural, he reasserted his belief in "the diffusion of information and the arraignment of all abuses at the bar of public reason . . . [and in] freedom of the press."[61] In both cases, the freedom of the individual to assert and implement one's preferences was critical.

In effect, then, Jefferson placed particular trust in the outcomes, the institutions and practices, produced by liberal regimes, preeminently in those produced by his own American polity. Because the American people were free in this way, there was a presumption that their institutions were progressive and valuable and that slavery was just such an institution. It had become so deeply embedded in American life that any threat to it would threaten the health or indeed the survival of the republic. As the institution's fortunes waxed rather than waned, the Virginian had less and less to say, at least in public, on the subject of its evil character.[62]

Jefferson, of course, might have rejected all these arguments by denying the legitimacy of the preferences of southern whites. He could have asked, for example, how a threat in the future to the lives of some southern whites could justify their denying liberty in the present to all the African slaves. In fact, however, Jefferson took very seriously the right of white masters to property.[63] As early as 1781, he referred, matter of factly, to the Southerners' "land, slaves, and other property."[64] This stand, and particularly his

[58] J. C. Miller 1977, 37.
[59] Greven 1977, 353.
[60] Peterson 1987, 235ff.; see also J. C. Miller 1977.
[61] Peterson 1987, 294.
[62] J. C. Miller 1977, 130.
[63] Ibid., 15.
[64] Koch and Peden 1944, 272, 252, 255.

eventual silence on the slavery issue, was rooted in his perception, first put forth in his draft of the declaration, that American blacks and whites were separate peoples. In the terms of the declaration, this separation meant that the two had not mutually instituted a government—had not mutually given their consent—to observe and mutually enforce their natural rights, including that of liberty. For this reason, Jefferson could suggest that even conscientious whites like himself owed their primary obligation to other members of their own community. Similarly, he could support popular protests in France and elsewhere, while dreading the prospect of slave rebellions, because the protesters, unlike the American slaves, were full citizens of their political community. Indeed, if American blacks and whites were truly separate peoples, blacks who were eventually freed might well be expected to be particularly vengeful.

In making this pivotal distinction between blacks and whites, Jefferson relied on his ontological and epistemological premises. According to his epistemology, all assertions, even those about human equality and possible differences between the two races, were open to testing and verification by sense perception or empirical study. Even though the young, overtly antislavery Jefferson considered it to be an observable fact that blacks were intellectually inferior, his philosophical empiricism did not require him to read the facts that way. As Miller has pointed out, Jefferson could have reaffirmed his egalitarianism by treating the problems of the blacks as entirely the consequence of their bondage.[65] Indeed, he would have been driven to do so, had he regarded a belief in human equality as an unquestionable postulate from which to begin, a postulate that could not be challenged with empirical data. By rejecting all such postulates, Jefferson's empiricism enabled him instead to begin with what he thought were the evident facts of the case, colored though these facts might have been by his economic interests and racial fears.

Moreover, many of the obvious differences between blacks and whites that Jefferson observed and reported on in the *Notes* were physical. Given his materialist philosophy, he believed that these observed patterns of racial differences were likely to persist, that if human beings were essentially material entities, then their future development was likely to be consistent with their enduring physical characteristics. Here, too, his philosophic materialism did not require an emphasis on the *physiological attributes* of slaves or of any other individuals, but on the *persistence of the differences* between slaves and others. As did his sensationalism, this feature of Jefferson's philosophy helped prepare the way for his eventual shift on slavery by making his final position plausible, and persuasive, to himself and others. The im-

[65] Peterson 1987, 188; J. C. Miller 1977, 46–59.

pact of Jefferson's outlook, however, can be fully clarified only by comparing it to that of his friend from Massachusetts.

Adams's Reform Liberalism

Like Jefferson, Adams valued compromise and equilibrium. His theory of republicanism focused on the appropriate balance between and among political institutions and social groups. A moderating force in the administration of the Alien and Sedition Acts, Adams ended his presidency, and frustrated the belligerent Hamiltonians in his own cabinet, by deciding to avoid a bitterly controversial war with France. Still, Adams was no humanist liberal. The balance he sought was to be accomplished more by curbing dangerous human passions and immoral behavior than by accommodating the competing goals adopted by various individuals.

The attitudes of both Adams and Jefferson toward religion are revealing. Devoted to the dignity and autonomy of his species, Jefferson largely ignored the role of the deity. He created his own scripture by culling the ethical teachings of Jesus from the rest of the New Testament. In contrast, Adams, in Peterson's words, "was a zealot, not about any particular creed, but about religion. It was in his blood and had weighed on his mind all his life."[66] Without religion, Adams thought, there could be no philosophy, and he repeatedly praised his Puritan forebears for their morals, courage, intellectuality, and even their anti-Catholicism.[67]

Most revealing of all, the Yankee moralist embraced much of the traditional piety of the New England orthodoxy. Although Adams disagreed with orthodox Calvinists on many issues, he shared their sense of human inferiority and ignorance when compared to God's infinite and inscrutable majesty. There "never was but one being who can Understand the Universe," he wrote Jefferson in 1813. "And . . . it is not only vain but wicked for insects to pretend to comprehend it."[68] Because "the World is . . . a Riddle and an Enigma," he thought humility was the only appropriate response.[69] Rather than celebrate his species, he believed that the human soul "ought to fill itself with a meek and humble anxiety."[70] Here was an almost Kantian focus on the limits of the human mind, a focus that anticipated the Transcendentalism of the next generation.

Not surprisingly then, Adams insisted on the responsibility of the individual to act on moral standards that were transcendent, because they were

[66] Peterson 1976, 123.
[67] Cappon 1959, 358, JA to TJ 15 July 1813; 435, JA to TJ 16 July 1814; 571, JA to TJ 3 Feb. 1821; 573, JA to TJ 18 May 1821.
[68] Ibid., 375, JA to TJ 14 Sept. 1813.
[69] Ibid., 376, JA to TJ 15 Sept. 1813.
[70] Haraszti 1952, 302; cf. J. Adams 1850–1856, 4:22.

divinely ordained. As much as he valued happiness, he held that it "consists in virtue"; that is, he *defined* the state of happiness as virtuous activity, thus rejecting the idea that it could be determined subjectively.[71] Indeed, Adams was deeply ambivalent about pleasure as the criterion for happiness, and thus as the goal of human life. At one point, he proclaimed his own devotion to "business alone."[72] As he wrote in his diary in 1756, "He is not a wise man . . . that has left one Passion in his Soul unsubdued."[73] In that spirit, he was willing to limit the individual's pursuit of pleasure.

Nor could Adams accept Jefferson's view of freedom as simply minimizing restraint. To be sure, negative liberty, including particularly the right of conscience, was a necessary condition for true freedom. Further, the negative liberty of some had sometimes to be abridged in order to protect that of others. "I have a right," Adams wrote, "to resist him" who "shall take it into his head . . . that he has a right to take my property without my consent."[74] Nevertheless, full liberty for Adams also had a positive side. He accepted the familiar argument that the genuinely free person is not a slave to passion; and emancipation from the passions entailed the development of one's moral and, of course, physical and intellectual faculties. "Liberty, according to my metaphysics," he wrote, "is an intellectual quality . . . it is a self-determining power in an intellectual agent. It implies thought and choice and power."[75] "Thought and choice and [self-determining] power" imply an obligation, a goal, to foster general self-improvement, including the improvement of his own, and other people's, moral faculties.

The contrast with Jefferson is clear. Given Jefferson's belief in negative liberty and tranquility, the Virginian placed less emphasis than Adams on the possibilities for fundamental changes in individuals. On Jefferson's humanist liberal view, education and experience would surely help the individual to pursue his or her goals more effectively. Even without assistance, however, all normal individuals could be trusted to identify their own goals—that is, to define happiness for themselves—but also to act altruistically where appropriate. For Adams, however, his belief in a positive side of liberty did not just allow but required the active improvement of oneself and others through assiduous emancipation from the passions and systematic cultivation of the faculties.

The result was a different approach to the issue of competing claims. As Adams's view of public service makes clear, the true moral imperative for him was not to balance such claims but to make sure that individuals did their duty and conformed to an appropriate moral law. Whereas Jefferson

71 J. Adams 1850–1856, 4:197; cf. Chinard 1933, 90.

72 J. Adams 1850–1856, 9:368, JA to Mercy Warren 25 Nov. 1775.

73 Butterfield 1961, 1:33, 14 June 1756.

74 J. Adams 1850–1856, 4:96; cf. Haraszti 1952, 144, 147.

75 Peek 1954, 196, JA to John Taylor 15 Apr. 1814.

sometimes regarded political office as a burden imposed on him by others for their benefit, the Yankee saw it as an opportunity for conscientious individuals to undertake self-improvement. The obligation of the rulers, he wrote John Taylor, is "to exert all their intellectual liberty to employ all their faculties, talents, and power for the public, general universal good, . . . [and] not for their own separate good or the interest of any party."[76] There was no pressing need, that is, to strike a balance between the public's interest and that of the individual official, because public service offered individuals this opportunity. There was no *imbalance*, according to Adams, between self-interest and public service.

These differences between Adams and Jefferson were reinforced by Adams's epistemology and ontology. In an 1816 letter, Adams dismissed Jefferson's materialism as inconsistent with human liberty, conscience, and morality.[77] At other times, he resorted to skepticism. The "question between spirit and matter," he wrote Jefferson in 1820, was "nugatory because we have neither evidence nor idea of either."[78] Nor could sensory experience resolve matters. Against Jefferson's sensationalism, Adams held that the "essences of mind and body" cannot be penetrated by "our senses or instruments." "Incision, knives, and microscopes make no discoveries in this region."[79] Indeed, the mind also provided a knowledge independent of sensory experience.[80] "Phylosophy which is the result of Reason," he wrote to Jefferson, "is the first, the original Revelation of The Creator to his Creature, Man."[81] In sum, Adams rejected any effort such as Jefferson's to ground notions of human well-being in sensory experience. There was, instead, "a law of right reason common to God and man" that was essential for "all human reasoning on the moral government of the universe."[82]

Slavery and Reform Liberalism

To recapitulate, Jefferson's humanist liberalism asserted the self-sufficiency of humankind in three forms that supported a tolerant disposition toward slavery. First, for Jefferson, the human *will* was self-sufficient, because individuals were able to decide on legitimate goals for themselves. Whatever a person found to be a source of temperate pleasure counted as well-being, provided it be consistent with the rights of others. Here, for egalitarians like

[76] Ibid., 197.
[77] Cappon 1959, 465, JA to TJ 2 Mar. 1816; cf. 551, JA to TJ 21 Dec. 1819; Haraszti 1952, 77.
[78] Cappon 1959, 563, JA to TJ 12 May 1820; cf. Haraszti 1952, 66, 106.
[79] Haraszti 1952, 66.
[80] J. Adams 1850–1856, 10:141, JA to James Lloyd 26 Mar. 1815; see also 147, JA to James Lloyd 29 Mar. 1815.
[81] Cappon 1959, 412, JA to TJ 25 Dec. 1813.
[82] Haraszti 1952, 71–72.

Jefferson, was the warrant for balancing competing claims and interests, including those of the friends of slavery. Second, human *rationality* was self-sufficient, because its task was instrumental, and free individuals could generally be trusted to implement the goals they adopted. Given this rationality, exchanges of either goods or ideas would produce beneficent outcomes—hence the presumption in favor of the institutions and practices, including American slavery, that flourished in a liberal society. Third, human *cognition* was self-sufficient, because ordinary sense perceptions accurately conveyed reality, and therefore the phenomenal world of material objects was the real world. It followed, for Jefferson, that the differences he observed between physiologically distinct races were real differences, and the liberal theory of rights and consent could be applied accordingly.

Adams's reform liberalism, however, supported an ultimately critical disposition toward slavery by denying each of these three claims. First, it rejected the sufficiency of the human will, because individuals could not simply determine their goals for themselves. Whatever an individual's pleasures and pains might be, religious and ethical duty commanded that individual not only to cultivate his or her own moral, intellectual, and physical faculties, but to help others to do so as well. Because he thought this injunction applied to slaves as well, Adams, like his Puritan forebears, favored educating slaves.[83] Most slave owners, of course, denied this opportunity to their chattel and denounced the idea as pernicious. For Adams, there could be no question of weighing competing claims. His comments implied—and the abolitionists later openly insisted—that the institution blighted the moral development of the masters, even as it blighted the intellectual development of the slaves.

Second, the emphasis on self-development led to a larger view of human rationality. Given a commitment to self-development, it was not enough just to note whatever goals individuals had adopted, and then ask factual questions about how well these goals were being implemented. However gratifying some object or goal might be, pursuing it was not morally acceptable if it subverted the obligation to promote self-development. Here was the source for much of Adams's animus against any individual or group having undue power over others, be it husbands or wives, the British colonial authorities, lawless American mobs, or French revolutionaries.[84] Excessive power, and the pride that went with it, often tempted the powerful to act on desires that were contrary to the course of their own or others' self-development.[85] It was in order to limit political power that Adams had insisted, at great political cost to himself, on an elaborate system of republi-

---

[83] Peek 1954, 207–8ff., JA to John Taylor 15 Apr. 1814.
[84] Cappon 1959, 10, JA to TJ 29 June 1778; 334, JA to TJ 25 June 1813.
[85] See, for example, J. Adams 1850–1856, 4:444; 3:448.

can checks and balances. According to this criterion of undue power, the institution of slavery was surely suspect. Implicit in Abigail Adams's letter to Adams, in 1776, was the claim that the institution was ungodly, indeed impious, because it elevated some human beings to a position of power over others, a station that belonged to God alone.[86] This criterion condemned slavery without regard for its popularity, for the desires of many that it persist, or for the fact that it had flourished in a free society.

Third, and perhaps most decisively, Adams's doubts about human cognition made it difficult for him to agree that blacks and whites were two separate peoples with different rights and destinies. Jefferson could assert this separation because many of the racial differences he emphasized were physical and empirically observable. For Adams, who rejected his friend's materialist ontology and sensationalist epistemology, human equality meant not the possession of certain observable skills but the moral equality of souls. Because Adams believed human souls to be immaterial objects not directly observable, it was beside the point to ask whether Jefferson's observations about the slaves were accurate. Adams's claim about human equality was a postulate from which he *began* to reason, not, as in Jefferson's case, the conclusion of an inquiry that relied on sense experience. Consequently, for Adams, empirical tests were simply irrelevant.

Furthermore, Adams's reform liberalism did more than immunize its devotees against a rationale for tolerating slavery. Most of the founders thought slavery immoral, yet the issue remained largely quiescent before the 1820s. It became pressing only when a later generation launched an emotional crusade that succeeded in enlisting the support of relative moderates, such as John Quincy Adams and Charles Francis Adams. Nevertheless, the crusading impulse was to be found in the doctrine of piety, that element in Adams's creed most at odds with a humanist celebration of the individual. To the humanist, the reform belief in humankind's insignificance when compared to an ultimately inscrutable God may not have seemed a likely source for a moral crusade. If the divine will was beyond human knowledge, how could a conscientious believer confidently adopt any militant cause? How could any human being presume to launch a moral crusade against established social institutions and practices?

In practice, however, the distance between the believers and the divinity increased the anxiety of the believers to be included among the redeemed. The profound tension between the human and the divine could be relieved best by throwing oneself into the activity and drama of a crusade for moral reform. Moreover, the sinfulness, the deficiencies, of the human condition made the exhibition of righteousness through militant activism especially important. Complete personal success might be beyond hope; every

[86] Butterfield et al. 1975, 120.

achievement might be only provisional; but these facts meant that every step forward left many more to be taken.

As skeptical as Adams was about political enthusiasms, he recognized just this connection. "The faculties of our understanding," he wrote Jefferson in 1825, "are not adequate to penetrate the Universe." After thus expressing his piety, he moved immediately to the issue of moral conduct: "Let us do our duty which is, to do as we would be done by."[87] In the right circumstances—those, for example, of his children and grandchildren after 1830—this sentiment became more than a demand for good conduct in one's usual calling.

All of Adams's beliefs were consistent with his New England heritage. Orthodox Calvinism, which emphasized the control or moral superintendency by a favored elite over a less worthy multitude, did not readily dispose its believers to war against slavery. Adams, however, was not orthodox. As a young man, he had embraced a moderate Unitarianism, an act that left him without a future in the orthodox ministry.[88] Like many of his Yankee contemporaries, he particularly abhorred the doctrines of predestination and election—the former decreed that each individual's salvation was wholly determined in advance by God's will and the latter that God had chosen to save only a few saints. As Adams himself put it, he could not believe in a harsh divinity who "created and preserves, for a time, innumerable millions [of sinners, only] to make them miserable."[89] According to his more liberal theology, "God created man in his own image," and took a strongly nurturing attitude toward his human creatures.[90]

With these theological changes, Adams's reform liberalism was capable of sustaining an antislavery disposition. While extending the opportunity and obligation of sainthood to all, reform liberalism still affirmed both the reality of sin and the moral duties of the saint. From this perspective, slavery was sinful because it prevented its victims from following the path of saints. Not surprisingly, the Second Great Awakening of the early 1800s, which powerfully advanced this new creed, also spawned the abolitionist agitation of the 1830s. For many of those swept up in the enthusiasm of the revival, the command to do God's work obliterated the distinction between religious and political obligations.

Adams himself remained cautious on the issue of slavery, partly, perhaps, because the resemblance between his creed and that of the Awakening was only approximate. Whereas the Awakening was enthusiastic and trinitarian, Adams's Unitarianism was rationalistic. Moreover, as Peterson has pointed out, Adams was more skeptical about human nature in his political theory

[87] Cappon 1959, 607, JA to TJ 22 Jan. 1825; cf. 376, JA to TJ 15 Sept. 1813.

[88] See Peterson 1976, 121; Chinard 1933, vi, 18, 21–22.

[89] Cappon 1959, 373–74, JA to TJ 14 Sept. 1813.

[90] Ibid., 382, JA to TJ Sept. (i.e., 4 Oct.) 1813.

than in his theology.[91] His children and grandchildren, who shared much of his rationalism, never became outright abolitionists; influenced by the rising democratic ethos of their culture, they combined a reform liberal sense of moral obligation with a belief in the legitimacy of the pursuit by popular movements of righteous goals. In that spirit, they became antislavery Whigs and, later, Republicans.

In the end, then, John Adams laid a foundation for a militant politics that he himself did not, perhaps could not, fully embrace. Still, his correspondence with Jefferson identified the basic premises and assumptions that came to be shared by other reform liberals in his family, his region, and his cultural tradition, a group that later included western Whigs like Abraham Lincoln. According to the still more egalitarian ethic of reform liberals after Adams, slavery was not just unfortunate or regrettable. It was profoundly offensive to God and to their own transcendent moral commitments. To be sure, slavery remained a peripheral issue in American politics during much of the antebellum period. It came fully to command political attention only after humanist and reform liberals had each addressed one of two sets of issues that had been left to them by the generation of Adams and Jefferson. One set of issues involved political democracy; the other involved morality in politics.

[91] Peterson 1976, 20–21, 6.

PART THREE

INTRODUCTION TO PART THREE

I N THE generation after Jefferson's death, the Jacksonian Democrats emerged as his humanist liberal successors. The Jacksonians' devotion to political equality, to the sovereignty of individual preferences, and to universal male suffrage, also continued the work of the founders. Whatever the Federalists' fears of popular excesses, whatever the Hamiltonians' private skepticism about democratic principles, the new republic had a popular foundation. Relying at every point on the ultimate authority of the people, the Constitution swept away every vestige of a hereditary order.[1]

The Jacksonian Democrats confronted two problems the founders had been spared. The first problem was that of the diversity of the population, stressed by Madison in the *Federalist Papers*.[2] By 1830, the electorate had been enlarged to include men without property; Jefferson's purchase of Louisiana had doubled the nation's territory; the population had increased dramatically between 1790 and 1830; and revolutions in transportation and manufacturing had multiplied the number of competing economic interests in the country.

The second problem the Jacksonians confronted was leadership. A large democratic electorate can effectively work its will only if its choices among groups of leaders are reduced to a manageable number. This problem had been mitigated for the first generation electorate, both by the standing its leaders had acquired during the revolutionary and constitutional periods and by a custom of social deference that survived from the colonial era. Except for the painful election of 1800, presidential succession had moved straightforwardly from Washington to Adams, and from Jefferson to Madison to Monroe. By the time Adams's son John Quincy Adams was elected in 1824, matters had become much more complex. As the founding generation left the stage, deference was on the decline.

The issues of diversity and leadership were technical matters at one level and, as such, posed two questions that are addressed by contemporary rational choice theory. One was how voters could agree on leaders who could best aggregate and implement the increasingly complex popular preferences of citizens. The other was how leaders might best proceed to form a viable majority on policy questions. The two-fold task was complicated by a third problem: transformation in the interests and desires themselves. As the Jacksonians themselves recognized, their era was marked by a seemingly unprecedented and unbridled material acquisitiveness—an insistence that all white Americans should be free to pursue material prosperity as avidly as

---

[1] See, for example, Diggins 1984 and Wood 1969.
[2] See, for example, *Federalist* No. 10.

they could. This spirit expressed the Jacksonians' egalitarian rejection of elitist constraints on the ambitions of common people.[3] The new acquisitiveness, however, not only aroused the democratic hopes of the Jacksonians, it also fed their republican fears. They were openly worried about the very lack of restraint that they eagerly sought. Those who benefited from the "spectacular commercial and industrial growth of the American economy" were nevertheless haunted by "the possibility of violent revolution always . . . a grinning death's head at the rich feast."[4] They made up a "laissez-faire society" that "look[ed] upon law as an attempt to contain the special boundlessness of American opportunity."[5] Given their lust for riches—indeed their outright selfishness—how would society or polity continue to cohere? In a society "where a form of naive, self-willed exploitation was coming increasingly to be identified with the true meaning of the republic,"[6] where would the new republic find the loyalty and self-sacrifice that it required? How, indeed, could the regime satisfy these new, intense demands?[7]

For the present purposes, the Jacksonians are especially interesting in three respects. First, they were torn even more than other generations between inherited norms and current enthusiasms. On the one hand, they looked for moral guidance to a partly republican, partly rationalist, partly Protestant, and thoroughly liberal union of autonomy and restraint, described here as the founding synthesis—the political legacy that gave their republican experiment its integrity. On the other hand, they also looked to the new opportunities for material gain offered them by their dynamic capitalist society, opportunities that made the country a beacon to others. Here, indeed, was the complex ambivalence so remarkably described by Meyers as the Jacksonian persuasion.

Second, the Jacksonians were interesting because they were democrats committed to popular rule; they were humanist liberals devoted to satisfying individual desires; and they were Americans of the second generation confronting a welter of intense and conflicting interests. In the language of contemporary social science, they were the first politicians anywhere to face the preference coordination problem in something like its full complexity. The two problems of diversity and leadership were in fact closely connected. Coordinating preferences meant imposing limits on some or all citizens, in part by forcing on them the substantive concessions or compromises that were also demanded by a republican ethic.

---

[3] See Benson 1971, ch. 5; M. L. Wilson 1974, 6, 40–43, 121–29.
[4] Somkin 1967, 36.
[5] Ibid., 46; see also Meyers 1960, ch. 6, esp. 140–41.
[6] Somkin 1967, 48.
[7] Benson 1971, 87.

Third, the Jacksonians are interesting because they had to face the problem of chattel slavery. Here, as Jefferson had recognized, the confrontation between morality and ambition was especially acute. On this issue, as the Jacksonians themselves saw, preferences were so intense and conflicting that coordinating them became the supreme test of a democratic politician's skills.

Three Jacksonian variants are considered here: William Leggett's insistence on strict laissez-faire; Stephen A. Douglas's belief in popular sovereignty based in states' rights; and Martin Van Buren's system of cohesive, competitive parties. From one perspective the three men were very similar: compared to Jefferson, all three affirmed a humanist liberalism less constrained than Jefferson's by the other elements of the founding synthesis. Although all three espoused a republican concern with limiting certain individual preferences, their republicanism was attenuated by a utilitarian concern for the satisfaction of individual desires. They relied less on the ethics of the individual citizens than on arranging the context in which these desires could be pursued. For Leggett, that context was a free market-like social process; for Douglas, an invigorated federal system; for Van Buren, the political party as an organization. The humanist liberalism of these men, that is, moved them closer to the Federalists' reliance on institutional constraints than to the anti-Federalists' stress on individual citizen virtue.[8]

Leggett, Douglas, and Van Buren, in short, each adopted and refashioned Jefferson's politics, de-emphasizing in the process its republican and Protestant elements and emphasizing its humanist liberal, utilitarian side. The refashioning nevertheless took three different forms. Leggett's belief in laissez-faire invoked Jefferson's egalitarianism and utilitarianism, his distaste for luxury and indulgence, his insistence on almost complete negative freedom, and a trust in unconstrained social processes. Douglas's popular sovereignty stressed a form of Jefferson's materialism, his consequentialist evaluation of an action or institution in terms of its effects, and his devotion to both the nation and its constituent states and communities. Finally, Van Buren emphasized Jefferson's willingness to build political parties as intersectional alliances, his concern with restraining political ambition, his emphasis on instrumental reasoning, especially in politics, and, most importantly, the implementing and concerting of individual preferences.

With all these differences, however, there was a further commonality among the three men. The strongly humanist liberal side of each man's politics both motivated and ultimately undercut his efforts to address the issue of human slavery.

[8] Cf. Ericson 1987 on this point.

FIVE

WILLIAM LEGGETT

PROCESS, UTILITY, AND LAISSEZ-FAIRE

WILLIAM LEGGETT was the radical conscience of Jacksonian democracy. Seaman, poet, short story writer, and New York theater critic, he made his political mark as an editorial writer, first on William Cullen Bryant's *Evening Post* and then on his own *Plaindealer*. Leggett wrote his editorials only during the early and middle 1830s, before ill health overtook him. Yet, more than any other Jacksonian theorist, Leggett expanded on Jefferson's belief in equality, utility, and universal individual rights, just at a time when the Virginian's fellow Southerners were turning against such doctrines as subversive.[1]

Jacksonian Politics and Humanist Liberal Principles

Leggett's rigorous laissez-faire creed spoke to both a particular constituency and to a much broader audience.[2] During the 1830s, many of New York City's artisans and small entrepreneurs felt threatened by freely extended credit, a rapid expansion of the money supply, and a wave of speculative ventures.[3] Because many of them blamed New York's chartered corporations, and especially the banks, for these developments, Leggett's attack on all governmentally created privileges, and indeed on all interventions in the economy, seemed to them to be a powerful demand for equality and social justice.[4] Still, Leggett's carefully wrought arguments acquired a "significance," as Hofstadter put it, "far out of proportion to his small direct influence."[5] In particular, Leggett powerfully influenced the radical Loco Foco and Barnburner wings of the New York Democracy.[6] His attack on special charters of incorporation helped prepare the way for New York's general incorporation law.[7] Finally, his demand that government cut all ties

---

[1] Trimble 1919, 399–401, 415–16; White 1986, 309; cf. Leggett 1984, 18, 54–55.
[2] White 1986, 307, 316; Meyers 1960, 186.
[3] Rifkin 1951, 45, 52; Beckner 1977, 34.
[4] Hofstadter 1943, 586–87.
[5] Ibid., 582.
[6] Cf. Leggett 1984, 258ff.; Rifkin 1951, 52; Trimble 1919, 399, 409.
[7] Hofstadter 1943, 594.

to the banks, which were creating a "script nobility" and sapping the vitality of economic and social life, anticipated Martin Van Buren's sub-treasury plan.[8]

Leggett was a good Jacksonian on other issues as well. He admired the Old Hero, he attacked Jackson's political enemies, and he depicted the Jacksonian coalition as honest producers struggling against sometimes fraudulent economic parasites.[9] Leggett considered the rule of the people to be the essence of good government, labeled himself a democrat "in the fullest and largest sense of the word," and ridiculed the idea that "the people are . . . incapable of self-government."[10] His particular watchword, therefore, was "equal rights," by which he meant giving the weak an equal political voice with the strong, and securing "a complete equality of civil privileges."[11] The Whigs, by contrast, stood for special favors for the already privileged.[12] "The one party [the Jacksonians]," he wrote in 1834, ". . . is composed, in a great measure, of the farmers, mechanics, labourers, and other producers of the . . . middling and lower classes . . . and the other [the Whigs] of the consumers, the rich, the proud, and the privileged."[13]

Leggett also embraced the Jacksonians' strict construction of the Constitution, a construction that ruled out a strong federal government. He hailed the veto by which Jackson killed the Bank of the United States, and he opposed federal programs of internal improvements and all versions of the protective tariff.[14] On cultural issues, Leggett abhorred all forms of religious prejudice, especially anti-Catholicism, and he opposed any efforts to exclude from participation the often pro-Jacksonian immigrants.[15] Leggett also insisted on the separation of church and state, he espoused the "voluntary principle" in religion, and he even rejected Thanksgiving Day as a religious intrusion on public life.[16]

These Jacksonian political views rested on humanist liberal principles. " 'I am a man,' " Leggett wrote, quoting Terence, " 'and nothing can be indifferent to me which affects humanity.' "[17] Consistent with Jefferson's sensationalist and materialist outlook, Leggett emphasized the solid, observable elements of experience and thus favored, for example, tangible gold and silver coins over paper bank notes.[18] Whereas banks were very often secre-

---

[8] Leggett 1984, 17, 63–64, 74, 93, 98, 117; Rifkin 1951, 53–54.

[9] Leggett 1984, 235, 270, 244, 72, 83.

[10] Ibid., 24, 20.

[11] Ibid., 9, 12, 17, 6.

[12] Ibid., 242–43, 260–61.

[13] Ibid., 244; cf. 171.

[14] Ibid., 42, 121, 237–38, 234–36, 27, 38, 241–42.

[15] Ibid., 21, 271–72.

[16] Ibid., 126, 141, 329–30.

[17] Ibid., 57.

[18] Cf. Meyers 1960 on Andrew Jackson, esp. 26–27 and 32.

tive and lent out "twice, and sometimes three times, the amount of their actual capital," the credit of "the humblest mechanick" could be relied on because his economic means were "visible."[19] In an agonized discussion of the copyright laws, Leggett accepted Locke's emphasis on physical relationship: "a distinctive and exclusive right" to real property depended upon the individual's "occupying it and mixing his labour with it." The author's right was "to the results of his manual labor," that is, his "corporeal" rather than "incorporeal" property. Only the former has "exact, definite, and always ascertainable" limits.[20]

Leggett's ethics were explicitly utilitarian.[21] His editorials repeatedly appealed to "the greatest good of the greatest number" as the right standard of evaluation, and he recognized that Benthamite doctrine was essentially aggregative.[22] "The object of all politicians," Leggett wrote, ". . . is . . . the greatest possible sum of happiness of which the social condition admits."[23] Accordingly, he accepted economic changes in which "individual suffering was atoned for by the inestimable augmentation of general good."[24] It followed that liberty should be understood in negative terms as the absence of constraint. "Unnecessary restraints," he wrote in 1835, "are the essence of tyranny."[25]

Jacksonian and humanist liberal principles were joined in Leggett's "great principle of equal political, civil, and religious rights."[26] For example, once established, a property right was so weighty that Leggett himself would tolerate even the despised chartered monopolies—until their charters expired. This devotion to rights also helped to identify those extraordinary cases of legitimate government intervention in economic affairs—for example, when a flour monopoly threatened the citizens' rights to self-preservation.[27] Rights, in short, were so important that Leggett's Loco Foco followers adopted the formal name of the Equal Rights party.[28]

As we have seen, a belief in individual rights is part of American genus liberalism. In a purely rights-oriented account, an individual's right to act, speak, or write as he pleases cannot be taken away or given up, because such a move would decrease the general utility or happiness. For that reason, Leggett's insistence on universal rights might seem to undermine his utilitarian, humanist liberal concern with satisfying individual desires. As one

[19] Leggett 1984, 76, 132–33.
[20] Ibid., 399.
[21] Ibid., 52; cf. 393.
[22] Ibid., 55, 142, 351, 398.
[23] Ibid., 56.
[24] Ibid., 160.
[25] Ibid., 20; cf. Meyers 1960, 192.
[26] Leggett 1984, 16.
[27] Ibid., 374–75, 380.
[28] Hofstadter 1943, 588.

thoughtful commentator has put it, Leggett treated utility as the "junior partner" in his theory, invoking it only in those cases where the "senior partner," equal rights, offered no useful guidance.[29] Leggett himself wrote that arguments for monopolies "as means of effecting 'great objects of public utility,' " only illustrated the "stale cant" of "those who desired to cheat the people of their rights."[30] He opposed some prison labor, "even though the whole community will eventually be benefitted," on the ground of "fundamental equal rights," pointing out that the goods so produced would compete with those produced by law-abiding citizens.[31] If the government's only criterion for action was "the benefit of the people," the government could "do any thing" advocated by "designing politicians."[32] The question for Leggett, then, was "not whether [some] . . . practice may not occasionally lead to public, or social, or individual benefit" but whether it will infringe "the sanctity of Equal Rights."[33]

Yet Leggett's utilitarianism went deeper than these remarks suggest. He argued for equal rights, in fact, from a distinctly humanist liberal perspective, by defending them *in terms of their utility*. As he wrote in 1837, the right to property, to "the exclusive use and benefit of the fruits of one's own labour, is the great and secure foundation of social order and happiness."[34] So, too, equal rights restrained men "from injuring one another," while leaving them otherwise free to their "own pursuits." It was a "great . . . regulating principle [that] harmoniously arranges the various parts of the stupendous whole."[35] Moreover, as Jefferson had pointed out, the rights to free speech and inquiry would lead to reliable knowledge. "Leave error free to flow where it listeth," Leggett opined, "so that truth is not shut out from the same channels . . . and who can doubt" the victor?[36]

Laissez-Faire: Leggett's Attenuated Republicanism

Like other good Jacksonians, Leggett looked to Jefferson's republican creed for his political ethic. It was the people's "virtue and intelligence," he argued, that "constitute the avowed basis of our institutions."[37] Admittedly, his laissez-faire policy benefited those ambitious, rising entrepreneurs who resented the practice of awarding special government charters to favored

29 White 1986, 310–11.
30 Leggett 1984, 278.
31 Ibid., 317–18.
32 Ibid., 11.
33 Ibid., 282.
34 Ibid., 392.
35 Ibid., 178.
36 Ibid., 398.
37 Ibid., 22.

competitors. As Meyers has pointed out, it was just those men on the make who epitomized the apparently unrestrained and unprecedented individualism of the Jacksonian era, and who therefore offended Leggett's republican sensibilities.[38] "A gaming spirit has infected the whole community," he lamented in 1837—to which development one possible response was a republican assault on the indulgence, luxury, and (in the sexist idiom of the time) effeminacy that had displaced the manliness of a healthy society.[39] The "present luxury," including lavish homes, expensive furniture, and fine wines, must be attributed to "speculations," which in turn reflected "the passion of avarice," and a desire to get rich rapidly, through investments rather than hard work.[40] Invoking the authority of the leading Old Republican, John Randolph of Roanoke, Leggett assailed "this insane desire of acquisition and display," that is, the avid acquisitiveness that amounted to simple human greed.[41] The "feverish avidity for sudden wealth," he maintained, fostered "a spirit of wild and dishonest speculation," distorted economic life, and ultimately blunted "men's moral perceptions."[42] In this excessive form, the "selfish feeling" was indeed "the root of all evil."[43]

Leggett, then, experienced in acute form the Jacksonian dilemma identified by Meyers. Given Leggett's humanist insistence on the sovereignty of individual preferences, he could hardly dismiss the goals of his contemporaries, however self-regarding and excessive. Given Leggett's emphasis on negative liberty, the chief republican virtue for him was individual autonomy. Leggett called on his fellow Americans to be "independent citizens" rather than "puppets" of the legislature.[44] He ridiculed the claim "that no man can possibly find his way in broad day light without being tied to the apron-string of a legislative dry-nurse."[45] How could he keep any form of republican faith when these individual goals so often exhibited an unrepublican passion of avarice?

Leggett's answer to that question simultaneously justified laissez-faire and attenuated his republicanism. As a seaman, he had suffered from the cruelty of his superior officers, and hostility to government authority marks all his political thought.[46] "The selfish feeling," he thought, became dangerous when involved "in . . . [the] struggle of party for . . . ascendancy."[47] Selfishness, that is, crossed "its proper bounds" when it became politicized,

[38] Meyers 1960, 202–4.
[39] Leggett 1984, 309, 49.
[40] Ibid., 172; see also 117, 249.
[41] Ibid., 149–50.
[42] Ibid., 58, 87.
[43] Ibid., 3.
[44] Ibid., 4.
[45] Ibid., 20.
[46] Rifkin 1951, 46; Hofstadter 1943, 583.
[47] Leggett 1984, 4; see 5.

when it emphasized political power and authority. At times, this antipolitical stance invoked familiar republican arguments. Indirect taxation, he maintained, is pernicious, partly because it spawns "a host of useless officers," making competition between parties a struggle "for place instead of principles."[48] Appointment of a weighmaster general in New York would not only limit trade but produce still another "band of placemen," like the patronage "army" in the post office.[49]

Leggett also spoke as a genus liberal. The government's "power of intermeddling with . . . private pursuits . . . may at pleasure elevate one class and depress another," thus violating the rights of the people.[50] The Whigs' great sin, in Leggett's eyes, was to favor a policy of "special privileges . . . which grants peculiar facilities to the opulent."[51] The results were illegitimate inequalities unrelated to real differences of ability and effort. In such a case, Leggett would regard as oppressive even the American republic he admired.[52]

Leggett's response to any policy of special privilege was his own version of the republican devotion to the public good. The evil was in the "frequent exercises of partial legislation"; therefore, there must be only general laws that treated every citizen in the same way. The same burden must be placed on the rich and poor alike. A graduated, direct tax (on property, for example) was thus superior to indirect taxes (import taxes, for example), because the latter discriminated in favor of some consumers against others.[53]

Unlike Jefferson, who more or less grudgingly supported government action if he thought the situation demanded it, Leggett did more than proscribe discriminatory government actions. He also went on to attack almost all government interventions in private life, except support for education.[54] In his view, the one sure "remedy" for all social ills was to "confine government within the narrowest limits of necessary duties."[55] His motto was simply: "*We are governed too much.*"[56] The state, of course, should protect "person[s] and property from domestic and foreign enemies" and establish the framework for "private business and pursuits."[57] Though it could proscribe fraud, the government could not legitimately regulate trade.[58] Protecting each individual "from the aggression of others" and

---

[48] Ibid., 23; see 26.
[49] Ibid., 313, 363.
[50] Ibid., 4, 23.
[51] Ibid., 256; cf. 5, 6, 244.
[52] Ibid., 20, 154; see White 1986.
[53] Leggett 1984, 3–6, 20–24, 38–41.
[54] Ibid., 39, 291.
[55] Ibid., 58.
[56] Ibid., 292.
[57] Ibid., 3, 8–9, 54–55, 32.
[58] Ibid., 123.

"punishing" the offenders did not mean assisting the victims of such aggression.[59] Compensation of victims would require taxes and would therefore punish—violate the rights of—those general taxpayers who had harmed no one.

Despite the belief of most other Jacksonians in states' rights, Leggett held that even state governments were prone to patronage abuses and the conferring of chartered monopolies. Nor should the states take care of the insane, rich or poor, lest governmental intermeddling have no end. Even pensions for revolutionary war veterans, including his own father, were unacceptable.[60] "The people ought not to . . . be led away by their sympathies. . . . The nearer they keep all power to their own hands . . . the more secure are they in their freedom and equal rights."[61] Indeed, Leggett wanted to privatize almost every species of public enterprise, including the post office, ferries, state prisons, and the military academy at West Point.[62]

Here was a seemingly republican standard with which to resist the "avid acquisitiveness," the lust for special governmental favors, that beset Jacksonian society. This version of laissez-faire required that citizens sacrifice some of their own objectives for the common welfare, specifically, that they sacrifice those preferences that involved government assistance to individuals in achieving their objectives. In effect, Leggett's republicanism added a moral dimension to his laissez-faire beliefs. Unsound taxes, he wrote in 1836, only "encourage lavish expenditure and . . . corruption."[63] Just as bad, government meddling in economic life would surely "promote excessive and luxurious refinement among a few," who would then become idle parasites.[64] Nevertheless, this same move also exhibited the tendency of the Jacksonians to dilute the republican creed; the prohibition Leggett asserted had a very restricted scope. Its object was to combat only those cases of excessive individual ambition, and lust for luxury, that relied on governmental assistance.

Leggett's Humanist Liberalism: Preferences and Process

At the same time that Leggett attenuated Jefferson's republicanism, he extenuated to a certain extent the Virginian's humanist liberal stress on the autonomy of individual preferences. Whereas Jefferson assigned a guiding political role to an intellectually gifted natural aristocracy, the New Yorker rejected any form of elite tutelage. "The prosperity of rational men," he

[59] Ibid., 44, 46–47.
[60] Ibid., 26, 75, 141, 292, 296ff.
[61] Ibid., 289–92.
[62] Ibid., 365, 303, 315, 42.
[63] Ibid., 41.
[64] Ibid., 50, 171.

wrote, "depends on themselves. Their talents and virtues shape their fortunes. They are therefore the best judges of their own affairs, and should be permitted to seek their own happiness in their own way."[65] Quite unlike Jefferson, who relied on an altruistic moral sense, Leggett held that "in its proper exercise," human selfishness "is the parent of all worldly good."[66]

This emphasis on satisfying the preferences of autonomous individuals led Leggett naturally to a vision of social life as a free, unconstrained process. "Society," as Leggett saw it, "is daily, hourly, momently, changing its constituent individuals. The particles which compose the stream of life are continually passing away to be succeeded by other[s]."[67] The social status and condition of individuals could also change. Claims to "hereditary distinction" amounted to little, for even the most presumptuous would-be aristocrats know that tomorrow "they themselves might be beggars . . . or at all events their children may become so."[68]

Leggett relied on such unconstrained processes because he took as their model the perfectly competitive market of political economists. "Democracy and political economy," he argued, "both assert the true dignity of man. They are both the natural champions of freedom, and the enemies of all restraints on the many for the benefit of the few."[69] Indeed the regular and legitimate operations of trade in a free market increased happiness and utility by adjusting, and thus promoting, equity and predictability in the allocation of goods and services.[70] Certainly, the harmonious operation of a free banking system would regulate trade much more satisfactorily than any government intervention.[71]

There were clear implications in these views for political action. Leggett recognized that because "men agree in their theory of Government, they must also agree to act in concert."[72] As chapter seven will show, the great organizational innovation of the Jacksonians was a system of cohesive parties whose competition would help coordinate voter preferences. Leggett shared traditional republicanism's distrust of parties. He had no use for party spoils, including patronage, and he thought party conflict was all too often marred by "immorality and licentiousness."[73] Moreover, he took his own principles too seriously to accept the compromises on issues that party organizations typically require to resolve conflicts among their members over preferences. As much as he admired Jackson and preferred the Demo-

---

[65] Ibid., 5.
[66] Ibid., 3.
[67] Ibid., 321.
[68] Ibid., 247.
[69] Ibid., 32; cf. 285.
[70] Ibid., 146, 118, 106–7, 308.
[71] Ibid., 128; cf. 54.
[72] Ibid., 33.
[73] Ibid., 57.

crats to the Whigs, Leggett intended his newspaper to "contend for men, as well as principles; but for the former as the means, and the latter as the object." Though he supported Van Buren in 1836, he would allow the new president "no deviation, however slight, from the straight and obvious path of democratic duty."[74] Exasperated by his attacks, Democratic leaders "excommunicated" him.[75]

Nevertheless, Leggett's trust in laissez-faire and social process carried with it a different type of solution to the problem of coordinating conflicting preferences. The whole matter of preference coordination became an issue only when it was necessary to form a stable majority to make choices among competing candidates or policy options. In the case of policies, laissez-faire ruled out just such coordination. Because only one policy option—government inaction—was typically legitimate, there was no need to resolve a conflict over what actions the government should take.

Leggett recognized, of course, that citizens would have conflicting objectives, even if none sought government help in resolving them. Here, market-type social processes offered a solution, even when the preferences were especially intense or extravagant. Monopolistic "combinations" that sought to control an economic market offered an excellent case in point. To begin with, Leggett's distaste for all governmental intermeddling meant that monopolistic combinations could not be forbidden legitimately. On the contrary, "men have a perfect natural right to do by combination, what they have a right to do by separate, unconcerted action."[76] Then again, some of these privately organized efforts had entirely legitimate goals, the collective efforts of workers, for example, to prevent employers from paying them with depreciated bank notes.[77]

More importantly, because markets and other social processes were inherently self-correcting, these combinations posed no real threat, even when they had unreasonable objectives. Whatever artificial gains might initially be achieved, even "extortionate and intolerant combinations" would be controlled "by the effect of competition and the influence of publick opinion."[78] Workers seeking extravagant wages or flour merchants trying to monopolize their product would be "answerable . . . to the inevitable penalties of a violation of the laws of trade."[79] In the end, then, coordination would be achieved because unreasonable claims would either have to be changed or else go unsatisfied.

---

[74] Ibid., 120.
[75] Rifkin 1951, 51; cf. Hofstadter 1943, 584.
[76] Leggett 1984, 379.
[77] Ibid., 85–86.
[78] Ibid., 348; cf. 44.
[79] Ibid., 110; cf. 336.

There was always some tension in Jefferson's thought between his belief that rationality and republican virtue should constrain individual conduct, and his utilitarian focus on satisfying individual desires. Leggett resolved this tension by following the lead of the political economists and giving free social processes a special importance. Thanks to such processes, Leggett argued, in good humanist liberal fashion, the pursuit of strictly private preferences regularly promoted the general good.

Most often, Leggett defended this claim in utilitarian terms by pointing to beneficent effects such processes produced, but he also offered an ultimately materialist rationale. Given a proper and rightful government, America would be "a nation founded as the hills, free as the air, and prosperous as fruitful soil, a genial climate, and industry, enterprise, temperance and intelligence can render us."[80] Like so many of his contemporaries, then, Leggett treated nature as a controlling moral standard and the source of equal rights. Rather than calling for "poems . . . heaped with elaborate ornaments of diction," he called for works that "breathe the unstudied sweetness of nature," and he identified progress with ever more closely approximating nature's "simple order."[81] Fortunately, this same natural order included free, market-like processes, "those natural principles of commercial intercourse which are called the laws of trade."[82] Citing a biography of Adam Smith, Leggett claimed that any government interference in private economic life would "disturb nature in the course of her operations with human affairs."[83] Even if "artificial" systems such as monarchy and aristocracy "produce a seeming . . . prosperity for a time . . . nature avenges her violated laws sooner or later."[84] Indeed, Leggett's ultimate objective was to have American life approximate just such self-regulating processes in order to secure progress, equity, and social peace. Here was the final element of his humanist liberalism. Leggett's argument for free social processes rested on a materialist claim about ultimate reality: free social processes were beneficial because they very closely resembled the physical processes of the natural world.

Slavery

Leggett's laissez-faire vision can be readily attacked, and defended, with by-now-familiar arguments. In his own time, as he came to see, any doctrine that emphasized rights and utility would meet its sternest test in its treat-

---

80 Ibid., 24.
81 Ibid., 179; cf. Meyers 1960, 186, 193–95.
82 Leggett 1984, 166.
83 Ibid., 37.
84 Ibid., 178.

ment of chattel slavery. At first, Leggett took the prosouthern stand of most northern Jacksonians. In 1834, he denounced "the . . . mad schemes of the immediate abolitionists," including their "revolting" advocacy of "promiscuous intermarriage."[85] At the very least, he thought, the assaults by the abolitionists on the South could be reduced if the United States postal system were to charge the abolitionists for the full cost of mailing their inflammatory tracts.[86] Not surprisingly, Leggett appealed to both rights and utility. Just as he admitted the rights of monopolies under still valid government charters, he recognized the "rights of the planters of the south" who had acquired their property without government help. There was also the welfare of the northern workers. If freed blacks moved north, they would depress wages, thereby enriching the business "aristocracy."[87] Rather than abolition, Leggett favored a plan of gradual colonization that would have included compensating the owners and sending the freed slaves to Africa.[88]

Leggett, however, preached his gospel of utility and equal rights with a rigor that few other Jacksonians could match. The very abstractness of his argument, his view of all individuals as bundles of rights and preferences, left him relatively uninterested in either racial differences or issues of implementation. In Leggett's case, the premises he shared with both Jefferson and other northern Jacksonians set him on a course in which he gradually shifted his fire from the abolitionists to their critics.

Like the conversions of many others to antislavery, Leggett's began with a concern for the rights of the white opponents of slavery. However "wild and visionary" the antislavery fanatics were, he wrote in 1834, their arguments must be met with "temperate argument and authentic facts." As a good consequentialist, Leggett argued that persecution of the abolitionists would only encourage more agitation from them.[89] More fundamentally, Leggett considered the abolitionists' "constitutional right of free discussion" to be "absolute."[90]

By late 1836, however, Leggett was writing of slavery's "enormous wickedness . . . [and] its pernicious influence on . . . the south."[91] In early 1837, he praised the abolitionists for saintly "purity of motive" and "loftier devotion."[92] Even "with sole reference to the test of utility" the institution

---

[85] Ibid., 191–92; cf. 194.
[86] Ibid., 199.
[87] Ibid., 195–96.
[88] Ibid., 192.
[89] Ibid.; cf. 49 and 198.
[90] Ibid., 198; cf. 34.
[91] Ibid., 34.
[92] Ibid., 216.

retarded the South's progress.[93] Worse, it made the slaves suffer, particularly by breaking up their families.[94] Worst of all, slavery violated the "natural equality of rights of all mankind," denying to the slaves both their liberty and control over what they produced.[95] Eventually Leggett insisted that the federal government had the authority to decide the fate of slavery in the District of Columbia—and he even insisted on the power of the people to call for stripping all protections of slavery from the Constitution.[96]

The importance of this shift in Leggett's stand deserves emphasis. Leggett became the Democrats' most outspoken foe of slavery during the 1830s—at a time, that is, when such a stand was a Jacksonian heresy.[97] Moreover, Leggett influenced many of the radical Jacksonians, who, after his death in 1839, joined the Free Soil and Republican parties.

There were, nevertheless, revealing gaps in Leggett's later stand. Although he professed himself an abolitionist in 1835, he promised at the same time to pursue slavery's end "by all means not inconsistent with higher duty."[98] Evidently this same duty required respect for the political rights of the South, for Leggett could only hope that by some "just and gradual measures of philanthropy their [the slaves'] fetters, one by one, may be unlocked."[99] As he wrote in his next editorial on the subject, the "highest obligation" was to discuss the institution "temperately but thoroughly."[100] Even in the essay in which he cited Congress's power over the District of Columbia and the people's power to amend the Constitution, Leggett did not actually call for any specific actions.[101] At one point, he did endorse the right of slaves to undertake armed rebellion, but in their condition of subjugation such a stand was of little practical use.[102] At another point, Leggett argued that if maintaining the Union meant "dismissing all hope of ultimate freedom to the slave; [then] let the compact be dissolved."[103] This dramatic step, however, as the ex-slave Frederick Douglass pointed out, would have left the slaves subjected to a political system entirely controlled by southern whites.

Douglass himself, of course, leveled this same charge of impracticality at the Garrisonian abolitionists, who actually preached disunion. Even many of those abolitionists who shunned political action felt free to assail slavery

---

[93] Ibid., 226.
[94] Ibid., 209.
[95] Ibid., 225, 192; cf. 229.
[96] Ibid., 227.
[97] Hofstadter 1943, 592.
[98] Leggett 1984, 206–7.
[99] Ibid., 210.
[100] Ibid., 212.
[101] Ibid., 227.
[102] White 1986, 318; Leggett 1984, 230.
[103] Leggett 1984, 211.

without sharing Leggett's concern for southern sensibilities. Douglass's indictment, however, did not apply at all to the political abolitionists with whom he himself was affiliated. Their position, moderated by the Republican party, was eventually reflected in Lincoln's determination to have the Union itself pass moral judgment on slavery, a step contrary to Leggett's strong inclinations to restrict the scope of government.

Leggett's regard for southern sensibilities can be attributed in part to four features of the radical Jacksonian and humanist liberal creed that Leggett had fashioned so carefully. Although the creed encouraged a cast of mind that made his inclination more difficult to follow, these four features by no means logically precluded an open political or moral attack on slavery, since some of Leggett's own Jacksonian admirers later made their way into the Republican party.

The first of these features was Leggett's continuing Jacksonian aversion to mixing morals and government coercion, even though he saw slavery as a moral issue. Two examples provide evidence of this continuing aversion. First, as much as Leggett despised gambling, he nevertheless opposed all government efforts to stop it. "Public opinion"—the "moral sense of the community"—he noted, was "the great and only salutary corrective" for activities such as gambling.[104] The second example is provided in an editorial written well after Leggett had acknowledged his abolitionist leanings. In it he suggested the case of a poor fisherman, who could "rescue a hundred men from certain death" but would not "do so unless each promised to pay him his weight in gold." In this case, too, the correct remedy was not government enforcement but "publick opinion" and the fisherman's "own notions of humanity."[105] If government coercion was inappropriate in a case involving life itself, it would be equally problematic in the case of slavery. In this case as well, there should presumably be a reliance on "publick opinion" and the slave owners' "notions of humanity."[106]

The second of these features was a celebration of the natural processes of the market in which Leggett largely overlooked the possibility of purely *social* exploitation. As White and Hofstadter have pointed out, Leggett had a theory of political rather than social class conflict. Accordingly, structured inequalities were unacceptable only if produced by government actions.[107] He had no complaint, for example, against the rich or successful if their prosperity had been secured through their own efforts.[108] To be sure, he despised the "kidnapper on the coast of Africa," whose illegal actions started

---

[104] Ibid., 311.
[105] Ibid., 349.
[106] Ibid., 213.
[107] White 1986, 318–19; Hofstadter 1943, 588–89.
[108] Leggett 1984, 261; cf. Meyers 1960, 192.

the slave trade;[109] yet, according to Leggett's position, slave owners who had purchased their chattel legally and did not benefit from government charters presumably belonged in a different, less offensive category.

Third, Leggett's enthusiasm for self-regulating processes indicated a desire for social harmony rather than conflict.[110] For all the asperity of his own rhetoric, he disliked partisan strife. For all his sympathy for the weak and poor, he regarded mob violence, even against extortionate merchants, as "disgraceful."[111] This same attitude evidently encouraged "a spirit of conciliation and compromise," indeed, of "brotherhood and national amity," with the South.[112] Such a spirit, according to Leggett, could apparently legitimately limit the discussion on the slavery issue. It was just such limits that even moderate Whigs like Lincoln later denounced.[113]

Finally, Leggett had an essentially static vision of both individual and society. Hofstadter has noted that Leggett "had no conception of history as an evolutionary process."[114] Though not explicitly opposed to industrial progress, Leggett did not advocate a dynamic role for entrepreneurs or call for a more complex capitalist order. For him, freedom was "an investment in the familiar and reliable."[115] So, too, he rejected a dynamic conception of the individual personality. Instead, his emphasis on social processes assumed the utility of *existing* preferences and the equal right that all individuals had to try to satisfy those preferences. The Whig position, in contrast, emphasized the development of an individual's faculties and skills. Moreover, the Whigs believed that the process of improving their abilities and understandings might well lead the individuals concerned to change their preferences. Leggett evidently detested this view, because it valued the preferences of some individuals over those of others, and it therefore seemed to license interference in private social and economic affairs. In any case, Leggett's discussions of convict labor concentrated on its impact on the economic situation of particular citizens, while ignoring the question of the redeeming or transforming effect such work might conceivably have on the convicts themselves.[116]

Most antislavery activists invoked the Whigs' developmental view in justifying their attack on an institution as vital and entrenched as slavery. To them, slavery was a sin because it denied the slaves the opportunity to develop their God-given abilities at the same time it deformed the moral

---

[109] Leggett 1984, 263.
[110] See ibid., 335.
[111] Ibid., 43.
[112] Ibid., 202.
[113] Johannsen 1965, 300–322.
[114] Hofstadter 1943, 593.
[115] Meyers 1960, 194–95, 191–92.
[116] Leggett 1984, 316–17.

capacities of the masters. The abolitionists believed, therefore, that the preferences of southern whites could be justly ignored. For all Leggett's disgust with slavery, he could never quite adopt an attitude that would legitimate meddling in so much of private life.

These several concerns reveal a common theme: Leggett's willingness to expand upon his genuinely critical stand on slavery was limited at every point by his consideration for individual autonomy and his suspicions of all but the most minimal government interventions in private life. By the mid-1830s, Leggett's critique of slavery certainly went well beyond anything Jefferson had ever asserted publicly after the 1780s. Yet there were similarities between the positions of the two men. Although both men thought the institution bad in principle, each had trouble translating those feelings into concrete programs of action. In both cases, their difficulty in advocating government action was supported by their political principles. The source and character of each man's ambivalence, however, were very different. Jefferson's attack on the institution invoked a rationalist and republican concern with individual virtue. The "unremitting despotism" of masters over their slaves, he complained, subverted self-control and self-restraint.[117] Moreover, Jefferson always left room for government action if it could eliminate social ills or accomplish social goods. He therefore defended his shift to a protective attitude toward slavery in terms of a conflict between the slaves' right to liberty and the owners' right to life and property. In addition, as we have noted, Jefferson's argument rested on certain humanist liberal premises, notably on a materialist and empiricist account of racial differences and on utilitarian claims about the costs of emancipation.

Leggett, however, came to have little if any use for such arguments. He saw slavery as plainly inconsistent with the idea of equal rights and as too harmful to be justified by any utilitarian defense. Nevertheless, his hesitancies on the slavery question did reflect his humanist liberalism. In effect, his devotion to the sovereignty of individual preferences left almost no room for virtue or morality—or the government—to play a role in solving social problems. For Leggett, the use by a government of its coercive powers, even in the form of taxes, to advance some moral vision would surely be calamitous. Even though Leggett denounced the selfishness of his contemporaries, he did not believe that the remedy for that selfishness lay primarily in the moralistic reactions of fellow citizens. The solution lay rather in the restoration of social equilibrium by the equally self-regarding, but counter-vailing, behavior of others—behavior that would make such transgressions unprofitable. Charity and altruism had to be essentially individual, private matters.

The slavery issue, however, could not be addressed by the restoration of a

[117] Koch and Peden 1944, 278.

social equilibrium. Restoring an equilibrium, or even modifying it slightly, meant leaving the institution largely intact. Although self-interest eventually mobilized some Northerners against the institution, it had not motivated the more radical opponents of slavery who first forced the issue onto the political agenda, thus goading Southerners into responses that eventually alienated more moderate Northerners. For the antislavery militants, the decisive considerations were ethical: first, a determination to follow a moral code that stressed the welfare of others, rather than one's own; and, second, a willingness to carry the struggle into public life by insisting that the government adopt their moral stand. Leggett came to oppose slavery vehemently, but his opposition was rooted firmly in humanist liberal principles. In his rejection of these two ethical considerations in the militants' stance, Leggett's views converged with those of Jacksonians, such as Stephen A. Douglas, who denounced abolitionism root and branch.

SIX

STEPHEN A. DOUGLAS AND
POPULAR SOVEREIGNTY

W ILLIAM LEGGETT'S problems with slavery anticipated the difficulties slavery eventually posed for all of Jackson's northern followers. Among those followers, none paid more attention to the issue than Lincoln's great opponent in Illinois, Stephen A. Douglas. Douglas's solution to the problem of slavery was popular sovereignty, the doctrine that the white voters of each state and federal territory should decide for themselves on the issue of slavery. As Douglas readily acknowledged, the doctrine had been introduced into the national debate by his fellow Democrat, Lewis Cass, but Cass's other interests had led to his appointment as secretary of state, a position not directly concerned with slavery policy, in the critical period from 1857 to 1860.[1] Douglas, as one biographer has written, thus became the "peculiar guardian" of popular sovereignty.[2] For Douglas, the doctrine was "a theory of government, a prescription for settling territorial questions, a framework . . . [for settling] disputes over slavery, and a philosophical extension" of his own "political personality."[3]

Because the issue of slavery could so easily divide major sections of the country against each other, the objective of the doctrine of popular sovereignty was to remove slavery from the national agenda and leave the decision about it to state and local majorities. The objective was not, of course, to have local and state majorities make separate decisions on genuinely national issues, on those for which advocates on all sides could be found in each section.[4] Douglas said at Galesburg in 1858, "If Illinois will settle the slavery question for herself, and mind her own business, and let her neighbors alone, we will be at peace."[5] In contrast, the polemics of the Republicans, he noted, did much to encourage divisive outrages such as John Brown's raid at Harper's Ferry.[6]

[1] Douglas 1860a, 49; Wells 1971, 58–59; Johannsen 1960, 384. References to Douglas 1860a and 1860b are to *The Life and Speeches*. The book comprises two volumes that are bound as one but are paginated separately.

[2] Johannsen 1960, 382–83.

[3] Wells 1971, 56.

[4] Douglas 1860b, 143.

[5] Johannsen 1965, 218–19.

[6] Douglas 1860a, 252ff.

As Jaenicke has observed, popular sovereignty offered the safety of pro-
ceduralism.[7] The doctrine appealed to moderates everywhere, because it
emphasized the prerogatives of local majorities rather than calling for any
evaluation of slavery itself. Douglas bolstered this appeal with additional
appeals to general usefulness and precedent. In the case of internal improvements, for example, he argued on behalf of an active role by state governments, where the people wanted it, as a middle path between the federal
programs supported by Whigs and Leggett's laissez-faire.[8] Popular sovereignty was also sanctioned by precedent. Jefferson's Northwest Ordinance,
for example—despite its explicit provisions to the contrary—had not actually excluded slavery in Indiana and Illinois.[9] Slavery persisted in both states
until the two legislatures expressly abolished it. Further, the Missouri Compromise, which outlawed slavery in the northern Louisiana Purchase, was
not a true intersectional compact, because, in fact, most northern legislators
voted against the Compromise of 1820.[10]

In any case, Douglas continued to support the doctrine of popular sover-
eignty until the onset of secession. In 1848, Douglas broke with the former
leader of his party, Martin Van Buren, when the New Yorker opposed any
expansion of slavery.[11] In 1850, Douglas arranged for the organization of
Utah and New Mexico as states without reference to slavery. In 1854, his
Kansas-Nebraska Act explicitly repealed the antislavery provisions of the
Missouri Compromise. Subsequently, he denounced Kansas's proslavery
Lecompton Constitution because, and only because, most white settlers
clearly opposed it.[12] The doctrine, Douglas's principle, was the centerpiece
of his successful campaign against Lincoln for the Senate in 1858 and of his
unsuccessful race against Lincoln for the presidency in 1860.

Jacksonian Politics and Humanist Liberalism

Douglas's devotion to local majority rights was linked to his Jacksonian
belief in equality. Jackson and the Democratic party, he thought, had per-
petuated Jefferson's crusade on behalf of the interests of the people against
an aristocracy of money and birth.[13] Like other Democrats, Douglas extended his egalitarianism to include immigrant aliens; he supported not
only their right to vote even before they became citizens but also the demo-

[7] Jaenicke 1986, 100.
[8] Johannsen 1973, 342–43.
[9] Johannsen 1961, 292–93; Douglas 1860a, 46, 47; Douglas 1860b, 86.
[10] Douglas 1860a, 106–22.
[11] Johannsen 1961, 84, 157.
[12] Douglas 1860a, 114–15, 118–19, 128; Johannsen 1961, 386–87, 403.
[13] Johannsen 1961, 14, 28, 42–44, 84; Douglas 1860a, 27.

cratic struggles of white people everywhere, notably of those in Hungary.[14] Douglas himself epitomized the Jacksonian's egalitarian ideal of the self-made man. Arriving in Illinois almost penniless in 1833, he had become a justice of the Illinois Supreme Court just eight years later at the age of twenty-eight. Elected to the House of Representatives in 1843, Douglas was soon chairing a major committee. In 1847, he entered the United States Senate, where he headed its Territories Committee until 1859, and he won his party's presidential nomination in 1860.

Except on internal improvements, where regional interests dictated some flexibility, Douglas also followed his party's line on other issues.[15] He admired Jackson's attack on the Bank of the United States, and he generally affirmed a strict constitutional construction to limit the powers of the federal government.[16] He also celebrated the independence of a republican citizenry, exemplified by independent farmers, and he insisted on a separation of church and state.[17] Finally, Douglas accepted Van Buren's demand that Democrats abide by the decisions of their party's conventions. Confusion and lack of discipline, he held, would only cripple the party's efforts to represent the people's interests.[18] Especially in his presidential campaign in 1860, he worried about the party's unity almost as much as about national unity.[19] Northern Jacksonians repaid Douglas's loyalty by supporting him throughout the struggle that eventually led to his presidential nomination.[20] At the height of the secession crisis, citizens and editorialists alike turned to him as their party's true leader and the champion of national unity.[21]

Douglas's Jacksonianism, however, cannot fully explain his popularity. By the late 1850s, he himself regarded the Jacksonian heritage as a wasting asset, largely because the party's positions on economic issues had lost much of their relevance.[22] Douglas, in fact, also espoused the more fundamental values of humanist liberalism. To begin with, he insisted on self-determination, on each person's formulating and acting on her or his own preferences without the tutelage of some divinely inspired and broadly shared moral standard.[23] As a young man, he thought that individuals must be free to choose their own occupations, including occupations in the liquor trade, though the latter was "in these days of Temperance not very honor-

[14] Douglas 1860a, 101; cf. 222–24; Johannsen 1973, 329–30; cf. 63, 83.
[15] Johannsen 1961, 67–68, 114, 273, 275; cf. Johannsen 1973, viii, 53.
[16] Johannsen 1961, 9, 29; Johannsen 1973, 52.
[17] Douglas 1851, 3, 8–9; Johannsen 1961, 318.
[18] Johannsen 1961, 25–27; Douglas 1860a, 88; Johannsen 1973, 26–28, 38–43.
[19] Johannsen 1973, 41, 42, 67; cf. Wells 1971, 246.
[20] Johannsen 1973, 738; cf. Wells 1971, 52.
[21] Johannsen 1973, 381, 383, 388–90.
[22] Johannsen 1965, 37, 187.
[23] Douglas 1860b, 27; Wells 1971, 127; Johannsen 1961, 311–13.

able, particularly among your Eastern People."[24] During the slavery controversy, he conceded that the law of God might speak to each individual privately; however, that eventuality did not authorize the recipients of such divine messages to issue moralistic instructions to others—still less did it justify attacks on provisions of the Constitution that were quite clearly stated.[25]

For Douglas, in other words, politics was primarily a matter of interests rather than morals. Because the responsibility of politicians was to accommodate these interests as equitably as possible, the test of a policy was consequentialist, or, as he put it, "qui bono?"[26] Douglas's consequentialism had a utilitarian cast. As he wrote in 1834, Illinois was likely to supply "all that can be made subservient to the wants, and that can conduce to the comfort and happiness of man."[27] He once commended agriculture as an occupation both "dignified and pleasurable."[28] He himself drank liquor freely, threw rather lavish parties, and, despite a substantial private income, sometimes lived beyond his means.[29]

Because individual preferences were primary for Douglas, rationality was instrumental. Even if goals could not be challenged, there was always the question of means or effectiveness. In politics, for example, Douglas shared the Jacksonian belief in hard money, but only as a means to promote the economic development of Illinois. When circumstances changed, he supported a state bank. So, too, he supported practical innovations in agriculture, and he evinced a spirit of experiment, inquiry, and inventiveness that was to be stimulated by one of his favorite projects, the Smithsonian Institution.[30]

Douglas approached the doctrine of popular sovereignty in the same terms of effectiveness. Even if national government could legally assert a uniform slavery policy for the territories, it lacked the means for enforcement.[31] In practice, neither Congress nor even the Supreme Court could impose such a policy on an unwilling population.[32] Similarly, slave owners might have the right to bring their slaves into any federal territory, but state and local governments had the powers, including that of taxation, to drive the slave owners out.[33]

---

24 Johannsen 1961, 19.
25 Douglas 1860b, 27–28; Douglas 1860a, 260–61.
26 Douglas 1860b, 185; Douglas 1860a, 154, 157; cf. Johannsen 1967, 34.
27 Johannsen 1961, 7.
28 Douglas 1851, 4.
29 Wells 1971, 139; Johannsen 1973, 690, 620.
30 Douglas 1851, 4–6, 22–25, 31; Johannsen 1973, 466–67.
31 Johannsen 1965, 29–30.
32 Johannsen 1973, 571; Johannsen 1965, 207, 210, 288, 298.
33 Dickerson 1913–1914, 202–3; Wells 1971, 119–21, 151–52, 222.

Popular sovereignty was also useful for Douglas himself. Throughout his political career, he had systematically courted the South. He repeatedly denounced abolitionism—making reference to "separate, distinct, and fanatical parts, called Abolitionists"—and cast an antiabolitionist vote in the Illinois legislature; he supported the gag rule against antislavery petitions in the House of Representatives; and he voted in the Senate for strong fugitive slave laws.[34] Above all, the doctrine of popular sovereignty reopened the question of the possible settlement by slave holders of the northern Louisiana Purchase, from which slavery had been excluded by the Missouri Compromise. Not surprisingly, many southern Jacksonians repaid Douglas by supporting his presidential candidacy at the 1856 Democratic convention.

Nevertheless, Douglas needed the support of the North at least as much as he needed that of the South.[35] Popular sovereignty was thus particularly useful, because he could also depict it as a device for arresting the spread of slavery. In the first place, because most of the west was inhospitable to slave-grown crops, few Southerners were likely to move there and be eligible to vote for slavery.[36] Second, Douglas held that the old Mexican law against slavery still applied, at least in California, until the people in each locale explicitly decided otherwise; the implicit ban thus further discouraged the migration of Southerners.[37] Finally, the North was so much more populous than the South by the 1850s that northern migrants to the western territories were very likely to outnumber southern migrants.[38]

Douglas understood that the uncertain impact of his doctrine made it all the more useful. During the Kansas-Nebraska debates, he refused to say exactly when the people of a territory could exclude slavery—before statehood (thus discouraging a southern migration before it started), or at the point of statehood itself (thus encouraging an increase in the number of southern migrants). Recognizing the ambiguity, his southern friends demanded a federal code that would protect slavery in the territories before statehood.[39] Douglas's response was unsatisfying: they must rely on the federal courts to enforce their rights.[40]

If Douglas was indisputably a humanist liberal, he nevertheless had obvious differences with William Leggett. The most obvious of the differences was the Illinois politician's rejection of laissez-faire. State governments, Douglas believed, should act not just to promote internal improvements

---

[34] Johannsen 1961, 79–80, 84, 255; Johannsen 1973, 54–55; Douglas 1860a, 57, 54; Douglas 1860b, 166–67.

[35] Douglas 1860a, 216.

[36] Johannsen 1961, 182, 289.

[37] Johannsen 1973, 275–76.

[38] Ibid., 279.

[39] Dickerson 1913–1914, 201, 209–10; Johannsen, 1967, 37.

[40] Johannsen 1965, 31–32; Johannsen 1967, 39.

but also to regulate marriage and alcohol consumption—and slavery as well. Because the powers of the government in these matters were clearly legitimate in Douglas's eyes, the appropriateness of a policy depended entirely on what the people of a particular locale happened to prefer.[41] Nor was he concerned about the liberties of the minorities on such issues. "Coercion," he remarked during the secession crisis, "is the vital principle upon which all Government rests."[42]

Douglas's stand on laissez-faire, however, did not make him any less a humanist liberal. Almost all liberal theorists have recognized that individuals must be restrained when they threaten the legitimate rights and interests of others. More to the point, although Douglas focused on the liberty of particular communities rather than of individuals, he still defined that liberty in negative terms. Each community, he insisted, had a right to decide about slavery for itself, without outside "meddling" or "interference."[43] He argued that the "right [of popular sovereignty for states] was conferred with the understanding and expectation that inasmuch as each locality had separate interests, each locality must have different and distinct local and domestic institutions, corresponding to its wants and interests."[44] No matter how excellent it might be, outsiders had no right to impose an institution or practice on others.[45] Finally, and most importantly, Douglas applied the doctrine, which served as his principle, to just those issues on which most states and communities were united internally but differed radically from each other. As a result of the internal unity, the governments would have to coerce only a few dissenters, thus maximizing the number allowed to enjoy a negative liberty.

Douglas's Attenuated Republicanism

For all his devotion to negative liberty, however, Douglas expressed little of Leggett's concern about the "avidity" or acquisitiveness of the Jacksonians. His adopted state, he remarked in 1845, was the place for people "who wish to change their condition."[46] A man of "capital . . . can make money with or without work."[47] Nevertheless, popular sovereignty did have a republican side, although it was a republicanism very different from Leggett's view of

[41] Douglas 1860b, 144; see Douglas 1859, 531.
[42] Johannsen 1973, 820.
[43] Johannsen 1965, 24–27, 300, 73.
[44] Ibid., 288.
[45] Douglas 1860a, 120–21; Johannsen 1965, 292.
[46] Johannsen 1961, 131.
[47] Ibid., 23.

republicanism. Whereas Leggett stressed republican autonomy, Douglas emphasized a republican devotion to the political community.

Through his form of republicanism, Douglas revealed the influence of his adopted region. Whereas he and Lincoln were both self-made men of the west, they traveled opposite cultural paths. Born to a frontier, border-state family, Lincoln looked to the northeast, and to the civility and education of the Whigs. Douglas was reared in Vermont and "found Jacksonville's New England atmosphere congenial." His "real affinity," his biographer added, "was with the farmers of the countryside . . . [rather than with] trans-planted New Englanders."[48] Along with the farmers, Douglas became a confirmed nationalist whose constant objective was both to preserve and to expand the Union. Almost all northern Jacksonians were expansionists, but those in thinly settled and less economically developed areas were especially devoted to a strong, growing union. It would not only protect them as a nation militarily and secure them access to the Gulf of Mexico for their farm products, but it would help build the railroads that would link them to eastern markets.

Douglas's own "vision," as Johannsen has observed, "was always directed toward a greater and stronger America."[49] His goal, Douglas announced, was a nation that would reach from ocean to ocean.[50] Indeed, his demand for the annexation of all of Oregon was "a matter of deep conviction, reflecting . . . [the] emotional expansionism and wild Anglophobia" of his section, a conviction that also appealed to Irish Democrats.[51] Douglas thus supported acquiring Texas and even Cuba for the South, as well as Oregon for the North.[52] His major achievements as a congressman and senator—helping to develop new railroads, and to organize a number of federal territories and admit several new states—were all specifically western goals.[53]

Douglas's nationalism also, however, reflected a broader loyalty common to Jacksonians. While he affirmed the nation's providential character—in the idiom of the Jacksonians, its manifest destiny to expand—he also celebrated its other achievements and prospects.[54] He reveled in the industrial development that had spread to Chicago from the northeast by 1850. He prized Americans' solidarity with each other, and he declared the people of

[48] Johannsen 1973, 24; see Johannsen 1960, 380, and Johannsen 1967, 29.
[49] Johannsen 1973, 304; Douglas 1860a, 40–41.
[50] Douglas 1860b, 50–52; Johannsen 1973, 142.
[51] Johannsen 1973, 179, 167.
[52] Johannsen 1973, 144, 528; Wells 1971, 154; Johannsen 1961, 119, 473; Douglas 1860a, 185; on the northern expansion see Johannsen 1973, 172, 178.
[53] Johannsen 1960, 381–82; Johannsen 1963, 233.
[54] Johannsen 1965, 105.

all sections his brethren.[55] He also lavishly praised the economic interdependence that tied the sections together.[56] From his perspective, a doctrine that removed the apple of discord from national politics had compelling virtues.

Nevertheless, once secession began, Douglas's nationalism led him to abandon the doctrine of popular sovereignty. He sought first to woo the South by supporting a new proslavery version of the Missouri Compromise. When this effort failed, he made his last great speech, sternly upholding the ultimate authority of the Union, including its powers of coercion.[57] His error, Douglas thought, had been in tilting too far in favor of the South.[58]

Douglas's oscillation between conciliation and coercion was related to a basic tension within his overall stand. Although his support for popular sovereignty emphasized decision-making by local majorities, his overriding goal remained the preservation of union. Underlying this tension was Douglas's republican devotion to the prerogatives of political communities, national and local alike. As a radical individualist, Leggett was able to contemplate the break up of the Union over slavery. Douglas, however, not only did all he could to save the Union, he also affirmed at the same time the power and prerogatives of states and territorial majorities.

Douglas's presumption in favor of the political majorities of all communities was also partly a response to his experiences in the west. Many rural Americans relied on political communities, because as individuals they were too personally isolated to depend entirely on voluntary cooperation for what they needed. It was not enough to rely, as Leggett did, on the actions and countervailing reactions of particular individuals. In a more contemporary idiom, the limited development of their region sensitized westerners to their need for public goods—from roads and schools to law and order—for which government action was necessary. The doctrine of popular sovereignty thus was a reflection of the character of western life. As one of Douglas's biographers put it, the doctrine's "essential ingredients—localism and majority rule—were basic to the whole political experience of the frontier."[59]

In these matters, of course, the west only exaggerated what was already a national pattern. As Tocqueville had noted with some concern, if the individualism of Americans meant self-reliance, it also meant loneliness, vulnerability, and even dependence on others. In effect, by granting broad

---

[55] Douglas 1860a, 156.

[56] Douglas 1851, 10–11.

[57] Douglas 1860a, 42–43; Douglas 1860b, 89; Johannsen 1973, 814ff.; Johannsen 1960, 45.

[58] Johannsen 1963, 245–46; Johannsen 1961, 500, 512; Johannsen 1973, 820, 865–66.

[59] Wells 1971, 57; see Johannsen 1960, 380; Johannsen 1973, 240.

powers to the states and territories, Douglas expressed his version of the republican ambivalence of Jacksonians toward the unlimited individualism they themselves asserted. As much as Douglas sought the satisfaction of individual preferences, he insisted on subordinating the self to the collectivity, that is, to the decision of the majority, when individual desires threatened national unity.

Douglas's republicanism was in fact doubly attenuated. In the first place, whereas Leggett's laissez-faire proscribed only those preferences that called for government action, Douglas's version of popular sovereignty banned only those preferences that endangered union. Second, the trouble with these preferences was not that they were *intrinsically* self-regarding; Douglas himself expressed no great worry about the pursuit of luxury or of material welfare as such. Whereas others debated the morality of slavery, Douglas expressly and purposely avoided the issue. He offered instead an essentially consequentialist, even functionalist, account of slavery, in which the crucial issue was the effect of a preference on the polity. Policy demands were benign, whatever their content, if they could easily be reconciled by compromise, or if they were already consensual enough to leave the community relatively undisturbed. In that way, Douglas's remedy, like Leggett's, did not rely on self-restraint; rather, what counted was not what preferences people held but how preferences were distributed. In particular, any preferences about slavery were acceptable as long as their distribution allowed local units to implement them consensually.

Preference Coordination

As with other Jacksonians, then, Douglas's humanist liberal concern with coordinating preferences in order to satisfy as many of them as possible dominated his republican concern with self-restraint. A telling illustration of this domination is the way in which the doctrine of popular sovereignty transformed Jefferson's position on states' rights. Douglas himself, to be sure, praised the position that Jefferson had taken on states' rights in the Virginia Resolution.[60] Douglas recognized the place that rights held in any liberal theory, including the space those rights created for individual enterprise and initiative; and, in 1839, he paid homage to "the inalienable rights of man—political equality, freedom of thought, of speech, and of conscience."[61] Jefferson's position, however, had been essentially negative and defensive; he had sought to protect individual autonomy by limiting the power of the federal government, and, over time, his focus had changed. Douglas, as Wells put it, "did not so much deny the existence of natural

[60] Douglas 1860a, 251ff.; cf. Douglas 1860b, 160.
[61] Johannsen 1973, 74.

rights as he thought it [prudent] . . . not to insist fully on each and every one of them in practice."[62] Instead of natural rights, Douglas typically referred to rights established by, and within, a specific political community, such as the rights of Englishmen invoked by American colonists in the 1770s. In contrast to communally established rights, prepolitical individual rights—those rooted in nature or divine law—were a threat to national unity.[63] Accordingly, Douglas rejected both the natural right of slaves to liberty and southern claims about the right to property. In the 1850s, "isolated individuals" could not rightfully take slaves into a federal territory against the wishes of the people of that territory, just as British merchants had no right to import African slaves into America in defiance of colonial legislatures.[64]

Douglas also understood that the slavery issue cut too deeply to be resolved without appeal to a basic ethical maxim. In the terms of the Declaration of Independence, he emphasized less the rights of individual dissenters than the consent of the governed—a consent that manifested itself through a process of majority rule.[65] Although very late in his career Douglas defended his doctrine by appealing to constitutional provisions and prior colonial precedents,[66] he more frequently and more effectively talked of majority rule.[67] During most of the 1850s, Douglas repeatedly proclaimed the "exclusive right of a free people . . . to manage and regulate their own internal affairs and domestic institutions"; in short, the "great principle of self-government" on which the Union was formed.[68] Popular sovereignty was a political as well as a moral principle. Morally, it held that the rightness or wrongness of slavery in a particular area depended on the views of the white male electorate. Politically, given the uneven distribution of white preferences in different sections of the country, popular sovereignty promised to resolve the nation's most troublesome issues through the normal workings of the democratic process.

Popular sovereignty thus did more than assert the priority of individual preferences. It also provided a method and principled rationale for the coordination of preferences among individuals. For the Jacksonians, the problem of preference coordination came to this: how could a democratic citizenry agree on some single policy, when they had widely differing and

[62] Wells 1971, 128.

[63] Douglas 1860b, 179–80.

[64] Douglas 1859, 537, 522.

[65] Cf. Douglas 1860b, 28.

[66] Cf. Johannsen 1965, 292; I am grateful to Diane Rothleder for making this point to me.

[67] Only in 1859 and 1860 did Douglas wholly adopt the argument that the Constitution precluded federal regulation on this issue. See Douglas 1859, 531, 520–21, 525, 526–27.

[68] Johannsen 1965, 22; cf. Johannsen 1961, 185.

intensely conflicting sets of preferences, especially about slavery? Leggett's was a very general solution, one that made the divergence of preferences irrelevant, because his solution eliminated the possibility of different policy options and permitted only the single policy option of minimal government action. In contrast, Douglas's popular sovereignty offered a particular solution directed only at those issues where the problem was most troublesome. Douglas's remedy, that is, looked to constituencies where one and only one preference mattered. If jurisdictions could be found in which the voters were nearly unanimous on a single preference, there would be no coordination problem, because there would be no divergent preferences to reconcile.

Slavery

One of Douglas's biographers has noted that Douglas assailed slavery in private conversations because it was "alien" to his "instinctive sense of justice."[69] Certainly, a wide cultural gulf separated him from his southern allies. It was not just his "Vermont background. . . . The South was agrarian [and leisurely], while Douglas stood for the advancing forces of industrialization . . . [and] seemed to worship action."[70] However, precisely because it failed to censure the immorality of the institution, popular sovereignty helped Douglas exploit the racism that pervaded his country and his party. Moreover, this lack of moral concern reflected Douglas's own interests and sentiments. Financially, Douglas depended on the labor of the more than one hundred slaves he had inherited from his first wife in 1853.[71] Although he insisted on kind treatment of them, he granted blacks only the charity owed to a dependent population. He repeatedly described them as his natural inferiors, assailed the very idea of intermarriage, and denied that they had any rights under the Declaration of Independence.[72]

The link between popular sovereignty and Douglas's racial attitudes was his devotion to cohesive political communities. As he said repeatedly, the United States was a white political community, "established . . . for the benefit of white men," with only a subordinate role for people of color.[73] Douglas regarded native American Indians, for example, as an obstacle to national progress, and especially to territorial expansion.[74] He therefore

[69] Wells 1971, 108.

[70] Ibid., 142.

[71] Johannsen 1973, 211, 337–38.

[72] Johannsen 1961, 433–34; Johannsen 1965, 46, 216, 299; Johannsen 1973, 571; Johannsen 1965, 33–34, 46, 196, 215–16.

[73] Douglas 1860a, 154.

[74] Johannsen 1961, 270.

endorsed Jackson's policy of Indian removal.[75] While in Congress, Douglas moved to eliminate Indian land titles in much of the west.[76]

Douglas's support for popular sovereignty was therefore overdetermined: the doctrine expressed his racial feelings and his personal interests, as well as his belief in his nation, its local communities, and majority rule. The very intensity and depth of his commitment led him to overlook difficulties that were political as much as moral. One difficulty, of course, was the obvious tension between his nationalist goal and his localist means. If the local or state majorities in which Douglas put his trust had intense but opposing preferences about *national* policies, then the problem of coordinating preferences would not only persist, but Douglas's stress on local majorities would actually make things worse. As he himself noted, opinions on slavery in most areas were generally one way or the other, and the emphasis on these local opinions encouraged ambitious politicians to articulate and even foster the extreme views of their constituents. The result was just that clash of moralistic politics that Douglas sought to avoid. Moreover, at least one locale, Kansas, was itself sharply divided. As Lincoln kept reminding Douglas, allowing Kansas to decide on slavery for itself had produced a bitter conflict responsible for inflaming the entire nation.

One of Douglas's problems was political: how to defend a middle ground from erosion by sectional polarization. Another of his problems was ethical and intellectual, and it grew directly out of a humanist liberal outlook, in which Jefferson's philosophic materialism had been converted into a materialist interpretation of social and political life. In Douglas's view, material interests were important enough that, in 1861, he tried to distract both sections from the slavery controversy by proposing a free trade zone throughout the continent.[77] As for slavery itself, if he sometimes compared the issue to a decision about alcohol or family relations, he just as frequently treated it as an essentially economic matter. A major warrant for popular sovereignty was that slave labor was more suitable in some natural settings than others. Local communities must make their own key economic decisions about what crops to grow, what goods to produce, and what form of labor to use, because each locale's climate, soil, and so forth made some economic practices much more profitable than others.[78] There were certain natural laws, then, that human beings could ignore only at their cost.[79] By stressing these natural laws, Douglas connected narrow economic self-interest to the physical differences between regions.[80]

[75] Ibid., 29.
[76] Douglas 1860a, 43.
[77] Wells 1971, 268–69.
[78] Douglas 1859, 522–23; cf. Johannsen 1965, 288.
[79] Douglas 1860b, 89.
[80] Wells 1971, 9, 64–65; cf. 95; Johannsen 1965, 29, 44; Douglas 1860b, 170.

These natural laws mattered to Douglas because of his trust in the instrumental rationality of the people; in their ability, that is, to select the most profitable course of action given their local circumstances.[81] Implicitly affirming Jefferson's reliance on direct sensory knowledge, Douglas held that the people on the scene had the immediate experience and thus the requisite information to make instrumentally correct decisions.[82] In Illinois, such observations and reasoning produced a popular decision against slavery. In the South, different conditions led equally rational citizens to opposite conclusions.[83] In such instances humanist liberalism became strongly deterministic. Leggett had argued that excessive individual demands would be counteracted by the metaphorically "natural" processes of the market, but he assumed that the individuals involved would freely adopt whatever preferences they wished. For Douglas, an area's natural features determined what policy would benefit a particular people, and, given their instrumental rationality, what policies such individuals would then prefer.[84]

This approach—making explicit the connection between natural regional differences and instrumental reasoning—exacerbated the fundamental problem Douglas never solved: popular sovereignty demanded that any national policy accommodate itself to interests determined by local circumstances. In that spirit, he attacked Lincoln's free-soil position for being narrowly sectional, in effect because it was inconsistent with the natural conditions in the South that favored slavery.[85] Lincoln's reply, that by 1858 Douglas had lost much of his own southern support in the quarrel over the Lecompton Constitution, revealed the basic difficulty with emphasizing diverse local circumstances.[86] If the people of a state or territory chose its policy preferences on the basis of economic interests that were themselves determined by their physical setting, where was their republican devotion to union? Even an electorate's stand on slavery in its own area almost unavoidably affected its position on national issues such as the tariff, building western railroads, and the fate of slaves who fled to the North. These issues could not be easily resolved if the main concern was the immediate interests of one state or locality. The inevitable tension between the requirements for satisfying local interests and those for reconciling divergent interests could only contribute to an "irrepressible conflict."

The Jacksonians, however, had devised another more direct approach to preference coordination, according to which each political faction would

[81] Douglas 1860a, 254.
[82] Johannsen 1961, 289; Douglas 1859, 535; cf. Johannsen 1960, 385; Johannsen 1973, 287; Johannsen 1961, 279.
[83] Johannsen 1965, 213–15, 288.
[84] Douglas 1859, 535.
[85] Johannsen 1965, 211, 288.
[86] Cf. Johannsen 1965, 298.

sacrifice some of its own preferences for the sake of a larger agreement. Under Martin Van Buren's leadership of the party, that approach was explicitly connected to the development of cohesive, competitive, political parties. Douglas and his fellow moderate Henry Clay, in fact, adopted this basic approach in fashioning the Compromise of 1850, but party interests did not play a decisive role in that effort. Douglas then took a very different path in 1854 by implementing popular sovereignty in the Kansas-Nebraska Act. As we shall see next, Van Buren's reliance on political parties was just as consistent with humanist liberalism as Douglas's appeal to local majorities, but it was much more politically creative.

SEVEN

MARTIN VAN BUREN'S HUMANIST LIBERAL
THEORY OF PARTY

NEW YORK'S leading Jacksonian, Martin Van Buren, was by no means as philosophically sophisticated as Adams or Jefferson, or as theoretically gifted as his contemporary, John C. Calhoun. Van Buren, however, ranged creatively in a narrower sphere. Whereas William Leggett and Stephen A. Douglas elaborated on the familiar Jeffersonian themes of individual autonomy and states' rights, Van Buren broke new ground. In so doing, he argued for a *system* of competitive, equally legitimate political parties—a system that came to exemplify both the strengths and the limitations of American humanist liberalism. Divided from its opposition on basic principles, each party was to be united by the willingness of its members to compromise with each other, by the combined support of members for the party's nominees, and by an equitable division of patronage.

Theory shaped practice. In Van Buren's hands, this conception of parties helped the Jacksonians build an intersectional Democratic party, one their Whig foes were forced to imitate. In the process, Van Buren struck a balance between William Leggett's concern with individual preferences and Stephen A. Douglas's devotion to the political community.

Van Buren's career was marked by four paradoxes. First, in his own time, he was known as the Sly Fox of Kinderhook; a brilliant political tactician, Van Buren became governor of New York, a United States senator at thirty-eight, and a successful secretary of state. He was also the last sitting vice president until 1988 to win the presidency—although his presidential term was undistinguished; it was his last public office. However, Van Buren's real historical importance lies not in the successful political career on which he lavished great care and energy, but in the organizational tool he fashioned as theorist and founder of the Second American Party System.

Second, party loyalty and discipline had a central place in Van Buren's political understanding. Even in 1844, when the Democrats denied him the nomination for president he thought was his due, he worked hard for the election of the candidate the party did nominate for president. After 1848, and until his death in 1862, Van Buren consistently supported every nominee of the Democratic party.[1] Yet, despite his discipline and loyalty to party,

[1] Cole 1984, 419, 423–24, 425.

in 1848 he committed the ultimate party heresy by running for president as a third-party candidate.

Third, Van Buren avidly courted the South throughout his national political career, becoming the first of the great Democratic doughfaces—"northern men with southern principles." However, his 1848 campaign as a Free Soil candidate allied him with the moralistic, reform-liberal heirs of John Adams, men against whom he had fought his entire adult life.

Fourth, in spite of all his political cunning and genuine theoretical insight, Van Buren's political understanding nevertheless finally proved inadequate for the achievement of many of his goals. Along with his own defeats in 1840 and 1848, he lived to see the Democratic debacle in 1860 that left his the minority party for the next seventy years.

These four paradoxes were not only closely connected to each other; each can be traced to Van Buren's humanist liberal theory of party.

Jacksonian Democrat and Humanist Liberal

Like Jefferson, whom he regarded as the greatest of American politicians and statesmen, Van Buren sought to build his party on the foundation of a New York–Virginia alliance.[2] To that end, in 1824 he backed a Southerner for president, just as in 1821–1822 he had supported a Virginian for speaker rather than a fellow New Yorker who opposed the South during the Missouri crisis.[3] While a member of the Senate, Van Buren lodged with southern legislators and struck up close friendships with southern states' rights radicals and militants, such as John Randolph of Roanoke.[4] Van Buren asked for southern loyalty and understanding in return. In 1836, some of his slave-state friends opposed Richard Johnson of Kentucky as his vice presidential candidate, because Johnson had a mulatto common-law wife, but Van Buren held firm, because Johnson was popular among Van Buren's northern followers.[5]

As a good Jacksonian, Van Buren did not leave the Jeffersonian persuasion as he found it. For all Jefferson's egalitarianism, his era was marked by a profound political and social deference, symbolized in the presidential dynasty of Virginia planters. In contrast, Jackson and Van Buren were politicians of modest birth and native wit, as were Van Buren's allies in the Albany Regency. The Jacksonian Supreme Court affirmed the economic rights and opportunities of such men in the famous Charles River Bridge case.[6] Van

[2] Van Buren 1920, 168, 183; Van Buren 1867, 424.
[3] Niven 1983, 140, 107–8; Cole 1984, 109.
[4] Cole 1984, 104, 107; Harrison 1956, 440–41.
[5] Cooper 1978, 86.
[6] See Somkin 1967 and Meyers 1960.

Buren voiced the same sentiment in his sustained campaign against imprisonment for debt.[7]

Van Buren also adopted the Jacksonian rather than the Jeffersonian stance on more particular matters. Whereas Jeffersonians had feared the abuse of executive authority, Van Buren and his fellows saw the president as a popular tribune. Similarly, whereas Jefferson and his two Virginian successors had agreed to federal economic actions when circumstances seemed to demand it (including the renewal of the charter of the first Bank of the United States in 1811), Van Buren rallied most Jacksonians to the banner of states' rights and denounced federal programs for internal improvements and, in particular, the renewal of the bank charter.[8] Finally, Van Buren embraced the expansionism advocated by his followers among northern white workers and farmers, whereas the Jeffersonians had been more tentative. In the spirit of expansionism, Van Buren not only condoned the displacement of the native American Indians, who were said to be blocking national growth and development, but he ranked this brutal episode among Jackson's achievements.[9]

These Jacksonian stands were firmly rooted in Van Buren's humanist liberalism. As he wrote in his autobiography, "The most attractive as well as the proper study of mankind is man." If he had an epistemology, it was a Jacksonian devotion to the solid, readily observable world of honest toil rather than the deceptive, manipulative one of finance capital.[10] Van Buren was also a consequentialist in his ethics. Jaenicke, adopting a theological idiom, has observed that Van Buren was always concerned with works rather than faith, with actions rather than purity of motive.[11] Van Buren praised the Jacksonians for promoting "the [prosperity,] welfare and happiness of those for whom they were selected to act."[12] As he showed in his reaction to the irregular, if not illegal, government of San Francisco, what mattered was not the conformity of an action to some abstract moral code, but its likely effects on human lives.[13]

This consequentialism was strongly utilitarian, in the sense of accepting

[7] Van Buren 1920, 212.

[8] M. L. Wilson 1984, 32–33. For Van Buren's celebration of states' rights, see Van Buren 1920, 401 and Van Buren 1867, 420. Also see Van Buren 1920, 56, 735–36; Silbey 1971, 588; and Van Buren 1867, 132–35. On Van Buren's view of the Bank of the United States as the foe of all republican liberty, see Van Buren 1920, 651 and M. L. Wilson 1984, 36. On his hatred for the money power, see Van Buren 1867, 161–63, 165, 176, 230–31; for his Jacksonian attack on an elitist judiciary, see Van Buren 1867, 274, 312ff.

[9] Van Buren 1920, 275–88.

[10] Ibid., 35, 645, 648; see also Van Buren 1867, 71.

[11] Jaenicke 1986, 99.

[12] [Citation missing.]

[13] Van Buren 1867, 89ff.

popular preferences rather than imposing some conception of public good. Devoted to satisfying the preferences of as many citizens as possible,[14] Van Buren condemned Hamilton for not consulting the people as to how they themselves understood their condition, remarking, the "objection that [Hamilton's] actions . . . [set] at naught the declared will of the people had but little weight with [Hamilton]." Van Buren criticized Hamilton for holding the people "incapable of judging" and for promoting their welfare "in spite of themselves."[15] He scorned John Quincy Adams's attempt to impose schemes of personal and cultural improvement on a public that had other preferences.[16] "The long-continued support of a majority of the people," as he put it, was "the only test of political merit in a Republic."[17] Thus the obligation of politicians was to "struggle" with the "conflict of interests and feelings" among their constituents.[18] Certainly, Van Buren had little use for reform liberalism with its competing focus on the development of human faculties. He himself was no model of abstemious self-control in his private life, and he dismissed the religiously motivated reformers who tried to protect the Indians, labeling such reformers "a class . . . easily instigated to meddle in public affairs" against the people's wishes.[19]

Van Buren also embraced Jefferson's humanist notion of balancing competing interests and preferences in order to satisfy the largest number of citizens. The celebrated Jefferson Day dinner of 1830 offers a case in point. After President Jackson, the nationalist, toasted the Union, a disaffected Vice President Calhoun placed the Union "next to our liberty." Van Buren's toast, which followed Calhoun's, was soon forgotten, yet it epitomized his whole political outlook: "Mutual forbearance and reciprocal concessions; thro' their agency the Union was established—the patriotic spirit from which they emanated will forever sustain it."[20] Animated by Van Buren's outlook, it was the Democratic party, which Van Buren had done so much to create—not the more moralistic Whig party—that maintained its intersectional alliances during the slavery controversies of the 1850s.

Because Van Buren believed that individuals must be free to form their own preferences, he also accepted Jefferson's belief in negative liberty, that is, in the absence of restraint, moral or otherwise, on the individual. Invoking the Declaration of Independence, Van Buren asserted the Jacksonian commitments to "the security of rights of persons and of property as an

---

[14] Jaenicke 1988, 37–38; Van Buren 1867, 29–30, 349.
[15] Van Buren 1867, 137–38.
[16] Van Buren 1920, 195.
[17] Van Buren 1867, 370.
[18] Van Buren 1920, 551.
[19] Ibid., 284–85; see 293–94.
[20] Ibid., 416.

indispensable ingredient in good government" and especially to religious liberty of conscience.[21]

Van Buren thought of rationality as essentially instrumental. Because individuals chose goals for themselves, rational analysis was restricted to questions of means, of the best way, that is, to achieve a particular goal. His guide was always experience, and his reliance was on "the humble virtue of prudence."[22] Given that outlook, even his revered principle of strict constitutional construction might have to be set aside, if the best means to pursue some overriding goal required it.[23]

A preoccupation with rational calculation marked Van Buren's politics more dramatically than either Leggett's moral passion for laissez-faire or Douglas's exuberant devotion to community and polity marked their politics. In fact, Van Buren's animus against many of his political foes was so limited that his politics sometimes seemed almost bloodless. In the administration of civil affairs, as he put it, "statesmen of sober judgment and prudence though possessed of less shining talents are generally the most prosperous."[24] His central concern was always interest rather than passion. As Ceasar has pointed out, Van Buren thought that parties were more than groups united by particular principles. They were also collections of interests that ought to be satisfied regardless of the momentary, irrational enthusiasms of voters. Indeed, Van Buren disliked arousing popular feelings even in partisan political campaigns, and he never fully understood the populist techniques that were used by the Whigs to outmaneuver him and oust him from the White House in the election of 1840.[25]

Van Buren's Humanist Liberal Theory
of Party

During the 1790s, the Jeffersonians established the first party system, when they organized their own party to oppose Federalist policies and candidates; yet Jefferson never entirely abandoned his republican suspicion of parties. He was so confident, in fact, of the rightness of his own party's cause that, as Van Buren himself pointed out, Jefferson "almost always said, 'The Republicans' pursued this course, and 'Hamilton' that—not naming

---

[21] Van Buren 1867, 72 and Van Buren 1920, 153–54.

[22] Van Buren 1920, 203.

[23] Van Buren 1867, 219; for an amusing example early in his career, see Van Buren's account of the battle over patronage at the "Convention for the Revision of the [New York] State Constitution" of 1821 (Van Buren 1920, 106–8).

[24] Van Buren 1920, 203–4.

[25] Ibid., 532, 719, 736, 741, 747; cf. Ceasar 1979, 154, 164, 167.

the Federalists as a party."[26] In Jefferson's famous observation in the First Inaugural, "We are all republicans—we are all federalists," he actually anticipated the lapse of party conflict that occurred briefly after 1816.[27]

Van Buren himself, of course, came to a very different view of parties: he believed that a system of competitive parties spurred party cohesion and was therefore desirable. He thus placed more emphasis on commitment to political parties than Jefferson had, just as Douglas placed special emphasis on Jefferson's devotion to democratic political communities and Leggett on Jefferson's belief in laissez-faire. Van Buren thereby came to occupy a middle position among his fellow Jacksonians. Van Buren's belief in party unity, for example, contrasted directly with Leggett's insistence on almost complete individual autonomy and with Douglas's commitment to the sovereignty of the local community. As Jaenicke has observed, "Democrats" like Van Buren "suspected any claim to act according to individual conscience and judgment as camouflage for unrestrained desire."[28] These Democrats, in other words, "spurn[ed] an evangelical [radically individualist] faith in the possibility of literal self-government based on voluntary adherence to God's law."[29] One object of Van Buren's commitment to party unity was to restrain ambitious politicians who lacked partisan loyalty. All good Democrats, he insisted, must be willing to sacrifice their personal preferences where party unity required it, and, in turn, the preservation of party unity would promote sectional amity within the Union.

Van Buren also valued political parties as essential to satisfying individual preferences in a large polity. This side of Van Buren's humanist liberalism can be explicated by recasting it in the language of contemporary rational choice theory. The vocabulary of rational choice theory was unknown to Van Buren himself, of course, but the theory not only shares his concern with preference satisfaction, it illuminates the specific difficulties he set out to solve.

Much of rational choice analysis focuses on the following problem: a set of individual actors must cooperate with each other in order to achieve a mutually desired and advantageous goal, but the actions necessary for attaining such a goal are often contrary to the particular interests of each individual actor. The classic case is that of the "free rider." Tom, Dick, and Harriet may all stand to benefit if their community builds a public facility, or if they avoid a destructive conflict among themselves. Yet Tom would clearly be better off if Harriet and Dick did all the work to build the facility or made all the concessions to avoid the conflict. Tom's rational course, therefore, is to let the others be the "suckers" who do the building or take the concilia-

26 Van Buren 1920, 186.
27 Peterson 1987, 292.
28 Jaenicke 1986, 105.
29 Ibid.

tory positions, while as a free rider he shares in the benefits. If all three acted as free riders, of course, there would be no cooperation; the common project would fail or the costly conflict ensue, and all three would be worse off. What all three need, then, is some method of coordination by which each knows that if he or she contributes, the others will as well.

The politicians of Van Buren's time faced problems of coordination that their predecessors had not faced. The services performed by the older generation during the period of the revolution and the founding lent its leaders a commanding moral authority. For the generation of founders, that is, the free rider problem was attenuated. Because the authority the founders held made it easier for them to coordinate the actions of their followers, and because many of their contemporaries were strongly devoted to the same set of leaders, those leaders who supported a particular statesman could expect with confidence that their efforts on his behalf would be reciprocated to their own benefit at a later time. As a result, they were able to pass the presidency from one to another with relatively little conflict, excepting only the painful clash between Jefferson and Adams.

As the founding generation passed from the scene, however, such coordination became more difficult. In the first place, no obvious successors emerged, no leaders whom voters could not only support but confidently expect others to support as well.[30] Second, even when leaders did emerge, they could not expect to be accorded the widespread social deference enjoyed by the founders, because the democratic ethos of the Jacksonians encouraged all Americans to insist on their own particular interests. Third, as almost all white men became enfranchised, the electorate grew so large that cooperation among them became less feasible. Finally, new obstacles to coordination were introduced by westward migration and economic development, events that created new sets of important regional and material concerns. Taken altogether, these changes meant that cooperation was now much more difficult to achieve. The voters were so numerous, so divided in their interests, so assertively concerned with their own welfare that free riding became a highly attractive strategy. Particular individuals were more likely to look after their own interests, and there was much more reason to expect that others would do likewise.

Van Buren and his fellow Jacksonians, then, were the first democratic politicians anywhere to confront the problem of coordinating voter conduct in something like its full complexity. As Van Buren put it, the political crises of 1820 and 1824 raised a crucial issue: how to establish "a union and concert of action . . . looking to the public good as the end of our labours."[31] In any event, the Jacksonians' humanist liberal concerns made

[30] For Van Buren's view on this point, see Ceasar 1979, 158.
[31] Van Buren 1920, 576.

them see the problem as one of coordinating the preferences of a diverse and complex polity; this instrumental construction proved more effective in political conflicts than the approach adopted by their reform liberal foes.

Van Buren's own analysis began with the crisis of 1820. At one level, of course, the crisis was simply a sectional dispute over whether to admit Missouri to the Union as a slave state. Van Buren, however, offered a different diagnosis. Because both the Federalist party and the Democratic-Republican party were intersectional coalitions, each party had an incentive to avoid sectional divisions in order to win elections. As Van Buren observed, "Party attachment in former times furnished a complete antidote for sectional prejudices."[32] Van Buren noted, "Formerly attacks upon southern Republicans were regarded by those of the North as assaults upon their political brethren and resented accordingly"; just this partisan competition disappeared with the consensual reelection of James Monroe as president.[33] In the absence of serious opposition, party loyalty lost its point, so that ambitious politicians were freer to appeal, or even pander, to the sectional feelings of their constituents. The danger of sectional conflict persisted, therefore, even after the immediate issue of slavery in Missouri had been resolved. As Van Buren remarked, the 1820 crisis directly "colored all our conversations" about the 1824 presidential campaign.[34] In fact, John Quincy Adams won the presidency even though his electoral college votes came almost entirely from the north and east.

Moreover, the 1824 election signaled the existence of a still broader problem. Monroe's victory in 1820 did more than put an end to the Federalist party. In vanquishing their opposition, Jefferson's Democratic-Republicans had also destroyed themselves. By 1824, with no Federalist threat to hold them together, they had splintered into four factions, each of which supported a major candidate for president. Part of the problem, then, was that each of these candidates received a respectable share of the popular and electoral vote, but no one's share even approached an absolute majority. The more important part of the problem, however, was that a politics of "personal factions," in Van Buren's words, had replaced the politics based on larger "principles."[35] National politics thus came to resemble New York's politics, which had long been dominated by the highly personalist Clintonians.

The results of this change were deplorable, in Van Buren's eyes. First, there were few clear lines of factional cleavage; there was rather a "chaos," as

[32] Ceasar 1979, 138, n. 23, citing *Martin Van Buren Papers* in the Library of Congress, Van Buren to Thomas Ritchie, 13 Jan. 1827.

[33] Jaenicke 1986, 101–2, n. 71, citing Remini 1955, 132 and Hofstadter 1969, 202, 226–27.

[34] Van Buren 1920, 140.

[35] Van Buren 1867, 3–4.

Van Buren saw it, that denied the voters sharply defined choices.[36] Second, the bitterness of personal competition poisoned political life. "Resolution[s] aimed at one or the other of the departments" of Crawford, Adams, or Calhoun were introduced every day and "discussed with great bitterness."[37] Third, and perhaps most seriously, with four candidates of roughly equal strength, arbitrary outcomes were all too likely. In the event, John Quincy Adams won the White House by joining forces with another candidate, Henry Clay. Other alliances, however, might well have commanded a majority—for example, the three southern and western factions might have arrayed themselves together against Adams. Here, in the language of contemporary social science, is Arrow's cycling problem: depending on factional alignments and realignments (when there are more than two choices among candidates or issues), any one majority coalition can be replaced by a second majority coalition, some of whose members belonged to the first.[38]

To Van Buren, it was just such factional maneuvering that denied the presidency to Andrew Jackson, even though Jackson had the most popular votes. The result was that Adams was elected, "against the known wishes of a majority of the People."[39] The election of Adams, the "son of a statesman," suggested to Van Buren an alarming bias toward men of birth and connections—witness, as he put it, "the alacrity and exulting spirit with which [the] votaries [of the old federal party] rallied to the standard of Mr. Adams."[40] According to Van Buren, a system of personalist factions permitted social and economic elites to make arrangements among themselves with relative ease, a development that seemed to be confirmed by Adams's appointment of Clay as his secretary of state. By contrast, the common people could unite to act only if there were cohesive political parties.[41] Free from the restraints imposed by such parties, Adams had clearly felt able to ignore the "state of public opinion" and to try to impose on the people a political agenda based on his own moral code.[42]

Van Buren's observations can be rendered in rational choice terms. For simplicity, we shall consider the opposition, as Van Buren saw it, between his own Jeffersonians, who would soon become Jacksonians, and their partisan opponents, who later became Whigs. As the crisis of 1820 made clear, the great threat to Van Buren's party was a north-south split. The northern and southern factions of Van Buren's party differed on particular

[36] Van Buren 1920, 449.
[37] Ceasar 1979, 132–33, Van Buren to Dudley 10 Jan. 1822, cited in Bonney 1875, 382–84.
[38] See, for example, MacKay 1980.
[39] Van Buren 1920, 192.
[40] Ibid., 193.
[41] Van Buren 1867, 226; cf. Ceasar 1979, 150–51.
[42] Van Buren 1920, 195.

policies and candidates, but they shared Jeffersonian and later Jacksonian principles, and they were both hostile to the Adams faction that later became the Whig party. In this situation, four main outcomes were possible:

(a) Both Democratic factions would make concessions, preserving party unity and making victory probable.

(b) Neither faction would make any concessions, so that the Democrats were likely to lose to another party.

(c) Northerners would make all the concessions, preserving party unity and making victory probable.

(d) Southerners would make all the concessions, preserving party unity and making victory probable.

Jefferson had confronted this problem in principle, of course, when he first put together a cross-sectional party coalition that joined New York and Virginia. In that case, too, each faction would have preferred to have its own way. The factions were bound together, however, by an egalitarian, democratic spirit and by an overriding enmity toward the Federalists because of the repressive Alien and Sedition Acts. Moreover, Jefferson's own great prestige meant that all factions wanted him as the party's standardbearer. As a result, unity was achieved particularly easily. This pattern is represented in terms of ordinal utilities in chart 7.1 and table 7.1, according to which factional agreement was preferred by both sides.[43] As a result, there was no serious factional conflict, no serious cooperation problem, and a theoretically trivial "harmony game."[44]

The situation was transformed by the events of 1820. The crisis over Missouri heightened sectional tensions; at the same time, the collapse of the Federalist party eliminated the Jacksonians' hated foes and reduced the costs of electoral defeat. The worst possible outcome for all concerned was the undesirable although not disastrous victory of someone like John Quincy Adams, who had been a Federalist but had joined the Jeffersonians in 1808. What mattered most to each faction, then, was the preservation of its independence, and the honor and preeminence of its leader; that is, no faction wanted to make unilateral concessions to another faction. This set of utilities is set out in the ordinal rankings in chart 7.2 and table 7.2. As table 7.2 shows, this game resembles the familiar prisoner's dilemma, in which if one side makes voluntary concessions, the other side's most advantageous re-

[43] [An *ordinal* ranking of utilities lists utilities in order of preference (first, second, third, etc.). An *interval* ranking of utilities also lists utilities in order of preference but, in addition, it assigns measures to the intervals: that is, it provides measures for how much the first is preferred to the second, the second to the third, etc., and, by interpolation, the first to the third, etc.]

[44] I would like to thank David Laitin and Duncan Snidal for their help on this analysis.

CHART 7.1
The Jeffersonians' Harmony Game

		North's utility	South's utility
Outcome 1:	Both make concessions, Jeffersonians win	4	4
Outcome 2:	Neither make concessions, Jeffersonians lose	1	1
Outcome 3:	North makes concessions, Jeffersonians win	2	3
Outcome 4:	South makes concessions, Jeffersonians win	3	2

TABLE 7.1
The Jeffersonians' Harmony Game

		South makes concessions	
		Yes	No
North makes concessions	Yes	4,4 (outcome 1)	2,3 (outcome 3)
	No	3,2 (outcome 4)	1,1 (outcome 2)

sponse is to offer nothing in return. As a result, the equilibrium or typical outcome is that in the lower right cell (outcome 2): mutual noncooperation, a party split, and the election of a crypto-Federalist (in Van Buren's eyes) such as Adams.

This situation confronted Van Buren with two main alternatives. The first was to accept the basic situation—a persistence of highly factionalized politics—and to trust in political education. Hopefully, he thought, the neo-Jeffersonian factions would learn to cooperate with each other as the game was repeated.[45] Given this set of utilities, however, stable patterns of cooperation were not very likely, unless the Jacksonians abandoned their acknowledged self-regarding ambitions. Equally important, the Jacksonians' emphasis on upward mobility, together with the highly personalist character of the new political factions, meant that key actors in one presi-

[45] Axelrod (1984) has noted the success of a "tit-for-tat" strategy, that is, reciprocity in kind for both cooperation and noncooperation.

CHART 7.2
The Prisoner's Dilemma Game of 1824

		North's utility	South's utility
Outcome 1:	Both make concessions, neo-Jeffersonians win	3	3
Outcome 2:	Neither make concessions, neo-Jeffersonians lose	2	2
Outcome 3:	North makes concessions, neo-Jeffersonians win	1	4
Outcome 4:	South makes concessions, neo-Jeffersonians win	4	1

TABLE 7.2
The Prisoner's Dilemma Game of 1824

		South makes concessions	
		Yes	*No*
	Yes	3,3 (outcome 1)	1,4 (outcome 3)
North makes concessions			
	No	4,1 (outcome 4)	2,2 (outcome 2)

dential election might well be replaced by a different set in the next. With discontinuity in personnel, continuity of political education was especially unlikely.

Van Buren's other major alternative was to address the problem of personal ambition directly—that is, by considering a change in the structure of incentives for individual politicians by reestablishing and reinvigorating partisan politics. In the language of rational choice, he had to transform the game of prisoner's dilemma into a game of chicken. There were, to be sure, continuities between the two games. Most importantly, Van Buren recognized that factional tensions among Jeffersonians, later Jacksonian Democrats, persisted, particularly those between the North and the South. He tried to reduce the impact of that split by insisting that what they shared outweighed what divided them. The major political split was between the people who were represented first by the Jeffersonians and then by the Jacksonians, on the one hand, and, on the other hand, the social and economic elites who were represented first by the Federalists and then by the Whigs. Given this split, both Democratic factions had a large stake in winning the election for president.[46] Accordingly, the most desirable outcome for either Democratic faction would still be a position of dominance within the party—but only as long as the party remained sufficiently unified to win the general election. The second best outcome would be party unity and victory in the general election, based on mutual concessions by the two factions. A party defeat would be so costly that a party split and Whig victory was least desirable. As a result, each faction would even prefer making unilateral concessions, if that was the only way to ensure unity and a Whig defeat. This pattern of utilities is presented, in ordinal terms, in chart 7.3 and table 7.3.

The chicken game is inherently unstable. If one faction of the party wants rationally to maximize its utility, it will demand a dominant place in the party, counting on the second faction to submit rather than precipitate a split and risk defeat of the party in the general election. The second faction would not agree to submit in this way, because, from its perspective, two of the three possible alternatives to submission—compromising, or forcing the other side to offer all the concessions—would improve its position. Even if one faction wins out over the other in a particular year, a federal system with independent state and local parties enables the losing faction to renew the contest almost immediately. If one faction tries to dominate, the other may well reply in kind. Here, then, is the chicken game in a nutshell: if neither faction blinks, the result is a split in the home party and a victory for the opposition party. All in all, each side has some incentive to make concessions and some incentive to stand firm, and the final outcome is highly indeterminate.

In his theory of party, Van Buren sought to remove the uncertainty from the chicken game by judicious modification of the incentive structure. As we noted above, Van Buren stressed the value of mutual incentives by emphasizing the basic opposition between the *parties*, and thus the devotion of the Democrats to those principles that originally united them.[47] The appeal to partisan principles and loyalty by itself, however, was insufficient to overcome a factional split. If one faction felt badly treated, it might still threaten to defect in order to force concessions from the other faction. The danger of defection could be avoided by offering compensation to the losing faction, in effect reducing the difference between making mutual concessions and submitting to an intraparty foe. In the language of the chicken game, Van Buren had to keep either faction from simply taking the role of the compliant sucker. But how? Van Buren's celebrated answer was an equitable divi-

---

[46] Van Buren 1920, 123.
[47] Ibid., 303, 678.

CHART 7.3
The Democrats' Unstable Chicken Game

	North's utility	South's utility
Outcome 1: Both make concessions, Jeffersonians win	3	3
Outcome 2: Neither make concessions, Jeffersonians lose	1	1
Outcome 3: North makes concessions, Jeffersonians win	2	4
Outcome 4: South makes concessions, Jeffersonians win	4	2

TABLE 7.3
The Democrats' Unstable Chicken Game

		South makes concessions	
		Yes	No
North makes concessions	Yes	3,3 (outcome 1)	2,4 (outcome 3)
	No	4,2 (outcome 4)	1,1 (outcome 2)

sion of the spoils that went with winning elections. In particular, he would compensate losing factions by offering them patronage side payments, if they failed to nominate their candidates but remained loyal to the party. All major groups in the party, beginning with the president's own cabinet, had to be accommodated.[48] For Van Buren, in other words, the real point of patronage was to cement party unity by opening public office to all party factions and thus reducing the gains obtained by one ambitious party faction at the expense of another. In this way, each faction could agree to the compromises that would ensure party unity.[49]

To present these moves in rational choice terms, we must introduce an interval analysis that ranks the utilities of the factions on a scale from 1 to 10.[50] In this way, we can show that some outcomes are relatively close to

[48] Ibid., 160ff., 448.
[49] Jaenicke 1986, 103; Van Buren 1920, 263, 265.
[50] [See note 43 above.]

CHART 7.4

Van Buren's Chicken Game: An Interval Analysis

		North's utility	South's utility
Outcome 1:	Both make concessions, Jacksonians win	8	8
Outcome 2:	Neither make concessions, Jacksonians lose	2	2
Outcome 3:	North makes concessions, Jacksonians win	7	9
Outcome 4:	South makes concessions, Jacksonians win	9	7

TABLE 7.4

Van Buren's Chicken Game: An Interval Analysis

		South makes concessions	
		Yes	*No*
North makes concessions	*Yes*	8,8 (outcome 1)	7,9 (outcome 3)
	No	9,7 (outcome 4)	2,2 (outcome 2)

each other, while others are not. In these terms, because differences within the party were small, securing factional dominance would have a utility of 9, but the availability of patronage side payments would mean that making all the concessions would still have the relatively high utility of 7. Accordingly, mutual concessions, that is, compromise on choosing candidates, would have a utility of 8. Given the differences between the parties, if the Democrats lost, each faction would have a utility of only 2. The harm done by a Whig victory, and the prospect of patronage for all factions if the Democrats won, made unity very much more preferable than division and defeat. This pattern is presented in chart 7.4 and table 7.4. (Utilities of 10 and 1 are not assigned, because the policy differences between the two parties were not absolute. Both parties, for instance, favored state government over federal, some help for some banks, and some internal improvements; the Democrats were mainly opposed to action by the *federal* government.)

These considerations help explain Van Buren's commitment to a *system* of two competitive parties. As he learned in the early 1820s, it was essential to maintain party unity; and it was the threat posed by the opposition party— the threat to both policies and patronage—that kept one's own party together. Accordingly, he regarded efforts to divide the opposition party as a "temptation."[51] Indeed, Van Buren prided himself on maintaining his personal friendships, even with his political foes when possible.[52] He also opposed any tendencies among factions in his own party to ally themselves with former party foes, whether Federalists in the 1820s or Whigs in the 1830s. In addition, because cohesion within each of the two major parties meant that only two serious candidates ran for each office, his system precluded the cycling problem evident in the election of 1824, in which there were more than two possible candidates.

Van Buren's Attenuated Republicanism

There was still the problem, however, of the intense, self-regarding individualism of the Jacksonians, still the chance that the party factions would not cooperate because each would insist on the dominant role in selecting party candidates and controlling patronage. Van Buren's answer was his own version of the attenuated republicanism of the Jacksonians. As Major Wilson put it, Van Buren refused to politicize morality.[53] As a good humanist liberal, he would not move a moral issue like slavery to the center of the political discussion. Van Buren did, however, again in Wilson's phrase, moralize politics. That is, he took a moral stand about the proper rules for political life, thus giving his theory an ethical, specifically republican cast that may well have increased its appeal. In Van Buren's eyes, the crucial republican virtue was neither Leggett's citizen autonomy nor Douglas's devotion to polity. It was, rather, the self-restraint of political leaders, their willingness to sacrifice their own policy preferences and candidacies for the sake of compromise.

Knowing how self-regarding partisan feelings might sometimes be, Van Buren admired the liberal sacrifice of extreme views that had made the Constitutional Convention such a success.[54] With respect to policy conflicts, his stand required the "mutual forbearance" that he had called for in his reply to the toasts of Jackson and Calhoun. The same concern also required emphasizing those economic or material matters, rather than moral issues like slavery, on which each side could make some sacrifice by

[51] Van Buren 1867, 119.
[52] Van Buren 1920, 567–68, 534.
[53] M. L. Wilson 1984.
[54] Van Buren 1867, 47, 237–38.

splitting the difference.[55] Characteristically, in reaction to the nullification issue in the 1830s Van Buren "recommended a reduction of the tariff and the observance by the federal government of a spirit of concession and forbearance as long as practicable."[56] He returned to this conciliatory posture toward southern Democrats after 1848.

Van Buren applied the same approach within political parties, demanding that individual members sacrifice their personal preferences for the sake of harmony.[57] Specifically, he laid down a rule that required submission to "the rigors of party discipline," that is, required a party member to support whomever the party nominated, even if the member had originally opposed the nominee.[58] It was this rule, Van Buren thought, that made his partisanship thoroughly republican. It limited self-aggrandizement by putting party unity ahead of the individual's own first preferences. The stress on party comity clearly shaped his own political practice. During his presidency, Van Buren made every effort to keep in step with his allies in the New York Democracy.[59] He also worked to maintain his southern ties. Even though he lost his party's nomination in 1844 to a Tennessean, he and his political friends rallied behind the eventual nominee, his old ally James K. Polk, immediately after the convention.[60] No claim need be made—Van Buren himself certainly made none—that this emphasis on party unity, by means of a republican limit on excessive individualism, made his theory of party philosophically profound. Nevertheless, many rank-and-file Jacksonians, in their predominantly rural society, turned to political parties, because political parties offered them both an organizational form for collective action and a republican limit on individual ambition.

If Van Buren's devotion to party discipline expressed his republican commitments, his republicanism was nevertheless at least as attenuated as Leggett's and Douglas's. John Adams and John Quincy Adams were surely right that traditional republican theory abhorred the spirit of party, which placed loyalty to one's own faction above conscientious devotion to the polity and the public good. More generally, Van Buren's political outlook exhibited little of the moral passion of eighteenth-century republicanism. He was, in fact, a consummate political professional, who was more often concerned with the skillful negotiation of compromises that would maximize as many preferences as possible, than with the substance of policy or with moral principle. To Horace Greeley, Van Buren was "the reconciler of

---

[55] Van Buren 1920, 241.

[56] Ibid., 552; see Van Buren's account of Madison's efforts to forge a middle position on the Bill of Rights in the First Congress (Van Buren 1867, 199).

[57] Jaenicke 1986, 103.

[58] Van Buren 1920, 116.

[59] See Cole 1984, 344; M. L. Wilson 1984, 132.

[60] Niven 1983, 394–95, 542.

the estranged, the harmonizer of those who were at feud among his fellow partisans."[61] In Ceasar's words, because "Van Buren understood a party to be . . . dedicated to certain general principles but differing widely on [specific issues] . . . the chief task of the party leader was to maintain consensus in the party."[62]

By attenuating his republicanism in the way he did, Van Buren took a position midway between Leggett's individualism and Douglas's devotion to the humanist liberal political community. On one side, Van Buren affirmed his "willingness to make liberal concessions [on policies], nay sacrifices, for the preservation of peace and reciprocal good will."[63] In this spirit, he offered almost extravagant praise for Clay, his respected foe, during the nullification controversy.[64] Van Buren himself developed a moderate stand on the tariff in order to reconcile New York's protectionist sentiments with the South's belief in free trade.[65] Indeed, this outlook resisted the introduction of divisive moral issues more effectively than Leggett's or Douglas's. For Leggett and Douglas, either individuals or state and territorial majorities had to be free to pursue whatever preferences they wished, including preferences about moral issues that required national solutions. Van Buren, by contrast, could explicitly regard such issues as politically illegitimate, simply because they threatened the cohesion of the parties that were essential to national unity. In that sense, his political ethic resembled "rule" rather than "act" utilitarianism. It made the long-term health of his party, the party system, and ultimately the Union, more important than any single policy, no matter how intense or numerous or moralistic its supporters. Indeed, his theory specified a mechanism for excluding divisive questions, by promoting political parties devoted to compromising over differences that could be resolved readily, while at the same time excluding efforts to translate moral visions into law.

On the other side, Van Buren was devoted to furthering party unity, because following that rule was the best way to satisfy as many preferences as possible, and it would also prevent such undemocratic outcomes as the election of John Quincy Adams in 1824. In that sense, both his tactical brilliance—whether it was in outmaneuvering Calhoun or in crafting broadly acceptable policies—and thus his reputation as the Sly Fox of Kinderhook, expressed his deepest political and even philosophical commitments.[66] Yet the "rule" side of his utilitarianism also mattered. Attenuated as it was, the republicanism of his emphasis on party unity and discipline

---

[61] Ceasar 1979, 162–63.
[62] Ibid., 158.
[63] Van Buren 1920, 552.
[64] Ibid., 556–57, 561.
[65] Niven 1983, 251–52, 254.
[66] See, for example, Cooper 1978, 13–15.

gave his humanist liberalism its distinctive cast, that is, its emphasis on party as the critical link between individual and community. It was this perspective that helped him refashion the party system as a major tool for resolving the looming crisis over slavery.

Slavery

Van Buren did more than offer his theory of party as a way of calming the recurring slavery controversy. He was indeed the first of the great dough-faces. His father, after all, had owned slaves before New York abolished the institution, and his son married into a slave-owning South Carolina family. Not surprisingly, then, Van Buren crafted a carefully formulated middle position on the issue. In the suffrage debates at the 1821 New York Constitutional Convention, he favored more stringent qualifications for blacks than for whites.[67] More generally, he thought the institution of slavery was so deeply implanted in the South that it was "positively and absolutely impossible to avoid." Certainly, "its existence was without fault on the part of those who had inherited it from ancestors,"[68] and many of his southern contemporaries had dealt with the problem quite liberally. As a good consequentialist, Van Buren saw no fruitful way to hasten slavery's end.[69] Any direct attack on slavery would only anger southern whites and, at the same time, frustrate slavery's northern foes, because such an attack would be futile.

Van Buren also took the prosouthern position on states' rights.[70] During Jackson's first term, Van Buren persuaded the Old Hero to veto federal funding for the Maysville road bill as a threat to the states' prerogatives, and, by extension, to their control over slavery.[71] After the nullification crisis erupted, Van Buren's stance toward South Carolina was notably more conciliatory than that of Jackson himself.[72] This conciliatory stance, to be sure, conveniently coincided with New York's economic interests. After New York had built the Erie Canal, the state no longer stood to benefit from a federally sponsored program of internal improvements; but even where the state's interests favored the exercise of federal powers—on the tariff, for example—Van Buren consciously straddled the issue to avoid offending the South.[73]

[67] Van Buren 1920, 112.
[68] Ibid., 131; see 131–33.
[69] Cole 1984, 425.
[70] Curtis 1970, 18; cf. Van Buren 1920, 315, 329, 550–53.
[71] Harrison 1956, 449, 451; cf. 444, 445.
[72] Niven 1983, 326, 327.
[73] Harrison 1956, 446, 444.

These views led Van Buren to assail the abolitionists for endangering "our blessed Union."[74] Responsible Northerners, he thought, had an obligation to denounce such agitation whenever it emerged. To reassure his southern friends, he voiced such sentiments repeatedly during his campaigns for the presidency in 1836 and 1840.[75] In the party statement he drafted for the 1836 election, he treated militant abolitionists as fanatics, and he praised the North for resisting them.[76] To the applause of the South, in his otherwise bland inaugural address, Van Buren singled out abolitionism for a direct attack.[77] As president, he was as good as his word. He supported the reelection of the Southerner, James K. Polk, to the speakership of the House, and he then supported the gag rule that prevented even discussion of antislavery petitions in the House. Further, he closed the southern mails to antislavery literature and withdrew the patronage of his administration from Leggett and other radical Democrats, when they began to defend the rights of abolitionists.[78] Later Van Buren favored a somewhat softened version of Calhoun's resolutions, which declared in favor of the permanence of slavery and the rights of slave holders.[79] For good measure, Van Buren appointed three proslavery Southerners to the Supreme Court.[80]

Nevertheless, Van Buren's stand on slavery was always complex. In 1820, for example, he did not simply directly defend the South's position on the Missouri question. Instead, he signed a call for a meeting to demand the exclusion of slavery from Missouri and then was conveniently out of town when it took place.[81] Personally, he believed that the institution was immoral, and he privately sympathized with the plight of the slaves, although he refrained from public comment until 1848.[82]

At the same time, Van Buren had always opposed the extension of slavery into new territories. He not only admired Jefferson for excluding it from north of the Ohio River, but he worked, first as vice president and then as president, to delay the annexation of Texas as a slave-holding area.[83] In the 1840s, his stand finally undermined his entente with the South.[84] Even in the 1830s there had been signs of trouble. Whereas Van Buren's predecessor in the presidency had been a decisive, straightforward war hero and a slave

---

[74] Van Buren 1920, 492.

[75] Cole 1984, 261; cf. Niven 1983, 400.

[76] Schlesinger 1971, 1:623–26. [Thanks to Douglas Jaenicke for this citation.]

[77] Richardson 1897, 3:317–18; see also Curtis 1970, 48. [Thanks to Douglas Jaenicke for these citations.]

[78] Cole 1984, 274; Niven 1983, 392, 401.

[79] Cooper 1978, 129.

[80] Cole 1984, 376.

[81] Cole 1984, 59; see Van Buren 1920, 99–100, 137–38, 140.

[82] Niven 1983, 79, 385.

[83] Van Buren 1920, 134, 136; Curtis 1970, 154–55, 158–59.

[84] Whitehurst 1932, 152.

holder to boot, Van Buren was a calculating, physically unimposing, professional politician from the northeast.[85] Understandably, some Southerners regarded his adroit political maneuvers on policies to be a real threat. He had skillfully used the Peggy Eaton affair to reduce southern influence in the cabinet and become Jackson's chief lieutenant. When Van Buren's enemies in the Senate rejected his nomination as ambassador to Great Britain, he exploited their blunder to become Jackson's running mate in 1832.

His tactical genius did not make Van Buren intrinsically antisouthern, but his obvious political skills underlined his image as the overly subtle northern rival to the South's Calhoun.[86] Because some Southerners viewed all Northerners with suspicion, his political foes regarded the Sly Fox as an inviting target.[87] In 1832, when they could not safely attack Jackson himself, they turned their fire on his New York running mate, denouncing him as unsound on slavery.[88] In several states, they ran slates of electors pledged to Jackson for president but to a candidate other than Van Buren for vice president.

Prior to the 1836 campaign, some southern leaders sought an alternative to Van Buren, such as Calhoun, to serve as the Democrats' presidential candidate.[89] Although Van Buren was nominated, his massive victory in the general election was marked by the same sectional tensions that in 1828 had been responsible for the defeat of the previous northern president, John Quincy Adams. Despite Van Buren's many southern electoral college votes, his share of the South's popular vote fell sharply compared to Jackson's performance in 1832. Nevertheless, Van Buren did as well as Jackson had in the middle states and notably better in New England, where his 45 percent was higher than any other Democrat would reach until after the Civil War.[90] This pattern, to be sure, did not hold in 1840, when Van Buren carried only six states, four of them in the South. As he recognized, the South had been the bastion of the Democrats since the party first emerged in 1828, and losing so much of it signaled substantial dissatisfaction.[91]

The sectional tensions proved fatal to Van Buren's presidential hopes in 1844. For many Northerners, the significance of the proposed annexation of Texas was that it threatened to boost the power of the slave states in both Congress and the electoral college. To Southerners, barring Texas from the Union would limit the further expansion of slavery and create a convenient

[85] McCormick 1966, 194–95; Cole 1984, 264.
[86] Cole 1984, 216–18.
[87] Cooper 1978, 141–43.
[88] Ibid., 15, 74.
[89] Ibid., 169, 171–72.
[90] McCormick 1966, 339–40, 48–49.
[91] Van Buren 1867, 372–73.

refuge for runaways.[92] Observing the conflict between his southern and northern supporters, Van Buren's enemies relentlessly pressed him to take a public stand on the issue.[93] When he reluctantly declared opposition to annexation, he dismayed his southern backers and forfeited an almost certain renomination at the Democratic national convention.[94] Even though a majority of the delegates were pledged to support him, a crucial block of them voted with his foes to retain the two-thirds rule for nomination. Because Van Buren could not muster that margin, his support drifted away after the first ballot, leaving his unhappy loyalists with the proannexationist Polk as the presidential candidate.[95]

Tensions worsened in 1848, when the leading issue was the place of slavery in the territories that had been gained in the Mexican War. Divided on this question as well as on economic issues, New York Democrats sent two delegations to the national convention: Van Buren's antislavery Barnburners and the more conservative Hunkers. Over the former's bitter protests, the convention offered an equal place to both factions and then nominated Lewis Cass, a Northerner who had favored annexation and opposed any general ban on slavery in the territories. Frustrated and humiliated, Van Buren's allies bolted and then joined forces with the antislavery Conscience Whigs and political abolitionists from the Liberty party. Because their new Free Soil party needed a standardbearer of national stature, Van Buren eventually agreed to become its candidate.

From one perspective, Van Buren's apparently shifting positions were consistent both with each other and with a part of the broad middle position that offered the prospect of sectional peace: the best way to avoid discord was to insist on the precise status quo ante that his generation had inherited from the founders. This stand meant opposing the expansion of slavery beyond its existing borders; but it also made Van Buren a doughface to many Northerners, because it fully protected slavery where it was already established—whence his implacable opposition to abolitionism. Even in the 1848 Free Soil campaign, Van Buren was concerned primarily with the threat that the expansion of slavery posed to white laborers. Rather than assail the institution or voice the concern of abolitionists for the slaves, his free-soil stand asserted, legalistically, the right of the federal government to control its own territories.[96] Van Buren even temporized on the status of

---

[92] Cooper 1978, 189–201, 241.

[93] Whitehurst 1932, 12–13.

[94] Niven 1983, 526; Whitehurst 1932, 19, 28–30; Van Buren 1920, 8; for the entire episode, see Cole 1984, 392–94.

[95] Whitehurst 1932, 46; Niven 1983, 537–40; Cooper 1978, 204–5.

[96] Niven 1983, 591, 569; Whitehurst 1932, 161–62, 169, 130–31.

slavery in the District of Columbia, where the federal government's power to act was clear.[97]

This complex position was consistent with Van Buren's virulent attacks on the abolitionists in the 1830s, his opposition to slavery's expansion in Texas, and therefore his willingness to run as the candidate of a free-soil coalition in 1848. Emphasizing Van Buren's stand on slavery itself leaves two questions unanswered. First, given his hostility to all forms of abolitionism, how could he make common cause with the political abolitionists who had joined the free-soil coalition in 1848? Second, given his opposition to the territorial expansion of slavery, how could he make such an abrupt reversal in his position during the 1850s?

For a time after the 1848 campaign, Van Buren's New York supporters did support a free-soil stand, partly because it proved popular even with many rank-and-file Hunkers.[98] To the dismay of antislavery militants, the Barnburners eventually softened their position and endorsed the Compromise of 1850.[99] That agreement included a remarkably harsh fugitive slave law and the organization of Utah and New Mexico as territories without explicitly prohibiting slavery there. Moreover, Van Buren himself readily acquiesced in this shift; he saw the Compromise as an effort to restore sectional comity.[100] A few years later, he even endorsed the Kansas-Nebraska Act, which repudiated his free-soil stand of 1848 entirely, by repealing the prohibition on slavery in the northern Louisiana Purchase. Still later, Van Buren even accepted most of the Dred Scott decision.[101] Finally, in 1860–1861 he favored the Crittenden Compromise that sought to stave off secession by offering concessions to the South.[102]

Here are the contradictions of Van Buren's position on slavery: if he had died in 1841, he would have appeared to be simply the first of the doughfaces. If he had died in 1849, his shift in 1848 would have been part of the rise of free-soil feelings among northern Democrats, a trend that eventually led many of them into the Republican party. However, Van Buren, who lived until 1862, reversed himself once again in 1850. His double reversal not only seems puzzling in terms of his position on slavery, but it also defies several seemingly plausible explanations.

As one possible explanation, Van Buren's Jacksonian nationalism, for example, certainly accounts for much of his conduct, but it cannot tell us why he broke sharply with the South in the 1840s, thus adding fuel to a growing sectional fire. Explanations based on Van Buren's careerist interests

[97] Whitehurst 1932, 175.
[98] Ibid., 195.
[99] Ibid., 185, 199–200.
[100] See Van Buren 1867, 355–70.
[101] Ibid., 355–57.
[102] Cole 1984, 425.

do little better. His defeat at the 1844 convention clearly ended his hopes in presidential politics, and his third party candidacy in 1848—and his later reversal—were little more than gestures. Finally, he had good reasons to be personally angry over his political demise and the rebuffs of his followers, first by the Polk administration and then in the Democratic convention of 1848.[103] Yet, rather than venting his feelings, he continued to calculate his actions—carefully and instrumentally. In 1848, for example, he insisted that his allies remain calm, act prudently, and seek party unity. The task of the Barnburners at the 1848 convention was to block President Polk's renomination at any cost, but they had to be ready to support any other candidate, even a Southerner or southern ally.[104] Provided Van Buren's political friends were treated with respect and seated at the convention as New York's sole representatives, the Van Burenites should not even insist on the exclusion of slavery from the Mexican territories.[105]

The questions persist: if Van Buren's actions were determined by nationalism, careerist expediency, or by commitment to union, how could he consort in 1848 with a party united only on the moral, sectionally divisive issue of antislavery? If he was always so opposed to slavery's territorial expansion, why did he later agree to the Kansas-Nebraska Act and even to much of Dred Scott? These puzzles can be solved by focusing on his calling as a professional politician and, more specifically, on his Jacksonian and humanist liberal theory of party.

Van Buren's entire career in fact epitomized his theory. The New York–Virginia alliance he carefully rebuilt did more than help form the Democratic party and make Jackson president in 1828. It helped promote Van Buren himself to the senior position in Jackson's cabinet, to the vice presidency, and finally to the presidency. His 1836 presidential campaign was particularly revealing. Because the Whigs nominated several favorite sons, Van Buren had to run against a Southerner, Hugh Lawson White of Tennessee, in the slave states. Although Van Buren did poorly in White's home state as well as in North Carolina, South Carolina, and Alabama, he carried most of the South.[106] More importantly, Van Buren's success in the South reflected just that party loyalty he had so fervently preached. In Virginia, he depended on the support of established Democratic leaders, notably Thomas Ritchie.[107] In other states, such as Mississippi and, apparently, Louisiana, he owed his victory to light turnout and voter ambivalence.[108]

[103] Whitehurst 1932, 77–79; cf. 96–101.
[104] Cole 1984, 410–15.
[105] Rayback 1954, 716; Whitehurst 1932, 136.
[106] McCormick 1966, 228–30.
[107] Ibid., 184–85.
[108] Ibid., 317, 302.

Here was the accommodation among party factions on which Van Buren's theory pivoted.

As a number of scholars have pointed out, a devotion to this conception of party influenced Van Buren's conduct in the 1840s as well. Certainly, slavery played a role. Some Van Burenites, for example, concluded that Polk intended all along to betray them after his election, because he could not trust them on the territories issue.[109] When Van Buren and Polk did fall out, it was not over slavery, however, or even over states' rights, but over the quintessentially partisan question of patronage.

To help Polk in 1844, Van Buren persuaded his ally and protégé Silas Wright to leave the Senate to run for governor.[110] With Wright at the head of the state ticket, the Van Burenites were able to deliver New York to Polk, and with it the election.[111] Acknowledging his debt, Polk had promised them suitable rewards once he was in office. In the end, however, Polk gave the position he reserved in the cabinet for a New Yorker to a Hunker rather than to a Barnburner.[112] Polk then also denied the Van Burenites most of the other posts that went to the New York Democracy.[113] This was the issue that really rankled. Here, after all, was where Van Buren had taken an ethical stand on the republican obligation to sacrifice some individual preferences for the sake of party unity. This obligation, moreover, was universal. It applied to Southerners, northern conservatives, and Van Burenites alike. Though Van Buren had always courted the South, he invariably insisted on the North's equal place in the party's councils: witness his choice of Richard Johnson, who was popular in the North, as a running mate, and his opposition to the annexation of Texas.[114]

Given this stand, Van Buren's bolting the party in 1848 was a natural response to the exclusion of his followers from the party's councils, an exclusion that began with Polk's ingratitude after the 1844 election.[115] After all, the Barnburners' foes at the 1848 convention not only demanded a pledge to support any nominated candidate who favored slavery in the territories, they rejected any comparable pledge from the southern delegates should the nominee have opposite views.[116] As Whitehurst observed, Van Buren interpreted this exclusion as a measure of how far the Democrats had

[109] Rayback 1955, 59.

[110] Niven 1983, 546.

[111] Whitehurst 1932, 52, 57; Cole 1984, 398–99.

[112] Rayback 1955, 51–52, 54–56.

[113] Cole 1984, 401–4.

[114] Whitehurst 1932, 149; Niven 1983, 570, 574; Rayback 1954, 711; Cole 1984, 358; Cooper 1978, 198–99.

[115] Jaenicke 1988, 52–53.

[116] Whitehurst 1932, 153.

strayed from his party theory. In consequence, the theory required him to teach his antagonists a lesson about conciliation.[117]

Once a party faction seized power and refused to make concessions to its opponents, the victimized group was not just entitled to retaliate, it was obligated to do so. In the language of the chicken game, once one faction rejected the cooperative solution, the other had to follow suit. Otherwise, the violator would benefit from its aggressiveness, and both sides would lose incentive to cooperate in the future. Slavery, then, was not the decisive issue. The real issue was the preservation of comity among the party's factions, so the party could best represent the preferences and interests of its supporters.[118] As Van Buren saw it, his faction alone represented the majority of New York Democrats, and the flagrantly unfair treatment it received at the convention indeed threatened the comity of the national party.[119]

Moreover, there was a corollary to this emphasis on party unity that can explain Van Buren's double reversal. For Van Buren, if not for his most intensely antislavery followers, a return to regular party politics was essential, once other Democrats had learned their lesson and begun to play again according to the old rules.[120] Van Buren's own faction, in other words, had to be willing to compromise on its own preferences. As Van Buren put it, "In 1852" his party "instructed by the . . . destructive tendency of the slavery agitations . . . united on General Pierce as their candidate, [and then] supported . . . their old and time-honored principles, and elected him by a triumphant majority."[121] In this sense, Van Buren's venture into antislavery politics in 1848 was the exception that proved his devotion to the Jacksonian party system he had done so much to build.

Van Buren's Failure: Slavery and Preference Coordination

In the end, the political fates of both Van Buren and the Democrats indicate a serious flaw in his theory of party. The point of his theory was to secure party unity, and with it electoral victory, by precluding conflict over divisive moral issues. We have seen that Van Buren personally lost out in 1844 when the party divided over slavery and Texas, and in 1848 the divisions in the party were followed by electoral defeat. In 1852 and 1856, of course, the Democratic factions came together to win the White House. When the party finally split on sectional lines in 1860, it lost the White House and remained a minority party until the 1930s.

[117] Ibid., 219; Mintz 1949, 440–41; see Rayback 1954, 716.
[118] Cf. Rayback 1955, 60; Jaenicke 1988, 41.
[119] Rayback 1954, 709; Niven 1983, 587, 590–91.
[120] Jaenicke 1988, 62–63, 68.
[121] Van Buren 1867, 354–55. [Thanks to Douglas Jaenicke for this citation.]

The flaw is obvious at one level. The efforts of the Democrats to keep the issue of slavery off the political agenda were futile and self-defeating. During the 1830s, most southern Democrats had accepted Van Buren's vision of competition between two great intersectional parties on relatively innocuous economic issues. Even the southern Whigs came to adopt a program with a strong economic emphasis.[122] Yet the direction of change in the South was clearly marked. The invention of the cotton gin, among other factors, had helped to make plantation slavery central to southern life and to perpetuate the region's mainly rural character. One result of this commitment to an agricultural economy was a bitter conflict with northern industry over the tariff. Another, even more ominous result was the more rapid growth of cities and expansion of industries in the North than in the South. As a result, the slave states began to fear for their political power and to view almost all Northerners with some suspicion. Stunned by occasional but bloody slave uprisings, southern whites turned their particular fury on the abolitionists for attacking their section and impugning their personal honor. Because any outside interference or criticism now seemed intolerable, southern whites demanded an end to the agitation by abolitionists, and they equated a free-soil position with abolitionism outright. Cooper has noted that, according to an *Address to the People of the Slaveholding States*, written by a committee of slave-state Congressmen, "a Whig victory portended ruin for the South because it meant the triumph of abolitionist principles. Southern salvation rested only with [those] . . . who had conclusively demonstrated their steadfastness to southern rights."[123] In effect, both the North and the South had begun to treat slavery in highly moralistic terms.

Here Van Buren's theory was confounded by its humanist liberal premise that all human preferences presumptively had the same standing. In slightly different language, his humanist liberal politics were in conflict with his humanist liberal ethics. Whereas his politics favored issues that could be negotiated readily, his ethics accorded respect to all, even to moralistic, preferences. If responsive politicians ought to satisfy as many preferences as they could, they were certainly entitled to take up those popular, ideological causes—those moralistic issues—that Van Buren himself found so troublesome. Voter attitudes on slavery, of course, were especially intransigent, but the upheaval of the 1850s was not the only time when American politics has been swept by ideological, moralistic currents. In the 1850s, the problem was not simply that Whig and Democratic parties tried to suppress the slavery issue and happened to fail. The important point is that once any major electoral constituency begins to focus on an issue, whether "moral" or

---

[122] Cooper 1978, 152, 162.
[123] Ibid., 145, 60–61, 52–53, 64, 74; Niven 1983, 384; see also Henig 1969, 42–43.

not, there is no principled reason—no humanist liberal warrant—for party politicians to resist the inclusion of that issue in political debate.

Many of Van Buren's contemporaries did not even try to resist. Instead, there were times when his party system itself exacerbated sectional tensions. Because the Democrats won by such landslides in the slave states in 1828, sheer political survival required their foes—who eventually became Whigs— to make an impression on southern voters. The strategy of these foes was to become even more "southern" than the Jacksonians themselves by wrapping themselves in the banners of slavery and states' rights. Van Buren, they charged, was the thin end of a northern wedge that would take over the federal government and then send the South to ruin.[124] Even though Van Buren won the election, the concerted efforts of the southern Whigs helped them as a group to emerge from the political wilderness.[125]

Van Buren noted this development in his autobiography, but he dismissed it as an aberration. What Van Buren lacked was an outlook that combined a devotion to party politics, and the unity it implied, with a clear moral stand on slavery. It was precisely this combination that the Lincoln persuasion would eventually supply, and a discussion of that development must be postponed until we return to Lincoln himself. It is clear, however, that even before the 1850s other partisan politicians were addressing the issue. At the same time that many southern Democrats were coming to defend slavery on moral grounds as a positive good, a number of northern politicians were helping to found a new, explicitly antislavery party.[126] The new Republican party, moreover, was Van Buren's apt pupil. As the career of its first elected president made clear, the party was open to men of modest background but great talent, very much like Van Buren and his friends in the Albany Regency. Like the Regency, the Republicans knew how to make effective use of patronage. As Lincoln insisted in his House Divided speech, the party's leaders demanded unity among its factions and rejected amalgamation with former foes, just as Van Buren had refused to join with the Clintonians and former Federalists in the 1820s.[127] As their choice of the Illinois moderate for their candidate in 1860 made clear, the leadership of the Republican party had learned how to compromise on factional differences for the sake of unity and victory.

The point is that although many particular features of the new party conformed to Van Buren's theory, its general outlook ran against everything that he stood for. Rather than committing themselves, as had Van Buren, to managing factional conflicts through intersectional compromises—rather than, that is, placing the Union ahead of some moral code—

---

[124] Cooper 1978, 58, 135–36 [on 1840]; cf. Silbey 1971, 589–90 [on 1836].
[125] McCormick 1966, 178, 206, 243.
[126] Sewell 1976; Foner 1970.
[127] Johannsen 1965, 14–21; see Fehrenbacher 1962, 70–95.

the Republicans mobilized a narrowly sectional coalition behind a moral crusade. Worse, from Van Buren's point of view, and as Douglas's troubles in 1860 made clear, it was Van Buren's own Democrats who continued to seek sectional accommodation, only to split apart and lose the most important election of the century.

Just how did this development confound Van Buren's theory? What in particular went wrong? An answer can be formulated by restating the situation in the terms of the prisoner's dilemma and chicken games. From this perspective, Van Buren clearly overlooked a crucial possibility: once a moral question like slavery comes to the fore, it may indeed hopelessly divide one political party, while binding another tightly together. If a party is united in that way, its factions can readily follow Van Buren's prescription for reaching an accommodation. For example, because the great majority of Republicans treated slavery as a moral evil, their differences in the late 1850s were perhaps even smaller than among Van Buren's Democrats in the 1830s. Conservative Republicans, to be sure, might be slightly less opposed to a Democratic victory than Republican radicals, but the partisan differences between Republicans and Democrats were clearly greater than those that divided Whigs and Democrats. The Republicans' failure to cooperate with each other, therefore, might mean a victory for the Democrats, who, the Republicans thought, had almost all refused, immorally, to condemn slavery. At the same time, no matter which faction won out within the party, the Republicans offered the other the consolation of patronage. This set of utilities encouraged the Republican factions to submit to the party's decisions on candidates and nominate a patronage-savvy moderate with a broad appeal; it is presented in interval terms[128] in chart 7.5 and table 7.5.

Because the Democratic factions sought to maintain an intersectional coalition while maintaining different stands on slavery, the Democrats faced a far grimmer prospect of success. On the slavery issue, the two wings of the party did agree that the national government should not denounce slavery as immoral—but that was all. Whereas most southern Democrats thought slavery a positive good and insisted on its continued expansion, most northern Democrats held that the morality of slavery, pro or con, was not a legitimate political issue.[129] Given this disagreement, each group stood to gain substantially if it could force the other to make all the concessions. The faction that blinked, that is, stood to lose heavily.

Moreover, mutual compromise offered relatively little to each side. A compromise agreement would presumably have committed the South to avoiding some aspects of the issue of the morality of slavery, while requiring the North to condone other aspects of slavery. Because Southerners viewed

---

[128] [See note 43 above.]
[129] Jaenicke 1986, 101–2; Formisano 1971, 245.

CHART 7.5
The Republicans' Chicken Game in the Late 1850s

		Conservatives' utility	Militants' utility
Outcome 1:	Both make concessions, Republicans win	8	8
Outcome 2:	Neither make concessions, Republicans lose	2	2
Outcome 3:	Conservatives make concessions, Republicans win	7	9
Outcome 4:	Militants make concessions, Republicans win	9	7

TABLE 7.5
The Republicans' Chicken Game in the Late 1850s

		Militants make concessions	
		Yes	No
	Yes	8,8 (outcome 1)	7,9 (outcome 3)
Conservatives make concessions			
	No	9,7 (outcome 4)	2,2 (outcome 2)

the issue in moral terms, presumably they would have been less pleased with such a compromise than would the accommodation-minded Northerners. The Southerners also had more to lose from victories by antislavery Republicans. To summarize this complicated situation: southern Democrats would be more adversely affected by *either* a factional compromise *or* a Republican victory. Each faction found compromise with the other—which was more likely to lead to a Democratic victory—to be only moderately preferable to insisting on its own position, even if that insistence led to a Democratic defeat. This set of utilities, presented in interval terms in chart 7.6 and table 7.6, shows that the likely outcome was a Democratic party split that would enhance the Republicans' prospects.

Indeed, if these preferences are restated ordinally, as in table 7.7, we have the familiar prisoner's dilemma. Assuming that one side makes concessions, the most rational strategy for the other is to make no concessions. As a result, a compromise typically does not occur and the party splits. Here,

CHART 7.6
The Democrats' Prisoner's Dilemma in 1860

		North's utility	South's utility
Outcome 1:	Both make concessions, Democrats (more likely) to win	5	4
Outcome 2:	Neither make concessions, Democrats lose	4	3
Outcome 3:	North makes concessions, Democrats win	2	10
Outcome 4:	South makes concessions, Democrats win	10	2

TABLE 7.6
The Democrats' Prisoner's Dilemma in 1860

		South makes concessions	
		Yes	*No*
	Yes	5,4 (outcome 1)	2,10 (outcome 3)
North makes concessions	*No*	10,2 (outcome 4)	4,3 (outcome 2)

TABLE 7.7
The Democrats' Prisoner's Dilemma in 1860: An Ordinal Analysis

		South makes concessions	
		Yes	*No*
	Yes	3,3 (outcome 1)	1,4 (outcome 3)
North makes concessions	*No*	4,1 (outcome 4)	2,2 (outcome 2)

then, was substantially the same situation as that created by personalist politics prior to the founding of the second party system. In effect, the inability of Van Buren's party to deal with the moral issue of slavery led it back into the predicament from which Van Buren's theory of politics had tried to rescue it.

How, then, did Lincoln and his fellow Republicans escape a similar fate? How, in fact, were they able to address slavery in moral terms, while still adopting the Jacksonians' view of party? How did they find a place for morality in politics, without abandoning the vision of political democracy elaborated by Van Buren and his allies? These questions will be taken up in the chapters that focus directly on the Lincoln persuasion. A satisfactory answer must take into account the Whig tradition with which Lincoln and most other Republicans first identified. We must first trace, in other words, the evolution of the New England reform-liberal tradition that led from Harvard-educated John Adams to the self-educated Whig lawyer from Illinois.

PART FOUR

INTRODUCTION TO PART FOUR

I N THE antebellum era, the Jacksonian and Whig perspectives formulated the basic problems of democratic politics in sharply different ways. For the Jacksonians as humanist liberals, the essential problem was always posed by an existing set of political choices. Respect for the autonomy of the individual meant that one question always came to the fore: what practices, policies, and institutions were necessary to satisfy as many citizens as possible? Their political problem thus was always *internal* to the existing set of preferences; one always began with the existing distribution of preferences; and the goal was always how best to aggregate them.

For most northern Whigs, at least for those influenced by Yankee political culture, however, the ruling questions took a different form: Could some or all of these existing preferences be reconciled with the commands of morality, and thus of duty? And, if so, how? Their emphasis was both on the larger good of the commonwealth and on the rights and opportunities of all its individual members, regardless of the preferences a majority happened to have at a particular time. These commands, these moral rules, in other words, were *external* to existing preferences, and they represented legitimate limits on such preferences. In practice, the limits took the form of moral duties that controlled the conduct of individuals toward each other and toward the larger political community. In contrast to the preferences that determined the actions of humanist liberals, it was these commands of conscience and morality, these psychological and ethical limits, that structured the actions of the reform liberals.

As I suggested earlier, the two sides of the American liberal community elaborated conflicting versions of their common faith, partly in response to developments in their society and polity. As the logic of rapid capitalist development took hold, as the character of vigorous democratic politics emerged, the central tenets of the founders' genus liberalism no longer offered satisfying answers to the most pressing political questions. For the earlier generation, the basic issue had been how to establish a liberal polity, how, that is, to forge the common bonds among liberal individuals that would make a stable liberal regime feasible. The question for the following generation, however, was not how to establish such a regime, but how to determine what course it should take, what policies it should adopt, in response to rapid social and political change. Here humanist and reform approaches offered different answers.

This point is illustrated, in a negative way, by the politics and political thought of Frederick Douglass.[1] From the standpoint of the liberal bi-polarity being explored here, the extent to which Douglass avoided making a choice between these two perspectives is remarkable. As I shall argue in the chapter on Douglass and Lydia Maria Child, one major reason is that Douglass's project did not require that choice. His object was not to shape the Union to move in a particular direction but to find a place in it for himself and his people. The fact that Douglass recurred to the genus liberalism of founders like Jefferson and John Adams, therefore, is far from surprising. Douglass's was also a founding project: to make sure that the bonds that citizens share would come to include what Child had called "that class of Americans called Africans."

Nevertheless, reform and humanist liberals shared a problem they both tended to conceptualize in terms of their common, though attenuated republican heritage: was the appropriate focus to be on (loyalty to) the liberal political community or on the (autonomy of the) liberal individual? Taken as a whole, northern Whigs, northern reform liberals, were much more hostile to slavery than were their humanist, Jacksonian political foes. Within the Whig tradition, the answer to this question—community or individual?—had important implications for how vocally and how insistently one voiced and acted on one's opposition to slavery.

Part four, then, [would have examined] three different kinds of reform liberals. The first, represented by abolitionists Lydia Maria Child and Frederick Douglass, exemplified a concern for individual duty and moral purity that overshadowed commitment to the preservation of the country's liberal regime. The second kind, represented by mainline politician Daniel Webster, displayed just that loyalty to the American republican experiment that Child, for instance, came to scorn; and he did so ultimately at the cost of all those in his state and in the broader cultural community for whom the slavery issue had become increasingly paramount. The third kind of reform liberal is exemplified by John Adams's son, John Quincy Adams. In much the same way that Van Buren offered the Jacksonians a middle course between Leggett's individualism and Douglas's devotion to the polity, the younger Adams marked out a middle road between Child and Webster. Although each of the reform liberal approaches had its intellectual and political strengths, each also suffered from intrinsic, even crippling, difficulties as the question of slavery finally came to dominate the antebellum political agenda.

---

[1] [JDG planned to include here one chapter on Frederick Douglass and Lydia Maria Child and one chapter on Daniel Webster, to accompany the chapter on John Quincy Adams; in the last paragraph of this introduction to part four, JDG indicated where these figures were to fit in the scheme of the book.]

EIGHT

JOHN QUINCY ADAMS

N O ANTEBELLUM FIGURE better illustrates the tensions between political morality and democratic polity than John Quincy
Adams. From 1781 to 1828 Adams served his country with intelligence, effectiveness, and at times real distinction: as minister, in turn, to
the Netherlands, Prussia, Russia, and Great Britain; as the chief United
States negotiator in the Treaty of Ghent; as a member of the Massachusetts
legislature, which in turn elected him to the U.S. Senate; and as secretary of
state under James Monroe. Adams also declined an appointment to the
Supreme Court. Yet historians, biographers, and Adams himself have all
regarded his presidency (1825–1829) as a clear failure.[1] Adams was in fact
ill-suited for that office. He won the White House in a four-man race, even
though Andrew Jackson received more popular and electoral votes, because
Adams's three opponents split the votes in the south and the west. Despite
the fact that Adams was a minority president, he insisted on pressing for an
ambitious program of internal improvements, cultural and economic development, a protective tariff, and a national bank. The program had little
popular appeal outside his own New England, and it therefore fared poorly
in Congress. Not surprisingly, then, Adams's bid for reelection was resoun-
dingly defeated by Jackson, just as his father, in his bid for a second term,
had been defeated by Thomas Jefferson.

Adams's problem was only partly his stubborn, often humorless and self-
righteous stand on policy questions.[2] Despite his burning political ambition,[3] he was an inept, even self-destructive politician during most of his
presidency. In 1824, Adams's campaign had suffered from a lack of coordination and leadership. Four years later he largely ignored those able anti-
Jackson politicians who might have helped his cause. As a generally sympathetic biographer has put it, because Adams never really knew how to
handle even his political allies and supporters, he tended to avoid them all.[4]

Two years after he lost the presidency, however, Adams's political fortunes reversed themselves, and he began a markedly successful, nine-term
career in the House of Representatives. Adams served as chair of the Committee on Manufacture, the Committee on Indian Affairs, and then the

---

[1] Hofstadter 1969; see also Nevins 1969, 454.
[2] Bemis 1956, 8.
[3] Richards 1986, 6–8.
[4] Bemis 1956, 22, 74, 100.

Committee on Foreign Affairs; he had considerable influence on tariff policy during the early 1830s; and he did much to shape the development of the Smithsonian Institution.[5] He became the spokesman for the North and the voice of its conscience in the country's struggle over slavery. In the late 1830s, Jackson angrily concluded that Adams's stand against the annexation of Texas had helped to delay its admission as a slave state.[6] Adams also waged a decade-long, ultimately successful fight against the House's infamous gag rule—which prevented discussion on the floor of any petition pertaining to slavery—and he thereby secured his place in American political history.[7] Moreover, the apparently self-righteous, moralistic stuffiness that had marred his presidency made Adams a respected congressman and a political success. By the 1830s, as Maclean has noted, Adams had become an American institution, at least in the eyes of his fellow Northerners. In his tours in 1843 through upstate New York and Ohio—areas that would supply the core of antislavery sentiment through 1865—Adams discovered an unwonted popularity, one never achieved by his father.[8] Paradoxically, in light of his success and contrary to his own earlier hopes, Adams's role in American politics remained largely negative: his was a continuing opposition to the claims and demands of the slave-holding interests. The positive articulation and affirmation of doctrine was to be left to Lincoln.

This paradox reveals a second. Adams achieved his success largely by confronting the slavery issue head-on, yet his own position on that issue remained clouded with ambiguity throughout his time in Congress. He never stated, for example, the connection between his stand and that of the abolitionists whose petitions he persistently submitted to Congress. As Maclean has perceptively observed, Adams has received relatively little attention from historians, in part because of his "complex and paradoxical" nature, including both his "stand on anti-slavery" and the related issue of native Americans.[9] As I shall try to show here, it is by understanding these paradoxes, and with them both the strengths and weaknesses of Adams's position on slavery, that we can fully understand the task confronting Lincoln in the decade after Adams's death.

Adams's Whiggish Loyalties

The paradoxical features of Adams's career resemble the complexities of his father's political and moral outlook. The policies and candidates of the

[5] Ibid., ch. 23.
[6] Parsons 1973, 372.
[7] Bemis 1956, chs. 13 and 17, 326–27.
[8] Maclean 1984, 158; Richards 1986, 145.
[9] Maclean 1984, 146; see Parsons 1973.

Whigs were an effective challenge to those of the Jacksonians,[10] although through most of the antebellum period the Whigs' coalition of forward-looking entrepreneurs and socially conservative but moralistic Protestants remained a political minority, with little strength in the growing and populistic south and west. Whereas the Democrats' rhetoric of political equality and equal economic opportunity helped them to win six of the eight presidential elections between 1828 and 1856, the Whigs were able to capture both houses of Congress at the same time only in 1840. Despite the political drawbacks, Adams generally shared the Whigs' socially conservative and mildly elitist stance throughout his service in Congress, even though his position on slavery was radical and at times disruptive.

On some aspects of the slavery issue, of course, Adams did break with most of his fellow partisans. However, contrary to some historical accounts and the somewhat self-pitying picture conveyed by his own diary, Adams often enjoyed widespread Whig support. Only a small band of loyalists *consistently* supported him, but he was not as politically isolated as he is usually portrayed. Almost all northern Whig representatives opposed the Mexican War and any territorial expansion of slavery, for example, yet during the Mexican War they joined Adams in voting supplies for the army in the field. Too, when the House adopted the gag rule in 1836, northern Whigs voted with Adams against the rule, 46 to 1, and they also voted 38 to 4 to keep open the possibility of regulating slavery in the District of Columbia.[11] The same group, with one exception, supported the Wilmot Proviso for excluding slavery from all the formerly Mexican territories, whereas eighteen northern Democrats opposed it.

On these issues, the differences between Adams and his fellow partisans were mostly verbal, as Richards has noted, with Adams more openly than others attacking the South and its peculiar institution. There were times when Adams's stand on slavery isolated him from his more moderate colleagues, but even in these cases he had support from a core of like-minded Whig moralists, particularly those who appealed to the anti-Masonic—that is, the populist, reformist, and evangelical—side of the Whig coalition. Adams had demonstrated his own ties to the anti-Masonic faction in 1833, when he prevailed on twelve of them to join with other Whigs in choosing the printer for the House of Representatives.[12] Similarly, in 1836 Adams and a few of these colleagues argued that the use of federal forces under the War Powers Act to put down a slave rebellion would justify other federal intervention on the issue of slavery. Such intervention, it was widely claimed, was prohibited under the principle of states' rights, but Adams and his allies argued that either the federal government could intervene or it

[10] J. R. Howe 1966.
[11] Richards 1986, 124.
[12] Ibid., 123; Nevins 1969, 435.

could not, and if the South asked for federal intervention to put down a slave rebellion, they in turn left themselves open to other kinds of federal intervention. Adams's allies "were not typical [Webster-Clay] Whigs"; they had abolitionist or broadly moral reformist leanings, "and all but one represented districts in which Anti-masonry had run rampant."[13]

However, when it came to economic issues, as Richards put it, Adams "was invariably on the side of the Webster men when the 'yeas and nays' were called in Congress."[14] Entirely hostile to the Jacksonians' doctrine of laissez-faire and their strict construction of the Constitution, Adams strongly espoused the essentials of Clay's celebrated American system.[15] Indeed, on certain points Adams went well beyond Clay. Adams, for example, embraced the Whigs' argument for a protective tariff that would encourage the nation's and especially his own region's emerging manufacturing industries. Such measures, he assured his supporters in Braintree, Massachusetts, would secure the jobs of northern workers.[16] Although Adams proved willing to compromise on the tariff when intersectional comity seemed to demand it, he whole-heartedly joined other Whigs in supporting the second Bank of the United States against Jackson's ultimately successful onslaught.[17]

For Adams, however, these elements of the American system were clearly less important than that system's call for internal improvements. Indeed, for this sixth president of the United States, improvement did not mean simply of the roads and canals so important to Clay; it meant, instead, a comprehensive vision of government support and stimulation for economic, social, and even cultural development.[18] Like most of the Whigs, Adams insisted that the federal government's public lands must be sold at a fair price rather than be given away. His object in this insistence, however, was not so much to maintain a supply of workers by restricting western migration as it was to use the proceeds of the land sales, together with the revenue yielded by the protective tariff, to support "continual progressive improvement, physical, moral, political, in the condition of the whole people of this Union."[19] The goal included both the "promotion of domestic industry" and the acquisition and diffusion of knowledge through "public institutions and seminaries of learning;" Adams considered the "improvement of human knowlege" to be a "sacred" cause.[20]

---

13 Richards 1986, 123.
14 Ibid., 57.
15 Ibid., 58–59, 10–11.
16 J. Q. Adams 1842a, 22, 53.
17 Lipsky 1950, 103; Richards 1986, 59–60, 78–88.
18 Richards 1986, 56–57.
19 J. Q. Adams 1842a, 22–23.
20 J. Q. Adams 1874–1877, 8:273; Koch and Peden 1946, 361–62.

Even as tensions over slavery mounted, Adams maintained his party ties. Because his hostility to Jackson was personal as well as political, Adams had no trouble supporting Whig candidates throughout the 1830s and 1840s.[21] In 1844, even after Adams had emerged as the North's tribune against the slave power, he supported the slave-owning Whig candidate, Henry Clay, against the political abolitionist of the Liberty party.[22] As Adams himself noted, he was one of the Whig leaders who gathered in 1841 to assess the impact of President Harrison's death on their party and to decide on the right course for Daniel Webster to pursue as secretary of state.[23]

Adams's position was sustained by his allegiance to what Howe called Whig political culture, notably the Whig belief in the social, historic, and organic bases of the human community. Adams emphasized, for example, "the influence of Society upon the condition of man. . . . It is only in society that man can exercise his prerogative of reason and his faculty of speech."[24] He also put great emphasis on the links between the generations and on the pivotal social role of the family.[25] "From the experience of the past," he observed in his inaugural address, "we derive instructive lessons for the future."[26] So, too, he emphasized to his children "the debt . . . every generation owes to its predecessors."[27]

The conservative implication of Adams's position becomes clear when we turn to his view of the family, that is, of the immediate link between the generations. A Whig rather than a Federalist, Adams spoke more readily than his father had about political equality and popular rule. Moreover, his view of women was partially—but only partially—tempered by his belief in their basic rights and the need for their consent in forming marriages. Nevertheless, in a well-ordered social world, Adams thought, "the *permanent* family compact" would be "formed by the *will* of the man and the *consent* of the woman"; thus, the "wife is not qualified to vote, because, by the nuptial tie and the law of God, her will has been subjected to that of her husband."[28]

Adams's stand on women more or less faithfully reflected the mores and prejudices of his own time, but his stands on property and especially on imprisonment for debt seem elitist, even when measured against those of his contemporary, that paragon of cautious calculation, Martin Van Buren. As

21 J. Q. Adams 1842a, 28; Richards 1986, 55–56.
22 Richards 1986, 173; Bemis 1956, 473.
23 Nevins 1969, 529–30.
24 J. Q. Adams 1845, 80–81.
25 Lipsky 1950, 98.
26 Koch and Peden 1946, 355.
27 J. Q. Adams 1874–1877, 2:10.
28 J. Q. Adams 1842b, Letter of transmittal.

a relatively young man, Adams had valued, in Lipsky's words, "order and stability," and in a letter to his father Adams had praised social "peace and a regulated liberty"; throughout his career, he construed that liberty to mean the protection of property.[29] In the 1780s he had referred disdainfully to "the idle and extravagant and consequently poor," and he feared any conflict that sharply divided the poor and the wealthy.[30]

Adams's position on property and liberty followed from his Lockean belief that the security of one's property was a "natural right."[31] Although he sympathized with the poor—and he thought that owning property entailed obligations to the community—Adams held that such ownership was essential to both liberty and democracy. "The protection and security of property," he wrote, "is not less the purpose of the social compact than that of persons."[32] He thus supported the Bank of the United States, as Bemis has said, because "it was a protector of private property and the sanctity of contract."[33]

Such a position led Adams to a stand on imprisonment for debt far less generous than the stands of many of his Jacksonian contemporaries, although he contemplated—however grudgingly—ending the practice. If there were to be such an end to imprisonment for debt, he felt, it would be necessary to "provid[e] some other substitute for the security which it gives to credit."[34] Indeed, the existing practice, he argued, permitted the poor to obtain credit not otherwise available, because they could promise to forfeit their freedom if they defaulted. This somewhat hardhearted concern for the poor, Bemis has noted, "seems almost medieval."[35] Be that as it may, Adams's stand on the issue underlines his lifelong ties to the conservative, and hierarchical, side of the Whig creed.

Adams and Slavery

Although Abigail Adams had been troubled by the prospect of miscegenation, she had taken a more explicit and liberal stand on race and slavery than her husband.[36] John Quincy had his own reservations about interracial marriage, and he believed strongly enough in the superiority of Anglo-Saxons to attempt to justify their displacement of the American Indians

[29] Lipsky 1950, 92; Koch and Peden 1946, 245.
[30] J. Adams 1850–1856, 1:185–86; Lipsky 1950, 91, see n. 18.
[31] Lipsky 1950, 166, quoting Adams 1837, 56.
[32] J. Q. Adams 1842b, 20.
[33] Bemis 1956, 252.
[34] Nevins 1969, 425.
[35] Bemis 1956, 257.
[36] Maclean 1984, 147; Richards 1986, 96–97.

from the northeast.[37] Like his mother, however, he believed that no human being could rightly enslave another, because each and every one had an immortal soul.[38] Indeed, every person was born with "natural rights, even against the patriarchal power of the father."[39] As a result, Adams scorned interpretations of the Declaration of Independence that restricted its applicability to a particular racial group.[40] To be sure, Adams did not express these sentiments early in his career; they emerged first in the privacy of his diary. In 1804, for example, he prepared a statement that voiced the standard northern Federalist complaint against the three-fifths rule—that rule by which three-fifths of the slaves enumerated in a census were counted in the apportionment of congressional seats. In his complaint, however, Adams seemed to emphasize the injury to northern white interests rather than the plight of the slaves. Indeed, some of the very early references to slavery in his diary were notably matter-of-fact and even dispassionate in tone. In 1816, for example, he reported British complaints about the slave trade without any comment of his own.[41] Three years later, he noted somewhat critically the activities of the Colonization Society, but he took no stand of his own.[42]

As the crisis over Missouri emerged, however, Adams's attitude shifted. In his journal, on January 24, 1820, he referred to slavery as "that outrage upon the goodness of God."[43] In a conversation with John C. Calhoun two months later, Adams attacked the institution, because it confounded "the ideas of servitude and labor" so that, in the South, much valuable work could only be performed by slaves. In his diary he went on to reflect that the Southerners' "condition of masterdom" had encouraged a "pride and vainglory" that disfigured their souls. Slavery, that is, not only prevented slaves from developing their faculties, it also had a deleterious effect on slave owners. Adams noted that it was "among the evils of slavery that it taints the very sources of moral principle. It establishes false estimates of virtue and vice: for what can be more false and heartless than this doctrine which makes the first and holiest rights of humanity to depend upon the color of the skin?"[44]

Over time, these private reflections became more militant, and Adams's public statements made him the leading foe in Congress of the slaveholding interests. By the mid-1830s, Adams held that if poor whites could vote, free

---

[37] Maclean 1984, 148; see Richards 1986, 183.
[38] Lipsky 1950, 100.
[39] Ibid., 96.
[40] Maclean 1984, 152; see J. Q. Adams 1874–1877, 5:10–11; cf. 9:349–50.
[41] Nevins 1969, 177–78.
[42] Ibid., 221–22.
[43] Ibid., 226.
[44] Ibid., 231–32.

blacks should be able to as well.[45] From the 1830s on, Adams openly expressed disdain for the doughfaces—that is, any politician like "Mr. Van Buren" who was "a Northern man with Southern principles."[46] By the 1840s, Adams regarded the admission of Texas as a slave state as "the heaviest calamity that ever befell myself and my country."[47] At the end of his career, he voted repeatedly for the Wilmot Proviso, which would have barred slavery from all the territories won in the Mexican War.[48]

By 1842 Adams could denounce the South's peculiar institution, because it regarded "men, women, and children" as "things to be treated by their owners . . . like tables, chairs and joint-stools." The resulting accumulation of "twelve hundred millions of dollars of property" that was *acquired by crime,* Adams held, "is daily becoming more and more odious."[49] Thus, the conspiracy to incorporate Texas into the Union illustrated the malign control of the slave-holders over every branch of the national government.[50] "The extinction" of slavery itself, he wrote on July 4, 1843, would be "nothing more nor less than the consummation of the Christian Religion."[51] By the end of his career, he was very discouraged over the rising political influence of the slave power; he even began to doubt his early comfortable belief that Anglo-Saxon civilization was truly and distinctively devoted to the cause of human liberty and was thus more advanced and deserving than that of the American Indians who had been driven from their native land.[52] Here, surely, were the attitudes that sustained Adams in his assaults in the House of Representatives on both the gag rule and the morality of slavery itself, the attitudes that inspired as well his successful plea before the Supreme Court for the freedom of the Africans who had ended up in federal custody after revolting against the crew of the slave ship *Amistad.*[53]

Adam's Liberalism

The apparent tensions between the importance of property rights for Adams and his stand on slavery can be understood in part in terms of the obvious, Lockean commitment to genus liberalism. Adams insisted that the principles of his nation's revered revolution had been "especially expounded

[45] Richards 1986, 97–98.
[46] J. Q. Adams 1842a, 16.
[47] Nevins 1969, 574.
[48] Bemis 1956, 499.
[49] J. Q. Adams 1842a, 20–21, 24.
[50] Ibid., 10, 20, 25–26.
[51] Bemis 1956, 465–66.
[52] Parsons 1973, 368–70.
[53] Bemis 1956, ch. 19.

in the writings of Locke," and Locke's theory permeated his own thought.[54] As a young man, Adams had held that every nation has "a natural and unalienable right to form a constitution . . . because government [is] . . . instituted for the common security and natural rights of every individual."[55]

His concern with individual rights encouraged the two sides of Adams's politics. As much as he valued energetic government, any regime that invaded property rights was clearly usurpatious.[56] More specifically, Adams celebrated "civil, political, commercial and religious liberty," as well as freedom of the press and free inquiry generally.[57] Moreover, Adams tied a belief in these freedoms to the doctrine of popular consent, hence his support for Jefferson's acquisition of Louisiana was qualified.[58] By the same token, a woman's prerogative of consenting to a marriage imposed limits on the authority of the father, that is, a woman's rights modified a father's authority. In general, consent, whether popular or individual, rightly imposed limits on those in positions of authority.

These considerations by themselves, however, underline a familiar point: genus liberalism is sufficiently rich and complex to have offered support and legitimation for both sides of Adams's politics—much as it did for Jefferson's. On one side, the slaves' right to freedom and the fact that they had not consented to their bondage argued for emancipation; on the other side, the owners had a clear right to their property and had consented to joining a union whose constitution represented an intersectional compromise. With these points in mind, the Jacksonians, who were just as good genus liberals in their ways as Adams, could argue for caution and prudence rather than for an all-out assault on slavery. That Adams resolved these tensions as he did, that he put aside his concern for property rights and his revulsion at miscegenation, may be traced in large part to his reform liberalism. Adams's reform liberalism, like his parents' and especially his mother's, strongly resembled Lydia Maria Child's, whose particular creed turned the broader tenets of genus liberalism in a militantly antislavery direction.

More overtly than her husband, Abigail Adams had been a remarkable precursor of those reform liberal foes of slavery, mainly from New England stock, who joined a stern Protestant conscience to a belief in the equality of human souls. Partly because of her husband's duties abroad, Abigail played a decisive part in John Quincy's early upbringing; she remained his intellectual companion the rest of her life, and she established an emotional tie with

[54] J. Q. Adams 1839, 40.
[55] Koch and Peden 1946, 231.
[56] Lipsky 1950, 142.
[57] Ibid., 166; J. Q. Adams 1874–1877, 7:492; Koch and Peden 1946, 228.
[58] J. Q. Adams 1941, 37, 81.

her son that stayed with him into his old age.[59] When he eventually attacked the slave-holding interests, the son was giving voice not only to his parents' specific views on race but also to their more far-reaching, reform liberal faith. The first letter of *Publicola*, for example, which affirmed a people's right to establish their own constitution, also denied—in the same sentence—that "a whole nation has the right to do whatever it chooses to do."[60] As that remark suggests, John Quincy Adams focused on the reform liberals' concern with moral duty rather than the humanist liberals' celebration of preferences.

Indeed, Adams's reform liberal commitment was indisputable. He read the Bible almost every day of his life. His discussion of American political parties invoked the very biblical passage—"a house divided against itself cannot stand"—that Lincoln was to make a centerpiece of his 1858 campaign for the Senate.[61] Like that of his father, Adams's faith, in the words of Edward Everett, followed the "milder" path of liberal Calvinism.[62] In particular, Adams affirmed the basic goodness and perfectability of human nature, and he denied the orthodox doctrines of original sin and eternal damnation.[63] For all his theological liberalism, however, Adams's life was dominated by the Puritans' moral concerns, their focus on duty, conscience, and rigorous self-examination. Human beings, rather than doing just as they pleased in pursuit of whatever preferences they happened to have, must be controlled—by their duties as well as their rights, and thus by the moral law to which any conscientious person would gladly submit.

Adams's outlook rested on a moderated version of his father's piety. However much he acknowledged the strength of natural reason, Adams joined his father in pointing up its limits, for "it cannot discover" the "sacred and important truths . . . in all their clearness."[64] The "dispensations" of Providence, he insisted in a *Discourse on Education* in 1839, were "wise" but ultimately "inscrutable," and one's duty as a human being was to submit to that will, that is, to proffer obedience to the "transcendent power of the Supreme Being." "Justice," he said, "has no other foundation than piety . . . *piety* becomes as rational as it is essential" and "becomes the first of human duties."[65]

Indeed, here also was the foundation of his duty and, therefore, his ethics. Adams prayed in his diary, near the end of his life, "May I . . . never murmur at the dispensation of Providence. . . . [I] implore [God's] . . . forgiveness

[59] Bemis 1956, 4–5; Nevins 1969, 555.
[60] Koch and Peden 1946, 231.
[61] J. Q. Adams 1941, 31.
[62] Lipsky 1950, 6, n. 6.
[63] Ibid., 77, n. 71.
[64] Koch and Peden 1946, 279.
[65] J. Q. Adams 1941, 10; Koch and Peden 1946, 281.

for all the errors and delinquincies of my life!"[66] Much earlier in his life he had expressed thanks to God for "lay[ing] his chastening hand upon me and . . . try[ing] me with bitter sorrow."[67] The result was a rigorous self-examination, a self-critical attitude, that subordinated Adams, in his own eyes, to God if not to other men, and that dominated his diaries from beginning to end.

These obligations held for others as well. In Lipsky's words, Adams believed that "governments were 'subordinate to the *moral* supremacy of the People,' [but] the People were in turn subordinate to a moral law."[68] For all his enthusiasm for universal human rights, which in turn sustained his hostility to slavery, Adams nevertheless linked that notion to one of moral duty. He therefore celebrated the Reformation, in part because it "was an advance in the knowledge of [humankind's] . . . *duties* and . . . *rights*."[69] As Bemis remarked, "duty" was the strongest word in Adams's vocabulary.[70] Adams's sense of obligation, for example, led him to attend the House of Representatives with a faithfulness rare among his colleagues.[71]

Adams's conception of duty helped to sustain his anti-utilitarian, anti-consequentialist ethic. He focused on intention, rather than on consequences or desires. As he put it in a letter to his mother, "the *virtue* of all action depends upon the motive of the actor."[72] Although Adams enjoyed a glass of good wine, he rejected pleasure or desire as a guide to moral conduct. Europe seemed a dangerous place to him, because people there were incited "to dissipation, intemperance, sensuality, and idleness; [which were] destructive of the will to self-control and self-denial."[73] Adams berated himself in his diary for his own "life of . . . irregularity and dissipation."[74] His goal was to control the appetites,[75] and he denounced "that odious discrimination between the sexes, which supposes one of them to have been created merely for the pleasure of the other."[76] More generally, Adams dismissed "indiscriminate sexual intercourse" as "the primitive law of the savage."[77]

This posture had clear implications for slavery. Like his father's, John Quincy's theology and ethics prepared him to dismiss the essentially utili-

---

[66] Koch and Peden 1946, 410.
[67] Nevins 1969, 103.
[68] J. Q. Adams 1837, 26.
[69] Koch and Peden 1946, 309.
[70] Bemis 1956, 284.
[71] Lipsky 1950, 61, 63.
[72] J. Q. Adams 1913–1917, 4:529.
[73] Lipsky 1950, 74, citing J. Q. Adams 1913–1917, 6:414.
[74] Nevins 1969, 69; cf. 157.
[75] Lipsky 1950, 76, citing J. Q. Adams 1842b, 7–8.
[76] J. Q. Adams 1845, 85.
[77] Ibid., 88.

itarian arguments for tolerating slavery—for example, that the institution was favored by important elements of American society and that emancipation would entail major social and economic costs. For both Adamses, on the contrary, all human beings were so remote from God's power and goodness that allowing some of them to have dominion over others was, quite literally, impious. Moreover, a care for one's own character and moral purity, for one's ethical duty, required just that course Adams followed in Congress: an often provocative resistance to the demands of the slave holders, no matter what the cost in the enmity of his fellow citizens.

In acting as his duty commanded, Adams followed the examples of his parents, and especially of his mother, by minimizing those racial differences that he was not entirely able to overlook. Some of the differences were physical, or, more properly, physiological; others were behavioral dissimilarities, produced by the opposed experiences of slavery and freedom. Adams approached these issues with an ontology and epistemology quite similar to, if less developed than, his father's.

Specifically, Adams had little use for the materialism and emphasis on sense perception that many Jacksonians shared with Jefferson. Despite Adams's enthusiasm for the empirical inquiries of natural science, he relied heavily, in Lipsky's words, on "the capacity of the rational mind to arrive at truth . . . through the logical inspection of principles" rather than the efforts, as Adams put it, of "political empirics."[78] This view clashed directly with the empiricism of his personal acquaintance, Jeremy Bentham. The English philosopher, Adams reported, favored a "positive" or sensory "knowledge of the physical world," whereas religious claims depended on the less reliable inferences of human reason. Adams replied that "the mere testimony of the senses" was unreliable and required the corrective of reason.[79] Twenty-six years later, Adams still referred slightingly to the "stubborness of man's belief in the testimony of his senses."[80]

In looking beyond the senses, Adams relied on the emphasis on immaterialism central to his faith. Our "Creator must be a spiritual and not a material Being," Adams wrote in 1811, suggesting the importance of each human being's "immortal soul."[81] Without such a soul, as he wrote in his diary, man would be "a mere tameable beast of the field"; he told Bentham that the immaterial human intellect molds and controls our world but is "nowhere perceptible to the sense." It followed that the physiological and behavioral differences between the two races, however often observed, were essentially unimportant. As Adams put it, "the fallacy" of the slave

---

[78] Lipsky 1950, 73, citing J. Q. Adams 1810, 1:23 and J. Q. Adams 1874–1877, 4:370.
[79] J. Q. Adams 1874–1877, 3:564.
[80] J. Q. Adams 1843, 18.
[81] Koch and Peden 1946, 278.

holders—what they overlooked—was that the "soul of one man cannot be made the property of another."[82]

Instead, therefore, of relying on sense perceptions and preferences, Adams joined other reform liberals in celebrating the cultivation of human faculties, or, as he typically put it, intellectual, physical, and moral improvement. Like many other heirs of the Puritan tradition, Adams had a burning ambition, a drive for success that would testify to his own worth, if not his own sanctity. The concern with worldly success led him to urge his children to "methodize your studies."[83]

Adams's ambition, however, had a distinctly intellectual cast. He retained a lively interest in science to the end of his life. As Lipsky has noted, Adams's *Memoirs* reveal a "drive for education [that] never ceased."[84] More broadly, Adams's was a partially secularized and endlessly reiterated concern for "improvement" that reproduced the concern of his ancestors for the cultivation of human faculties—rather than the satisfaction of human preferences—as the true object of one's ethics. Witness, for example, Adams's declaration that "all the powers of the body and all the faculties of the mind of every individual . . . should be exercised to the utmost extent . . . in improving the condition of his kind."[85] "Improvement" thus was not only of oneself but of more general human conditions that would enable others to improve as well. Adams's European travels, he recalled in 1809, had left him with a vivid impression of the "excellence" that could be achieved by the use of one's artistic "faculties."[86]

His concern for human improvement shaped Adams's own public actions. Even though he initially favored the removal of native American Indians from their ancestral lands, he later took a much more protective attitude toward the "civilized" tribes, precisely because they had cultivated their faculties as well as their lands.[87] So, too, his first annual message called for "public institutions and seminaries of learning" to promote "the acquisition of knowledge" and thus contribute to "the improvement of the condition of men."[88] This concern also accounts for his intense interest and influential role in the founding of the Smithsonian Institution.[89]

As a liberal Calvinist, Adams construed the outlook in voluntarist terms. He insisted on freedom of worship and the "right of private judgment, in other words the privilege of every reader, to exercise the faculties of his own

---

[82] Koch and Peden 1946, 408; J. Q. Adams 1874–1877, 3:565.

[83] J. Q. Adams 1874–1877, 2:17.

[84] Richards 1986, 201; Lipsky 1950, 66.

[85] J. Q. Adams 1845, 87; see Koch and Peden 1946, 406.

[86] Koch and Peden 1946, 266.

[87] See Koch and Peden 1946, 358, and Nevins 1969, 526.

[88] Koch and Peden 1946, 361.

[89] Bemis 1956, 512; cf. 523.

understanding in what he reads."[90] While Adams believed, that is, in one's obligation to develop *some* faculty or other; he also believed that one was free to choose the particular project for oneself. The "opportunities and dispositions of individuals for the cultivation of any one specific art or science are infinitely diversified."[91]

As in the case of his parents, and of Lydia Maria Child, for Adams the emphasis on the self-development of human faculties rather than on the satisfaction of preferences had important implications for Adams's stand on slavery. Whereas a focus on preferences often led to concern with balancing competing claims (e.g., for and against slavery), Adams's strict ethical premises led in a very different direction. Witness his remarks to John C. Calhoun on the aversion of southern whites to performing the physical work typically undertaken by slaves. Adams's concern with improvement—moral as well as physical and intellectual—suggested that people of all sections would benefit from emancipation, no matter what their preferences. John Randolph of Roanoke, the perceptive southern militant, recognized the force of this argument and just this danger to his own section.[92] Randolph was one of many who understood liberty in negative terms, as the absence of constraint, and who often thought of abolition as the coercing of southern whites and thus the limiting of their freedom. As a result, the issues of balance and preferences reemerged. The value of giving the slaves their liberty had to be weighed against the constraints such a step would impose on the preferences of both Southerners and their many northern sympathizers.

The absence of restraint, to be sure, was part of Adams's understanding of liberty. There could be no liberty, he suggested in the Cincinnati oration, if one's "hands . . . [were] manacled or tied" or if one's feet were "fettered or cramped into impotence."[93] Liberty defined only as the absence of constraint, however, was clearly incomplete. Drunkards did not suffer from external coercion to drink, for example, but their enslavement to drink meant they were still not meaningfully free. Accordingly, like so many of his fellow Yankees, Adams understood freedom more positively: one has the liberty to perform a complex action only if one has the ability or capacity to do so. The liberty of one individual could not be opposed to the liberty of another, therefore, just because the two individuals had conflicting preferences. From Adams's perspective, such an opposition would not readily arise, because the way to increase the liberty of any two individuals would be to help both improve themselves. In the case of slavery, as John Randolph feared, increasing the liberty of both sides would mean intellectual im-

[90] J. Q. Adams 1839, 27–28.
[91] Koch and Peden 1946, 406.
[92] Bemis 1956, 132.
[93] Koch and Peden 1946, 401.

provement for the slaves and moral improvement for their masters—and consequently the end of the institution. Cultivating the faculties of all would increase freedom in general, and society as a whole would acquire a more developed capacity for action. In Adams's words, "individual liberty is individual power, and as the power of the community is a mass compounded of individual powers, the nation which enjoys the most freedom must necessarily be in proportion to its numbers the most powerful nation."[94]

Adams's watchword as president, not surprisingly, was "liberty is power."[95] His political enemies, who typically deplored his attitude on slavery, clung to the idea of simple negative liberty—the absence of constraint; a major opposition paper, for example, insisted that "power is always stealing from the many to the few." To Jacksonians more generally, as Bemis has noted, "liberty meant the least government possible in Washington."[96]

Reform Liberalism and Politics

John Quincy Adams may have been a paradigm of reform liberalism, but his calling as a public man—as a politician—kept him from becoming a true abolitionist. Over time, as Adams attacked the slave-holding interests more and more openly, and as he came to recognize an emotional and moral affinity with reformers like Child, he came to despise Daniel Webster. Yet certain affinities between Adams and the Whig statesman persisted. The two men agreed not just on the Whigs' economic program and the sins of the Democrats, but also on the importance of protecting the Union from the divisive consequences of the conflict over slavery.

Adams's approach to slavery as a public issue, in fact, revealed a basic ambivalence that endured, though in varying forms, throughout his career. Early on, Adams's position was hardly hostile to the South, either on the issue of slavery itself or on the issue of removing American Indians from the southeastern United States.[97] As secretary of state, Adams supported Jackson's aggressive efforts to secure Florida, and as president Adams supported the acquisition of parts of Texas, even though both territories were likely to become slave states.[98] The unionism that Adams inherited from his father surely played a role in these actions. On the question of the federal territories, despite his doubts and reservations, Adams "favored this Missouri

[94] Ibid., 342.
[95] Bemis 1956, 69.
[96] Ibid., 142, 152.
[97] Richards 1986, 147–51.
[98] Ibid., 151–52.

Compromise," as he wrote in his journal, "believing it to be all that could be effected under the present Constitution, and from extreme unwillingness to put the Union at hazard."[99] As Bemis noted, Adams was "an abolitionist at heart but a constitutionalist in practice."[100]

Additional considerations affected Adams's position. As Richards has summarized Adams's conduct up to the mid-1830s: "whenever there was a conflict between liberty and the law, or liberty and his position in government, or liberty and his political career, the cause of liberty was abandoned."[101] Adams, after all, confronted essentially the same social order that ostracized the hitherto influential and celebrated Child, as well as the aristocratic Wendell Phillips, once they declared themselves abolitionists—and, unlike Child and Phillips, Adams was a politician who remained dependent on public approval. As a result, in 1837 Adams explicitly valued "prudence and caution," in general and with regard to slavery—much in the spirit in which as a presidential candidate in the early 1820s he had kept his antislavery feelings to himself.[102] Similarly, Adams responded with cautious hesitation to an invitation to attend an abolitionist meeting: "Upon this subject of anti-slavery my principles and my position make it necessary for me to be more circumspect in my conduct than belongs to my nature."[103] Several weeks later, he complained that "the abolitionists . . . are constantly urging me to indiscreet movements, which would ruin me and weaken and not strengthen their cause."[104] Adams suggested to a political sympathizer that the abolitionists' extreme demands were counterproductive.[105] The fight over the right to petition in Congress therefore served Adams admirably. Because the right to petition was only a collateral issue, it allowed him to attack the slave-holding interests "without alienating his own constituents, divided as they still were on the issue of abolition."[106] The motives that produced Adams's equivocal position on slavery were, on the one side, his burning political ambition and his obvious caution as a result and, on the other side, his hatred of slavery and the tensions between the institutions of New England and the South. Once again, however, our question is how Adams could maintain this tension-ridden position, convincing both himself and his constituents that he was acting on principle and not just political convenience.

Part of the answer follows from his reform liberalism itself, in particular

[99] Nevins 1969, 232.
[100] Bemis 1956, ix.
[101] Richards 1986, 105.
[102] Bemis 1956, 350; Richards 1986, 103.
[103] Nevins 1969, 479.
[104] Ibid., 483.
[105] Bemis 1956, 375, 382.
[106] Ibid., 335; see Nevins 1969, 466.

from its injunction that he devote his energies and faculties to improving himself and his society. Such a project entailed the pursuit of success in the world, both as a way of rendering service to others and of demonstrating Adams's own morality and his genuine commitment to achieving that goal. After all, the ethics of the New England orthodoxy, heavily modified but never abandoned by Adams, instructed God's souls not to retreat to a private world of individual purity, but to reform—to purify—their nation's official church. The insistence on success in the world meant, in turn, a concern with instrumental rationality—with finding the most effective means of pursuing one's goals—that marked Adams's entire career. The instruction to pursue reform effectively in the world was a central element of the reform liberal outlook, an instruction that would inspire a crusading enthusiasm in many of its partisans.

Adams's religious sensibility always had a practical cast, as he himself noted in a letter to his father.[107] His attention to means and ends, for example, accounts for Adams's slighting reference to that whole range of "partial associations" that characterized his era—from "Native Americans" and "Irish Catholics" to "abolition societies" and the "Liberty party" that "are sealing the fate of this nation."[108] Adams's skeptical attitude grew out of a broader intellectual skepticism. He described Ralph Waldo Emerson, for example, as a "young man [who had failed] . . . in the everyday avocations of a Unitarian preacher" and only then declared "all the old revelations superannuated and worn out."[109] Adams's own tendency, instead, was to consider the "necessity" of a particular case, as he did in defending Jackson's actions against the American Indians in Florida.[110] Just these considerations led Adams to take a cautious stand on the tariff—and on slavery—during his campaign for the presidency in 1824.[111] So, too, Adams devoted considerable energy to winning support in Congress, especially among former Federalists. He willingly struck the highly political—though certainly not corrupt—bargain with Henry Clay, in the controversial 1824 election, for example, the bargain according to which Clay threw his support for the presidency to Adams, in exchange for the appointment as secretary of state.[112]

Adams's commitment to worldly success had a broader consequence for his political outlook. The world in which he sought political success and effectiveness was not only broadly liberal, it was, more specifically, still republican—although to a diminished degree. Adams's reverence for Locke

[107] See J. Q. Adams 1913–1917, 6:111–16.
[108] Nevins 1969, 572–73, 564–65.
[109] Ibid., 511.
[110] Ibid., 199.
[111] Bemis 1956, 34.
[112] Ibid., 43–44, 58, 130–31.

was matched by his admiration for the great republican theorist Algernon Sidney.[113] Adams characterized the spirit of the English revolutionaries as thoroughly republican, and from that perspective he denounced all claims to "absolute, irresistable, despotic power," arguing that "unlimited power belongs not to the nature of man; and rotten will be the foundation of every government leaning upon such a maxim for support." Certainly Adams endorsed the republican insistence on the separation of powers compounded by a division of "the [legislative] power [into two houses] to prevent legislative tyranny."[114] Adams was thus a republican constitutionalist; he was devoted to arrangements for limiting all political power rather than committed to any single faction, even the democratic majority.[115] Not surprisingly, Adams expressed his own political values in a clear, if somewhat attenuated, republican rhetoric. And that attenuated republicanism reinforced and legitimated his complex and paradoxical stand on slavery.

In his republicanism, Adams emphasized the independence and virtue of every individual citizen. This position, first, ruled out the enslavement of one individual by another and, second, encouraged moral stands, such as those of the abolitionists, against the blandishments of political parties and authorities. Thus for Adams republican virtue was connected to a strict morality. As Adams said in his "Jubilee of the Constitution," the people's "virtue . . . was the foundation of republican government," and that virtue was itself "the natural and inalienable rights of man, of the indefeasible constituent and dissolvent sovereignty of the people [which must] always [be] . . . subordinate to a rule of right and wrong, and always responsible to the Supreme Ruler of the universe for [its] . . . *rightful* exercise."[116]

For himself, Adams tried to implement this outlook, at least in part by following a rule of republican simplicity. As president, he "made the journeys to [and] from New England as unostentatiously as possible . . . by common stage and steamship accommodations and suffering inconveniences like any ordinary traveler."[117] Richards added that Adams was "the epitome of republican simplicity in his dress and his treatment of servants."[118] To be sure, Adams feared a regime "that would give expression to the will of a tyrannical popular majority"—yet he had little sympathy for overtly aristocratic institutions, and he could berate "the idleness of the rich and prosperous."[119] There was a thread of consistency here: all segments of

---

[113] J. Q. Adams 1842b, 27.
[114] J. Q. Adams 1831, 19, 13, 26; Lipsky 1950, 234, 202.
[115] Lipsky 1950, 222; J. Q. Adams 1839, 115.
[116] J. Q. Adams 1839, 54.
[117] Bemis 1956, 100.
[118] Richards 1986, 209.
[119] Lipsky 1950, 110, 112.

society—all citizens—must subordinate their own passions and interests to the society's limits on individual aggrandizement, to a rule of right that was essential to a republican polity. From this perspective, the unlimited power of masters over slaves—and the unlimited indulgence of passions that such power sometimes encouraged—was essentially unrepublican. Equally unrepublican was the reluctance of both the Jacksonian Democrats and the conservative Whigs to disturb the nation's social and economic interests by raising the slavery issue.

This insistence on individual virtue helped sustain Adams's classically republican hostility to the principle of party loyalty, since that loyalty, as Adams saw it, could all too often lead to compromising one's independent standpoint, principles, and virtue in the pursuit of party unity and electoral victory. The most flagrant case in point, of course, was the question of patronage. Personally, Adams thought that the "besetting sin of popular governments" was the tendency of "cunning" politicians to "fatten upon the public spoils" by removing partisan opponents from office regardless of their abilities or virtues. Adams noted that "Mr. Jefferson made numerous removals from office of good and efficient officers, to put partizans of his own, not better qualified, in their place."[120] True to this sentiment, Adams himself made every effort, with some real success, to keep the issue of party loyalties and patronage from affecting the Smithsonian Institution.

By the same token, however willing Adams was to cooperate with the Whigs in Congress on many issues and to support their party's congressional candidates, he never hesitated to break with them when his policy position seemed to demand it.[121] In just that way he had broken with both Federalists and Democratic-Republicans in an earlier era. As a senator in the first decade of the 1800s, Adams recalled in 1809, "the part which I acted was that of an *independent* member," leading him to support part of Jefferson's program—the Louisiana Purchase, the Non-Importation Act of 1806, and the Embargo Act of 1807. In 1808 that support cost him reelection by a Massachusetts legislature dominated by Federalists.[122] Although Adams supported Jefferson on foreign policy issues, however, he had no regular contact with the Republican order during this period; instead, he joined his one-time Federalist allies against the Republicans over domestic sectional issues, such as the constitutional scope of the national government's powers and the three-fifths rule, which increased the South's representation in the House of Representatives.[123] So, too, in his later career Adams broke with the Whigs to support Jackson on the issue of foreign

[120] Nevins 1969, 455; J. Q. Adams 1941, 36.
[121] Bemis 1956, 313–15.
[122] Koch and Peden 1946, 265; cf. Nevins 1969, xxi, 48–49.
[123] Nevins 1969, 50; Richards 1986, 37.

reparations.[124] As Adams himself put it, "My course in the House of Representatives has put me to the ban of *all* the Presidential parties."[125]

As Adams himself saw rather early on, his scorn for "caballing, bargaining, place-giving," and the like cost him dearly in national popularity, and one biographer has argued that Adams "was blissfully ignorant of the party manipulation, largely the project of Thurlow Weed," that helped Adams win the presidency. Once in the White House he spurned such maneuvering, especially the use of patronage.[126] This stand reflected Adams's basic political principles. Indeed, he said, "I have made moral principle, and not party or selfish purpose the standard of my conduct throughout my political life"; he was not about to become "a mere partizan."[127] More broadly, Adams believed that by demanding the absolute loyalty of their members, parties made war on the individual conscience. For the young Adams, partisan feeling was responsible for "the impossibility of pursuing the dictates of my own conscience without sacrificing every prospect, not merely of advancement, but even of retaining that character and reputation I have enjoyed."[128] Adams had such distaste for parties that his *Parties in the United States* was a political history of the republic's first three decades, in which, according to Adams, parties played a notably limited role. In so far as this stance represented republicanism's traditional hostility to party, it also provided a republican basis for Adams's opposition to slavery. Any specific attack on the slave power in the 1830s and early 1840s was an act of individual conscience that required one to defy the two major parties of the Jacksonian era—both of which were committed to intersectional amity and thus to keeping slavery off the political agenda.

As with almost all of his contemporaries, however, the republican creed that Adams followed was attenuated by more characteristically nineteenth-century concerns that, in various ways, tempered his willingness to take a public stand against slavery. In particular, Adams's concept of "improvement" more closely fitted his Protestant conception of vocation than it fitted a republican conception of virtue. As we observed earlier, the republican outlook was largely static. It tended to speak to the traditional public-spiritedness and self-restraint of a citizenry concerned with protecting their existing property and privileges against the machinations of self-aggrandizing politicians. Indeed, the latter's greed led them to welcome the new forms of economic activity that would provide new sources of material gain—often through corrupt bargains between the entrepreneurs and well-placed public officials.

[124] Nevins 1969, xxvi.
[125] C. F. Adams 1902, 88.
[126] Nevins 1969, 239; Lipsky 1950, 185; Bemis 1956, 135–36.
[127] C. F. Adams 1902, 88–89.
[128] Nevins 1969, 21.

Although Adams had only scorn for such corruption, there was a fundamentally dynamic element to his thought that looked on economic innovation itself as essential to improvement—and Adams's stand, in turn, meant a view of government far from that of orthodox eighteenth-century republicanism. The point here is not just that Adams sought the "stimulation of domestic activity to the fullest extent," such that during his presidency he advanced an ambitious program of economic development through government-sponsored improvements.[129] The real significance of his outlook was his enthusiasm for the more dynamic elements of the American economy. Adams, for example, flatly rejected Jefferson's view that commerce ought to be agriculture's handmaid.[130] So, too, Adams argued that cities were a distinctive and indispensable—though not the only—element of a civilized country.[131]

In fact Adams's outlook was closer to the redeemed Calvinists' unremitting service to God's moral order than to the more comfortable stability of a virtuous republican order. As he put it in 1834, his administration had sought a program of "progressive and unceasing internal improvement." From that perspective the impotence of the American government would place "the nation itself on a footing of inferiority" with others.[132] This stand, in turn, led Adams away from republicanism's almost congenital fear of political power. Early in his career he supported Jefferson's position on the embargo as a legitimate exercise of presidential leadership and governmental activity—despite the bitter opposition of his Federalist friends. Somewhat later, his one real criticism of President Monroe was that the chief executive was "perhaps too reluctant to exercise" the powers of office.[133] Whereas the hatred of most Whigs for "King Andrew" Jackson encouraged a traditionally republican suspicion of executive power, Adams remained sympathetic, at least until 1837, to Hamilton's vision of a strong executive. Even when, as a congressman, Adams attacked Jackson's and Van Buren's policies and asserted legislative prerogatives, he never attacked the powers of the executive in general.[134]

Here, then, were two further constraints on Adams's antislavery zeal. First, a belief in economic progress, which in the American case meant the growth of an economy in which cotton—as an export and as the raw material for New England industry—played a crucial role; and second, a respect for and devotion to government authority and political compro-

---

[129] Lipsky 1950, 116; see Koch and Peden 1946, 374.
[130] J. Q. Adams 1941, 39; cf. 105.
[131] J. Q. Adams 1845, 86–87.
[132] Nevins 1969, 454; Koch and Peden 1946, 374.
[133] Koch and Peden 1946, 48–49, 243.
[134] Lipsky 1950, 198, 270–71, 201.

mise, both of which the abolitionists found incompatible with a crusade animated by purely moral principles.

As we have seen, these attitudes represented an attenuation of Adams's republican faith. As it was, some features of Adams's republicanism actually reinforced the attenuation. But even in those respects in which he remained close to traditional republicanism, that creed did not always support immediate abolition. Adams's republican opposition to the spirit of party, for instance, did not simply assert his right to individual, private judgment; parties were so suspect in his eyes, because loyalty to the party displaced loyalty to the regime. In fact, Adams's ultimately "organic view of society" made him hostile to any interpretation of the polity that emphasized contending factions.[135] As the young Adams wrote to his father, the various occupational groups and interests "are all so mutually dependent upon one another" that only "partial politicans," who were animated by misguided partisanship, could erect "an imaginary wall of separation between them."[136] As Lipsky put it, Adams saw "party conflict as a threat to the national union," so that, in his own words, he did not seek to be "a man of party" but rather a "man of . . . [his] whole country."[137] Here, in short, was the familiar Whig appeal to the common good, or to what Adams came close to calling the public interest. All Americans, he wrote in 1804, "have . . . a deep permanent and a paramount interest in *Union*."[138] For him, moreover, there was a direct connection to the republican tradition, since "upon the republican principle, every individual has a stake, an interest, and a voice in the common stock of society," that is, a "common interest."[139] Once again, though, his broad concern for the whole community did not readily support a regime-rending attack on an institution that had become central to much of his nation's social and economic life.

Moreover, this same reluctance to support such an attack was reinforced by those elements of Adams's view of his whole polity, elements that moved him away from a wholly republican stand. Adams himself—who witnessed the Battle of Bunker Hill with his mother—was deeply committed to the Union. In his view the Union was founded by the whole of the American people. Adams connected republicanism with loyalty to the Union—to the Declaration of Independence and the Constitution as expressions of "republican virtues" (Lipsky's words) that solved the problem of antirepublican factionalism so prominent under the Articles of Confederation.[140] In

[135] Ibid., 113.
[136] J. Q. Adams 1913–1917, 1:63.
[137] Lipsky 1950, 183.
[138] J. Q. Adams 1913–1917, 3:88.
[139] J. Q. Adams 1874–1877, 2:12.
[140] J. Q. Adams 1837, 33; see Lipsky 1950, 219 and J. Q. Adams 1941, 5, 7.

fact, however, traditional eighteenth-century republicanism had celebrated the small polity—in which citizens could reasonably be expected to determine the common good, monitor the course of political life, and intervene effectively against their leaders when those leaders succumbed to corruption and the selfishness of factionalism. Adams, however, was too much a child of the revolution and, finally, too much a devotee of the Union to give this view any credence at all. More than merely political or economic, his nationalism was emotional and cultural as well.[141] His enthusiasm for expansion led him to boast in his inaugural address about the nation's territorial spread.[142]

He had no use whatever for the "hallucination" of nullification or its states' rights variants, whether it was advanced by slave-holding Southerners or his fellow Yankees.[143] "Philosophically, politically, morally" he considered it "an inversion of all human reasoning . . . [a] self-contradiction."[144] Adams scorned the idea that he was "merely a man of" Massachusetts; "the longer I live," he wrote his father in 1816, "the stronger I find my national feelings."[145]

The upshot for the slavery issues was Adams's preference for sectional accommodation rather than for conflict, a preference Adams never quite abandoned. This posture, to be sure, led him to assail states' rights extremism in Calhoun's South Carolina, but it also encouraged conciliation as a general policy. Despite his own belief in protection, Adams favored compromise during the tariff quarrels of the early 1830s—most of all, Bemis noted, because Adams feared "that the Union might not last five years longer under existing tensions."[146] Moreover, there is a striking analogy between this attitude and the position Adams took while a senator during the administration of Jefferson, when he reluctantly advocated repealing the embargo to conciliate the New England Federalists. As Bemis noted:

> Senator Adams had not agreed with his Federalist constituents that the Embargo was unconstitutional, but he knew how determined they were to resist it, some of them to the point of separation from the Union; therefore he had advised his new Republican friends in Congress to repeal or modify the obnoxious measure. Similarly in 1831 Representative Adams of the Plymouth district thought the tariff perfectly constitutional, but whatever the right of the matter, he feared that the Nullifiers of South Carolina had the will, and the means, to resist a law of the Federal Government. . . . The only way to preserve

---

[141] Richards 1986, 65.
[142] Koch and Peden 1946, 354.
[143] Bemis 1956, 234; see Nevins 1969, 459; J. Q. Adams 1831, 22–23.
[144] J. Q. Adams 1831, 35.
[145] Koch and Peden 1946, 287.
[146] Bemis 1956, 241.

PART FIVE

INTRODUCTION TO PART FIVE

Dave Ericson

LINCOLN always claimed that the free-soil policy of the Republican party had been the policy of the founding fathers. He engaged in extensive historical exegesis to prove that point in his Cooper Union address of 1860, and he earlier had clashed with Douglas on the point several times during the course of their famous 1858 debates. The third-generation controversy over the founders' position on slavery discloses three important facts about American political culture and Lincoln's central place within it.

One, that controversy suggests the power of the myth of the founding fathers. Later generations debated (still debate!) political issues in terms of the founders' positions on those issues. We suspect that if the founders had formulated a clear, national policy on the slavery issue, it would have been determinative for later generations. Two, lacking such a policy, the founding synthesis was loose-jointed enough that a Lincoln and a Douglas could translate it into significantly different policies even on such a fundamental issue as slavery, and each could claim to be following the example of the founding fathers. The myth did not preclude conflict; at times it even exacerbated conflict. Three, it was the very lack of a clear, national policy on slavery in the founding synthesis that demarcates the way in which Lincoln transcended his "fathers" and began to create his own myth.

Lincoln's definitive political act was to attempt to make the founders' free-soil policy a clear, national policy. Whether or not that actually had been their policy—he was undoubtedly right about their prevailing anti-slavery preferences—he surpassed them in his public advocacy of and insistence on that policy. He also surpassed them in voicing the presuppositions of that policy; in bearing witness to the fact that slavery was an evil institution that must eventually be eradicated from the American subcontinent. Lincoln's intention, of course, was to persuade the American people, as a whole, to accept that definition of slavery and its fate. Primarily, he sought to solve the issue on the level of public meaning, not policy. This is not to say that he believed the correct policies were unimportant. He felt that they should be well-calculated to end slavery as expeditiously as possible without destroying the Union. He recognized, however, the deep tensions between those two criteria, tensions that permitted legitimate disputes over the correct policies. What became critical, then, was that the public mind be settled on the right course, and for him the right course was a matter that was not open to dispute. A public commitment to the ultimate end of slavery was the minimum requirement necessary to overcome the polity's inevitable temporizing on the issue. In his sensitivity to the importance of public language and in his ethical perfectionism, Lincoln not only distinguished himself from the founders but exhibited stronger affinities to the abolitionists than to the commanding presences of the second generation.

Yet, Lincoln was not an abolitionist. Unlike the abolitionists, and like the founders and such second-generation figures as Webster and Van Buren, Lincoln was relatively flexible on specific policies, charitable to dissenting preferences, especially in the South, and vague about the time frame for ending slavery. Those matters were properly subject to the intersectional compromises and intergenerational adjustments endemic to American-style politics.

By all indications, Lincoln believed that the specific policies the founders had adopted on the slavery issue had been the best possible ones in 1787, just as the Missouri Compromise of 1820 and the Compromise of 1850 had, situationally, been the best policies. Those policies had met the dual obligation of preserving the Union without compromising the evolutionary trend toward extending the sphere of freedom. Political circumstances, though, continued to change. In the late 1850s, the requirements of liberty and union defined the optimal policy as the exclusion of slavery from all the territories. And if that policy did not have the desired causal effect in strangling slavery in the Southern states—still a heavily debated proposition among historians—it would be left to future generations to formulate policies better calculated to maintaining the delicate balance between liberty and union.

In Lincoln's view, the general direction of national policies on slavery had been toward ending the institution; that is, until 1854. The Kansas-Nebraska Act, which to Douglas seemed perfectly consistent with a succession of intersectional compromises on the slavery issue, was to Lincoln a disastrous retrogression from the direction of those compromises. It was but one small step to insisting that the act was part of a conspiracy to explicitly reverse that direction. Lincoln, thus, only had to expose the conspiracy and reassert the policy direction.

Of course, not all Americans shared Lincoln's assessment of the situation. Where he saw a policy direction they saw policy drift. In truth, prior national policies on slavery appear to have been the by-product of a series of intersectional compromises on the issue and not the result of a publicly identified and agreed-upon policy goal. Lincoln distinguished himself from his predecessors by elevating the status of their compromises. This departure, in turn, required a new inflexibility about the direction of national policies on slavery as well as more explicit condemnations of the institution. Indeed, his predecessors' silence about slavery had always been more expressive than their utterances. The Lincoln-abolitionist parallel, again, seems to be the stronger one.

Lincoln appeared genuinely surprised when the Southern states seceded from the Union rather than accept his presidency. He was surprised because of his declared intention to honor existing political and economic arrangements in the South, his charity toward southern, proslavery opinion, and his flexibility on specific policies in light of that opinion. He thought that free soil was the policy that would "clear the market" and undermine slavery without also undermining the Union. In this, he assumed that southern preferences were more right on slavery than they actually were; that despite the rabid racist rhetoric of the fire-eaters and their own prideful opposition to free soil, most Southerners still shared Jefferson's "necessary evil" views on slavery. He also assumed that the "rule of law" was stronger in the South than it actually was. Together, these two assumptions led him to believe that most Southerners could, and would, accept a free-soil president. Lincoln underestimated, however, the degree to which they might be inflexible exactly where he was—on the territories question.

Obviously, Lincoln's options were limited. He had to work within the parameters of the existing state of public opinion—North and South—and he had to work with the cultural resources available to him, to attempt to place slavery on the road to extinction while preserving the Union. On the one hand, his powerful commitment to the Union precluded the "South be damned" solution of many of the abolitionists (which arguably was a "slaves be damned" solution). On the other hand, he was committed, as Douglas was not, to a certain kind of union, to a union that was itself committed to liberty. He also realized, as Douglas did not, that the Union could no longer stand divided on the slavery issue. Given the existing state of public opinion, the founders' "house" would soon fall even under status quo arrangements, and especially under Douglas's "squatters' sovereignty." No matter how wrenching it might prove to be, a national decision had to be made on the fate of slavery. Lincoln quite skillfully used the cultural resources available to him to try to prejudice the right decision without destroying the house. He sought to make the decision less wrenching by postponing its implementation to an indefinite future. Slavery might be publicly condemned and yet linger for a hundred years in the South. Many Southerners, however, found that situation unendurable, too analogous to the situation of a prisoner on death row. Tragically, but understandably, they rejected Lincoln's solution. By 1860, probably no policy could have cleared the market. Nonetheless, it was a measure of Lincoln's success that the house could be rebuilt along his guidelines, even if those guidelines inevitably contained their own fractures and fissures.

The significance of Lincoln's solution to the slavery issue is not just that he developed a remarkably subtle response to a problem that had proven intractable to his predecessors. His solution also embodied a new cultural synthesis, or, perhaps better, resynthesis. In this very broad sense, he was simultaneously responding to the apparently deep-seated inability of the founding synthesis to effectively address the slavery issue and developing a more complex synthesis that could more effectively address that issue. Here, he, and not Douglas, was prototypically a third-generation figure.

In reworking the founding synthesis, Lincoln had to engage his moral absolutism in dialogue with the founders' inherently more relativistic concept of union. His solution was to elevate the Union itself to a higher moral plane. The Union was only viable, he insisted, to the extent that it shared certain basic moral commitments. Moreover, it was the duty of the Union itself—as a moral covenant—to chasten its own tendencies toward decay. Lincoln, finally, offered his solution in the name of the founders, tying himself securely to the founding myth even as he rewrote it.

Lincoln's solution to the slavery issue, then, operated on a number of different levels; as public policy and political philosophy, as electoral strategy and moral commitment, and as American history and cultural prophecy. It existed as both a reformulation of his predecessors' political ideas and a legacy upon which his successors could draw to address the salient issues of their day. In combining all these functions, it constituted a political persuasion. What were the contours of this Lincoln persuasion?

Like the humanist liberals—Jefferson, Leggett, Van Buren, and Douglas—Lincoln recognized the integrity of existing preferences. His free-labor ideology recast his party's exclusionary policy into a form that was more appealing to the northern democracy, just as that policy itself was intended to be more sensitive to southern preferences than immediate abolition was. Similarly, he was committed to party politics and its troublesome coordination of intra- and interparty preferences. Lastly, he was willing to honor the intersectional compromises of preferences upon which the Union was built. Nevertheless, Lincoln transcended the humanist liberals in his resolve to press the free-soil policy, to label slavery a moral wrong, and to portend its eventual doom. However much he might temper his language because of dissenting opinions, there were certain positions he would not yield to them. Lincoln meant to save the Union by rededicating it to liberty.

In his views on liberty and union, Lincoln, therefore, also drew on the Protestant face of American liberalism. Yet, unlike other reform liberals—the Adamses, Webster, and the abolitionists—he was able successfully to combine morality and politics. This feat was one that the Adamses and Webster had, in very different ways, been unable to accomplish, and one that the abolitionists had not even tried to accomplish. The relation between morality and politics had perplexed—in a sense, paralyzed—John Adams and John Quincy Adams. Webster was the more successful politician precisely to the extent that he artificially isolated the two domains, although it was a measure of his failure that morality kept intruding upon, and into, his politics. But, then, he was ensconced in a strongly Protestant Whig culture. For their part, the abolitionists evaded the problem. This is not to deny that many of them were politically astute men and women. They did not, however, engage in the normal politics of preference-coordination. Furthermore, they, implicitly or explicitly, violated the rule of law, just as the Southern secessionists were to do. Lincoln held true to his 1838 gloss on the abolitionists. They repudiated essential components of the founding synthesis—its thin theory of republicanism as well as its humanist liberalism.

The abolitionists' piety, their determination to achieve moral perfection despite the ambiguous and arbitrary features of human existence, really reached back beyond the founding synthesis to an earlier Puritan synthesis. Even here, though, Lincoln's position was the more complex one. His own piety more closely mirrored the seventeenth-century orthodoxy's uneasy blend of self and community; of instrumental and consummatory reasoning. Unlike the abolitionists—who, again, largely avoided the problem— Lincoln confronted, and sought to resolve as best he could, the ambiguities intrinsic to societal rules and their concrete applications.

We can now appreciate the full richness of the Lincoln persuasion. It reinvigorated the founders' liberal synthesis with a Puritan ethical perfectionism even as it realigned the humanist, reform, and republican elements within that synthesis. Lincoln's genius consisted in using the cultural— ultimately, philosophic—resources available to him to address the critical issue of his day in a way that was more compelling to more Northerners than the alternatives put forth by any of his rivals. The Lincoln myth continues to resonate not because of any specific policy, neither free soil nor emancipation (which truly was forced upon him by the march of events). It continues to resonate because his name is inextricably linked with "one nation conceived in liberty" in a way those who conceived this nation are not.

The final two chapters attempt to measure Lincoln's achievement as a cultural achievement. Chapter nine discusses two of the central concepts of the founding synthesis—liberty and union—and shows how Lincoln surpassed Webster and Douglas in rethinking the relationship between those two terms. Chapter ten explores the subtle differences between the ways in which Lincoln and the abolitionists drew upon their common Protestant heritage. Together, the two chapters reveal how Lincoln utilized his political culture not only to secure his own place within it but to bequeath a much richer culture to those who followed him.

NINE

LINCOLN AND THE NORTH'S COMMITMENT

TO LIBERTY AND UNION

FROM THE TIME of Daniel Webster's celebrated Second Reply to Hayne in 1830, almost every Northerner had rallied to his eloquent statement of their sectional creed: "Liberty *and* Union, now and for ever, one and inseparable!"[1] In linking the two major tenets of the North's liberal faith—individual freedom and enterprise, and the providential importance of the Union and its republican institutions—Webster expressed his profound political moderation. As much as he personally disliked slavery, his devotion to union signaled a willingness to tolerate the institution in the South in order to avoid a rending sectional conflict. National survival required that each section treat the other with discretion and tact.

By the 1850s, however, tensions between the two sections had mounted, and Northerners had become increasingly divided among themselves, especially over the possible expansion of slavery into the as-yet-unsettled federal territories. To some Northerners, the imperative remained compromise with the South. To others, slavery and liberty were so deeply opposed that the Union must ultimately attack the institution. In the ensuing debate over liberty and union, Lincoln, Douglas, and Webster each spoke in a particularly thoughtful way for one of the three parties that made appeals to the northern electorate in the course of the decade: the Republicans who nominated Lincoln in 1860; the northern Democrats who nominated Douglas; and the conservative Whigs (in 1860, the Constitutional Unionists), whose northern leaders had been Webster's associates and disciples.

To begin, the Lincoln persuasion must be defined in relation to the contrasting views of liberty and union held by the three men. In this chapter, we will see that whereas Douglas and Webster shared a processual view of politics—a view Hartz attributed to most Americans—Lincoln saw the inadequacies of that processual view, brought into focus by the issue of slavery. We will also see how a Wittgensteinian approach to American political culture partially confirms but also partially undercuts Hartz's consensus thesis. In chapter ten, we will see how the comparison between Lincoln and the abolitionists illuminates the multiple meanings and descriptions of politics that existed within the broader liberal consensus in the North.

[1] Webster 1864, 3:342.

Douglas: Negative Liberty and a Quantitative Union

Douglas was predominantly a humanist liberal who remained faithful to the secular libertarian and utilitarian principles of Jacksonian Democracy. Furthermore, Douglas articulated the ideas of liberty and union in his 1858 Senate campaign against Lincoln in a way that was consistent with this underlying philosophic position. Douglas believed in negative liberty; that is, in freedom from external restraint. He bitterly opposed the moralistic meddling of the political community in private affairs. Secure in their rights, individuals must be the judges of their own happiness, and they must unite to act accordingly. The danger came from intrusive moralists, Yankee or otherwise. "You must allow the people," Douglas said in his inaugural campaign speech at Chicago in 1858, "to decide for themselves whether they desire a Maine Liquor law[,] . . . to decide for themselves the relations between husband and wife, parent and child. . . . Whenever you put a limitation upon the right of any people to decide what laws they want, you have destroyed the fundamental principle of self-government." "If the people of . . . each State mind its own business . . . and not meddle with its neighbors," he added in his last debate with Lincoln, at Alton, "then there will be peace . . . throughout the whole Union."[2]

Douglas was a passionate nationalist for whom the need to preserve the Union was urgent. He said at Freeport in 1858, "The hope of the friends of freedom throughout the world rests upon the perpetuity of this Union."[3] As Major Wilson has pointed out, Douglas and other Democrats understood the Union in quantitative terms, and this understanding was linked to their belief in negative liberty. Even expansion southward, into areas in which slavery might flourish, was desirable because it would increase the total area in which white Americans could freely pursue their preferences. "This is a young and growing nation," Douglas continued. "It swarms as often as a hive of bees, and as new swarms are turned out each year, there must be hives in which they can gather and make their honey." Thus he was willing "to acquire more territory . . . without reference to the question of slavery."[4]

Douglas, however, faced a practical obstacle in implementing his principles. Expansion to the west was dependent on the construction of a transcontinental railroad. This, in turn, required the organization of the Nebraska territory—through which ran the projected route favored by Douglas and his Illinois constituents. The Nebraska territory, however, lay

[2] Johannsen 1965, 28, 300.
[3] Ibid., 105.
[4] Ibid., 91; M. L. Wilson 1974, 174–82, 227–31; Johannsen 1965, 326.

in the northern part of the Louisiana Purchase, which had been closed to slavery by the Missouri Compromise. In the end, Douglas agreed to the repeal of the compromise, in order to obtain the southern votes that were required to pass legislation necessary for the organization of Kansas and Nebraska. Douglas's action in this case might seem to have diminished liberty by imposing a hated policy on both blacks and antislavery whites. In fact, however, his action was principled as well as expedient. The question of the freedom of blacks did not pose a serious problem for Douglas, because he believed that blacks were "inferior beings." He instructed those "who believe that the negro is your equal . . . socially, politically, and legally" to "vote for Mr. Lincoln." "I care more for the great principle of self-government," he announced at Alton, "than I do for all the negroes . . . that ever existed."[5] Nevertheless, Douglas's position rested on something other than racism alone, since he was also willing to coerce antislavery whites by forcing them to accept slavery in Kansas, at least until its people formed a territorial government.

Douglas's stand was consistent with his belief in negative liberty. If individuals were free to pursue their preferences without undue restraint, there would inevitably be cases in which their preferences collided. Given such cases, some people would have to be restrained so that others could pursue their goals. Even a Lockean government, whose principal task was to umpire these conflicts, had to use some coercion to enforce its decisions. Once a legally binding decision is made, said Douglas of the Dred Scott case, "my private opinion, your opinion, all other opinions, must yield to the majesty of [the Court's] authoritative adjudication."[6]

In effect, then, Douglas referred to the total measure of liberty in the society much as one might refer to its overall technological development or to the extent of its transportation system. In the case of liberty, the unavoidable conflicts among individuals and groups meant that there was an upper limit to the total measure of liberty that could be allowed. Liberty, in other words, was not a public good; increasing the supply of liberty to some would not necessarily make it more available to all. Because any national policy on slavery would necessarily coerce some group, Douglas advocated developing the west without specific regard for the preferences of antislavery whites. Such a policy, Douglas believed, would boost the net liberty of white Americans.

Nevertheless, as a good Jacksonian, Douglas sought to minimize coercion by a creative reshaping of the connection between liberty and union. His instrument, as we saw, was the famous and fateful doctrine of popular sovereignty. Because white Americans overwhelmingly favored slavery in

5 Johannsen 1965, 216, 93, 326.
6 Ibid., 31.

some areas but overwhelmingly opposed it in others, the optimal way to minimize restraint and maximize freedom, Douglas thought, was to let local majorities decide the issue for themselves. The preferences, in other words, of almost all white Americans with regard to the legality of slavery would be decisive in their own area. Moreover, localizing decision-making would help save the Union by removing an extremely divisive issue from national politics.[7]

In themselves, these features of Douglas's position are fairly well known. What can be added here is that Douglas treated the connection between liberty and union as both empirical and causal. The connection was causal, because extending liberty by allowing local white majorities to follow their own preferences on slavery (the cause) would preserve the Union (the effect). The connection was empirical or contingent—rather than necessary or conceptual—in three related senses. First, the meanings of the two terms were obviously very different. *Liberty* referred to the degree of restraint experienced by individual white Americans. *Union* designated a specific political regime. Second, the phenomena of liberty and union were only contingently related, since there were readily conceivable circumstances in which extending liberty might not have helped save the Union. Suppose, for example, that the white residents in some areas were bitterly but evenly divided on the slavery question, whereas in other areas the sentiment was overwhelmingly for or against slavery. By Douglas's reasoning, the total measure of liberty might be increased by permitting the residents of each locality to decide the question for themselves. Such a policy in the divided areas, however, might well spawn intense conflict, which could then inflame feelings elsewhere—a result that would threaten instead of save the Union. Lincoln, in fact, made just this charge against popular sovereignty. As he saw it, the bloody conflicts over slavery within the Kansas territory had actually set the North and South at each other's throats.[8]

Third, even though Douglas believed in liberty and union, those values by themselves did not and could not determine the morally correct course of action on the slavery issue. Rather than simply consulting his conscience or moral code and then applying its rule to the existing situation, however, Douglas began with certain empirical observations. His object, of course, was to minimize coercion. Therefore, before acting, Douglas had to take note of the actual geographical distribution of white opinion—and, indeed, it was the sharp, observable North-South split on the slavery issue that led him to consider popular sovereignty such an attractive policy. As we shall see, Webster, and Lincoln even more, understood morality quite differently.

[7] See Potter 1976, 341ff.; see also Lincoln and Douglas 1958, 18–28; cf. 54–55, 110–14, 364.

[8] Basler 1953–1955, 2:270.

Webster: Positive Liberty
and a Qualitative Union

Webster, too, valued the idea of negative liberty that was central to the northern liberal consensus. He celebrated "freedom of human thought" and recognized the right of individuals to move where they wished. Taken alone, however, the liberty to do what one pleased could lead to disruptive conflicts. Allowing everyone the "liberty of judging and of deciding exclusively" for themselves, of acting "during pleasure" or *"during feeling,"* might all too easily destroy the Union. Against this threat, Webster preached cooperation on behalf of the "good, and the harmony, and the union of the whole country," a unity of interest such that the American people were "one in making war, and one in making peace . . . [and] one in regulating commerce."[9]

In addition, however, Webster, like many Yankee Protestants—and unlike Douglas and other leading Jacksonians—understood liberty in positive as well as negative terms. Webster, that is, tended more to the reform pole of the liberal consensus than to the humanist one. He reiterated, in a highly secularized and less restrictive idiom, John Winthrop's seventeenth-century Puritan belief, not in a "natural liberty" to do what one pleased, but in a "civil liberty" to do "that only which is good, just, and honest."[10] Like most other northern Whigs and abolitionists, Webster believed that increasing one's freedom meant developing one's physical, moral, and intellectual faculties, as much through cooperation as competition.

A simple example illustrates Webster's position: although negative liberty, the absence of restraint, is necessary for an individual to be free to read, it is not sufficient. A person can actually read only if he or she also has the positive liberty to do so—that is, only if he or she has mastered reading as a skill. Americans are free, Webster said at Plymouth, because they are "intelligent, educated, freeholders, freemen, republicans, possessed of all the means of modern improvement, modern science, arts, literature." He thought his generation ought to emulate Jefferson and John Adams through "the cultivation of every good principle and every good habit." A command of "literature, ancient as well as modern," he observed, not only helps secure "private happiness" but "render[s] its possessor . . . more accomplished also for action in the affairs of life, and especially for public action."[11]

---

[9] Webster 1864, 2:214; 3:324; 5:385; 3:472.
[10] P. Miller 1961a, 426; see also P. Miller 1961b, 1956a and 1956b; and D. W. Howe 1979.
[11] Webster 1864, 2:212; 1:147, 143.

As was true for many other Yankees, for Webster this belief in positive liberty was joined to a dislike of slavery. According to him, the institution violated natural law and the "natural equality of man." Both the slaves and the white Southerners had suffered. How, he asked, could Southerners try "to prove that the absolute ignorance and the abject slavery of the South are more in conformity with the high purpose and destiny of immortal, rational human beings than the educated, the independent free labor of the North?"[12]

Yet, as the sectional crisis intensified in the late 1840s, Webster's basic moderation emerged. He opposed the Wilmot Proviso, which would have barred slavery from the territories acquired in the war against Mexico, because it would "wound the pride . . . of the Southern States." Rather than celebrating the Protestant conscience, Webster berated antislavery "agitators" for their moralism, their "belief that nothing is good but what is perfect," a belief that led only to "useless, irritating controversies." This moderation reflected Webster's deeply felt nationalism. "The union of these states," as he put it, "gives us power at home and credit abroad." Beyond such practical benefits, the American regime had a providential role in the history of freedom. In a world dominated by monarchical and barbaric regimes, the Union was the great defender and advocate of republican freedom, the bulwark upon which freedom everywhere depended. The American government, Webster claimed, "is an experiment of such remarkable and renowned success . . . that he is a fool or a madman who would wish to try that experiment a second time."[13] Like Douglas, Webster feared that public attacks on slavery would encourage sectional strife and thus threaten the Union.

Webster devoted much of his political career, and the greatest of his speeches, to securing sectional comity, but he did not seek Douglas's goal of territorial expansion. The government, Webster thought, was "very likely to be endangered . . . by a further enlargement of the territorial surface." The Union's true mission was to increase positive freedom through uncoerced social, moral, and capitalist progress. For that reason, the cause of individual development or liberty was linked to that of the nation.[14] Secession, therefore, was unacceptable because it threatened the Union's capacity to extend liberty to all citizens through enrichment of their cultural and economic life.

Webster's distinctly Whiggish patriotism reinforced his rationalist's latitudinarian distrust of moralistic attacks on the culture of another region. Out of deference to northern opinion, slavery had to be excluded from the free states, and it could not be treated as a positive good. However, espe-

[12] Ibid., 5:360, 308.

[13] Ibid., 5:382, 352, 332, 385; 2:209, 208.

[14] Ibid., 5:56; 3:321–22, 324; see also M. L. Wilson 1974, 159–71.

cially in the early 1850s, the same reasoning led Webster, for all his dislike of slavery, to oppose abolitionism, or any other perfectionist stance on the issue, because such a stance might enrage the South.

In summary, despite Webster's more positive conception of freedom and his well-known policy differences with Douglas, he agreed with Douglas that: (a) human freedom importantly depended on the healthy development of the American Union; (b) this development depended on sectional comity; and (c) such comity depended on each section's refraining from attacks on the other's distinctive institutions. Webster's views on these matters have frequently been noted. There were also other substantial, if less obvious, points of convergence with Douglas. Both men thought about liberty in terms of a total quantity—in Webster's case, in terms of the sum of the opportunities for self-development enjoyed by the society as a whole. For both men, the goal of the nation was to increase that total. Neither man, however, thought that liberty was a public good that would be available to all (including blacks) once it was made available to some. On the contrary, there was a limit to the feasible extension of liberty, a limit to be determined empirically by assessing the relationship between the two sections. Also, according to Webster's own assessment, attempts to emancipate the slaves would not extend liberty but would instead only exacerbate sectional tensions, weaken the Union, and thus endanger freedom by harming its great republican bulwark.

Webster also joined Douglas, therefore, in treating the "inseparable" connection between liberty and union as a causal and empirical one. For Webster, the connection was causal because preserving the Union (the cause) would have the effect of maintaining and expanding liberty. (For Douglas, the causal direction was reversed.) Furthermore, the connection was empirical and contingent for Webster in the same three ways that it was for Douglas.

First, Webster believed the two terms had very different meanings. Whereas *liberty* described the condition of individual members of the American regime, *union* referred to the regime itself and included its established republican institutions. Second, the causal relationship Webster asserted was contingent; it would not hold in all plausibly conceivable circumstances. Assume, for instance, that the demographic trends had been reversed and that the South had an increasing majority of the nation's white population. In those circumstances, it is by no means clear—given Webster's dislike of slavery—that preserving the Union would have been the most effective way to promote positive liberty. Third, the values of liberty and union did not by themselves dictate Webster's stand on the slavery issue. Before he could take a policy position, he had to make an empirical judgment—specifically, about how best to decrease sectional tensions. After examining the politically relevant facts, Webster chose almost complete public silence on the moral aspects of the issue.

The convergence between Webster and Douglas was behavioral as well as theoretical. By 1850, their agreement on the causal and empirical connection between liberty and union had begun to overshadow their traditional conflicts. Toward the end of his life, Webster opposed the formal exclusion of slavery from the territories, and he warred politically with the antislavery Conscience Whigs, who later were to join Lincoln in the Republican party. In addition, Webster was contemplating an alliance with the Douglas Democrats in an explicitly unionist party; and, following Webster's death in 1852, many of his family and associates opposed first the Republican candidate for president in 1856, John Fremont, and then Lincoln himself in 1860.[15]

At one level, Jacksonian Democrats like Douglas and conservative Whigs like Webster shared the belief that antislavery agitation threatened the Union. At a second level, their convergence signaled the exhaustion of their original ideologies; that is, it signaled the decline of the economic issues that had initially divided their parties. Through the 1830s and 1840s, the Whigs maintained that the federal government could and should help launch the process of capitalist development through an American system of banks, protective tariffs, and internal improvements. In reply, the Democrats denounced the special charters and the privileges allegedly conferred by such policies, and they argued for the unalloyed competition of the free market. As the economy continued to mature, however, the positions of the two parties shifted. The Whigs began to view government intervention as less essential to development, while the Democrats began to embrace some forms of government assistance, notably in the development of the railroads. As Douglas noted in 1858, by the early 1850s the old issues had simply begun to recede.[16]

The analysis offered here adds a third level consideration. Webster and Douglas were also linked by the more general approach to politics described by Hartz as the Lockean liberal consensus. For all Webster's belief in positive liberty and government intervention in the economy, his conception of politics, like Douglas's, was ultimately processual; politics, that is, was the interaction of individuals and groups in pursuit of their own, self-determined goals and interests. In Webster's view, the federal government might assist the process, but it should not try to determine it. Political life should be free of the intrusive moral preaching that exalted the goals of one

---

[15] See Potter 1976, 263, 416–17.
[16] Johannsen 1965, 37ff.; see Meyers 1960, 253–75.

faction over another. Ultimately, political disputes should be resolved through negotiation and compromise rather than conflict.

Stated more explicitly, this shared understanding accepts three of the propositions viewed by Hartz as central to the American liberal tradition. First, the great "moral" imperative in American politics is to preserve liberal institutions as the framework within which individuals can freely pursue their own goals (including, in Webster's case, self-development). Second, desirable outcomes can be produced only through a process in which each individual, group, or section identifies its own interests and goals and then decides what compromises are acceptable to it. Thus, both Douglas and Webster thought the feasible extension of liberty depended on what might be called the ethical facts of the matter. If the basic position of any particular interest or section were violated, supporters would react so negatively that the process could not survive. Finally, the more ethically radical solutions, such as the attempt to impose a moral direction on the process, were unacceptably dangerous to the process. It was on this last point that Lincoln dissented most thoroughly.

Lincoln on Liberty and Union: A Conceptual Connection

Lincoln, Douglas, and Webster

The character of Lincoln's political thought and action supports Huntington's claim, noted in chapter two, that the decade of the 1850s was not a period of creedal passion. Apart from a few notably moderate speeches on temperance, Lincoln had little to do with any antebellum movement for moral reform; as a young Whig, he spoke out for law and order and against unreasoning passion of any kind.[17] Given his allegiance to the Constitution, Lincoln was firm but cautious in his condemnation of slavery. He did insist that the institution be restricted to the slave states and branded as a moral wrong; at the same time, he sought to conciliate the South over other matters, even over the Fugitive Slave Act, which the abolitionists publicly denounced and he privately detested. Lincoln also refused to denounce the Constitution and polity that tolerated the institution. Slavery, he once said, might well persist for a "hundred years at least." Until the Emancipation Proclamation, which meticulously exempted all those areas of slavery under Union control, Lincoln consistently rejected immediate, uncompensated, universal emancipation. By today's standards, Lincoln even occasionally spoke in racist terms; in 1858, for example, he disclaimed any idea of

[17] Basler 1953–1955, 1:108–15.

introducing "political and social equality between the white and black races."[18]

Lincoln's stand on the slavery question helped advance both his career and his party's interests. Certainly, Lincoln knew how to adapt to changing circumstances. Whereas the followers of both Douglas and Webster preferred the safe, familiar economic issues of the 1830s and 1840s, Lincoln had no trouble taking up the new issue. In fact, as Foner has observed, Lincoln's firm but cautious stand placed him at the ideological center of the new party. To Lincoln's right, conservative Republicans and the other major parties in the 1860 election urged a more conciliatory attitude toward the South. To his left, radical Republicans called for more dramatic antislavery measures such as the repeal of the Fugitive Slave Act. Lincoln's position, then, was far from idiosyncratic. His caution attracted those voters in the lower North whom the Republicans needed to win the White House, while his commitment to universal equality as an eventual goal, and his eloquent insistence on the slaves' humanity, made him acceptable to the more militant Republicans of the upper North.[19] He offered an effective solution that involved the political mechanism of party, a way of confronting slavery without drifting into antipolitical moralism. He thus harnessed a concern with both individual preferences and romantic conscience to effective political life. Most of all, Lincoln solved the problem that had dogged John Quincy Adams: how to reconcile individual with community and the zeal to do one's duty with rational calculation.

Lincoln was also loyal to his society's institutions. A successful lawyer, a loyal Whig, and then a loyal Republican, he consistently supported the procapitalist policies of these parties. Moreover, his complex position on slavery can be understood instrumentally, as (causally) advancing his economic interests. On the one hand, northern capital had long resented southern resistance to a protective tariff, to a strong banking system, and to the Whig program for economic development; on the other hand, many capitalists feared secession would be economically disruptive, if not catastrophic, and they therefore urged moderation.[20]

Lincoln's passion for success also tied him to his society and its institutions in a broader way. Consider, for example, one difficulty confronting any narrowly economic explanation of the adamant refusal of the Republicans to compromise on the territories issue: the particular issues that divided the sections, such as the tariff and the western railroads, were both limited in scope and ultimately resolvable. If purely material interests had been the only real consideration, then quarreling economic elites might well

[18] Ibid., 3:181.

[19] Foner 1970, 205, 225, and ch. 6; see Sewell 1976, ch. 13; Potter 1976, 424, 427; Oates 1977, 192–93.

[20] Hacker, in Stampp 1959, 64; Oates 1977, 58.

have reached a sectional compromise that would have shifted the economic costs to the lower classes. Indeed, after Lincoln was elected and the South began to secede, many eastern capitalists urged sectional accommodation for the sake of economic tranquility. Lincoln and his allies, however, angrily rejected this concern with immediate economic costs.[21]

This difficulty suggests an alternative approach, namely that specific interests are subordinate to—or better defined by—the modes of action and conceptual meanings that constitute a social practice. The real struggle in these discussions was between two contrasting ethics that had cultural and moral as well as economic dimensions: the ethic of the seemingly aristocratic southern planter versus the ethic of the self-made, self-employed northern entrepreneur.[22] This conflict of ethics was most intense at just that point where Lincoln and his political friends were most rigid; that is, on the territories question. Because southern society assigned the highest social prestige to the largest planters, it encouraged investment in land and labor—in more slaves and bigger plantations rather than in capital such as new machinery. Consequently, new slave territory was crucial both for ambitious planters whose status depended on owning land and for the slave breeders of the upper South, whose plantations would remain viable only if there were a market for their excess slaves.[23]

The sparsely settled federal territories, however, were equally vital to the North. The free states defended their competitive capitalist order by emphasizing the opportunities open to every enterprising individual, opportunities that were greatest, and most equally available, in the west. No other Northerner better articulated this defense of the section's capitalist life form, exemplified it in his own life, and linked it more clearly to the territories issue, than Lincoln himself. Most Northerners, Lincoln observed, "work for themselves . . . taking the whole product to themselves" and neither work for, nor hire, others.[24]

The accounts of Lincoln's motives addressed here and in chapter one stress Lincoln's attachment to this institutional order. Lincoln's determination to refound the Union on more elevated principles that excluded slavery can be interpreted as an ultimately successful effort to secure his generation's psychological independence from the towering achievements of its predecessors. As for Lincoln's political aspirations, his ambition for elective office made sense only within a popular republican regime in which every citizen could freely pursue political success. As Lincoln told an Ohio regiment in 1864, "Nowhere in the world is presented a government of so much liberty and equality. To the humblest and poorest amongst us are held

21 Moore 1966, ch. 3; Stampp 1959; Oates 1977, 205.
22 See Genovese 1965, 28–29; Potter 1976, 454–57; Hofstadter 1974.
23 Genovese 1965, 28–29, 246–47.
24 [Citation missing.]

out the highest privileges and positions. The present moment finds me at the White House, yet there is as good a chance for your children as there was for my father's."[25] Restated in this way, these ulterior motive accounts affirm Lincoln's commitment to the institutions of his society and polity rather than to a politics of creedal passion. In very different idioms, these accounts emphasize just those liberal, petty bourgeois values that united most Northerners and divided their section from the South.

Lincoln and Principles of Action

Up to a point, therefore, Lincoln agreed with Douglas and Webster—and with many white Northerners—about liberty and union. All three men asserted the value of negative freedom, as well as of their existing republican institutions, a mobile society, and a capitalist economy. They also agreed on the Union's providential importance as the home of republican liberty, especially after the failure of the 1848 revolutions in Europe. These American institutions and practices exemplified the equation between efficiency and self-help, between success and self-reliance, which in their view accounted for the North's relative social and economic progress. Just as self-reliance helped individuals to become efficient, and thus economically successful, so too hard work and careful planning helped them to secure an independent social position in which they could rely on their own efforts. As Lincoln said in 1859:

> The prudent, penniless beginner in the world, labors for wages awhile, saves a surplus with which to buy tools or land, for himself; then labors on his own account another while, and at length hires another new beginner to help him. This, say its advocates, is *free* labor—the just and generous, and prosperous system, which opens the way for all—gives hope to all, and energy, and progress, and improvement of condition to all.[26]

Lincoln, Douglas, Webster, and many contemporaries extended the shared perspective of their allegiance to American institutions to the slavery issue; given their common devotion to the Union and its social system, they acknowledged a necessity for tolerating slavery indefinitely in the southern states. Because all three men were impatient with abstract moralism, they regarded both the separatism of the abolitionists and the secessionism of the fire-eaters as equally unacceptable heresies. Yet they also had little tolerance for the aristocratic southern culture in which the slave owners held the preeminent position: slavery fostered the South's aristocratic pretensions, blocked its economic progress, and—worst of all—undermined its loyalty

25 Basler 1953–1955, 7:528.
26 Ibid., 3:478–79.

to the Union. As Foner has put it: "In their devotion to the union and their bitter opposition to southern domination of the government, Republicans and [Douglas Democrats] stood close together in 1860."[27] So, too, many of the conservative ex-Whigs who had admired Webster and regarded the Republicans as too extreme nevertheless rallied to the Union cause after the Confederacy attacked Fort Sumter.

These areas of agreement, however, did not resolve the debate among Northerners over slavery, liberty, and union. For that reason, the areas of agreement are insufficient to support a strong version of Hartz's consensus thesis. On the contrary, the elections of 1856 and 1860 witnessed a realignment—based on the meaning and interpretation of slavery, liberty, and union—that transformed northern electoral politics. The upheavals of the 1850s exposed the fault lines within the northern liberal consensus, and by 1860 the Republicans had replaced the defunct Whigs and reduced the Democrats to the minority status they were to hold until the 1930s. An examination of the Lincoln persuasion—in particular, the ways in which Lincoln crafted a transformation of American politics—will help us understand Lincoln's role in these realignments.

Most obviously, the substance of Lincoln's liberalism, as both an ethical and political outlook, was deeply opposed to that of Douglas and Webster. Foner, for example, has quoted a Republican newspaper of the time to the effect that Douglas rejected the "moral element in politics." Lincoln agreed with the observation. Lincoln thought Douglas would be welcomed by Republicans whenever "he and we can come together on *principle*. But clearly, he is not *now* with us—he does not *pretend* to be—he does not *promise* to *ever* be."[28]

The principle to which Lincoln referred concerned slavery. In 1854, Lincoln announced his campaign against the Kansas-Nebraska Act in terms that neither Douglas nor Webster could ever use in public: "This . . . covert *real* zeal for the spread of slavery, I can not but hate. I hate it because of the monstrous injustice of slavery itself. I hate it . . . especially because it forces so many really good men amongst ourselves into an open war with the very fundamental principles of civil liberty." He added that Douglas's support of slavery and its spread "shows that the Judge has no very vivid impression that the negro is a human; and consequently has no idea that there can be any moral question in legislating about him."[29]

From that point on, Lincoln asserted "the profound central truth that slavery is a wrong and ought to be dealt with as a wrong." We must act, he said, "with the fixed idea that it must *and will* come to an end," primarily by

---

[27] Foner 1970, 307; see also Potter 1976, 547–48; cf. Holt 1978, 215–16.
[28] Foner 1970, 307; Basler 1953–1955, 2:468.
[29] Basler 1953–1955, 2:255.

arresting its further spread. There were certain principles, he declared in his last public speech, on which one must be "inflexible." On two key issues, Lincoln was as good as his words. When the southern states began to secede from the Union after his election, neither conservative Republicans nor eastern businessmen could persuade him to yield on the question of slavery in the territories. During the war, he was equally adamant about not re-enslaving any person who had been freed by the Emancipation Proclamation.[30] These indeed were the key issues, and the principle of action, that separated him from Douglas and Webster.

Lincoln, like Webster, understood liberty in terms of individual development. He preached the Yankee gospel of opportunity and the importance of education or "cultivated thought." "We wish," he declared in a "Fragment on Slavery," "to give *all* a chance . . . the weak to grow stronger, the ignorant wiser; and all better and happier together."[31] Douglas, true to his belief in negative liberty, saw only a clash of competing preferences; for Lincoln, however, this clash of preferences was not decisive. From Lincoln's perspective, slavery was triply evil. It denied all intellectual opportunity to the slaves; it corrupted the morals of their masters; and it threatened the prospects of poorer whites. Because whites as well as blacks were hurt by slavery, there was no solution in simply mediating among the preferences of the friends and foes of slavery.

Lincoln and Webster shared a reform liberal belief in positive liberty, but they were divided in more subtle ways. At the rhetorical level, from 1854 on, Lincoln addressed the slavery question more publicly, much more often, and with much greater feeling than Webster had ever done. This difference was only partly a reflection of the increased sectional tensions that developed after Webster's death. Because Lincoln believed in freedom for all peoples everywhere, he was simply less concerned than Webster with determining an upper limit to liberty, that is, with determining the point at which trying to extend liberty would be self-defeating. Instead, Lincoln used the term "liberty" to describe the extent to which any particular individual had a meaningful opportunity to develop his or her capacities. He then appraised his society in terms of the proportion of its members who actually had such opportunities. Lincoln, Douglas, and Webster, then, provide a clear case of the multiple meanings of "liberty."

Yet how could Lincoln have ignored Webster's concern about the Union, when he shared the older Whig's nationalism and recognized the Union's contribution to economic and social progress? Lincoln sounded like Webster, when in 1845 he held "it to be a paramount duty of us in the free states,

---

[30] Ibid., 281; 3:368, 366, 369, 370 (emphasis added); see Oates 1977, 216; B. P. Thomas 1952, 288.

[31] Basler 1953–1955, 2:222.

due to the Union . . . *and perhaps to liberty itself* (paradox though it may seem) to let the slavery of the other states alone." And he conceded at Peoria in 1854 that "I would consent to the extension of [slavery] . . . rather than see the Union dissolved, just as I would consent to any GREAT evil, to avoid a GREATER one."[32]

That they held these sentiments about the Union in common, however, did not mean that Lincoln and Webster described the Union in the same way. After Kansas-Nebraska, Lincoln talked mainly about the Union's moral and political rather than its territorial or even economic importance. Slavery, he complained in 1854, "deprives our republican example of its just influence in the world—enables the enemies of free institutions, with plausibility, to taunt us as hypocrites." In the same paragraph of the Peoria speech in which Lincoln characterized the Union's dissolution as a greater evil, he went on to contrast the "love of justice"—asserted in the Declaration of Independence—with the "selfishness" on which slavery was founded. "These principles are in [such] eternal antagonism," he continued, that their "collision" over the extension of slavery produced "shocks, and throes, and convulsions" that endangered the Union.[33] For Lincoln, in other words, true devotion to the Union meant requiring the Union to maintain its moral stance whatever the impact on sectional conflict.

Lincoln, then, accepted but went beyond Webster's and Douglas's description of the Union. Lincoln's version did not simply refer to some existing regime with a specific set of republican institutions. It also included the Union's commitment to equality of rights, to the love of justice, and to the extension of positive liberty to all. Moreover, *Lincoln's loyalty was to this description*. Consequently, for Lincoln the real danger was that the Union might no longer deserve to be so described—not because of a geographically divisive sectional quarrel but because of an assault on the Union's basic ethical principles. At Peoria in 1854, Lincoln predicted that if the nation returned to "practices and policy" consistent with the Declaration of Independence, "we shall not only have saved the Union, but we shall have so saved it as to make . . . it forever worthy of the saving." Or, as he put it in an 1861 speech in Philadelphia, if the Union "can't be saved upon that principle, it will be truly awful. But, if this country cannot be saved without giving up that principle—I was about to say that I would rather be assassinated on this spot than to surrender it."[34]

Lincoln's differences with Webster and Douglas over the description of the Union paralleled his and Webster's disagreement with Douglas over the

---

[32] Ibid., 1:348 (italics added); 2:270.

[33] Ibid., 2:255, 271.

[34] Ibid., 2:276; 4:240; see also 2:126.

meaning of liberty. In both cases, there was a tension between a static and a dynamic outlook. Douglas's concept of negative liberty implied a static conception of the individual personality. Given an individual's preference for some object, the only questions that were possible concerned (a) whether obstacles (such as external constraints) existed that would prevent an individual's acting on that desire, and (b) how to remove such obstacles if they were not legitimate. Apart from this, however, neither the individual concerned nor others had a responsibility to change themselves in any particular way. The concept of positive liberty, in contrast, required acquiring certain crucial skills. Fully pursued, it required an ongoing, self-reflective, and self-critical effort to cultivate one's faculties. As Webster suggested through his repeated references to education and economic mobility, pursuing positive liberty involved dedication to a *project* of continuous self-improvement. By embracing positive as well as negative liberty, Webster and Lincoln, although not Douglas, transcended the limits of Hartz's Lockean liberal consensus.

Nevertheless, although Webster rejected Douglas's static understanding of liberty, the two men shared a static description of the Union. Webster, to be sure, affirmed the orthodox Whig doctrine that the Union, as then constituted, would contribute to a dynamic process of *economic* development. Political development, however, was another matter entirely. When it came to the Union itself, Webster favored no such transformation. Like Douglas, he seems to have thought that the Union had taken the right course from the beginning. As he said at the end of his Second Reply to Hayne, the Union "had its origin in the necessities of disordered finance, prostrate commerce, and ruined credit. Under its benign influence, these great interests immediately awoke. . . . Every year . . . [offers] fresh proofs of its utility." "Governments," Webster stated on another occasion, "are instituted for practical benefit, not for subjects of speculative reasoning merely."[35] Webster, as we have seen, was suspicious of noble-sounding crusades. Such enterprises might well involve just that moralism that, he feared, would enrage the South and tear the Union apart. On the question of the Union, then, Webster and Douglas remained within the limits of Hartz's Lockean consensus. Sufficient, for their own time at least, was a regime that maintained republican political institutions and upheld the rights of its white citizens.

Lincoln, however, was not content with a union so described, and it is on this issue that his break with Hartz's version of the liberal consensus is most apparent. Just as the genuinely free individual had to have a project, *so too* did a union that Lincoln could fervently support. The emphasis on a sustained, morally informed project for the Union appeared repeatedly in

---

[35] Webster 1864, 3:341, 13.

Lincoln's speeches of the 1850s, as, for example, at Peoria in 1854: "Our republican robe is soiled, and trailed in the dust. Let us repurify it. . . . Let us re-adopt the Declaration of Independence and . . . the practices, and policy which harmonize with it. . . . let all Americans . . . join in the great and good work." At Chicago, two years later, he declared that "our government rests in public opinion." However much public opinion acquiesced in the existing necessity of slavery, its "constant working has been a steady progress toward the practical equality of all men." Six months later at Springfield, this Kantian perfectionism in his ethic emerged still more clearly. The authors of the declaration, he asserted, "meant to set up a standard maxim for a free society which should be . . . constantly looked to, constantly labored for, and even though never perfectly attained, constantly approximated, and thereby constantly spreading and deepening its influence, and augmenting the happiness and value of life to all people of all colors everywhere." Although this goal did not mean equality "in all respects," it did include the declaration's "inalienable rights, among which are life, liberty, and the pursuit of happiness." By asserting this continuing task for "all lovers of liberty everywhere"—and for their political regime—Lincoln converted Douglas's and Webster's static picture of the Union into a dynamic political enterprise.[36]

These considerations help us understand the way in which Lincoln could both affirm his liberal culture and yet embrace a politics that was fundamentally at odds with that of Douglas and Webster. In Wittgenstein's terms, the three men's uses of *liberty* clearly exhibit a family resemblance; there was similarity of usage, that is, but there was also notable divergence. At the same time, the three men described the Union very differently. Most important of all, Lincoln's consistently teleological approach broke decisively with the idea of a causal and empirical connection between the meaning of *liberty* and the description of the Union.[37]

Lincoln, to be sure, did think instrumentally and causally both about his own career and about slavery, and his analysis argued for moderation. In the first place, the institution was too entrenched to be easily removed; that is, it would be causally difficult to uproot. Second, the moralistic demands of the abolitionists threatened to unleash a chain of causes and effects that might well devastate the Union. We have already noted three strict conditions that qualified this conciliatory position.[38] First, the political community—the Union—had formally to declare the institution to be an unmitigated evil. Second, the federal government had to adopt policies that would ensure the eventual demise of slavery, primarily by restricting it to the existing slave

[36] Basler 1953–1955, 2:276, 385, 406.
[37] See Jaffa 1959.
[38] I would like to thank Nathan Tarcov for suggesting this formulation of Lincoln's position.

states. Third, there could be no retrogression on either of the first two conditions; once adopted, no antislavery stand or law could be reversed. If any of those conditions were violated, as happened in the case of Douglas's Kansas-Nebraska Act, they must be restored, even at the cost of southern secession.

By these conditions, Lincoln subordinated his causal thinking about the Union to an overriding moral imperative. His House Divided speech indeed made a causal prediction: the Union could not exist indefinitely half-slave and half-free. Nevertheless, that prediction was premised on an un-wavering moral position: eventually the Union must be wholly free. Read-ing from that speech, in his first debate with Douglas at Ottawa, Lincoln said, there is "no more excuse for permitting slavery to go into our own free territory, than [for] . . . reviving the African slave trade." Moreover, "if we could arrest its spread" through such a territorial restriction, slavery "*would be* in the course of ultimate extinction."[39] This position, of course—which Lincoln associated in 1858 with "the moral constitution of men's minds"—had causal consequences.[40] It made his election unacceptable to so many Southerners that most of the slave states seceded within a few months of his election. In word and deed, however, Lincoln ignored these possible conse-quences. Before his election, he simply insisted on keeping slavery out of the territories. Once he was elected and secession had begun, he spurned all efforts at compromise.

In the end, then, Lincoln treated the connection between liberty and union as more than either a causal or an empirical one. There was no single outcome with respect to slavery that he was determined to bring about at once. Although he personally hated slavery and wished for its immediate end, he would allow it to persist in the slave states because it was protected there by the Constitution. The preservation of the Union, however, also was not an absolutely overriding goal. Lincoln insisted on branding slavery as a wrong and barring its expansion, even if the consequence was southern secession and civil war. Rather than taking steps that would cause the Union to be saved or cause slavery to be ended by some specific point in time, his goal was to keep the Union true to the course and direction of its moral project. The point on which he remained adamant was that slavery be treated as a wrong.

If Lincoln did not consider the connection between liberty and union to be simply causal, neither did he consider it to be fully empirical. In his description, the Union was dedicated to an egalitarian version of positive liberty. As a result, the terms *liberty* and *union* did not have entirely separate meanings in his discourse. Instead, *Lincoln's concept of liberty was an essential*

[39] Basler 1953–1955, 3:15, 18.
[40] Johannsen 1965, 54, 52, 55.

part of his description of the Union. As we have seen, he believed that the American regime would be truly "worthy of the saving," would merit description as the Union, only insofar as it was committed to liberty for "people of all colors everywhere." Because Lincoln thought of *both* liberty and union as very closely related, morally informed projects, there were no plausibly conceivable circumstances in which one's commitments to liberty and union could be sharply distinguished. A devotion to the Union's fundamental project simply meant a devotion to extending liberty. By the same token, any true friend of liberty must necessarily participate in the Union's essential project.

Finally, Lincoln did not follow the examples of either Douglas or Webster, both of whom made empirical facts central to their judgments about liberty and union. According to Douglas, one could decide the appropriate extension of slavery only after discovering which local communities preferred to have slavery and which did not. For his part, Webster called for an accommodating policy on slavery after observing the South's bitter reaction to the abolitionists. In developing his position on the issue, Lincoln of course took some general facts into account—the intense southern feelings about the Fugitive Slave Act, for example. Given the substance rather than the style of his moral position, however, such factual considerations could not be decisive; on the contrary, Lincoln's concept of liberty and his description of the Union were ethical norms to be used in evaluating the facts he observed. However much Lincoln shunned moralistic politics, there were no facts that for him could possibly justify the Union's renouncing its determination to end slavery.

Conclusion: Rule-Ambiguity and Liberal Politics

Lincoln's position had both consensual and dissensual elements. By embracing the inseparable connection between liberty and union, he affirmed the pervasive liberalism of American political culture. His particular conception of liberty, his particular description of the Union, and the way in which he joined them, however, illustrate the importance of multiple meanings and multiple descriptions in American political culture. Nevertheless, the discussion to this point has not offered a unified framework that simultaneously distinguishes Lincoln from both those contemporaries who remained entirely within the prevailing dispensation and those who were committed to radical protest. The point here is to consider the issue of rules and rule-teaching as central to one kind of liberal thought. In order to identify such a framework, it may be helpful to return to the philosophical explication and critique of Hartz's consensus thesis presented in chapter two.

That discussion maintained that to use words correctly, to participate appropriately in a social practice, individuals must master relevant, inter-subjectively shared sets of rules. Such a Wittgensteinian perspective empha-sizes the essentially social character of human life and language; yet, because rules are never complete and definitive and can therefore be changed, the perspective also accords an indispensable role to the individual. Moreover, verbal formulas can never state the rules unambiguously. There will always be some cases that the rules have not anticipated; on other matters, the rules are simply silent. Partly for these reasons, there are limits on the extent to which a community and its teachers can transmit and enforce the commu-nity's norms. Because no completely unambiguous interpretation of the rules is possible, a teacher can only cite a series of examples or particular applications, invite the individual students to grasp the basic point of the examples, and hope that the students can go on for themselves. It is a central feature of human life that most students catch on, but some do not.

This discussion recasts a familiar liberal concern. Instead of focusing on the competing claims of personal autonomy and of social order and security, the focus is shifted to the different roles of the individual and the commu-nity in providing for the continuity, transmission, and transformation of linguistic and social rules. Rule-ambiguity bears on liberal politics in an-other way as well: because the rules do not always speak clearly, a conflict over their interpretation is always possible.

The issue of rule-ambiguity was not fundamental, however, either for northern abolitionists and southern secessionists, or for political moderates such as Douglas and Webster. On the one hand, northern abolitionists and southern secessionists avoided problems of interpretation simply by rejec-ting the prevailing rules. During the sectional crisis of the 1850s, the aboli-tionists openly defied the Fugitive Slave Act and denounced the Constitu-tion, just as the southern fire-eaters threatened secession and then made good on their threat. On the other hand, Douglas and Webster, and other political moderates, avoided the question in a different way. Because they both endorsed the Union as it was, they were committed to accepting the prevailing rules, the implementation of which, according to Douglas and Webster, was essentially unambiguous. Moreover, on many issues, there was sufficiently broad agreement to establish a framework within which social and political life could take place. Importantly, this stand did not require either Webster or Douglas to ignore the fact of rule-ambiguity itself. Where the rules were silent or unclear, a genuinely liberal polity would rely on individuals and groups to interpret the ambiguities for themselves. They should exercise their private judgment or initiative, with the greatest re-wards going to the most enterprising. To establish some official interpreta-tion on issues that were bitterly contested would be to indulge in just that moralism that Webster and Douglas decried. Accordingly, Douglas favored permitting individuals and groups to pursue their own preferences; whereas Webster hoped they would seek economic and cultural development over time. Here, indeed, was a processual politics.

Lincoln, in contrast, rejected both the militants' repudiation of the rules and the moderates' reliance on process. For him, the problem of rule-ambiguity and the need to resolve it by interpretation were central issues of social and political life. Lincoln recognized, of course, that the common practices of his society with respect to some matters were clear evidence of the Union's basic rules on those matters. Nevertheless, his primary political aim after 1854 was to resolve a persistent ambiguity about the declaration's promise of certain inalienable rights; specifically, how widely—that is to whom—should those rights apply? Lincoln also demanded that the Union itself provide this resolution by applying the declaration's guarantees to "all peoples of all colors everywhere."

Here then is the distinguishing complexity of Lincoln's politics: his ability to position himself successfully between moderates and militants. Unlike Webster and Douglas, on the one hand, Lincoln refused to treat the ambiguities of the basic rules of his social and political order as if those ambiguities were politically irrelevant. Unlike the abolitionists and secessionists, on the other hand, he refused to ignore the issue of rule-ambiguity by disavowing the rules themselves. Instead, Lincoln focused directly on two of the ambiguities—the meaning of liberty and the description of the Union. The result of this focus was to highlight a fundamental political conflict, a substantive conflict over the tenets of liberalism—a conflict for which Hartz made no provision in his analysis.

The problem with the consensus thesis, however, is not just that it overlooked the possibilities of family resemblance and multiple description. The real difficulty is that its essentially processual vision of American politics left matters of rule-ambiguity entirely to private judgment. As we have seen, this processual view cannot account for the Protestant substance of Lincoln's politics, however firmly his style placed him in the political mainstream. Moreover, there is reason to regard conflict over the meaning of particular rules or institutions as a permanent feature of American politics. Because the mastery of language and participation in social practices are central to human life, ambiguity in the interpretation of some of the rules is a constant feature of that life, and, thus, the substantive character of American liberalism will remain an enduring issue. In consequence, there will continue to be challenges to the processual view of politics that, as Hartz argued, has so powerfully shaped the course of American political development. Lincoln appears not only to have understood the limits of the processual view of politics but also to have prepared us for future challenges to that view.

The task that remains is to show, more precisely, how Lincoln differed both in substance and style from the abolitionists, who were more directly influenced by the New England Protestant tradition and who could make stronger claims to being critics of the processual view of politics. The next chapter will discuss the cultural resources available to Lincoln that enabled him to position himself between the abolitionists and the more conservative Yankees, and it will explore the side of American liberalism that evaded Hartz's analysis.

TEN

LINCOLN'S POLITICAL HUMANITARIANISM

MORAL REFORM AND THE

COVENANT TRADITION

THE ARGUMENT to be developed in this final chapter makes two basic claims. The first claim is that Lincoln's position on slavery, like the position of the abolitionists, reflected a broadly humanitarian ethic. Unlike the humanitarianism of the abolitionists, however, Lincoln's humanitarianism was political rather than personal. It required dedicating and when necessary rededicating the American regime to the moral, material, and intellectual self-improvement of every citizen. The second claim is that Lincoln's political humanitarianism achieved coherence and intelligiblity—and attracted great popular support—because it drew broadly on beliefs and practices deeply rooted in American culture. That is, whereas the personal humanitarianism of the abolitionists was an expression primarily of the tradition of Protestant separatism and piety, Lincoln's ethic asserted a *union* of piety with prudential rationality, and of sainthood with citizenship. This outlook, initially articulated in America by New England's colonial orthodoxy, was further developed in the nineteenth century by Lincoln's Whiggish political culture.

Together, these two claims offer important support for a much more general proposition: in American political culture, the humanitarian or reform tradition has been a major liberal alternative to the dominant, humanist version of American liberalism.[1] This is the same general proposition that has been argued, *pace* Hartz, throughout the preceding chapters. As we have seen, Lincoln's position combined reform, or humanitarian, liberal features with humanist liberal features. Our focus is now shifted to the reform side of the liberal bipolarity.

---

[1] [Despite the similarity between the terms *humanist liberalism* and *humanitarianism*, the two are quite distinct. *Humanitarianism* refers to a religiously rooted (although not necessarily self-consciously so) concern with helping others to develop their distinctively human capacities, in contrast to the humanist liberals' thoroughly secular concern with aggregating preferences.]

Lincoln's Political Ethic

Lincoln's ethic had both humanitarian and political features. Before discussing Lincoln's ethic, however, a consideration of the related but distinct position of the abolitionists will point up the significance of the humanitarian features of his ethic. Parts of the following section reiterate material from chapters one, two, and nine; in particular the section recalls the inadequacies of the existing explanations of Lincoln's actions that rely solely on his enthusiasm for capitalism and on his political ambition. The purpose of this and subsequent sections is twofold: first, to emphasize the similarities between Lincoln's position and actions and those of the abolitionists in order to highlight their common heritage; and second, to identify the distinctions between them in order to highlight Lincoln's particular political and ethical contributions.

The Abolitionists' Personal Humanitarianism

The abolitionists were America's quintessential humanitarians. They—and, for a time, they alone—denounced slavery as an intolerable sin, because it violated the most fundamental obligations human beings owe to one another. The peculiar institution, as William Lloyd Garrison maintained, bore "the awful guilt of debasing the physical and defiling the moral workmanship of the great God—creatures made little lower than the angels, and capable of the highest intellectual attainments." According to Elizur Wright, the essential humanity of the slaves made their bondage intolerable, and every free person had the unavoidable "duty . . . to urge upon slaveholders *immediate emancipation* so long as there is a slave to agitate the consciences of tyrants, so long as there is a tyrant on the globe." Instead of emphasizing the elaborate calculation of individual and social costs and benefits of emancipation, this attitude encouraged an ethical perfectionism. "Their attachment to the Union is so strong," Lydia Maria Child observed of her fellow abolitionists, "that they would make any sacrifice of self-interest to preserve it; but they never will consent to sacrifice honor and principle. 'Duties are ours; events are God's.' "[2]

The humanitarianism of the abolitionists extended to issues beyond slavery, precisely because it entailed that belief in the imperative ethical obligation of individuals to help others develop their fundamental, distinctively human capacities; to help others, that is, to make correct inferences and intelligent judgments, to help them to act deliberately and take responsibility for their actions, and to master socially defined skills and practices as

[2] Garrison 1830, 7; Wright 1833, 12; Child 1839, 69.

diverse as chess and statecraft.[3] The abolitionists accordingly denounced every apparent obstacle to individual self-development, including addiction to alcohol, discrimination against women, lack of education for the poor, and inhumane treatment of the indigent insane.[4] Most of all, they believed that the sin of slavery imposed on them a threefold obligation: first, to exhibit one's own saintliness by attacking a very evil institution; second, to free the slaves so they could develop their own rational faculties; and, third, to rescue the slave owners, regardless of the slave owners' own preferences, from a state of sin in which their enslavement of other human beings had subverted their morality.

These antislavery militants framed this obligation largely in individualist terms. At first they directed their moral suasion at those persons who owned slaves. When these overtures were angrily rebuffed, they began to stress the suffering and persecution their crusade had brought upon themselves. Later, in order to protect their personal moral standing, many of them withdrew from the political parties and the Protestant churches they judged to be hopelessly compromised on the slavery issue. For Garrison and his followers, the American polity—the Union and Constitution—was itself immoral.[5] Finally, abolitionist propaganda made the plight of the individual slave one of its staple themes and embraced its classic expression in *Uncle Tom's Cabin*, even though that book had been written by a relatively moderate New Englander.[6] Moreover, the militants' concern for the individual was not merely tactical. For them, the plight of the individual slave epitomized the thoroughly evil character of slavery, and, therefore, any effort to recapture fugitive slaves was morally unconscionable.

Because the abolitionists were ethical perfectionists, they rejected purely consequentialist, cost-benefit arguments about the social and economic costs that would follow emancipation and about the political catastrophe that would follow secession. For the abolitionists, some actions were simply imperative; other actions were simply unacceptable. It was the duty of the righteous to do the one and shun the other, confident, as Child implied, that God would ensure that their actions have ultimately beneficent results. For the Massachusetts Anti-slavery Society, the important point was to demonstrate "the purity of our motives" in order to "free ourselves of guilt."[7] As Wendell Phillips, with the self-assurance of the moralist, put it, "No matter if the charter of emancipation was written in blood and anarchy stalk abroad with giant strides—if God commanded, it was right."[8] "You must perform

---

[3] Greenstone 1982b, 13–18.

[4] See Greenstone 1979; Messerli 1972; and Walters 1976, chs. 3 and 4.

[5] Walters 1976, 23, 129–31.

[6] Garrison 1852.

[7] Massachusetts Anti-slavery Society 1844, 91–92.

[8] Quoted in Bartlett 1965, 112.

your duty faithfully, fearlessly, and promptly," Garrison told his followers, "and leave the consequences to God."[9]

Such a perfectionist ethic might strike modern readers as dangerously absolutist, but it sustained the abolitionists in their relentless agitation against an institution that most white Americans preferred to ignore. To be sure, many people in all sections of the country sympathized with the plight of the slaves, wished the slaves well, and recognized at least in the abstract their right to freedom. Such a charitable attitude, however, did not necessarily lead to an insistence on immediate emancipation; this is true whether the individuals in question were moved by benevolent feelings that emphasized the passive features of human experience, or they affirmed a more activist belief in individual rights. This ethical benevolence, that is, as distinct from humanitarianism, prescribes a course of personal charity toward others, primarily in order to alleviate the pain and suffering of those others.[10] However, because pain and suffering are intrinsic to the human condition, everyone is in need of succor and comfort. Accordingly, the duty of benevolence is "imperfect"; it does not indicate specific beneficiaries. Although it requires me to help others, I am relatively free to select the particular persons I wish to assist. There is no particular group, even slaves, whom I *must* help, regardless.

The abolitionists' humanitarian concern with helping others develop their faculties also differed from a rights-oriented liberal tradition in which all individuals are entitled to pursue whatever goals they choose, provided they do not infringe on the legitimate activities of others. From the rights tradition follow three main duties: (a) the obligation of each individual to respect the rights of others when properly invoked; (b) the obligation of the government to referee conflicts among individuals pursuing their privately chosen goals; and (c) the obligation of each citizen to support a government that respects individuals' rights and fulfills its responsibility to act as an umpire. These duties are "perfect" in that they require one to respect the rights of particular persons. One example, from contractarian theory, is the obligation to help those of one's fellow citizens whose rights have been denied. Nevertheless, rights rather than duties are still prior; that is, one has the duty to help another person only when that person invokes a right by identifying a goal and trying to pursue it.[11]

In the case of slavery, the rights perspective typically produced an equivocal result. In the abstract, there may have been a presumption that the slaves' right to liberty created a perfect duty to help them secure their freedom. In practice, since even running away was a crime, it was virtually impossible for

[9] Quoted in Chapman 1921, 142; cf. Barlett 1965, 116; Child 1839, 69; Garrison 1837, 77.

[10] Cf. Davis 1966, 334–57, 376–82; Davis 1975, 179–82, 245–46.

[11] Cf. Davis 1975, 257.

slaves to invoke their right to liberty. Moreover, the rights tradition was committed to weighing competing claims. The slaves' right to liberty, therefore, had always to be measured, first, against the property rights of slave owners and, second, against the right of all southern whites to self-preservation in the face of the potential revenge of the freed slaves. Many liberals who espoused a doctrine of rights, in fact, acknowledged only the imperfect duty of treating slaves with consideration.[12] Henry Clay, for example, recognized the suffering of the slaves, but he also emphasized the potential cost of emancipation to the slave owners, to other whites, and even to the ex-slaves if they should be freed and left to fend for themselves.[13]

More generally, because slavery was thoroughly enmeshed in the web of established social interests, one's dislike or contempt for the institution was not sufficient to require one to demand its immediate abolition.[14] As David Brion Davis has noted, a belief in "the ideas of utility, social equilibrium, and the moral economy of nature" was more likely to encourage a complex weighing of opposed interests, a fear of costly civil strife, and a quest for sectional compromise than it was to encourage abolitionist principles. Such was the dominant perspective not only of such southern Whigs as Clay but of Jefferson and his Jacksonian heirs.[15]

By contrast, the abolitionists thought it imperative to provide every American with the opportunity for intellectual and moral development. Accordingly, they recognized a perfect duty to help those particular individuals who lacked that opportunity. To the abolitionists, it was plain that the slaves needed such help the most. Moreover, this assistance was owed to the slaves not because of what the slaves did or demanded—not because they invoked their rights—but because of their condition, because of the fact that they were not free to develop their distinctively human faculties. For the abolitionists, the preferences of southern whites, or even of the slaves themselves, could not be decisive. Slavery was intolerable insofar as it blighted both the intellectual self-improvement of its black victims and the moral self-development of its white beneficiaries. As a result, the abolitionists were often as paternalistic, as intermeddling and intrusive, as moralistically concerned with the affairs of others, as their critics maintained. These vices of the abolitionists were nevertheless intimately connected to their virtues. By a relentless goading of the nation to confront the slavery issue more directly, the abolitionists, in their righteous and even self-righteous agitation, provoked Southerners into defending slavery as a positive good and secession as a political right.[16] As this southern apologia

12 Davis 1975, ch. 4; D. W. Howe 1979, 133ff.
13 Clay 1857, 5:151, 387ff.
14 Cf. Davis 1975, 256–57.
15 Davis 1975, 258; cf. Davis 1966, chs. 13–14.
16 J. L. Thomas 1965a.

turned into a sweeping indictment of the culture, society, and economy of the free states, it heightened sectional tensions, leading to the civil war that finally destroyed the institution.[17]

Lincoln's Humanitarianism

In many respects, Lincoln shared the humanitarianism of the abolitionists. Although he undoubtedly took a more moderate stance than the antislavery militants on the slavery issue, his disagreements with them were primarily questions of means rather than ends. The militants were not "properly" members of the Republican party, but Lincoln made it clear that the new party shared with the militants the belief that slavery was "a moral, social and political wrong." The militants and he differed, as he carefully put it, mainly on questions of "practical action."[18]

Lincoln's own hatred of slavery was linked both to his belief in the development of human faculties and to his ultimately perfectionist conception of ethical duty. "All nature—the whole world, material, moral, and intellectual—is a mine," he observed at the height of the slavery struggle in 1859. "Now it was the destined work of Adam's race to develope . . . the hidden treasures of this mine." During the course of this development, the triumph of reason over passion was especially important. "Every head," he said, "should be cultivated and improved by whatever will add to its capacity for performing its charge. In one word Free Labor insists on universal education." As a young politician many years earlier, Lincoln had emphasized the importance of education, and he made the government's responsibility for the common schools a tenet of his mature political thought.[19] Lincoln's actions illustrated his words. As a boy, he read avidly; after serving in Congress, he taught himself geometry; as president, he mastered military strategy—and all through his life he appeared to fear the loss of reason more than death itself.[20]

The concern with developing one's faculties rather than simply satisfying one's preferences also shaped Lincoln's attitude toward alcohol, and indeed generally toward the satisfying of mere desires. Although the style of his 1842 Temperance Address was charitable and ironic, he shared the common Whig fear that the passions and, more broadly, the lure of self-interest were capable of enslaving the intellect. His goal was to free every dramseller from the lure of "pecuniary interest" and every drunkard from "burning appetite" by appealing to their rational capacities. Personally, Lincoln found that

[17] Cf. Friedman 1982, 4.
[18] Basler 1953–1955, 3:313.
[19] Ibid., 3:358; 1:114; 3:480; 1:8; 2:221–22.
[20] Oates 1977, 21, 77; B. P. Thomas 1952, 130, 133, 292.

drinking left him feeling "flabby and undone."[21] In the same vein, he decried the "pleasure hunting masters of southern slaves," and he denounced indifference to slavery as assuming "that there is no right principle of action but *self-interest.*" Nevertheless, even though passion and self-love undermined the rational capacities and moral development of the slave owners, the experience of slavery itself visited a worse, and wholly undeserved, fate on the slaves. Bondage "clouded" their "intellects" and denied them the chance to develop their own faculties.[22]

Moreover, Lincoln's humanitarianism extended, at least in principle, to every human being. Like most of the abolitionists, he sympathized with a number of feminist objectives, including the right of women to vote. Lincoln also privately rejected the nativism that was attractive to many other antislavery Whigs.[23] In general, he felt it was the government's responsibility to provide "for the helpless, young and afflicted" who might be unable to improve themselves. Furthermore, he was confident that most people would respond positively if given a genuine opportunity to improve themselves. In his youth, he recalled, "I was a hired laborer. The hired laborer of yesterday labors on his own account today, and will hire others to labor for him tomorrow. Advancement—improvement in conditions—is the order of things in a society of equals."[24]

Lincoln formulated these maxims in perfectionist terms, which sharply distinguished the moral from the immoral. In the Garden of Eden, he reminded Douglas in 1854, there was a clear difference between right and wrong. God told Adam that "there was one tree, of the fruit of which he should not eat." Although Lincoln recognized that no individual could attain perfection, he adopted the command of the New Testament, "be ye . . . perfect," and interpreted it to mean that "he who did the most towards reaching that standard, attained the highest degree of moral perfection." There were, therefore, times when a concern for the consequences of one's actions must give way to one's duty to act in accordance with "the profound central truth that slavery is a wrong and ought to be dealt with as a wrong," that is, "with the fixed idea that it must and will come to an end." Despite his distaste for violence, Lincoln even found himself admiring John Brown's devotion to what Brown perceived to be his own divinely ordained mission.[25]

It was primarily this deeply humanitarian hatred of slavery that moved Lincoln to denounce the Kansas-Nebraska Act. The issue of principle was especially important because he and Douglas agreed on the specific issue of

[21] Basler 1953–1955, 1:274–75; B. P. Thomas 1952, 37, 111–12.
[22] Basler 1953–1955, 1:109; 2:255; 5:372; 2:222.
[23] Oates 1977, 33, 298; Basler 1953–1955, 2:323.
[24] Basler 1953–1955, 2:221.
[25] Ibid., 2:278, 501; 3:368, 370; Oates 1977, 182.

Kansas itself. Because Douglas's doctrine of popular sovereignty assigned control over the fate of slavery to a territory's white majority—and in Kansas that majority was antislavery—Douglas, too, opposed admitting slavery to the territory. As a result, Lincoln could distinguish himself clearly from Douglas only by invoking his own humanitarian commitments. Lincoln had to insist on the *moral* necessity of excluding slavery from the federal territories as a matter of *general* policy.

Lincoln's strategy, as Potter has observed, was to "shift attention" to the "philosophic aspects" of the slavery question, "where he believed that their differences were conspicuous and fundamental."[26] This strategy meant attacking Douglas's basic premise that slavery and its extension into the territories posed no significant moral issue. The conflict between them, however, was still more basic. Ultimately, Douglas's doctrine of popular sovereignty was rooted in a utilitarian concern with satisfying the preferences of as many individuals as possible. Against this position, Lincoln insisted that on the great issues—such as liberty and union—self-regarding motives and preferences had to be limited by overriding ethical concerns. In this regard, he was much closer to the abolitionists than to Douglas.

As we saw, the ulterior-motive accounts of Lincoln's actions by themselves are unpersuasive. Here, we will add another dimension to that argument: in the matter of motives it is difficult to distinguish Lincoln from the abolitionists, who traditionally have been considered the most principled of the opponents of slavery, because Lincoln and the abolitionists shared both an enthusiasm for capitalism and a passion for personal success.

Lincoln, we recall, explicitly disavowed moralistic meddling in the private affairs of others. As he said at Peoria in 1854, "My faith in the proposition that each man should do precisely as he pleases with all which is exclusively his own, lies at the foundation of . . . [my] sense of justice."[27] Again as we have seen, policy conformed to principle, and throughout Lincoln's political career he supported a Whig economic program explicitly designed to encourage entrepreneurial success in a capitalist system. By the 1850s, Lincoln voiced this economic vision in the free labor rhetoric of the Republicans that, as Hofstadter has noted, almost entirely failed to anticipate the coming importance of the giant industrial corporation.[28]

Lincoln's use of this rhetoric, however, does not disprove his humanitarianism. On the contrary, the social-economic vision that the rhetoric expressed closely resembled that of the abolitionists. In the view of many of the abolitionists, slavery's greatest evil was that it precluded the *voluntary* pursuit of a moral life in which human beings could meaningfully develop

[26] Potter 1976, 338.
[27] Basler 1953–1955, 2:265.
[28] Hofstadter 1974, 135–36.

their faculties. As the American government continued to equivocate on slavery, the abolitionists began to be suspicious of any exercise of power by the government and, in some cases, they even began to shift to favor laissez-faire.[29] Lincoln never went that far. He rejected individual self-determination on slavery if it meant the government must allow one person to enslave another.[30] Lincoln, that is, explicitly endorsed public as well as private action where necessary to improve American society. Equally important, both Lincoln and the abolitionists admired the successful capitalist for essentially humanitarian reasons. The capacity for the moral, intellectual, and social self-development of the self-made entrepreneur was for them simply a special case of the more general goal of self-improvement that Lincoln and other moral reformers of his time sought for every American. For Lincoln, "material prosperity . . . [was] the external sign of inner spiritual health"—and it had the same meaning for the antislavery radicals.[31]

To answer the second kind of objection to Lincoln's humanitarianism—that his was animated by ulterior, self-regarding motives that reflected his political ambition, his capitalist enthusiasm, and his unresolved Oedipal feelings—I have pointed out that these three accounts are not consistent with each other; and that in some cases they offer competing explanations, a fact that suggests that Lincoln had to rationalize his conduct and reconcile competing motives in terms of some principle. Further, the implication that Lincoln treated the slavery issue instrumentally, in order to satisfy these motives, is at least partially contradicted by his inflexibility on the slavery issue. On certain aspects of the slavery issue—his refusal to yield on the question of slavery in the territories, for example—Lincoln's moral convictions must have dictated his policy.

When Lincoln is compared to the abolitionists, it can be seen that they appear to have acted on ulterior motives very similar to Lincoln's. Although most antislavery militants shunned conventional politics, for instance, their notorious doctrinal and organizational rivalries indicate a desire for personal power and public influence comparable to Lincoln's own.[32] Some abolitionists evidently turned to the antislavery cause, in order to prove both the social and moral worth of an intelligentsia whose social position was being challenged by a new economic elite. Moreover, those abolitionists from New England stock had to compete psychologically with both the achievements of their parents during the revolutionary era and the errand into the wilderness of their Puritan ancestors.[33] Finally, we have already

[29] Walters 1976, 116ff.
[30] Basler 1953–1955, 2:266.
[31] Jaffa 1959, 304; cf. Forgie 1979, 72; Oates 1977, 180; cf. Basler 1953–1955, 5:51–52. On the abolitionists, see Walters 1976, 114ff.
[32] Walters 1976, ch. 1; J. L. Thomas 1965b, 76–98; Wyatt-Brown 1971, ch. 10.
[33] Walters 1976, 177, n. 17; P. Miller 1956a.

observed that the antislavery militants typically embraced capitalist values, including in some cases that of laissez-faire. In Lydia Maria Child's revealing words:

> The abolitionists . . . merely wish to have . . . the stimulus of *wages* applied instead of the stimulus of the *whip*. The relation of master and laborer [after emancipation] might still continue; but . . . even when human beings are brutalized to the last degree, by the soul-destroying system of slavery, they still have sense enough to be more willing to work two hours for twelve cents than to work one hour for nothing.[34]

The importance of these ulterior motives does not demonstrate that the abolitionists' actions were simply the product of their personal ambition. For one thing, we shall see that the antislavery militants exhibited the traditional piety of New England Protestantism.[35] It has also been a commonplace, at least since Weber's classic study of the Protestant ethic, that New England Calvinism strikingly combined morality and ambition. While demanding devotion to moral duty, the Puritans' creed simultaneously commanded unremitting pursuit of success in one's vocation—whether it took the form of the Protestant capitalist's worldly asceticism or the humanitarian reformer's piety. As we have already noted, such demonstrated commitment not only helped redeem the world for God, it signaled one's own worthiness. Devotion of just this sort helped the antislavery militants fuel the sectional crisis over slavery.

Equally important, whatever the motives of the abolitionists, they among all of slavery's enemies were surely the most idealistic and uncompromising. In order to appraise the difference between the abolitionists and other contemporaries in antebellum politics, it is not helpful to emphasize that *all* these groups acted on self-regarding motives. It is more important to distinguish between conduct that is and conduct that is not humanitarian in character. This distinction enables us to identify the group most clearly guided by moral principles in the instance—the struggle against slavery—in which moral commitments were the most evident. This move, in other words, permits us to distinguish between fundamentally different sources of human action—between idealism or fanaticism on one side, and instrumental, often egoistic calculations on the other. In sum, even though Lincoln and the abolitionists both shared their society's passion for success, we cannot fully understand the politics of the 1850s without distinguishing slavery's enemies from those Northerners for whom slavery was not an overriding issue.

[34] Child 1839, 63–64.
[35] Cf. J. L. Thomas 1965a.

Lincoln's Political Commitments

The argument that Lincoln shared a strong humanitarian concern with the abolitionists must meet a third possible objection. This objection, based on Lincoln's moderation on the slavery question, directly challenges the connection between Lincoln and the abolitionists and requires more extensive discussion. It asks the question, was Lincoln not simply too moderate, and therefore too offensive to the abolitionists themselves, to justify our calling him a humanitarian? Consider, for example, that when Lincoln was a congressman, he included a fugitive slave provision in a plan intended to provide for the compensated emancipation of slave children born in the District of Columbia. The plan was never formally proposed, but Phillips reacted to Lincoln's provision by denouncing him as the "slave hound of Illinois." Consider too the demand of Lincoln and his fellow Republicans that slavery be excluded from the territories. The policy, while it was meant to protect white settlers from having to compete with slave labor, left the slaves themselves in bondage. This issue has been extensively examined in the literature, but it seems particularly relevant to Lincoln.[36] He won his party's presidential nomination in 1860, after all, because he could appeal to those more conservative voters (especially those in the lower North) for whom most other Republicans—to say nothing of the abolitionists—were too extreme on the slavery issue. At Freeport, in his 1858 debates with Douglas, Lincoln had made his caution unmistakable: he did not favor the unconditional repeal of the Fugitive Slave Act; he did not flatly oppose the admission of more slave states into the Union; and he did not absolutely demand either the abolition of slavery in the nation's capital or the prohibition of the slave trade between the slave states.[37]

Clearly, Lincoln was not a single-minded moral reformer. Unlike Horace Mann or Dorothea Dix, he did not throw all his energies into political action on behalf of unschooled children, the indigent insane, or other individuals who were denied a genuine opportunity for self-development. Unlike many of the leading abolitionists, Lincoln was not one of the eastern intellectuals who, in jeremiads and solemn meditations, denounced the sins of the southern slave owners, the greed of the northern capitalists, and the inadequacies of the lower classes. The child of a mobile frontier society, Lincoln was unburdened, or unblessed, by the weight of a New England conscience. His ethical pronouncements were often relaxed, sometimes even playful, and his instincts as a politician led him to conciliate rather than alienate other members of his political community. On the temperance

[36] See Foner 1970; Sewell 1976; Potter 1976; Fehrenbacher 1962; Craven 1971.
[37] Johannsen 1965, 76.

question, he called for *"persuasion"* or a "drop of honey" rather than "anathema and denunciation," and he warned against trying to "dictate to the drunkard's judgment or to command his action."[38]

To the distress of many abolitionists, Lincoln was equally charitable toward the slave owners. "I surely will not blame" southern whites, he said at Peoria in 1854, "for not doing what I should not know how to do myself. If all earthly power were given me, I should not know what to do, as to the existing institution." As a good Whig, Lincoln supported his party's American System of economic development and revered its author Henry Clay as his "beau ideal."[39] This greatest of Whig politicians, however, was himself a slave owner and, not surprisingly, Lincoln's respect for Clay and his moderate position on slavery repelled most abolitionists; nor did many of them support Lincoln in 1860. Phillips called Lincoln a "huckster in politics," and Garrison denounced Lincoln's party as "cowardly." For his part, Lincoln always believed the abolitionists to be misguided. Protesting against the antislavery resolutions of the 1837 Illinois legislature, Lincoln claimed the abolitionists' demands would only increase the evils of slavery. Later, Lincoln pointed out that the New York abolitionists, by voting for the Liberty party's presidential candidate instead of for Clay in 1844, had made possible the election of the proslavery Democrat, James K. Polk.[40]

By itself, however, the abolitionists' view of Lincoln was one-sided and ignored his moralistic rejection of slavery, his broader humanitarianism, and, most of all, his inflexibility on just that issue of the territories that precipitated southern secession and brought about the eventual end of slavery. In light of these positions, the question of whether or not Lincoln was a humanitarian is less useful than the question of what kind of humanitarianism he embraced. Exactly how, in other words, did Lincoln differ from the abolitionists; how did that difference enable him to achieve greater political success; and how could he coherently and consistently assert humanitarian values and at the same time seek political success?

Briefly stated, Lincoln was able to reconcile his moderate positions on the slavery issue with his hatred of the peculiar institution, because his basic outlook was simultaneously both political and ethical. Furthermore, the political side of his outlook rested on two concerns of considerable importance to American Whigs: one, the centrality of appropriate institutions to a well-ordered society and, two, the crucial role of history—of a developmental process over time—in achieving worthy social goals.

---

[38] Basler 1953–1955, 1:273.
[39] Ibid., 3:29.
[40] Oates 1977, 202–3; B. P. Thomas 1952, 64, 112.

Given the first concern, Lincoln's immediate purpose remained constant: to secure the moral character of the Union. As a young man of twenty-nine, he had delivered the remarkable Lyceum address, which was devoted to "the perpetuation of our political institutions." In it, he voiced the Whiggish sentiment that "reverence for the laws . . . becomes the *political religion* of the nation" in order to sustain "the temple of liberty." Sixteen years later, he condemned the "monstrous injustice of slavery," in part because the existence of slavery in the United States "enables the enemies of free institutions, with plausibility, to taunt us as hypocrites."[41]

Lincoln's focus on institutions meant that his moral code did not require him to assist directly every individual whom he might be able to help, even when the cause was compelling. It has often been observed that Lincoln tolerated (however unhappily) the recapture of individual fugitive slaves; he sentenced war deserters to death (though he issued many pardons); he imprisoned Northerners who attacked the war effort; and he exempted from the Emancipation Proclamation the slaves of masters loyal to the Union. Above all, he led the nation into a war in which millions of people suffered.[42] Because the proximate object of his humanitarianism was political rather than personal, Lincoln gave highest priority to policies directed toward perfecting those social and political institutions that would, in turn, help all persons to develop their faculties. His immediate goal was not to abolish slavery but to insure that the regime cease to recognize slavery as a just or permanent institution. Accordingly, Lincoln called on the Union to adopt immediately those "practices and policies" that would declare slavery an immoral institution and guarantee its eventual end.[43] Lincoln's moral code, in other words, was intimately connected to his republicanism, to his belief in popular self-government. Humanitarian objectives could be truly secure, he held, only if they were adopted by a regime whose institutions were themselves thoroughly popular—that is, democratic and republican—in character.

This complex perspective found its expression in a political humanitarianism that concentrated more on the moral direction of policies and institutions than on the fate of particular individuals. Lincoln politicized his humanitarianism through a Whiggish concern with time and history. In his view, certain obstacles to securing some morally worthy objectives could be surmounted only by a struggle that extended over time. Indeed, a concern with time was central to Lincoln's moral vision. Ethical conduct, he believed, required continuous effort. The principles of freedom in the Declaration of Independence should be "a standard maxim for free society . . .

[41] Basler 1953–1955, 1:108, 112, 115; 2:255.
[42] Rogin 1982.
[43] Basler 1953–1955, 2:276; see 54.

familiar to all, revered by all . . . and even though never perfectly attained, constantly approximated, and thereby constantly spreading . . . its influence."[44]

Lincoln's perfectionism, therefore, was necessarily and explicitly gradualist. He interpreted not only the declaration's "unalienable rights" but also the Gospel's "be ye perfect" in this spirit. Lincoln approached the slavery issue in the same spirit. Slavery should be stigmatized immediately as a wrong, but it should be eradicated only through a gradual process. What counted was the *direction* of national policies, not immediate results. Although some delay was acceptable, retrogression was not. This stance, again, explains his intense negative reaction to the Kansas-Nebraska Act, as well as his later insistence that slaves freed by the Emancipation Proclamation must never be re-enslaved.[45]

Lincoln's position, thus, was that humanitarian reformers must first work to convert political institutions to the rightness of their cause and then seek, over time, to help particular individuals. In a sense, Lincoln's position was a variant of the familiar Republican doctrine of "freedom national" advanced by Salmon Chase and Charles Sumner.[46] Slavery, insisted Chase and Sumner, could be sustained and legitimated only by the authority of the states, never by that of the federal government. Lincoln's version of this position proved successful, partly because it appealed very powerfully to both wings of his party, and it was important because it was clearly an ethical and intellectual achievement as well as a political one. On the one hand, Lincoln's demand that the federal government stigmatize slavery as a wrong appealed to Republican militants. This demand enabled Lincoln to escape the moral relativism of Douglas's popular sovereignty. On the other hand, Lincoln's support of the nation's political institutions and of a gradualist approach toward ending slavery appealed to northern moderates. This stand acknowledged the danger of moral absolutism—the arrogance of the self-righteous—against which Lincoln had preached as early as his Temperance Address of 1842. Lincoln felt that only by respecting the tolerant and deliberative character of republican institutions could the antislavery movement avoid overriding, or appearing to override, the reasonable concerns of others.

[44] Ibid., 406; see 501.

[45] A similar gradualism seems to have shaped Lincoln's policies on reconstruction. He contemplated extending to the ex-slaves some civil rights but not full political and social equality. He also evidently believed that any progress beyond that point would require the revival of the South's political institutions (see Basler 1953–1955, 8:402–4). In some ways, his position was at least as advanced as that of Garrison who (unlike Phillips) favored dissolving the American Anti-slavery Society once all slaves were legally free. Lincoln thus cannot be grouped with those Republicans who assumed that after the war the problems of the ex-slaves would take care of themselves without extensive government intervention.

[46] Donald 1974, 227ff.

In all this, Lincoln's most crucial move was to make humanitarianism politically relevant. He provided his contemporaries with an ethic that embraced rather than shrank from the institutional and temporal complexities of political life, an ethic that nevertheless maintained the integrity of its moral commitment.

Lincoln's Protestant Ethic

The preceding explanation of Lincoln's political humanitarianism itself remains incomplete, because it does not indicate how he was able successfully to combine political moderation and ethical perfectionism. Lincoln's self-regarding motives are only a partial explanation of his moderation on the slavery issue, and explanations in terms of these motives are more convincing when applied to specific positions—his opposition to the expansion of slavery, for example—than when applied to his broader political outlook. Many Republicans, after all, shared Lincoln's motives and policy goals, but few if any developed so complex and subtle a political ethic. A more complete account of Lincoln's success, then, must ask other questions: why, for example, was *any* type of humanitarianism relevant to a *political* debate over slavery? Why did Americans, North and South, take the militant attacks on slavery so seriously that they felt compelled to denounce the abolitionists as fanatics?

As these questions suggest, our concern is not primarily with Lincoln's personal goals, that is, with what causes impelled him, or the abolitionists, to take specific policy positions. Our focus instead is on the substance of his politics and how his broader political outlook differed from that of the abolitionists. We shall ask, on the one hand, how the abolitionists were able to develop a critique of slavery that they and some of their contemporaries found intelligible and persuasive but that others found truly threatening. We shall ask, on the other hand, how Lincoln was able to formulate a competing political ethic. In particular, what were the conceptual and cultural resources upon which he drew, and how did they resemble and differ from those drawn upon by the antislavery militants?

The Abolitionists' Religious Tradition

The brief answer to the two questions is that, for all their differences over politics and political institutions, Lincoln and the abolitionists both were powerfully influenced by the Protestant religious tradition that shaped their common Yankee culture. To develop this claim, we will first consider the rationalist, individualist, and perfectionist values that were inherited by the abolitionists from New England Calvinism and from northern Protestant-ism more generally.

A New England Calvinist heritage, it must be emphasized, did not guar-antee support for abolitionism, and a large number of the abolitionists were not orthodox Protestants. Many antislavery activists, in fact, withdrew in disgust from their Protestant churches because those churches shunned any connection with the antislavery movement. Some of the abolitionists, in-cluding the Transcendentalist Theodore Parker, rejected the Christian belief in the Trinity, and most of the rest were heterodox on at least one major theological issue. Nor did abolitionism simply reproduce the seventeenth-century Puritan ethos; witness the affinity of many of the abolitionists for the secular enlightenment doctrine of laissez-faire. Nevertheless, it remains the case that the antislavery movement, like Lincoln's free-soil Republica-nism, found its most sympathetic reception in Calvinist New England and areas of Yankee settlement to the west. Equally important, the antislavery movement drew openly and substantially on the rationalist, individualist, and perfectionist elements of the Protestant religious tradition.[47]

The reigning theology of colonial New England had at its core a deeply rationalist concern with the development of human faculties. One of the orthodoxy's most pressing concerns was with the gulf between the future potential of natural human reason and the present reality of sinful, de-formed human intellects. According to the colonial orthodoxy, that gulf could be bridged only where God had freely chosen a small band of saints to do his will. The celebrated doctrine of predestination stated that God had directly singled out a few human beings for salvation, and by his grace he had largely restored their rational faculties. At the same time, however, sainthood required God's elect to exercise, and thus develop, their re-deemed faculties in accord with the Puritan doctrines of vocation and sanc-tification. These saints, the orthodoxy insisted, could not retreat from the world. Instead, just as God had restored order and rationality to their individual souls, they had a duty to bring order and rationality to social life by developing their faculties and performing in vocations that would glorify God. In the words of the seventeenth-century Puritan divine, John Preston, "The way to grow in any grace is the exercise of that grace."[48]

The content of the saints' duty—this obligation to develop their faculties—was deeply rationalist; its form was individualist and perfection-ist. Given God's sovereignty and infinite power, personal merit and good deeds were no guarantee of salvation. God's decisions about who should be saved, that is, could neither be understood by mere mortals nor influenced by the ability of certain human beings to perform more good deeds than

---

[47] J. L. Thomas 1965a.
[48] P. Miller 1956b, 82–92; see P. Miller 1961a, ch. 3; P. Miller 1956a, 88.

sinful deeds. Instead, his saints were "justified"—individually chosen for divine, and therefore ultimately unknowable, reasons—through an act of divine will. Salvation was conveyed directly to the individual by God's freely bestowed grace.

This individualism, however, this direct connection between God and each one of his saints, led not to anarchy but to a powerful system of ethical and social constraints. Too, a belief in the divine selection of a small band of saints encouraged not smug self-assurance but a remarkable activism. If only a few were chosen, and they were selected according to God's ultimately unknowable will, how could anyone be confident that he or she had really been singled out for redemption? As Weber and others have pointed out, many Calvinists tried to relieve this anxiety about their own salvation by acting as if God had indeed chosen them; that is, by relentlessly pursuing ethical perfection in their own conduct. The theologians, to be sure, held that such righteousness could only be a consequence and a sign, never the cause, of sainthood. Theology, however, powerfully shaped psychology, and any and every moral lapse was to be avoided lest it seem to reveal the would-be saint to be a doomed sinner. Everything depended on sanctification, a process of individual self-scrutiny and struggle for moral purity.[49]

One result of this process was the appearance in the Puritan orthodoxy of what Perry Miller has called an Augustinian strain of piety.[50] This piety was not fundamentally an emotion or enthusiasm; rather it was a belief that the saints must strive unceasingly to transform their fallible selves into worthy instruments of a divinity so infinitely majestic as to be beyond human ken. The obligation of the saints, that is, was not only to *develop* their moral, intellectual, and physical faculties—it was also to *perfect* them and thus to do God's will rather than their own. In this concept of duty, as paradoxical as it might seem, the Puritans' highly individualist concern with salvation led to a strong belief in the value of social constraints. For one thing, such constraints helped them to do their duty by precluding the outright egoism that catered to one's own pleasures and preferences. Equally important, that same duty required them affirmatively to serve God and to help others by rationalizing the broader community. Where necessary, moreover, duty required them to constrain other individuals, even if that meant a meddling concern with the development, moral welfare, or at least the right conduct of others.

This activist ethic, however, did not lead directly to abolitionism or to any other kind of moral reform. In the Puritan view, because most individuals were irredeemably mired in sin, they required the discipline of godly government and appropriate human authority to prevent them from doing evil.

---

[49] Bercovitch 1975, ch. 1.
[50] P. Miller 1961a, ch. 1.

Accordingly, for example, it was possible that some or all of the slaves had been providentially singled out for subordination, and there was therefore no clear or morally binding presumption against their enslavement. The move from the orthodox view to abolitionism required the modification of orthodox beliefs in two distinct ways.

The first of these two theological modifications, which reflected the powerful democratic and voluntarist currents in early nineteenth-century American society, rejected as elitist the orthodox belief that God would save only a few saints. Especially during the Great Awakenings, liberal Calvinists increasingly insisted that a truly loving God would offer salvation to every human being who willingly sought his grace. If this were true, then surely some of the slaves could also exercise this moral freedom by striving to develop their God-given faculties. The slaves could do so, however, only if they were liberated from bondage. Slavery was an unpardonable sin, in other words, because it prevented its victims from even attempting to seek sanctification by laboring under their own direction to rationalize the world. As a result, some of those liberal Calvinists who were moved by the Second Awakening took up the abolitionist banner, including several future leaders of the Liberty party, as well as the students who left Cincinnati's Lane Seminary to found Oberlin College.

The second of these two theological modifications shifted the focus of moral concern and, by implication, the Calvinist view of political authority. By itself, a belief in free moral agency did not support a thoroughgoing humanitarianism, primarily because freedom enabled the individual to follow either a sinful or a moral path. Some Calvinists, therefore, emphasized the *consequences* of the individual's moral choices. In general, this concern with consequences required restraining the sinful behavior of those who willfully remained unregenerate. The result of this concern was support for moral regulation, including for such conservative causes as protecting the integrity of the sabbath. In light of the disorder that seemed likely to follow as a consequence of emancipation, these Calvinists either ignored slavery or tended to favor African colonization without, however, insisting on an end to slavery.[51] For other Calvinists, in contrast, the central question emphasized the *conditions* that make genuine moral agency possible. These Calvinists sought to change those conditions—most notably slavery—that made it impossible for some individuals even to seek self-development.

Nevertheless, participation in the antislavery crusade required *both* the voluntarism and egalitarianism of liberal Protestantism *and* a traditional Calvinist concern with piety in the pursuit of worldly vocation. The Second Awakening's greatest preacher, Charles Finney, for example, despite his liberal theology, sought to combat evil through prayer, suasion, and reli-

---

[51] J. L. Thomas 1965a, 246–47.

gious conversion rather than through social activism. Finney detested human bondage, but he remained largely aloof from the antislavery movement. The abolitionists, in contrast, linked their cause with the pietistic objective of reforming the world as they labored to redeem their souls. Like more traditional Calvinists, they emphasized curbing the "lowest passions." "Restraints," wrote Theodore Weld, "are the web of civilized society, warp and woof."[52] For the abolitionists, however, the passionate, self-indulgent persons who needed restraint were not the slaves, who had never enjoyed freedom; they were rather the slave owners who had abused their freedom by exploiting their slaves socially, economically, and sexually. The standards of the abolitionists thus required their unceasing struggle against the peculiar institution, no matter how unpopular that struggle might become. In this respect, they had truly inherited the piety of the Puritans. Rigorously committed to moral perfection, they reproduced in a nineteenth-century idiom the seventeenth-century yearning to become deserving servants of an infinite God.[53]

Because most Northerners loved the Union, disliked blacks, and thought the abolitionists too extreme, many contemporary historians have concluded that the abolitionists had little direct influence on antebellum politics.[54] At most, according to these historians, the impact of the abolitionists was indirect; they goaded Southerners into more extreme defenses of slavery and more virulent attacks on the North. The polemic of the Southerners, in turn, antagonized moderate Northerners and contributed to the crisis.

How could the abolitionists have succeeded in goading Southerners in this way? Some Southerners, of course, may have felt guilty about owning slaves, but, as the nineteenth century wore on, fewer and fewer of them would concede that slavery was an evil institution.[55] If we focus on the religious roots of the abolitionists, however, another possibility emerges. Some Southerners may have recognized the antislavery potential in the voluntarist and egalitarian wing of Calvinism, and they may have perceived the danger to themselves of this potential, should the abolitionists prove successful in sparking the Yankee conscience. In all likelihood, anxiety helped produce just the outcome that was least desired. By reacting so harshly against the possible threat, the Southerners actually encouraged moderate Northerners in turn to view the slave power as a threat and to conclude that the otherwise detested abolitionists had morality on their side.

[52] Walters 1976, 77.
[53] P. Miller 1961a, ch. 1; Davis 1966, 294–99, 368–78; Davis 1975, 296, 335, 554.
[54] Friedman 1982, 45.
[55] Potter 1976, 39ff.

Lincoln and the Whigs' Protestant Culture

Assuming the foregoing argument to be correct, an analysis that emphasizes the religious roots of the abolitionists must overcome a double problem. Such an analysis says too much, if it implies that a belief in liberal Calvinism always led to a belief in abolition. Even among liberal Calvinists, abolitionism was not politically the most important antislavery movement; it was only the most radical. Such an analysis says too little if it fails to tell us precisely how and why liberal Calvinists were able conscientiously to oppose slavery and still reject abolitionism. Attention to Lincoln's humanitarianism will help resolve both of these problems.

Like many of the liberal Calvinists, Lincoln detested slavery without embracing immediate emancipation. Nevertheless, his political ethic can be traced, even if only indirectly, to the same New England Protestant tradition that spawned abolitionism. This claim about his political ethic, however, depends on two other, by no means self-evident, claims: first, that Lincoln was strongly influenced by Yankee religious values and beliefs, despite the obvious facts of his family background and personal religious affiliation; and, second, that an illuminating parallel can be drawn between the tensions within colonial Puritanism and the disagreements among Whigs, Republicans, and moral reformers of Lincoln's own time.

Lincoln was not a direct descendant of New England Protestantism. His seventeenth-century Massachusetts ancestors were Quakers, not Puritans, and his immediate forebears were Baptists from rural Kentucky and Virginia, not the cultured offspring of Yankee Calvinism. Personally, he had little to do with any organized denomination, although he may have been influenced by the antislavery sentiments of his father's church, and his providential view of the Civil War may have derived from his mother's religious fatalism.[56]

Although the young Lincoln adopted some of his family's religious ideas, he fervently sought to rise above their social and cultural status. Starting out in the Illinois village of New Salem, he chose to associate with the town's elite rather than with the "meaner sort" who liked his humor. As a young man, he sought out better-educated lawyers as teachers and colleagues, and the two women he courted came from upper-class backgrounds. As a father, he was proud of his oldest son Robert's cultivation and easy familiarity with Harvard classmates from established eastern families; most of these new upper-class associates were Whigs. Lincoln himself had joined the Whig party as a youth, and he stayed with it until its collapse in the mid-1850s, serving the party as a floor leader in the state legislature, as a presidential elector, and as a national committeeman. During this period, he also

---

[56] Oates 1977, ch. 1; B. P. Thomas 1952, ch. 2.

adopted the unionism and procapitalist policies of its leading national spokesmen.[57]

Although Lincoln gave his allegiance to a political party and not a church—to a secularized ethic and not a theology—Whiggery meant more to him than an economic program or a chance for political advancement, or even a route to higher social status. His partisanship was a cultural as well as a political phenomenon—one that reflected his aspirations rather than his family background. As Daniel Walker Howe has argued, the Whig party offered Lincoln an entire culture with which to shape his life.[58] The Whigs, for example, had little patience with the self-indulgent, undisciplined individual. Instead, they were simultaneously concerned with self-control and social progress, which together they thought were essential to a well-ordered society. Especially in the North, Whig culture had strongly Protestant roots, and, at the least, Whiggery powerfully reinforced Lincoln's moral earnestness as well as his commitment to learning; that commitment dated from his youth but had not been highly valued in the frontier society where he grew up. Moreover, Lincoln's orientation toward the Whigs was not accidental but intentional on his part. Significantly, Lincoln defended the Whig culture against the derision of Douglas and his followers, even in the late 1850s after the Whig party itself had disappeared.[59] Lincoln's Whig partisanship, therefore, appears to have been a major vehicle by which he confirmed a self-identification with the New England cultural tradition that he adopted rather than inherited from his family.

The Whigs believed as strongly in the community and its institutions as in individual development. It was in the name of community that the party's early leaders denounced the self-serving factionalism of the Jacksonian Democrats and, as an alternative, called for a devotion to the common good. At the same time that the party justified its procapitalist economic policies by claiming that the policies would bring prosperity to all, it also appealed to other social classes by celebrating community and polity as the source of essential moral standards.[60] This dual appeal, however, was just what the abolitionists found so upsetting about Lincoln and his fellow Whigs. A question arises, therefore, about how the same Protestant culture that helped sustain abolitionism was also able to foster the Whigs' commitment to social institutions. Another question arises about why so many of his contemporaries regarded Lincoln's marriage of humanitarian individualism and Whiggish institutionalism as not only a coherent but also a compelling political ethic. Why did Lincoln's contemporaries not dismiss his

[57] Oates 1977, 5, 19–21, 34; B. P. Thomas 1952, 56, 73, 78–80, 96, 105; Basler 1953–1955, 2:322, 400.

[58] D. W. Howe 1979, ch. 2.

[59] Basler 1953–1955, 3:356ff.

[60] D. W. Howe 1979, ch. 2; Greenstone 1982b; Benson 1973, ch. 5.

ethic as simply the transparent attempt of an ambitious politician to collect diverse factions under a single banner?

Covenant Theology and the Dilemmas of the New England Way

The claim being advanced here is that Lincoln's position drew upon a tradition of religious thought and a conception of sainthood and citizenship that occupied a central place in New England culture. From this perspective, the religious tradition common to both Whigs and abolitionists constituted a family of related belief systems. This point has not been well understood. Starting with Weber's study of the Protestant ethic, the tendency has been to consider this tradition as a single pattern of influence. For our purposes, it will be necessary to consider seventeenth-century Puritanism within a more complex framework.

The general goal of the piety of the Puritans was to glorify God by rationalizing his world; the specific goal, from which they derived their name, was to purify an institution, their own Church of England.[61] This project, however, suffered from two problems that sorely troubled English Calvinism. First, how could fallible men and women combine rationality with saintly devotion? Second, how could saints who were devoted to religious purity involve themselves in a corrupt church without being contaminated by it?

The first question pitted the mystical, pietistic character of the saintly life against the rational content of the mission of the saints. The Puritans were dedicated to making their church more rational. They sought to abolish the magical ceremonies conducted by an ignorant, sinful priesthood and to substitute the intelligible preaching of a competent, learned clergy. Puritanism thus embodied a rationalist Aristotelian strain that respected the human mind and the natural order as products of divine intellect.[62] The obligation of the saints was to reason carefully and instrumentally about the most effective way to proceed in their task—herein was a major source of the nineteenth-century humanitarians' devotion to the development of human faculties.

If the content of the Puritans' mission was rationalist, however, the means were not. The mission had to be pursued by human beings who had fallen into sin and who could not, as a result, genuinely comprehend God's actions. As Miller noted, whatever the theological warrants for this conception of God as arbitrary and capricious, it was a valid description of the Puritans' perception of a world that was often harsh and unpredictable.[63] In any case, this perception of an almost unbridgeable gap between the human

---

[61] P. Miller 1961a, ch. 1.

[62] Morgan 1965, 5–12; P. Miller 1961a, ch. 6.

[63] P. Miller 1961a, 17.

and the divine led in its turn to the Puritans' Augustinian strain of piety. Deformed by sin, human beings could hope to perceive, reason, and act correctly on important questions only if they had been transformed by the exalting, yet humbling, experience of receiving God's grace.

The sign of this grace was piety, and an unquestioning determination to become one of the worthy instruments of the infinite God, by striving relentlessly both to purify his church and to bring order to his world. Neither grace nor piety, however, could be attained solely through the individual's own efforts, not even through systematic rational reflection on moral issues. On the contrary, attaining grace and piety required the genuine devotion of one's whole self and soul to God. It required, that is, the kind of zeal for purity that was exhibited by the abolitionists two centuries later. There was, then, a clear and inherent tension in the creed of the Massachusetts orthodoxy, between the calm, reflective rationality of their religious objectives, on the one hand, and, on the other, the piety, the zealous religious and ethical commitment, with which they sought to achieve those objectives.

The second question, about the participation of saints in a corrupt church, pitted the universalistic scope of the Puritans' project against the particularistic character of their religious community; the reform of the whole Church of England, that is, against the reliance of the project on a select band of saints whose success demanded religious purity. The duty of the Puritans was evangelical: not merely to found a new sect but to redeem the religious life of an entire society.[64] The scope of their religious obligation, therefore, was defined politically, by the boundaries of the nation served by the Church of England. How were the regenerate to fulfill this obligation if they risked falling into sin by participating in the corrupt national church? The answer, at least for the Puritans who later immigrated to New England, was separation—the development of a congregational form of church polity in which the regenerate prepared and sustained themselves by worshipping in religious communities uncontaminated by the old order. This separation, they believed, would protect their purity, without which they could not pursue their mission. There was, consequently, conflict between the separatism of the New England Puritans and their evangelical goal of redeeming the whole society.

A prominent feature of New England religious history was the colonial orthodoxy's determination to overcome these two tensions—between rationality and devotion, and between the purity of the church and the reform of society—through a complicated and subtle theology. As Miller repeatedly observed, the New England Way insisted on maintaining both piety

---

[64] Morgan 1965, ch. 5.

and rationality, both the zeal and saving experience of grace and the discipline of reason and law.[65] As Bercovitch has emphasized, the saints called themselves nonseparating congregationalists; they treated their religious communities both as select congregations of the regenerate and as part of the established church of the colonial polity. The theological device by which they accomplished this synthesis was the concept of the covenant, according to which God contracted with his saints to grant them salvation in exchange for their acceptance of his grace and their conscientious dedication to achieving the perfection of a holy life.

With respect to the tension between rationality and piety, the covenant theology provided scope for human freedom and rational calculation by making God knowable. By proffering the covenant, God had agreed to choose saints intelligibly, not arbitrarily—that is, in accordance with the provisions of the covenant. As a result, an individual could freely accept those provisions and struggle to live up to them. Not only had God bound himself to observe the Covenant of Grace, but he had made its terms understandable to the (redeemed) human intellect. In this way, the orthodoxy affirmed its commitment to the purposeful and (at least partly) voluntarist use of human reason. To serve God within the covenant, and to conform to its terms, one had to demonstrate a rational concern with effective, instrumentally rational action. At the same time, because God chose to offer the covenant, he retained his ultimate sovereignty. Sainthood still required a supreme act of faith and consequent moral commitment; the most profound of religious experiences still entailed an uncompromising zeal to serve this infinite and finally mysterious being. The orthodoxy thus reasserted the saintly yearning for holiness and the passionate quest for perfection.[66]

With respect to the second tension between the purity of the church and the reform of society, the orthodox theology singled out as regenerate only those who individually accepted the Covenant of Grace and were therefore entitled to receive the sacraments. Those outside the covenant remained "dead in sin," as in original Calvinist theology. By continuing to distinguish sharply between saints and sinners, the orthodoxy preserved the obligation of each believer to seek moral purity. The colonial Puritans, however, also emphasized God's interest in human history as well as in individual biographies. He had covenanted not just with particular saints but with the whole nation of New England.[67] Accordingly, the Puritans had a collective, corporate role to play in secular history, although the playing out of that role had

[65] P. Miller 1961a.
[66] Ibid., ch. 13.
[67] Morgan 1965, ch. 3.

to be judged by the transhistorical standards of God's providential plan rather than by the standards of worldly success alone. From this *national covenant* between God and all of New England flowed the responsibility of every member of the church-nation—not simply of every saint—to do God's work in a historical drama of sacred significance. Consequently, the citizenship of the New Englanders in this new Israel assumed a special spiritual importance. The result was a political project in which the quest for individual perfection took on a communal form at the same time that community life acquired an ethical content.

The first generation of Puritans may have been able to suppress major dissent from this covenantal position, because they had migrated to a remote colony. Even our abbreviated discussion, however, suggests the extent to which New England Calvinism experienced a variety of theological and ethical challenges, each of which dissented in some way from the orthodoxy's insistence both that piety be linked with rationality and that purity be joined with citizenship.

The tension between rationality and piety is indicated by the different columns of table 10.1. Arminianism (the left-hand column) asserted the value of human rationality and freedom. Human beings could save themselves if they freely sought to glorify God in the course of pursuing their worldly vocations, a task that required reasoning instrumentally about how best to reshape the world. Among New England's rationalist clergy to whom this position appealed, sainthood came to mean an emphasis on properly calculating the consequences of one's actions so that one truly furthered God's ends. Sociologically, this relatively calm, restrained doctrine appealed to the socially and economically successful. Theologically, it spawned Unitarianism, whose liberal creed produced comparatively few abolitionists in the nineteenth century.[68] Although the orthodox theologians recognized the importance of the rationalist position, they argued in favor of piety by maintaining, first, that God's will remained ultimately mysterious and, second, that those outside the covenant remained mired in sin. It then followed that sainthood continued to demand unremitting zeal from those who experienced God's grace and accepted his covenant.

To those early Puritans who were to be found on the pietistic side of this dimension (the right-hand column of table 10.1), rationality, learning, and even godly government were unnecessary in directing the actions of saints, because the saints had been touched by God's grace. Most of these pietistic, antinomian sects were so rebelliously individualistic, so supportive of personal intuition, that they were either destroyed by internal dissent or suppressed by the civil authorities. The Quakers survived and flourished, however, precisely because they tempered their antinomian belief in an inner

[68] Heimert 1966, 17, 32–33, 169, 205, 326, 335.

TABLE 10.1
A Typology of Political/Ethical Positions that Evolved out of Puritanism

	Affirms the saints' rationality	*Affirms rationality and piety*	*Affirms the saints' piety*
Affirms the saints' obligations to the polity (national covenant)	Conversative, proto-Unitarian rationalists (colonial patriots vs. England)	Seventeenth-century Presbyterians, Solomon Stoddard	Evangelistic nationalists
Affirms both obligations (both covenants)	Democratic nationalists (John Wise), secularists, Benj. Franklin	The colonial orthodoxy (New England Way)	Evangelical reformers, antislavery Edwardseans
Affirms the saints' ethical obligations as individuals (Covenant of Grace)	Secular anarchists	Separatists, Roger Williams, early Plymouth Colony	Quakers

light with a subtle pattern of informal, communal discipline.[69] Both the orthodoxy and the antinomians acknowledged the decisive importance of God's grace, but, in contrast to the antinomians, the orthodoxy insisted on the rational features of the covenantal relationship and thus on the central role of the rational faculties of the believers.

The second tension, between purity and inclusiveness, is indicated by the three rows of table 10.1. The separating congregationalists (the bottom row) believed that they had to withdraw from the hopeless corruption of the established church into communities of the regenerate, each of whom individually had been saved by the Covenant of Grace. Although some of these separatist groups affirmed the civil authority of the state and the importance of learning and human reason, those that *remained* separatist turned inward, religiously and ethically. In effect, they rejected the evangelical obligation to redeem society by participating in its established religious and political institutions; nor did they believe in the religious mission of the citizen.[70] Indeed, the greatest American separatist, Roger Williams, thought political institutions were so prone to sin, that he preached religious toleration as a way of protecting true believers from government persecution. What mattered to Williams was sainthood rather than citizenship.[71] Yet, even though the orthodoxy embraced the Covenant of Grace,

[69] Davis 1966, 299; see Davis 1975, 206, 226.
[70] Morgan 1965, 142ff.
[71] P. Miller 1970.

they rejected separatism because it overlooked the significance of the national covenant and thus denied the political responsibilities of the saints.

In contrast to the separatists, the seventeenth-century English Presbyterians (the top row of table 10.1) held that God alone could distinguish true from counterfeit saints. For that reason, the church could not rightfully deny membership and the sacraments to any well-behaved, professing Christian. In New England, Solomon Stoddard imposed a similar doctrine on the Connecticut Valley after 1677.[72] To Stoddard and the Presbyterians, the church's spiritual jurisdiction was territorial; its responsibility was to embrace and supervise all individuals within that jurisdiction, whether or not they had been individually saved. In this sense, citizenship, indeed *residence*, replaced sainthood as the qualification for church membership. The orthodoxy, however, although they also upheld the central importance of the national covenant and thus the connection between citizenship and sainthood, insisted that full church membership could be extended only to true saints who were participants in the Covenant of Grace. Moreover, the religious and ethical responsibilities of God's elect *included* the duties every citizen owed to the civil authorities.

As the position of the orthodoxy makes clear, the tensions in Puritan theology were not outright contradictions. Some separatists like the Quakers, for instance, emphasized piety; others, like Williams, joined the orthodoxy in combining piety with rationality.[73] There were, that is, at least three possible positions that could be taken on each dimension (hence, the middle row and column of table 10.1). One could choose either piety or instrumental rationality, or one could join Williams in affirming both values; or one could seek either purity or evangelical inclusiveness, or one could follow the orthodoxy in seeking both. These possibilities defined the complex ethical-religious framework bequeathed to subsequent generations, including the generation of Lincoln's Whigs.

Two Tensions in New England Political Culture

Lincoln and the colonial orthodoxy lived in widely separated worlds. There is no specific evidence that Lincoln was familiar with the subtleties of seventeenth-century Puritan theology. In common with many New England Protestants who were influenced by the great eighteenth-century theologian Jonathan Edwards, Lincoln did not invoke the explicitly contractual features of the covenant tradition. More generally, whereas Puritan thought and practice was elitist and still medieval in some respects, Lincoln's ideology was universalistic and egalitarian. Further, Lincoln and most of his contemporaries believed in the American republican experiment

---

[72] P. Miller 1961b, chs. 14, 16.
[73] P. Miller 1970, 241–53.

rather than in a theologically sanctioned errand into the wilderness. Finally, whereas the Puritans focused on the religious duty of the saint, Lincoln was concerned with the humanitarian obligation of the truly ethical person.

Despite these differences, however, a substantial case can be made that the Puritan legacy had great importance for Lincoln in at least two respects. First, the New England tradition had created a *structure* of political and ethical *choices* that continued to shape debate among Whigs, Republicans, and Yankee moral reformers until the Civil War. When Lincoln became a Whig and embraced the party's cultural values, he did not commit himself to a monolithic doctrine. Instead, he acquired a distinctive set of questions that framed a continuing debate about politics and ethics. Second, Lincoln's own position—the answers he fashioned to the dilemmas of his day, especially after 1854—closely resembled the stance that had been adopted by the colonial orthodoxy.

It is by now a commonplace that, from its inception in the early 1830s until the party's death a generation later, Whig culture exhibited both a conservative concern with social discipline and some more liberal, egalitarian, and voluntarist tendencies—a duality that paralleled the theological split within New England Calvinism. As a result, the Whigs' Protestant outlook no more surely entailed a commitment to antislavery than had a Calvinist theology. Many conservative or Cotton Whigs, particularly in the eastern cities, for example, tried to preserve national unity by supporting sectional accommodation and opposing moralistic attacks on the South. The Conscience Whigs of Massachusetts, in contrast, along with their allies in the party's rural and western bastions, held that the ideas of universal equality and self-improvement made slavery intolerable. Furthermore, this conflict was only one of several that divided different Whig factions from each other; the conflict similarly divided various groups of moral reformers and, later, the factions that made up the Republican party. It is with regard to these divisions that a comparison between Puritanism and Lincoln's political ethic becomes relevant, because the issues once again involved the tensions between sainthood and citizenship and between rationality and piety. We will examine the pattern of these tensions according to the terms of the typology set out in table 10.2. The partitions of table 10.2 correspond to those of table 10.1: the nineteenth-century political divisions replace the more explicitly theological divisions of the seventeenth century.[74]

---

[74] It must be emphasized that this analysis does *not* apply to nineteenth-century groups who were not strongly influenced by the Yankee religious tradition—the utilitarian foes of slavery such as Richard Hildreth, for example, or those northern Democrats who viewed slave owners as a competing economic and social interest; far less did it apply to Democrats like Douglas who urged sectional accommodation. Furthermore, it should be recalled, both Leggett and Van Buren were antislavery, but on utilitarian rather than perfectionist grounds.

TABLE 10.2
A Typology of Nineteenth-century Political/Ethical Positions
that Evolved out of Colonial Calvinism

	Affirms place of instrumental reasoning in morality	Affirms place of instrumental and consummatory reasoning in morality	Affirms place of consummatory reasoning in morality
Affirms moral obligations to the polity	Daniel Webster and the Cotton Whigs	Henry Clay	Evangelistic supporters of Manifest Destiny
Affirms both obligations	William Seward and the Whig modernizers (Lincoln before 1854)	Lincoln in 1854 and after	Joshua Giddings at the end of his career
Affirms obligations of individuals to seek moral purity	Secular (antislavery) utopian communities	Garrisonian Abolitionists	Quakers

THE FIRST DIMENSION: UNIONISM VS. MORAL PURITY

One dimension of antebellum politics in the North exhibited conflicting conceptions of moral duty: how essential was it to maintain one's ethical purity as opposed to fulfilling one's obligations as a citizen? In much the same way that the preceding generation of New Englanders had oscillated between the nationalism of the early Federalists and the secessionist tendencies of the Hartford Convention, the antebellum generation witnessed a struggle between unionism (top row of table 10.2) and separatism (bottom row of table 10.2).

At one extreme, New England's Cotton Whigs, including Webster, Rufus Choate, and Edward Everett, disliked slavery and objected for prudential reasons to its territorial extension. Like Lincoln, these men tended to favor colonization rather than abolition as a solution to the problem of slavery. Unlike Lincoln, however, they resisted attempts to make slavery a moral issue, lest it tear the Union apart. Without the Union, they feared, liberty would not be secure for the people of any race. In particular, Webster and his allies believed that the moralism of the abolitionists would undermine the social basis on which freedom rested. Accordingly, many of his followers refused to vote for the Republicans in either 1856 or 1860.[75]

[75] Potter 1976, 263, 416.

At the other extreme, the antislavery militants insisted on a moral purity that was not to be found in most social, religious, and political institutions. Leading a genuinely holy life meant separating from those institutions and establishing communion only with the truly righteous. In the eighteenth century, the Pennsylvania Quakers, the first major group to condemn slavery in the new world, were offended by their colonial government's use of force against the Indians. Later, these Friends were unable to accept the constitutional compromises (explicitly embraced by Lincoln and Webster) that tolerated slavery in the South. From the mid-1700s on, therefore, the Friends followed a separatist course in politics and took little part in the political side of the antislavery struggle in the 1800s. Instead, as Digby Baltzell has pointed out, the Friends sought ethical purity—and attacked slavery—not through political institutions but by reforming their personal and religious conduct.[76] They purged their own religious community of slave holders, and they issued moral appeals against slavery while helping individual fugitive slaves to escape to Canada.

In some ways, the abolitionists resembled the Quakers. Some of the abolitionists, including the strongly antislavery Transcendentalists, were directly influenced by the Friends—Garrison himself had been converted to abolitionism by a Friend. Indeed, Harriet Martineau thought Garrison acted like a Friend, and one of Garrison's own converts compared him to the Quakers' founder, George Fox.[77] On the issue of unionism versus moral purity the two groups had similar beliefs. Although most antislavery militants acknowledged the value of private organizations that were maintained on righteous principles, the militants also believed that American society's established institutions were ethically compromised. In particular, the militants were suspicious of political institutions. Garrison, who declared his country to be mankind, held that "the governments of this world . . . are all Anti-Christ."[78] Even worse from the point of view of the abolitionists, their own government tolerated slavery within its borders. Not surprisingly, a separatist creed was adopted by a congeries of radical antislavery anarchists and perfectionists who withdrew into utopian communities.

Other antislavery groups took positions somewhere between the abolitionists and the unionist Whigs. Some non-Garrisonian abolitionists read the Constitution as an antislavery document; others, notably members of the Liberty party, carried the campaign against slavery into electoral politics.[79] Nevertheless, few Liberty party activists emphasized the Union's role as a republican experiment of world-historical significance. Although some of their leaders eventually became radical Republicans, most Liberty party supporters could not accept the maneuvering and compromises essen-

[76] Baltzell 1979, 154ff.
[77] See Walters 1976, 51–52; Martineau 1835, 116; Child 1839, 68.
[78] Garrison 1837, 78.
[79] National Liberty Party Convention 1843, 95–96.

tial to institutional life. They withdrew from the major churches, just as they "came out" from the major parties—a step the politically ambitious Lincoln evidently never considered. To members of the Liberty party, the Missouri Compromise—by allowing slavery into the southern part of the Louisiana Purchase—revealed the Union's hypocritical default on its republican commitment to freedom.[80] As a result, the Republican and Liberty parties differed over both the intrinsic moral worth of the Union and the policies the Union had adopted. Lincoln bitterly lamented the repeal of the Missouri Compromise. In his eyes, the important point of the compromise was that it had stigmatized slavery as immoral by barring it from the northern part of the Louisiana Purchase. For the Republicans, therefore, as for the nationalist but antislavery Whigs before them, the Union continued to be the great republican experiment, rightly deserving of their allegiance, even if commitment to it meant that the extinction of slavery could be accomplished only gradually.

THE SECOND DIMENSION: INSTRUMENTAL VS. CONSUMMATORY ACTION

The second dimension of the typology involves disagreements among Northern Whigs, Republicans, and moral reformers over the character of social action. Specifically, the second dimension exhibits the competing instrumental and consummatory conceptions of moral reasoning.[81] Should one reason in consummatory terms in order to obey the commands of the moral law; that is, should one do only that which is intrinsically right, without engaging in an elaborate analysis of the likely consequences of one's actions? Or, ought one to view one's actions instrumentally, as means for achieving desirable ends, and reason instrumentally only about the most likely way to achieve those ends?

On the instrumental side of the division were most of those conservative Whigs whom Howe has called Whig modernizers[82] (left-hand column of table 10.2). These Whigs evaluated legal arrangements and political actions instrumentally, in terms of likely consequences. For them, a stable polity was essential for social progress and economic development. Politics, thereby, was less an exercise in morality than an applied science that focused on securing beneficent outcomes. One's political duty was to shun the fanatical pursuit of ethical perfection and to pursue instead a considered course of dispassionate reasoning about how best to achieve such outcomes. To con-

---

[80] J. L. Thomas 1965a, 247; Walters 1976, 15–16; Ball 1982, 34, 32, 20.

[81] [Instrumental reasoning is reasoning according to means-ends calculations; consummatory reasoning is reasoning according to moral duty and perfectionist principles. Humanist liberal reasoning is instrumental; reform liberal reasoning is consummatory. See also Apter 1965 and Apter 1971.]

[82] See D. W. Howe 1979, 181–209.

vert politics into a morality play, as Webster thought the abolitionists wanted to do, was reckless and self-defeating. It was reckless because it risked destroying the Union. It was self-defeating because destroying the world's only viable large republic would make it much more difficult to realize a humane, genuinely free society. Not every instrumentally oriented politician, however, took such an unwavering stance. William H. Seward, for example, joined his nationalism to a universalistic belief in individual development, a position that led him to reject nativism and denounce slavery. In the early 1850s, Seward, unlike Lincoln, opposed Webster on the Compromise of 1850 in a celebrated appeal to a law "higher" than the Constitution. Nevertheless, Seward displayed a somewhat serene trust in the ability of instrumental reasoning to direct social and economic modernization. As the crucial decade wore on, he came to dwell on the negative consequences of moralism, almost as much as Webster had done; and, especially during the secession crisis, Seward proved less militant than Lincoln.

Proponents of the consummatory conception of action (right-hand column of table 10.2), in contrast, insisted that one's actions must be valued because they profess or affirm one's moral commitments and in this sense are right in themselves. What is required of the actor is consummatory reasoning by which he or she decides on a certain action after determining whether or not its salient features are in accord with moral law or duty. To the humanitarians who espoused this view, an undue concern with the effectiveness of one's actions could become a form of idolatry, in which concern for efficiency displaced concern for duty. Many Quakers, for example, believed that instrumental, political calculations led inexorably to moral compromise and, in particular, to the use of force as the most effective means of achieving one's preferred ends. The Quakers avoided this trap by bearing personal rather than political witness against slavery. This consummatory view was shared by others with more positive, even unionist, feelings toward their regime, such as Joshua Giddings, a leading antislavery Whig who later became a Republican congressman from Ohio. Although Giddings drifted out of conventional politics as he underwent religious conversion and increasingly focused on achieving spiritual purity, he came to justify political actions entirely in terms of their ethical content.[83]

As with instrumental action, there is a spectrum of positions consistent with consummatory action. Among Republicans, such radicals as Sumner also merged moral and political concerns, athough they did so somewhat less singlemindedly than did Giddings at the end of his career. Moreover, many Garrisonians did not fully share the Quakers' negative view of political action; political action was acceptable, that is, as long as it did not involve

[83] Stewart 1970, 280ff, ch. 12.

a commitment to the Union or its slavery-tainted institutions. As the Garrisonians saw it, their commitment to developing and exercising human faculties required them to reason instrumentally themselves to advance their cause against slavery. Given, thus, a responsibility to present the moral case against slavery as effectively as possible, they paid close attention to public opinion and political developments. Phillips, in particular, developed a persuasive argument that agitation and propaganda were the most effective tools available to them in bringing their cause before an indifferent if not hostile society.[84]

Even among the Garrisonians, then, there were detectable shades of difference. Garrison's doctrine of nonresistance expressed the pacifist's distaste for all violence and, by extension, for political actions that could readily lead to it.[85] Phillips, however, was more troubled by the sinfulness of the American regime than by the intrinsic defects of political action. His emphasis on disunionism rather than on nonresistance suggested he could support a government that had redeemed itself by separating from the South.[86]

Lincoln's Covenantal Synthesis

For all their differences, the political ethics of Lincoln and the seventeenth-century New England Puritans had striking parallels. At least by 1854, Lincoln had rejected all those alternative positions that failed either to join political and moral duties or to combine instrumental rationality with a commitment to ethical perfectionism. As we have seen in our detailed discussion of his humanitarianism, Lincoln fully shared the enthusiasm of many moral reformers for individual development and self-improvement. Equally important, Lincoln believed that implementing those values required communion with others—specifically, with fellow partisans who shared and publicly professed the same ethical vision. As Lincoln said in his last senatorial debate with Douglas:

> The real issue in this controversy . . . is the sentiment on the part of one class that looks upon the institution of slavery *as a wrong*, and of another class that *does not* look upon it as a wrong. . . . [That antislavery position] is the sentiment of the Republican party. It is the sentiment around which all their actions—all their arguments circle—from which all their propositions radiate.

It was essential, moreover, that this sentiment be openly declared. What Lincoln detested about the Democrats was their doctrine that

[84] Filler 1965, 34ff.
[85] Walters 1976, 26.
[86] I should like to thank Diana Schaub for making this point to me.

you must not say any thing about . . . [slavery] in the free States, *because it is not here*. You must not say any thing about it in the slave States, *because it is there*. You must not say any thing about it in the pulpit, because that is religion and has nothing to do with it. You must not say any thing about it in politics, *because that will disturb the security of 'my place'*.[87]

In short, Lincoln insisted, against the conservative nationalists, that the Union must face its ethical responsibilities with respect to slavery, come what may.

Lincoln combined his humanitarian concern for individual improvement with the unionist's devotion to social and political institutions—in such a way, however, that both abolitionists and conservative Whigs found his position unacceptable. Lincoln, that is, combined citizenship with morality—in part by rejecting all forms of separatism. He was convinced that an acceptable ethic must seek to redeem both the American republic and particular individuals within it.

As a nationalist and a Whig politician, Lincoln believed fervently in the importance of social and political institutions. He praised education because it fostered in citizens an appreciation of the nation's free institutions, and on economic issues he supported using those institutions to help expand opportunities for individual, capitalist enterprise.[88] Sentiment reinforced social vision. As Potter has observed, Lincoln adopted from Clay and Webster a romantic reverence for the Union and its government, and he shared that sentiment with other Republicans and antislavery Whigs such as John Quincy Adams, Seward, and Giddings (all of whom occupy the middle row of table 10.2).[89] Lincoln could also be as sentimental about the fate of the republic as he was about the fate of particular individuals. "Our republican robe is soiled and trailed in the dust," he lamented in 1854, after passage of the Kansas-Nebraska Act. "Let us repurify it. Let us turn and wash it white, in the spirit, if not the blood, of the revolution, so . . . that succeeding millions . . . shall rise up and call us blessed to the latest generation." The Civil War, he so memorably asserted at Gettysburg in 1863, would test "whether . . . any nation," "conceived in Liberty" and dedicated to democratic principles, "can long endure."[90]

The point is not that Lincoln's enthusiasm for institutions overrode his belief in individual development; on the contrary, as a devotee of Whig culture, Lincoln believed that the improvement of individual and society were almost inseparably joined. He considered the collective activities of past and present generations to be morally worthy, because they were indis-

[87] Johannsen 1965, 316, 318.
[88] B. P. Thomas 1952, 15; D. W. Howe 1979, chs. 8, 11.
[89] Potter 1976, 343.
[90] Basler 1953–1955, 5:424; 2:276; 7:528; see B. P. Thomas 1952, 268–69.

pensable for the cultivation of individual human reason. In his most interesting discussion of this question, at the height of the slavery crisis in 1859, Lincoln examined the connection between the "habit" of ratiocination and "the most important discoveries and inventions," that is, between *reflection* and *experiment*. In his view, the process of rational inquiry was essentially communal. Not only was "the inclination to exchange thoughts with one another . . . probably an original impulse of our nature" but, especially when language becomes written, it was this exchange—sometimes across generations—that enabled "different individuals to . . . combine their powers of observation and reflection, greatly [facilitating] useful discoveries and inventions. . . . What one observes . . . he [then] tells to another . . . [and a] result is thus reached which neither *alone* . . . would have arrived at."[91]

This view casts in a progressive and egalitarian form the familiar Whig belief in the importance of social and historical development. Anticipating the arguments of the late-nineteenth-century Pragmatists, Lincoln emphasized the importance of a community of inquiry and practice that depended on both socially established habits and socially shared language. As a number of authors have suggested, Emerson can be seen as a link between the Puritans' focus on nature as God's handiwork and the Pragmatists' emphasis on naturalism. Similarly, Lincoln represents a link between the Puritans' focus on society and the Pragmatists' emphasis on community and scientific collaboration.[92] Lincoln's argument about the nature of this community is indicative of perhaps his most fundamental justification for unionism; it is an argument that echoes that of the tenth Federalist paper: the full exercise and development of human reason requires not the intimacy of a small, morally homogeneous community, but the diversity and freedom of a geographically and temporally extended republican society.

For Lincoln, in other words, there was a symbiotic relationship between individual development and the institutional life of a community. Lincoln thought that only a regime devoted to improving the capacities of its members for self-development could rightfully be called the Union. His emphasis on the social dimensions of inquiry, however, also suggests the converse: that the humanitarian cause of individual improvement could flourish only in a republican society large and complex enough to sustain human inquiry and progress.[93] Lincoln's explicit arguments that secession had to be resisted—both because the Union had a world-historic mission as an exemplary republic, and because an independent South would perpetuate slavery indefinitely—are joined here by an equally compelling reason for resistence:

[91] Basler 1953–1955, 3:358–60.
[92] I wish to thank David Tracy for making this point clear to me.
[93] I am grateful to Gayle McKeen for making this point to me.

the South's withdrawal from the Union would reduce the numbers and diversity of that society in which liberty and the pursuit of individual self-development could be most vigorously pursued.

As he combined his moral obligations to individuals and to institutions, so Lincoln combined the perspectives of instrumental rationality and consummatory ethics. Lincoln affirmed, that is, the roles of both rationality and piety in morality (as indicated by the middle column of table 10.2). Throughout his life, Lincoln was concerned with assessing the consequences of his political acts. In the Lyceum speech of 1838, Lincoln sounded the typically Whiggish call for the rule of law and reason, in part because responsible political action required a due concern for the results of one's deeds.[94] In his Temperance Address of 1842, as noted above, Lincoln explicitly shunned moral denunciation of the drunkard and dramseller and favored instead appealing to their good sense. Throughout his political career, Lincoln reveled in the instrumental reasoning, the legal tactics, and the political strategies that most abolitionists could not stomach. When the Free Soilers of 1848 insisted that "they would do their duty and leave the consequences to God," Lincoln countered that duty required us to rely "on our most intelligent judgment of the consequences."[95] We have seen that Lincoln argued that the efforts of the minor antislavery parties were counterproductive because they helped elect proslavery Democrats.

Lincoln never abandoned this commitment to instrumental reasoning. Lincoln objected, for example, to the slogan of the Garrisonians, "no union with slaveholders," an objection voiced in instrumentalist terms by abolitionist Frederick Douglass: allowing the South to become independent, dissolve the Union, would simply "leave . . . the slave to free himself."[96] Provided that both his party and his nation demonstrated their fundamental opposition to slavery, Lincoln believed that the most effective way to oppose slavery was to concentrate on building political coalitions. Before Lincoln entered the White House, he extended an appeal for support to all Republicans, regardless of their positions on issues other than slavery. Later, his concern with political success led him to join forces with both the Northern Democrats and the border-state unionists, who could be rallied to the cause of the Union, if not of antislavery.

Until 1854, this instrumentalist orientation seems to have almost completely dominated Lincoln's political outlook. Until then, he was for the most part a Whig modernizer who had adopted a calculating attitude toward his career, as well as the somewhat complacent loyalty toward his regime that one might expect of a provincial lawyer of apparently limited

---

[94] Basler 1953–1955, 1:115.
[95] Ibid., 2:3.
[96] Douglass 1855, 127.

moral passion.[97] The continued existence of slavery in the South could be comfortably rationalized by claiming that the federal laws excluding it from the rest of the territories would lead gradually to its extinction. Even during his presidency, Lincoln relied on his formidable abilities as a political tactician and strategist in confronting major crises.

Ultimately, however, these instrumental concerns formed only one side of Lincoln's position. In the very speech in which he argued in instrumental terms against the Liberty party's campaign of 1844, he went on to concede that on issues where "divine law, or human law" had spoken, its command would be decisive.[98] By 1854, slavery had become just such an issue. Once Lincoln reemerged in that year as a major figure in Illinois politics, he repeatedly asserted the compelling force of ethical maxims. The essence of his position was that, regardless of other considerations, the Union must adopt "practices and policies" that would both stigmatize slavery as immoral and eventually end it. On this point, compromise and, therefore, elaborate calculations about consequences were irrelevant. One must profess one's moral code in part by acting in accord with it.

Against conservative unionists, then, Lincoln insisted that all political action must be taken according to moral principles that could not be compromised. Without such principles, one could try to calculate the consequences of one's actions, but there would be no clear standard by which to measure whether existing institutions and practices were truly unacceptable. Conversely, against the abolitionists' preoccupation with piety and perfection, Lincoln insisted that without some attention to political realities freedom itself would be lost.

In this dual emphasis, there is an important structural parallel between Lincoln's political humanitarianism and the creed of the seventeenth-century colonial orthodoxy. In both cases, the values of instrumental rationality were joined to those of piety, just as a devotion to sainthood was joined to a strong belief in the obligations of citizenship. To be sure, the substantive concerns in each case were very different—for Lincoln, the concerns were slavery, liberty, and union; for the orthodoxy, the concern was the role of the citizen-saint in the new American Israel. It bears reemphasis that the colonial orthodoxy did not bequeath to Lincoln, any more than to the abolitionists, a predisposition for or against slavery. Many factors other than a Calvinist ethic—the egalitarian currents of eighteenth- and nineteenth-century American society, for example—encouraged a dislike of the institution of slavery; further, many individuals from Yankee, Calvinist backgrounds shunned all forms of antislavery activity. What can

---

[97] B. P. Thomas 1952, 143.
[98] Basler 1953–1955, 2:4.

be traced to the Puritan strain in American culture was not a substantive belief but a *conditional* proposition that powerfully shaped Lincoln's political ethic. According to this proposition, *if* one took an ethical stand, for instance, against slavery, *then* it was necessary to frame that stand in terms of both one's responsibilities as a citizen and one's moral duty. It was, in other words, the very complexity of Lincoln's position—his synthesis of widely differing political and ethical concerns—that struck a responsive chord in so many members of his Yankee culture, a culture whose own roots could be traced back to the comparably complex synthesis of the Puritan orthodoxy.

As this last remark suggests, there were at least three ways, none of them strictly causal, in which the colonial orthodoxy can be said to help account for both the emergence and the success of Lincoln's ethic: first, a connection between the Puritan ethic and Lincoln himself; second, the impact of that ethic on his relations with other political leaders; and, finally, the way in which it shaped his appeal to the northern electorate.

First, as an individual, Lincoln sought a response to the slavery crisis that would unite genuine moral intensity with a concern for political reality and the preservation of the Union. Lincoln found the resources from which to fashion that connection when he embraced a Whig culture that itself had been powerfully shaped by the New England Protestant tradition. In that tradition, linkages between piety and instrumental rationality, and between moral and political obligations, were central assumptions rather than paradoxical curiosities. The orthodoxy's covenantal theology provided a pattern of thought within American political culture that was broadly accepted by individual citizens, even though it was not always recognized as explicitly Puritan in origin. Lincoln found that pattern useful—once he had adapted it to radically changed conditions—as he attempted to reconcile his very different objectives.

Second, as a political leader, Lincoln drew on this same cultural tradition to forge a preeminent position among the political elites of his section with whom he had to compete and cooperate. The slavery crisis was so complicated and finally so difficult to resolve, because for most northern politicians it posed at least two separate dilemmas. One dilemma pitted the claims of nationalism and the consequent need to conciliate the South against the moral revulsion of the North with regard to the peculiar institution. The other dilemma pitted the familiar and quite general requirement that politicians proceed cautiously in order to maintain their political alliances against the need to contend with an issue that was rapidly radicalizing the northern electorate in the 1850s. Lincoln's political success in the late 1850s reflects his articulation of an ethic that compellingly addressed these dilemmas by combining moral commitment with political realism. Here, too, the New England Calvinist tradition made a valuable contribution. The worldview of that tradition, which began with a quest for sainthood, made that saint-hood worldly by requiring the exercise of prudential, calculating reason in order to reshape political as well as social life. Similarly, Lincoln's political humanitarianism, his dedication to an ethic that was both unionist and concerned with political calculation seemed very well designed to respond to the crisis of the 1850s.

Third, as political actors seeking votes, Lincoln and his party drew on the Puritan tradition in their campaign for political support among northern voters. As the crisis over slavery intensified, many Northerners sought to interpret the crisis by drawing on the terms of their inherited values and symbols. Because so many of them shared a political culture shaped by the Puritan idea of the covenant, Lincoln was able to provide them with such an interpretation. It is well-known that Lincoln repeatedly invoked the Decla-ration of Independence in his attacks on slavery. For him, the declaration was not simply a rational statement of universal truths about the natural rights of particular individuals—it also proclaimed his nation's covenantal status as a special people with "an ancient faith," a status that imposed solemn responsibilities on them. This interpretation enabled him to appeal to a wide range of his fellow Northerners by affirming the simultaneous importance of both morality and nationhood to a people who had come to value each of those and were prepared to see them as intimately connected—in part because of the continuing cultural influence of the Puritans.

Conclusion: Lincoln's Piety

There is one sense in which this account of Lincoln's political ethic remains overly intellectual, in which it fails to grasp the most important way in which he spoke to his contemporaries. The sectional crisis of the 1850s did not simply present to Lincoln's generation a political puzzle for which his humanitarianism represented a complex but intellectually satisfying solu-tion. More deeply, the crisis was a wrenching individual and collective trauma that challenged fundamental beliefs and loyalties and made it diffi-cult to sustain a purposeful course of action. Much of Lincoln's greatness lay in his ability to come to terms with this deeper issue both by addressing its moral dimensions and by connecting the ethical debate to such immediate political questions as the status of slavery in the territories. Here, too, Lincoln's relation to the Puritan tradition played a significant role.

After 1854, Lincoln found himself wrestling with changes that had be-come genuinely bewildering. As had the colonial orthodoxy, Lincoln came to find reality, indeed God himself, unfathomable. As I have already sug-gested, this attitude was not very pronounced before 1854, but the repeal in that year of the Missouri Compromise by the Kansas-Nebraska Act shattered Lincoln's complacency about the Union's commitment to human freedom. To a person with Lincoln's belief in human progress and his intense hatred of slavery, the act must have made history seem regressive rather than progressive. Whereas America had hitherto been on a forward course, as had Lincoln's own career, the forces determining the fate of the Union in 1854 must have appeared arbitrary and threatening. The result for Lincoln must have been a profound disorientation, a "bewilderment and confusion," shared by many other Northerners.[99]

Six years later, Lincoln recalled that "in 1854, his [legal] profession had almost superseded the thought of politics in his mind, when the repeal of the Missouri Compromise aroused him as he had never been aroused before." There is also the revealing letter of 1855 to his old friend, Joshua Speed, in which Lincoln confessed both political uncertainty and deep personal disquiet about the advance of both slavery and nativism. "Our progress in degeneracy appears to me pretty rapid," he wrote. Should the nativist "Know Nothings get control . . . I should prefer emigrating to some country . . . where despotism can be taken pure, and without the base alloy of hypocrisy."[100]

It was in response to precisely these developments that Lincoln began to move away from a primary concern with economic modernization toward a political humanitarianism in which he joined instrumental calculation with a perfectionist ethic, and political obligation with moral duty. This intellectual development became still clearer as the crisis of the 1850s gave way to the even more traumatic struggle over secession and the horrors of civil war. His response was, in effect, a new statement of the Puritans' Augustinian piety. Gripped by a sense of responsibility for the nation's suffering, Lincoln articulated the connection between his perfectionist ethic and the finally inexplicable character of human affairs. In his Second Inaugural, in an eloquent invocation of God's ineluctable judgments, as well as in his repeated calls for days of national fasting, Lincoln connected the duties of citizenship with moral dedication, in language that both recalled and extended Puritan rhetoric. As he so movingly put it as early as 1862,

> God's purpose is [possibly] . . . different from the purpose of either party— and yet the human instrumentalities, working just as they do, are the best adaptation to effect his purpose. . . . He could have either *saved* or *destroyed* the Union without a human contest. Yet the contest began. And having begun He could give the final victory to either side any day. Yet the contest proceeds.[101]

[99] Charnwood 1916, 114.
[100] Basler 1953–1955, 4:67; 2:323.
[101] Ibid., 5:404.

Epilogue

Hofstadter has written that had Lincoln "lived to seventy he would have seen the generation brought up on self-help . . . build oppressive business corporations, and begin to close off those treasured opportunities for the little man . . . [even as] his own party [became] the jackal of the vested interests." Lincoln himself, Hofstadter added, "presided over the social revolution that destroyed the simple equalitarian [sic] order of the 1840s."[102] For Hofstadter, Lincoln is largely irrelevant to modern politics. Lincoln may have resolved the issues of slavery and the supremacy of the national government, but he and his party's "free labor" ideology had little to say about the questions of class, ethnicity, and race that so troubled later generations.

Lincoln's vision of a society of small entrepreneurs certainly failed to anticipate either the structure or the human costs of late nineteenth-century industrial capitalism; but at a more general level Lincoln contributed to an ongoing American humanitarian tradition. Witness his importance for the settlement-house movement—some of whose leaders influenced the New Deal—which in its own day emphasized the development of each individual's distinctively human faculties.[103] Hofstadter's reading of Lincoln was plausible, but it was also inadequate, precisely because it ignored Lincoln's political humanitarianism. On Hofstadter's reading, one cannot explain— save by invoking sheer filial piety—the reverence in which Lincoln was held by the postbellum social reformers, who themselves explicitly addressed the crises of an urban, industrial society. In much the same way that Lincoln had insisted that the government must ultimately destroy the institution that had blighted the slaves' opportunities for self-development, Jane Addams and her colleagues believed in committing the government to fostering self-development, even among the least privileged members of their urban-industrial society. Similarly, just as Lincoln had joined perfectionist goals to gradualist political tactics, the settlement-house workers sought not the immediate transformation of their society but rather steady progress in building a new order that would encourage self-development for all its members.

These considerations do not support explanations based in cultural determinism: Lincoln's thought and practice did not somehow cause later social-reform movements, any more than the Puritans caused Lincoln's political humanitarianism. Such claims are clearly either false or meaningless. The argument here, instead, is that Lincoln inspired Addams and her colleagues by providing them with a model to emulate in addressing the problems of

[102] Hofstadter 1974, 135–36.
[103] Addams 1961, ch. 2; see Greenstone 1979.

their own time. In this way, the relationship between Lincoln and the settlement-house reformers parallels the relationship between the colonial orthodoxy and Lincoln.

The parallel is closer still. A number of the settlement-house workers, including Addams, were distinguished by their special devotion to a vocation that required them to spend their lives among society's victims in order better to understand and help them. In Addams's own case, the intensity of her vocation was partly a reflection of her experiences in a Calvinist school, which had imparted to her a perfectionist sense of moral duty. Yet, the vocation itself was a response to the bewildering, often paralyzing, pace of social change during the late nineteenth century; to the urbanization, industrialization, and new immigration from southern and eastern Europe that had so disrupted American life. On one account, Addams's vocation was a response to social changes too massive and too sudden to be adequately understood by the men and women of her generation. The nature of her response, however, can also be attributed to her Calvinist education, because piety was the Puritans' answer to the fact of human ignorance and, more particularly, to the reality of a mysterious and seemingly arbitrary God. Given God's remoteness, the truly worshipful response was to try to become his worthy instrument by seeking perfection.

There are thus strong parallels between both the situations Addams and Lincoln each faced and their pietistic responses to those situations. The two were linked in part by a common Yankee culture, planted in the New World by seventeenth-century Puritans and reworked throughout the eighteenth and nineteenth centuries, by Great Awakening preachers and founding fathers, by party tacticians and moral reformers. Lincoln, in turn, bequeathed this culture in an enriched form to later generations of Americans as a resource with which they would confront the uncertainties of their own times—in the process, in their turns, inevitably transforming anew the shape and substance of that culture.

REFERENCES

Adams, Charles Francis. 1902 [1819–1842]. *John Quincy Adams and Emancipation under Martial Law*. Published with *John Quincy Adams: His Connection with the Monroe Doctrine* by Worthington Chauncey Ford, 1823. Reprinted from the Proceedings of the Massachusetts Historical Society, January 1902. Cambridge, Mass.: John Wilson and Son.

Adams, John. 1850–1856. *The Works of John Adams*. Edited by Charles Francis Adams. 10 vols. Boston: Charles C. Little and James Brown.

———. 1876. *Familiar Letters of John Adams and his Wife Abigail Adams*. Edited by Charles Francis Adams. Boston: Hurd and Houghton.

———. 1955. Letterbook. *Microfilms of the John Adams Papers*. Reel 124. Boston: Massachusetts Historical Society.

Adams, John Quincy. 1810. Inaugural Oration. In *Lectures on Rhetoric and Oratory*. 2 vols. Cambridge, Mass.: Hilliard and Metcalf.

———. 1831. *An Oration Addressed to the Town of Quincy on the Fourth of July, 1831, the 55th Anniversary of the Independence of the United States of America*. Boston: Richardson, Lord, and Holbrook.

———. 1837. *An Oration Delivered before the Inhabitants of the Town of Newburyport, at their Request, on the Sixty-first Anniversary of the Declaration of Independence*. Newburyport, Mass.: Morss and Brewster.

———. 1839. *The Jubilee of the Constitution: A Discourse Delivered at the Request of the New York Historical Society; on Tuesday, the 30th of April, 1839; Being the Fiftieth Anniversary of the Inauguration of George Washington as President of the United States, on Thursday, the 30th of April 1789*. New York: Samuel Colman.

———. 1842a. *Address of John Quincy Adams to his Constituents of the Twelfth Congressional District, at Braintree, September 17th, 1842*. Boston: J. H. Eastburn, Printer. Reported originally for the *Boston Atlas*.

———. 1842b. *Address to the Norfolk County Temperance Society at Their Meeting at Quincy, 29 September, 1842*. Boston: Russell and Cutler.

———. 1842c. *The Social Compact, Exemplified in the Constitution of the Commonwealth of Massachusetts; with Remarks on the Theories of Divine Right of Hobbes and of Filmer, and the Counter Theorys of Sidney, Locke, Montesquieu, and Rousseau, Concerning the Origin and Nature of Government: A Lecture, Delivered before the Franklin Lyceum, at Providence, Rhode Island, November 25th, 1842*. Providence, R.I.: Knowles and Vose, Printers.

———. 1843. *An Oration Delivered before the Cincinnati Astronomical Society, on the Occasion of Laying the Cornerstone of an Astronomical Observatory, on the 10th of November, 1843*. Cincinnati: Shepard & Co.

———. 1845. Society and Civilization. *American Whig Review* 2:80–89.

———. 1874–1877. *Memoirs of John Quincy Adams, Comprising Portions of his Diary from 1795 to 1848*. 12 vols. Edited by Charles Francis Adams. Philadelphia: J. B. Lippincott & Co.

———. 1913–1917. *Writings of John Quincy Adams*. 7 vols. Edited by Worthington Chauncey Ford. New York: Macmillan.

———. 1941. *Parties in the United States*. New York: Greenberg.

Addams, Jane. 1961 [1910]. *Twenty Years at Hull House*. New York: New American Library.

Appleby, Joyce O. 1984. *Capitalism and a New Social Order: The Republican Vision of the 1790s*. New York: New York University Press.

Apter, David E. 1965. *The Politics of Modernization*. Chicago: University of Chicago Press.

———. 1971. *Choice and the Politics of Allocation*. New Haven: Yale University Press.

Axelrod, Robert. 1984. *The Evolution of Cooperation*. New York: Basic Books.

Bailyn, Bernard. 1967. *Ideological Origins of the American Revolution*. Cambridge: Harvard University Press.

Ball, Robin. 1982. Making Politics Religious and Religion Political: The American Anti-slavery Society and the Liberty Party. Bachelor's paper, Department of Political Science, University of Chicago.

Baltzell, E. Digby. 1979. *Puritan Boston and Quaker Philadelphia*. New York: Free Press.

Banning, Lance. 1978. *The Jeffersonian Persuasion: Evolution of a Party Ideology*. Ithaca: Cornell University Press.

Bartlett, Irving H. 1965. The Persistence of Wendell Phillips. In Duberman, ed., 1965, 102–22.

Basler, Roy P., ed. 1953–1955. *The Collected Works of Abraham Lincoln*. 8 vols. New Brunswick, N.J.: Rutgers University Press.

Beard, Charles A., and Mary R. Beard. 1936. *The Rise of American Civilization*. New York: Macmillan.

Beckner, Steven K. 1977. Leggett: 19th Century Libertarian. *Reason* 8(10): 32–34.

Bemis, Samuel Flagg. 1956. *John Quincy Adams and the Union*. New York: Alfred A. Knopf.

Benson, Lee. 1973 [1961]. *The Concept of Jacksonian Democracy: New York as a Test Case*. Princeton: Princeton University Press.

Bercovitch, Sacvan. 1975. *The Puritan Origins of the American Self*. New Haven: Yale University Press.

———. 1978. *The American Jeremiad*. Madison: University of Wisconsin Press.

Bonney, Catharina. 1875. *A Legacy of Historical Gleanings*. Albany, N.Y.: J. Munsell.

Boorstin, Daniel. 1953. *The Genius of American Politics*. Chicago: University of Chicago Press.

Boyd, Julian P., ed. 1950. *The Papers of Thomas Jefferson*. Vol. 2. Princeton: Princeton University Press.

Bushman, Richard L. 1967. *From Puritan to Yankee: Character and the Social Order in Connecticut, 1690–1765*. Cambridge: Harvard University Press.

Butterfield, L. H., ed. 1961. *Diary and Autobiography of John Adams*. 4 vols. Cambridge: Harvard University Press, Belknap Press.

Butterfield, L. H., Marc Friedlaender, and Mary-Jo Kline, eds. 1975. *The Book of Abigail and John: Selected Letters of the Adams Family 1762–1784*. Cambridge, Mass.: Harvard University Press.

Cappon, Lester J., ed. 1959. *The Adams-Jefferson Letters: The Complete Correspondence between Thomas Jefferson and Abigail and John Adams.* 2 vols. (1777–1804, 1812–1826). Chapel Hill: University of North Carolina Press.

Casmier, Stephen J. 1986. Reason and Structure in the Works of John Adams. Master's thesis, Department of Political Science, University of Chicago.

Cavell, Stanley. 1969. *Must We Mean What We Say?* New York: Charles Scribner's Sons.

Ceasar, James W. 1979. *Presidential Selection: Theory and Development.* Princeton: Princeton University Press.

Chapman, John Jay. 1921. *William Lloyd Garrison.* New York: Moffat Yard and Co.

Charnwood, Lord Godfrey. 1916. *Abraham Lincoln.* London: Constable and Co.

Child, Lydia Maria. 1839. *Anti-Slavery Catechism.* Newburyport, Mass: C. Whipple. Reprinted in J. L. Thomas, ed., 1965b.

Chinard, Gilbert. 1933. *Honest John Adams.* Boston: Little, Brown & Co.

———. 1946. *Thomas Jefferson: The Apostle of Americanism.* Boston: Little, Brown & Co.

Clay, Henry. 1857. *The Works of Henry Clay.* Edited by Calvin Colton. New York: A. S. Barnes and Burr.

Cole, Donald B. 1984. *Martin Van Buren and the American Political System.* Princeton: Princeton University Press.

Commager, Henry Steele. 1975. *Jefferson, Nationalism, and the Enlightenment.* New York: George Braziller.

Conkin, Paul K. 1968. *Puritans and Pragmatists: Eight Eminent American Thinkers.* Bloomington: Indiana University Press.

Cooke, J. W. 1973. Jefferson on Liberty. *Journal of the History of Ideas* 34(1):563–76.

Cooper, William J., Jr. 1978. *The South and the Politics of Slavery 1828–1856.* Baton Rouge: Louisiana State University Press.

Craven, Avery. 1971. *The Coming of the Civil War.* 2d ed. Chicago: University of Chicago Press.

Curtis, James C. 1970. *The Fox at Bay: Martin Van Buren and the Presidency, 1837–1841.* Lexington: University Press of Kentucky.

Dauer, Manning J. 1968 [1953]. *The Adams Federalists.* Baltimore: Johns Hopkins University Press.

Davis, David Brion. 1966. *The Problem of Slavery in Western Culture.* Ithaca: Cornell University Press.

———. 1975. *The Problem of Slavery in the Age of Revolution: 1770–1823.* Ithaca: Cornell University Press.

Dickerson, O. M. 1913–1914. Stephen A. Douglas and the Split in the Democratic Party. *Proceedings of the Mississippi Valley Historical Association* 7:196–211.

Diggins, John P. 1984. *The Lost Soul of American Politics: Virtue, Self-Interest, and the Foundations of Liberalism.* New York: Basic Books.

Donald, David. 1974. *Charles Sumner and the Coming of the Civil War.* New York: Alfred A. Knopf.

Douglas, Stephen A. 1851. *Address of the Honorable Stephen A. Douglas, at the Annual Fair of the New York State Agricultural Society, Held at Rochester, September, 1851.* Albany, N.Y.: C. Van Benthuysen, Printer.

———. 1859. The Dividing Line between Federal and Local Authority. Popular Sovereignty in the Territories. Detached from *Harper's New Monthly Magazine*, 519–38. New York: Harper and Brothers.

———. 1860a; 1860b. *The Life and Speeches of Stephen A. Douglas*. New York: H. Dayton. This work comprises two volumes bound as one but separately paginated.

Douglass, Frederick. 1855. The Anti-slavery Movement. In J. L. Thomas, ed., 1965b.

Duberman, Martin, ed. 1965. *The Antislavery Vanguard*. Princeton: Princeton University Press.

Dumbauld, Edward, ed. 1955. *The Political Writings of Thomas Jefferson: Representative Selections*. The American Heritage Series. Indianapolis, Ind.: Bobbs-Merrill.

Dunn, John. 1969. *The Political Thought of John Locke: An Historical Account of the Argument of the "Two Treatises of Government."* Cambridge: Cambridge University Press.

Elazar, Daniel J. 1970. *Cities of the Prairie*. New York: Basic Books.

Elster, Jon. 1982. Marxism, Functionalism, and Game Theory. *Theory and Society* 11:453–582.

Ericson, Dave. 1987. American Republicanism 1787–1833: The Federal Farmer and Daniel Webster. Ph.D. dissertation, Department of Political Science, University of Chicago. Revised and expanded to *The Shaping of American Liberalism: The Debates over Ratification, Nullification, and Slavery*. University of Chicago Press, 1993.

Fehrenbacher, Don E. 1962. *Prelude to Greatness: Lincoln in the 1850s*. Stanford: Stanford University Press.

Ferguson, Robert A. 1980. "Mysterious Obligation": Jefferson's *Notes on the State of Virginia*. *American Literature* 52(3):381–406.

Filler, Louis, ed. 1965. *Wendell Phillips on Civil Rights and Freedom*. New York: Hill and Wang.

Foner, Eric. 1950. *The Life and Writings of Frederick Douglass*. 4 vols. New York: International Publishers.

———. 1970. *Free Soil, Free Labor, Free Men*. New York: Oxford University Press.

Forgie, George B. 1979. *Patricide in the House Divided: A Psychological Interpretation of Lincoln and his Age*. New York: W. W. Norton.

Formisano, Ronald P. 1971. *The Birth of Mass Political Parties*. Princeton: Princeton University Press.

Frederickson, George M., ed. 1968. *William Lloyd Garrison: Great Lives Observed*. Englewood Cliffs, N.J.: Prentice-Hall.

Frege, Gottlieb. 1975. On Sense and Reference. *The Logic of Grammar*. Edited by Donald Davidson and Gilbert Harmon. Encino, Calif.: Dickinson.

Friedman, Lawrence J. 1982. *Gregarious Saints: Self and Community in American Abolitionism 1830–1870*. Cambridge: Cambridge University Press.

Gallie, W. B. 1964. Essentially Contested Concepts. In Gallie, *Philosophy and the Historical Understanding*, 157–91. New York: Schocken Books.

Gamwell, Franklin I. 1984. *Beyond Preference: Liberal Theories of Independent Associations*. Chicago: University of Chicago Press.

Garrison, William Lloyd. 1830. Henry Clay's Colonization Address. Reprinted in J. L. Thomas, ed., 1965b.

———. 1831. Opening statement of the first issue [of *The Liberator*]. Reprinted in Frederickson, ed., 1968.

———. 1837. No Union with Slave-Holders. Reprinted in J. L. Thomas, ed., 1965b.

———. 1852. Review of *Uncle Tom's Cabin*. Reprinted in Frederickson, ed., 1968.

Geertz, Clifford. 1973. *The Interpretation of Cultures*. New York: Basic Books.

Genovese, Eugene D. 1965. *The Political Economy of Slavery: Studies in the Economy and Society of the Slave South*. New York: Pantheon.

Goldstein, Robert. 1978. *Political Repression in Modern America*. Boston: G. K. Hall.

Gramsci, Antonio. 1971. *Selections from the Prison Notebooks*. New York: International Publishers.

Greenstone, J. David. 1977 [1969]. *Labor in American Politics*. Chicago: University of Chicago Press.

———. 1979. Dorothea Dix and Jane Addams: From Transcendentalism to Pragmatism in American Social Reform. *Social Service Review* 53:527–59.

———, ed. 1982a. *Public Values and Private Power in American Politics*. Chicago: University of Chicago Press.

———. 1982b. The Transient and the Permanent in American Politics: Standards, Interests, and the Concept of "Public." In Greenstone, ed., 1982a.

———. 1986. Political Culture and American Political Development: Liberty, Union, and the Liberal Bipolarity. *Studies in American Political Development* 1:1–49. New Haven: Yale University Press.

———. 1988. Against Simplicity: The Cultural Dimensions of the Constitution. *University of Chicago Law Review* 55:428–49.

———. 1991. Adams and Jefferson on Slavery: Two Liberalisms and the Roots of Civic Ambivalence. In Robert E. Calvert, ed., *"The Constitution of the People": Reflections on Citizens and Civil Society*. Lawrence: University Press of Kansas.

———. 1992. Lincoln's Political Humanitarianism: Moral Reform and the Covenant Tradition in American Political Culture. In *American Models of Revolutionary Leadership: George Washington and other Founders*, edited by Daniel J. Elazar and Ellis Katz, 195–225. Lanham, Md.: University Press of America for the Center for the Study of Federalism.

———. 1993. Covenant, Process, and Slavery in the Thought of Adams and Jefferson. In *What Happened to Covenant in the Nineteenth Century?* edited by Daniel J. Elazar. Lanham, Md.: University Press of America for the Center for the Study of Federalism.

Greenstone, J. David, and Paul E. Peterson. 1983. Inquiry and Social Function: Two Views of Educational Practice and Policy. In Lee S. Shulman and Gary Sykes, eds., *Handbook of Teaching and Policy*. New York: Longmans.

Greven, Philip. 1977. *The Protestant Temperament: Patterns of Child-rearing, Religious Experience, and the Self in Early America*. New York: New American Library.

Hacker, Louis M. 1935. Revolutionary America. In *Harper's Magazine*. Reprinted in Stampp 1959, 62–65.

Handler, Edward. 1964. *America and Europe in the Political Thought of John Adams*. Cambridge: Harvard University Press.

Haraszti, Zoltan. 1952. *John Adams and the Prophets of Progress*. Cambridge: Harvard University Press.

Harrison, Joseph Hobson, Jr. 1956. Martin Van Buren and his Southern Supporters. *Journal of Southern History* 22:438–58.

Hartz, Louis. 1955. *The Liberal Tradition in America*. New York: Harcourt, Brace & World.

——. 1964. *The Founding of New Societies*. New York: Harcourt, Brace & World.

Heimert, Alan. 1966. *Religion and the American Mind: From the Great Awakening to the Revolution*. Cambridge: Harvard University Press.

Henig, Gerald S. 1969. The Jacksonian Attitude toward Abolitionism in the 1830s. *Tennessee Historical Quarterly* 28:42–56.

Hofstadter, Richard. 1943. William Leggett, Spokesman of Jacksonian Democracy. *Political Science Quarterly* 58:581–94.

——. 1969. *The Idea of a Party System: The Rise of Legitimate Opposition in the United States, 1780–1840*. Berkeley: University of California Press.

——. 1974 [1948]. *The American Political Tradition*. New York: Vintage Books.

Holt, Michael F. 1978. *The Political Crisis of the 1850s*. New York: John Wiley & Sons.

Howe, Daniel Walker. 1979. *The Political Culture of the American Whigs*. Chicago: University of Chicago Press.

Howe, John R., Jr. 1966. *The Changing Political Thought of John Adams*. Princeton: Princeton University Press.

Huntington, Samuel P. 1981. *American Politics: The Promise of Disharmony*. Cambridge: Harvard University Press.

Jaenicke, Douglas W. 1986. The Jacksonian Integration of Parties into the Constitutional System. *Political Science Quarterly* 101(1):85–107.

——. 1988. *Partisanship, Free Soil and Defection: The Case of the New York Barnburners*. Manchester, United Kingdom: Manchester Papers in Politics, University of Manchester, no. 5/88.

Jaffa, Harry V. 1959. *Crisis of the House Divided: An Interpretation of the Lincoln-Douglas Debates*. Seattle: University of Washington Press.

——. 1965. *Equality and Liberty: Theory and Practice in American Politics*. New York: Oxford University Press.

Johannsen, Robert W. 1960. Stephen A. Douglas, Popular Sovereignty, and the Territories. *The Historian* 22:378–95.

——, ed. 1961. *The Letters of Stephen A. Douglas*. Urbana: University of Illinois Press.

——. 1963. The Douglas Democracy and the Crisis of Disunion. *Civil War History* 9:229–47.

——, ed. 1965. *The Lincoln-Douglas Debates of 1858*. New York: Oxford University Press.

——. 1967. Stephen A. Douglas and the South. *Southern History* 33:26–50.

——. 1973. *Stephen A. Douglas*. New York: Oxford University Press.

Kammen, Michael. 1972. *People of Paradox*. New York: Random House.

Katznelson, Ira. 1980. *City Trenches*. New York: Pantheon Books.

Kelley, Robert. 1979. *The Cultural Pattern in American Politics*. New York: Alfred A. Knopf.

Kerber, Linda K. 1980 [1970]. *Federalists in Dissent: Imaginary Ideology in Jeffersonian America*. Ithaca: Cornell University Press.

Kleppner, Paul. 1970. *The Cross of Culture: A Social Analysis of Midwestern Politics 1850–1900*. New York: Free Press.

Kloppenberg, James. 1982. The Virtues of Liberalism: Christianity, Republicanism, and Ethics in Early American Political Discourse. *Journal of American History* 87:629–54.

Koch, Adrienne, and William Peden, eds. 1944. *The Life and Selected Writings of Thomas Jefferson*. New York: Modern Library.

_____, eds. 1946. *Selected Writings of John and John Quincy Adams*. New York: Alfred A. Knopf.

Kramnick, Isaac. 1982. Republican Revisionism Revisited. *American Historical Review* 87(3):629–64.

Kripke, Saul. 1982. *Wittgenstein on Rules and Private Language: An Elementary Exposition*. Cambridge: Harvard University Press.

Lawrence, Roy P. 1972. *Motive and Intention: An Essay in the Appreciation of Action*. Evanston, Ill.: Northwestern University Press.

Leggett, William. 1984. *Democratick Editorials: Essays in Jacksonian Political Economy*. Edited by Lawrence H. White. Indianapolis, Ind.: Liberty Press.

Lenin, V. I. 1908 [1902]. What Is to Be Done? In Lenin, *Selected Works*. Vol. 2: *The Struggle for the Bolshevik Party 1900–1904*. Edited by J. Fineberg. New York: International Publishers, 1933.

Lincoln, Abraham, and Stephen A. Douglas. 1958. *Created Equal? The Complete Lincoln-Douglas Debates of 1858*. Edited with an introduction by Paul M. Angle. Chicago: University of Chicago Press.

Lipsky, George A. 1950. *John Quincy Adams: His Theory and Ideas*. New York: Thomas Y. Crowell.

Lorwin, Lewis. 1933. *The American Federation of Labor*. Washington, D.C.: Brookings Institution.

MacKay, Alfred F. 1980. *Arrow's Theorem, the Paradox of Social Choice: A Case Study in the Philosophy of Economics*. New Haven: Yale University Press.

Maclean, William Jerry. 1984. Othello Scorned: The Racial Thought of John Quincy Adams. *Journal of the Early Republic* 4:143–60.

Martineau, Harriet. 1835. An English Radical Describes a Meeting with Garrison. In Frederickson, ed., 1968.

Marx, Karl. 1843. On the Jewish Question. In Tucker, ed., 1978.

Marx, Karl, and Friedrich Engels. 1958. *The German Ideology*. New York: International Publishers.

Massachusetts Anti-slavery Society. 1844. Twelfth Annual Report. In J. L. Thomas, ed., 1965b.

Mathews, Donald G. 1965. Orange Scott: The Methodist Evangelist as Revolutionary. In Duberman, ed., 1965, 71–101.

McCormick, Richard P. 1966. *The Second American Party System: Party Formation in the Jacksonian Era*. Chapel Hill: University of North Carolina Press.

Messerli, Jonathan. 1972. *Horace Mann: A Biography*. New York: Alfred A. Knopf.

Meyers, Marvin. 1960 [1957]. *The Jacksonian Persuasion*. New York: Vintage Books.

———. 1963. Louis Hartz, *The Liberal Tradition in America*: An Appraisal. *Comparative Studies in Society and History* 5(3).

Miller, John Chester. 1977. *The Wolf by the Ears: Thomas Jefferson and Slavery*. New York: Free Press.

Miller, Perry. 1956a. Errand into the Wilderness. In Miller, *Errand into the Wilderness*. Cambridge: Harvard University Press, Belknap Press.

———. 1956b. The Marrow of Puritan Divinity. In Miller, *Errand into the Wilderness*.

———. 1961a. *The New England Mind: The Seventeenth Century*. Boston: Beacon Press.

———. 1961b. *The New England Mind: From Colony to Province*. Boston: Beacon Press.

———. 1970. *Roger Williams: His Contribution to the American Tradition*. New York: Atheneum.

Mintz, Max M. 1949. The Political Ideas of Martin Van Buren. *New York History* 30:422–48.

Moore, Barrington. 1966. *Social Origins of Dictatorship and Democracy: Lord and Peasant in the Making of the Modern World*. Boston: Beacon Press.

Morgan, Edmund S. 1965. *Visible Saints: The History of the Puritan Idea*. Ithaca: Cornell University Press.

Myrdal, Gunnar. 1964 [1944]. *An American Dilemma*. New York: McGraw-Hill.

National Liberty Party Convention. 1843. Emancipation Extra, Tract Number 1. In J. L. Thomas, ed., 1965b.

Nevins, Allan, ed. 1969 [1928]. *The Diary of John Quincy Adams 1794–1845*. New York: Frederick Ungar.

Niven, John. 1983. *Martin Van Buren: The Romantic Age of American Politics*. New York: Oxford University Press.

Norton, Anne. 1986. *Alternative Americas: A Reading of Antebellum Political Culture*. Chicago: University of Chicago Press.

Oates, Stephen B. 1977. *With Malice toward None: The Life of Abraham Lincoln*. New York: New American Library.

Ostrander, Gilman M. 1978. Jefferson and Scottish Culture. *Historical Reflections/Réflexions Historique* 5(2):233–49.

Padover, Saul K. 1942. *Jefferson*. New York: Harcourt, Brace & Co.

Parsons, Lynn Hudson. 1973. A Perpetual Harrow upon my Feelings: John Quincy Adams and the American Indian. *New England Quarterly* 46(3):339–79.

Peek, George A., ed. 1954. *The Political Writings of John Adams: Representative Selections*. New York: Bobbs-Merrill.

Perry, Lewis. 1973. *Radical Abolitionism: Anarchy and the Government of God in Antislavery Thought*. Ithaca: Cornell University Press.

Peterson, Merrill D. 1976. *Adams and Jefferson: A Revolutionary Dialogue*. Athens: University of Georgia Press.

———, ed. 1987 [1975]. *The Portable Thomas Jefferson*. New York: Penguin Books.

Pitkin, Hanna F. 1972. *Wittgenstein and Justice*. Berkeley: University of California Press.

Pocock, J. G. A. 1975. *The Machiavellian Moment*. Princeton: Princeton University Press.

Potter, David M. 1954. *People of Plenty*. Chicago: University of Chicago Press.

———. 1976. *The Impending Crisis 1848–1861*. New York: Harper and Row.

Przeworski, Adam. 1985. *Capitalism and Social Democracy*. Cambridge: Cambridge University Press.

Rawls, John. 1987. The Priority of Right and Ideas of the Good. Paper delivered at University of Chicago, 5 Nov. 1987.

Rayback, Joseph G. 1954. Martin Van Buren's Desire for Revenge in the Campaign of 1848. *Mississippi Valley Historical Review* 40:707–16.

———. 1955. Martin Van Buren's Break with James K. Polk: The Record. *New York History* 36:51–62.

Richards, Leonard L. 1986. *The Life and Times of Congressman John Quincy Adams*. New York: Oxford University Press.

Richardson, James D. 1897. *A Compilation of the Messages and Papers of the Presidents, 1789–1901*. 20 vols. Washington, D.C.: Bureau of National Literature and Art.

Rifkin, Lester Harvey. 1951. William Leggett: Journalist-Philosopher of Agrarian Democracy in New York. *New York History* 32:45–60.

Remini, Robert V. 1955. *Martin Van Buren and the Making of the Democratic Party*. New York: W. W. Norton.

Robbins, Caroline. 1975. The Pursuit of Happiness. In Irving Kristol et al., *America's Continuing Revolution: An Act of Conservation*. Washington, D.C.: American Enterprise Institute for Public Policy Research.

Rogin, Michael P. 1982. The King's Two Bodies: Lincoln, Wilson, Nixon, and Presidential Self-sacrifice. In Greenstone, ed., 1982a.

Schlesinger, Arthur M., Jr. 1945. *The Age of Jackson*. Boston: Little, Brown & Co.

———, ed. 1971. *History of American Presidential Elections*. 4 vols. New York: Chelsea House.

Sewell, Richard H. 1976. *Ballots for Freedom: Antislavery Politics in the United States, 1837–1860*. New York: Oxford University Press.

Shaw, Peter. 1976. *The Character of John Adams*. New York: W. W. Norton and Co.

Sidney, Algernon. 1751. *Discourses Concerning Government*. 3d ed. London: A. Millar.

Silbey, Joel H. 1971. Election of 1836. In Schlesinger, ed., 1971, 577–600.

Skocpol, Theda. 1985. Bringing the State Back In: Current Research. In *Bringing the State Back In*, edited by Peter B. Evans, Dietrich Rueschemeyer, and Theda Skocpol. New York: Cambridge University Press.

Somkin, Fred. 1967. *Unquiet Eagle: Memory and Desire in the Idea of American Freedom, 1815–1860*. Ithaca: Cornell University Press.

Sparrow, Bartholomew. 1991. From the Outside In: The Effects of World War II on the American State. Ph.D. dissertation, Department of Political Science, University of Chicago.

Stampp, Kenneth M. 1959. *The Causes of the Civil War*. Englewood Cliffs, N.J.: Prentice-Hall.

Stewart, James B. 1970. *Joshua R. Giddings and the Tactics of Radical Politics*. Cleveland: Case Western Reserve University Press.

Strozier, Charles B. 1982. *Lincoln's Quest for Union: Public and Private Meanings*. New York: Basic Books.

Tarcov, Nathan. 1984. *Locke's Education for Liberty*. Chicago: University of Chicago Press.

Taylor, William R. 1961 [1957]. *Cavalier and Yankee: The Old South and American National Character*. New York: Harper Torchbooks.

Thomas, Benjamin P. 1952. *Abraham Lincoln*. New York: Alfred A. Knopf.

Thomas, John L. 1963. *The Liberator: William Lloyd Garrison, a Biography*. Boston: Little, Brown & Co.

———. 1965a. Antislavery and Utopia. In Duberman, ed., 1965, 240–69.

———, ed. 1965b. *Slavery Attacked: The Abolitionist Crusade*. Englewood Cliffs, N.J.: Prentice-Hall.

Tocqueville, Alexis de. 1969. *Democracy in America*. New York: Vintage Books.

Trimble, William. 1919. Diverging Tendencies in New York Democracy in the Period of the Locofocos. *American Historical Review* 24(3):396–421.

Tucker, R. C., ed. 1978 [1972]. *The Marx-Engels Reader*. New York: W. W. Norton.

Van Buren, Martin. 1867. *Inquiry into the Origin and Course of Political Parties in the United States*. New York: Hurd & Houghton.

———. 1920. *The Autobiography of Martin Van Buren*. Edited by John C. Fitzpatrick. Annual Report of the American Historical Association for the Year 1918. Vol. 2. Washington, D.C.: U.S. Government Printing Office.

Walters, Ronald. 1976. *The Antislavery Appeal: American Abolitionism after 1830*. Baltimore: Johns Hopkins University Press.

Warner, W. Lloyd. 1961. The Cult of the Dead. In *The Family of God*, 216–59. New Haven: Yale University Press.

Weber, Max. 1987 [1930]. *The Protestant Ethic and the Spirit of Capitalism*. Translated by Talcott Parsons. London: Unwin Paperbacks.

———. 1978 [1968]. *Economy and Society: An Outline of Interpretive Sociology*. Edited by Guenther Roth and Claus Wittich. Berkeley: University of California Press.

Webster. Daniel. 1864. *The Works of Daniel Webster*. 6 vols. Boston: Little, Brown & Co.

Wells, Damon. 1971. *Stephen Douglas: The Last Years, 1857–1861*. Austin: University of Texas Press.

White, Lawrence H. 1986. William Leggett: Jacksonian Editorialist as Classical Liberal Political Economist. *History of Political Economy* 18(2):307–24.

Whitehurst, Alto Lee. 1932. Martin Van Buren and the Free Soil Movement. Ph.D. dissertation, Department of History, University of Chicago.

Wilson, Douglas L. 1981. The American *Agricola*: Jefferson's Agrarianism and the Classical Tradition. *South Atlantic Quarterly* 80(3):339–54.

Wilson, Major L. 1974. *Space, Time, and Freedom: The Quest for Nationality and the Irrepressible Conflict 1815–1861*. Contributions in American History, no. 35. Series editor, Jon Wakelyn. Westport, Conn.: Greenwood Press.

———. 1984. *The Presidency of Martin Van Buren*. Lawrence: University Press of Kansas.

Wittgenstein, Ludwig. 1958 [1953]. *Philosophical Investigations*, 3d ed. Translated by G. E. M. Anscombe. New York: Macmillan.

Wood, Gordon S. 1969. *The Creation of the American Republic*. Chapel Hill: University of North Carolina Press for the Institute of Early American History and Culture at Williamsburg, Va.

Wright, Elizur, Jr. 1833. The Sin of Slavery. In J. L. Thomas, ed., 1965b.

Wyatt-Brown, Bertram. 1971. *Lewis Tappan and the Evangelical War against Slavery*. New York: Atheneum.

Yarbrough, Jean. 1979. Republicanism Reconsidered: Some Thoughts on the Foundation and Preservation of the American Republic. *The Review of Politics* 41(1):61–95.

INDEX

abolitionists
—John Quincy Adams and, 205–6
—Douglas and, 139, 144
—Douglass on, 135–36
—founding synthesis and, 221
—Garrisonian, 135, 273, 275–76, 279
—humanitarianism of, 245–49
—laissez-faire and, 252, 253, 259
—Leggett and, 134, 135, 136, 137–38, 139
—Lincoln and: humanitarianism and, 254–55; motives of, 251; second leadership generation and, 218; unionism and, 17, 29, 238; Whigs and, 277
—motives of, 251, 252–53
—Quakers and, 273
—religious tradition of, 55, 243, 258–62, 273
—Republicans and, 249
—Van Buren and, 173, 175, 176
—Webster and, 227, 228
—white Southerners and, 180, 241
—women's suffrage and, xxiii
academies, 98
acquisitiveness. See material acquisitiveness
activism, 115–16, 276
Adams, Abigail: agrarian ideals of, 83; Polly Jefferson and, 72; Thomas Jefferson and, 106; John Quincy and, 199–200; on slavery, 99–100, 103, 115, 196
Adams, Charles Francis, 77, 115
Adams, John: *Dissertation on Canon and Feudal Law*, 80; Douglass and, 190; Jefferson and, xxv, 64, 71–117; Lincoln and, 220; Locke and, 52; philosophical heirs of, xxii, 155; Van Buren and, 154, 170; Webster on, 226
Adams, John Quincy, xxii, xxvii, 70, 115, 191–214; defeat of, 76–77; Democratic Republicans and, 73, 95; *Discourse on Education*, 200; election of, 161, 162, 171; Jefferson and, 97; "Jubilee of the Constitution," 208; Lincoln and, xxix, 192, 220, 231, 277; moral/political relationship and, 6; *Parties in the United States*,

210; party factionalism and, 163; slavery and (*see under* slavery); on social influences, xxvi; Van Buren and, xxvi–xxvii, 157, 170, 174, 190
Addams, Jane, 284, 285
Address to the People of the Slaveholding States, 180
African-Americans, xxiii, 63, 190. *See also* free blacks; slavery
agrarian ideals, 82, 90, 146
Albany Regency, 155, 181
alcohol consumption. *See* temperance movement
Alien and Sedition Acts, 71; John Adams and, 74–75, 76, 90, 111; Federalists and, 163; Jefferson and, 82, 108
American Anti-slavery Society, 257n.45
American Philosophical Society, 84
Amis des Noirs (society), 99
Amistad (ship), 198
anti-Masonic Whigs, 193, 194
antinomian sects, 268–69
aristocracy: John Adams and, 80, 91, 92, 93, 98; natural, 74, 100, 130; Southern, 233; Tocqueville on, 37
Aristotelianism, 265
armies, 9, 22, 81, 82
Arrow, Kenneth, 162
Articles of Confederation, 212
Augustinian piety, 260, 266, 283
authoritarianism, 39
autonomy. *See* freedom

Bacon, Francis, 97
Baltzell, Digby, 273
Bank of the United States, 125, 142, 156, also n.8, 194, 196
banks, 14, 124, 125–26, 131
Banning, Lance, 5
Baptists, 263
Barnburner faction, 124, 175, 176, 177, 178
Beard, Charles, 14, 43
Beard, Mary, 14
belief systems, 50